SPECIAL REPORT 254

MANAGING SPEED

Review of Current Practice for Setting and Enforcing Speed Limits

Committee for Guidance on
Setting and Enforcing Speed Limits

TRANSPORTATION RESEARCH BOARD
National Research Council

NATIONAL ACADEMY PRESS
WASHINGTON, D.C. 1998

Transportation Research Board Special Report 254

Subscriber Categories
IVA highway operations, capacity, and traffic control
IVB safety and human performance

Transportation Research Board publications are available by ordering individual publications directly from the TRB Business Office, through the Internet at http://www.nas.edu/trb/index.html, or by annual subscription through organizational or individual affiliation with TRB. Affiliates and library subscribers are eligible for substantial discounts. For further information, contact the Transportation Research Board Business Office, National Research Council, 2101 Constitution Avenue, N.W., Washington, D.C. 20418 (telephone 202-334-3214; fax 202-334-2519; or e-mail aarcher@nas.edu).

Printed in the United States of America.

NOTICE: The project that is the subject of this report was approved by the Governing Board of the National Research Council, whose members are drawn from the councils of the National Academy of Sciences, the National Academy of Engineering, and the Institute of Medicine. The members of the committee responsible for the report were chosen for their special competencies and with regard for appropriate balance.

This report has been reviewed by a group other than the authors according to the procedures approved by a Report Review Committee consisting of members of the National Academy of Sciences, the National Academy of Engineering, and the Institute of Medicine. The views expressed in the individually authored papers that are included in this report are those of the authors and do not necessarily reflect the views of the committee, the Transportation Research Board, the National Research Council, or the project's sponsors.

The study was sponsored by the National Highway Traffic Safety Administration and the Federal Highway Administration of the U.S. Department of Transportation and by the Centers for Disease Control and Prevention of the U.S. Department of Health and Human Services.

Library of Congress Cataloging-in-Publication Data

Managing Speed : review of current practice for setting and enforcing speed limits / Committee for Guidance on Setting and Enforcing Speed Limits, Transportation Research Board, National Research Council, National Academy Press.
p. cm.—(Special report (National Research Council (U.S.). Transportation Research Board) ; 254)
ISBN 0-309-06502-X
1. Speed limits—United States. 2. Roads—United States—Safety measures. I. National Research Council (U.S.). Transportation Research Board. Committee for Guidance on Setting and Enforcing Speed Limits. II. Series.
HE5620.S6M36 1998
388.3'144'0973—dc21 98-40323
CIP

Committee for Guidance on Setting and Enforcing Speed Limits

JOHN G. MILLIKEN, *Chairman*, Venable, Baetjer & Howard, McLean, Virginia
FORREST M. COUNCIL, University of North Carolina, Chapel Hill
TERRANCE W. GAINER, Metropolitan Police Department, Washington, D.C.*
NICHOLAS J. GARBER, University of Virginia, Charlottesville
KRISTINE M. GEBBIE, Columbia University School of Nursing, New York
JEROME W. HALL, University of New Mexico, Albuquerque
CHARLES A. LAVE, University of California, Irvine
JOHN M. MASON, JR., The Pennsylvania State University, University Park
FREDERICK MOSTELLER, Harvard University, Cambridge
SHARON D. NICHOLS, Western Highway Institute, Casper, Wyoming
CLINTON V. OSTER, Jr., Indiana University, Bloomington
RICHARD A. RETTING, Insurance Institute for Highway Safety, Arlington, Virginia
THOMAS B. SHERIDAN, Massachusetts Institute of Technology, Cambridge
WILLIAM C. TAYLOR, Michigan State University, East Lansing
GEORGE TSEBELIS, University of California, Los Angeles
DAVID C. VIANO, General Motors Corporation, Warren, Michigan
RICHARD P. WEAVER, California Department of Transportation (retired), Sacramento

*Formerly Illinois State Police, Springfield

Liaison Representatives

STEPHEN F. CAMPBELL, Sr., American Trucking Associations, Alexandria, Virginia
RICHARD P. COMPTON, National Highway Traffic Safety Administration, Washington, D.C.
MARK EDWARDS, American Automobile Association, Heathrow, Florida
DAVID J. HENSING, American Association of State Highway and Transportation Officials, Washington, D.C.
HENRY JASNY, Advocates for Highway and Auto Safety, Washington, D.C.
RICHARD PAIN, Transportation Research Board, Washington, D.C.

Transportation Research Board Staff

NANCY P. HUMPHREY, Study Director

Preface

With repeal of the National Maximum Speed Limit (NMSL) of 55 mph (89 km/h) in 1995, states once again have the responsibility for setting appropriate speed limits on major highways. Much has changed in the 20 years during which the NMSL was in effect. Passenger vehicles have become more crashworthy, and vehicles are equipped with more safety features like airbags. Improvements in highway design, roadside safety, and emergency medical services have made the highways safer and assistance to crash victims more rapid. Drivers and other vehicle occupants are buckling up more, and drunk driving is less widespread than it used to be. Together these improvements have contributed to a national reduction in highway fatality rates, although rates have stabilized in recent years and total numbers of fatalities and injuries have crept up. States have raised speed limits on many major highways, and several states report that driving speeds are up, particularly for those who drive well in excess of speed limits. Some drivers appear to have reacted to safer conditions on the highways by altering their perception of the riskiness of driving and engaging in more risk-taking behavior.

Methods for setting speed limits have essentially remained unchanged since before the NMSL came into effect. In the wake of the repeal of the NMSL, many states and some local governments are reexamining speed limit policies; most have already raised speed limits. Thus, it is an appropriate time to reevaluate speed limit and related enforcement policies not only for Interstate highways but for all road classes. The Transportation Research Board (TRB) undertook a major evaluation of the NMSL in 1984 to provide Congress with an assessment of the costs and benefits of speed limit policies in effect at that time. The primary objective of this study—requested and funded by the National Highway Traffic Safety Administration (NHTSA), the Federal Highway Administration, and the Centers for Disease Control and Prevention—is to review current practice for setting and enforcing speed limits on all types of roads.

There are numerous strategies for managing driving speeds. The charge of this study, however, is focused primarily on regulating speed through speed limits and enforcement. More specifically, and in response to the charge, the study reviews existing methods of setting and enforcing speed limits, taking into consideration relevant research, opportunities provided by new technology, and expected changes in highway travel. The findings of the study are presented in the form of guidance, rather than standards, to those who must make decisions about appropriate speed limits and related enforcement policies.

To conduct the study, TRB formed a panel of 17 experts under the leadership of John G. Milliken, Partner at the firm of Venable, Baetjer & Howard. The study committee includes experts in traffic engineering, highway design, traffic operations and highway safety, vehicle design and biomechanics, human factors, public health, traffic enforcement, highway users, economics, statistics, political science, and public policy. The committee was assisted during its deliberations by the input and advice of several liaison representatives. The committee also supplemented its expertise with invited presentations by state and local traffic engineers, local law enforcement officers, and a circuit court judge. The report that follows, however, represents the consensus view solely of the study committee.

The committee wishes to acknowledge the work of many individuals who contributed to the report. Nancy P. Humphrey managed the study and drafted the final report under the guidance of the committee and the supervision of Stephen R. Godwin, Director of Studies and Information Services. The committee also commissioned three literature reviews to inform its deliberations. The papers are appended to the report to make the information available to a broad audience. The interpretations and conclusions reached in the papers are those of the authors; the key findings endorsed by the committee appear in the main body of the report. David Shinar of Ben-Gurion University of the Negev, Israel, reviewed the theoretical literature on the relationship between speed and safety. The major findings of that paper are included in Chapter 2 with supporting detail in Appendix B. Patrick S. McCarthy of Purdue University reviewed empirical evidence of the effect of speed limits on vehicle speeds and highway safety. The major findings of that paper are included in Chapter 3 with the full review in Appendix C. William D. Glauz of the Midwest Research Institute reviewed experience with automated technologies for speed management and enforcement. The major findings of that paper are included in Chapter 4 with the full detail in Appendix D.

The committee also wishes to thank Suzanne Schneider, Assistant Executive Director of TRB, who managed the report review process. The report has been reviewed in draft form by individuals chosen for their diverse perspectives and technical expertise, in accordance with procedures approved by the National Research Council's Report Review Committee. The purpose of this independent review is to provide candid and critical comments that will assist the institution in making the published report as sound as possible and to ensure that the report meets institutional standards for objectivity, evidence, and responsiveness to the study charge. The review comments and draft manuscript remain confidential to protect the integrity of the deliberative process. We wish to thank the following individuals for their participation in the review of this report: R. Quinn Brackett, Brackett & Associates; Gary Byrd, Alexandria, Virginia; James H. Hedlund, NHTSA (retired); Lester A. Hoel, University of Virginia; Joseph Hummer, North Carolina State University; Gerald W. Hyland, Fairfax County Board of Supervisors; Herbert S. Levinson, Herbert S. Levinson Transportation Consultant; Bradley L. Mallory, Pennsylvania Department of Transportation; John A. Rice, University of California, Berkeley; Thomas C. Schelling, University of Maryland.

While the individuals listed above have provided constructive comments and suggestions, it must be emphasized that responsibility for the final content of this report rests solely with the authoring committee and the institution.

The report was edited and prepared for publication under the supervision of Nancy A. Ackerman, Director of Reports and Editorial Services, TRB. Special appreciation is expressed to Norman Solomon, who edited the report, and to Marguerite Schneider, who assisted in meeting arrangements, travel plans, and communications with the committee and provided word processing support for preparation of the final manuscript.

Contents

Executive Summary

In 1995 Congress repealed the National Maximum Speed Limit (NMSL) of 55 mph (89 km/h), returning to the states the responsibility for setting speed limits on major highways. Since then, 49 state legislatures have taken the opportunity to raise speed limits on Interstate highways—and, in some cases, on other major roads—often to levels that had been in effect before the NMSL was established in 1974. Some states are reexamining methods for determining appropriate speed limits. Several are monitoring the effects of changes in speed limits on driving speeds and safety outcomes.

In this study current practice in setting speed limits on all roads—not just major highways—is reviewed, and guidance to state and local governments on appropriate methods of setting speed limits and related enforcement strategies is provided. The study is intended for a broad audience of those involved in decisions about speed limits—state and local legislators, traffic engineers, and law enforcement and judicial officials, as well as the interested general public.

OVERVIEW OF CURRENT PRACTICE

Speed limits are one of the oldest strategies for controlling driving speeds. Connecticut imposed the first maximum speed limit of 8 mph (13 km/h) in cities in 1901. Since that time, primary responsibility for setting speed limits has remained with state and local governments. Nationally mandated speed limits such as the NMSL are exceptions to the rule.

The current framework for speed regulation was developed in the 1920s and 1930s. Each state has a basic statute that requires drivers to operate vehicles at a speed that is reasonable and prudent for existing conditions. Speed limits are legislated by road class (e.g., Interstate highway) and geographic area (e.g., urban district). They generally apply to all roads of a particular class throughout a jurisdiction. However, state and most local governments have the authority to change the limits by establishing speed zones for highway sections where statutory limits do not fit specific road or traffic conditions, and to determine alternative maximum speed limits in these zones.

Legislated speed limits are established by state legislatures, city councils, or Congress on the basis of judgments about appropriate trade-offs among public safety, community concerns, and travel efficiency. Legislated limits are established for favorable conditions—good weather, free-flowing traffic, and good visibility. Drivers are expected to reduce speeds as these conditions deteriorate. Speed limits in speed zones are determined administratively. The most common approach sets the limit on the basis of an engineering study, which takes into consideration such factors as operating speeds of free-flowing vehicles, crash experience, roadside development and roadway geometry (e.g., curvature, sight distance), and parking and pedestrian levels to make a judgment about the speed at which the limit should be set. In many speed zones, it is common practice to establish the speed limit near the 85th percentile speed, that is, the speed at or below which 85 percent of drivers travel in free-flow conditions at representative locations on the highway or roadway section. This approach assumes that most drivers are capable of judging the speed at which they can safely travel.

REGULATION OF DRIVING SPEEDS

If most drivers are assumed to be capable of making reasonable judgments about appropriate driving speeds, why are speed limits even necessary?

The primary reason for regulating individual choices is the significant risks drivers can impose on others. For example, a driver with a higher tolerance for risk may decide to drive faster, accepting a higher probability of a crash, injury, or even death in exchange for a shorter trip time. This driver's decision may not adequately take into consideration the risk his choices impose on the other road users. Even a driver traveling alone who is involved in a single-vehicle crash may impose medical and property damage costs on society that are not fully reimbursed by the driver. The imposition of risks on others that are not adequately considered when the activity of a person or a firm affects their welfare is a primary reason for government intervention in many areas besides traffic safety, such as environmental protection and product safety.

Another reason for regulating speed derives from the inability of some drivers to correctly judge the capabilities of their vehicles (e.g., stopping, handling) and to anticipate roadway geometry and roadside conditions sufficiently to determine appropriate driving speeds. This reason may not be as relevant for experienced motorists driving under familiar circumstances. However, inexperienced drivers or experienced drivers operating in unfamiliar surroundings may underestimate risk and make inappropriate speed choices. Even drivers familiar with a particular road can make inappropriate decisions because of fatigue or other factors.

A final reason for regulating speed, which is related to the issues of information adequacy and judgment, is the tendency of some drivers to underestimate or misjudge the effects of speed on crash probability and severity. This problem is often manifested by young and inexperienced drivers and may be a problem for other drivers.

The risks imposed on others and the adequacy of information about appropriate driving speeds vary by road class. For example, the risks imposed on others by individual driver speed choices are likely to be relatively small on rural Interstate highways where free-flowing traffic creates fewer opportunities for conflict with other road users. Moreover, under normal conditions, drivers typically have adequate information to determine appropriate driving speeds because these highways are usually built to the highest design standards, access is limited, and roadside activity is minimal. In contrast, the risks imposed on others by individual driver speed choices may be large on urban arterials where roadside activities are numerous and traffic volumes are high for extended periods of the day, increasing the probability of conflict with other road users. These differences are important factors for consideration in setting appropriate speed limits on different types of roads.

THE SAFETY CONNECTION AND THE ROLE OF SPEED LIMITS

Drivers' speed choices impose risks that affect both the probability and severity of crashes. Speed is directly related to injury severity in a crash. The probability of severe injury increases sharply with the impact speed of a vehicle in a collision, reflecting the laws of physics. The risk is even greater when a vehicle strikes a pedestrian, the most vulnerable of road users. Although injury to vehicle occupants in a crash can be mitigated by safety belt use and airbags, the strength of the relationship between speed and crash severity alone is sufficient reason for managing speed.

Speed is also linked to the probability of being in a crash, although the evidence is not as compelling because crashes are complex events that seldom can be attributed to a single factor. Many driver attributes and behavioral factors besides speed affect the probability of crashes—driving under the influence of alcohol or other drugs, age, attitudes toward risk, and experience of the driver—but speed has been shown to play an important role.

The concept of speed itself is complex. It can relate to the speed of a single vehicle or to the distribution of speeds in a stream of traffic. Crash involvement on Interstate highways and nonlimited-access rural roads has been associated with the deviation of the speed of crash-involved vehicles from the average speed of traffic. Crash involvement has also been associated with the speed of travel, at least on certain road types. For example, single-vehicle crash involvement rates on nonlimited-access rural roads have been shown to rise with travel speed.

The primary purpose of speed limits is to enhance safety by reducing the risks imposed by drivers' speed choices. Speed limits enhance safety in at least two ways. By establishing an upper bound on speed, they have a limiting function; the objective is to reduce both the probability and the severity of crashes. Speed limits also have a coordinating function. Here the intent is to reduce dispersion in speeds (i.e., lessen differences in speed among drivers using the same road at the same time) and thus reduce the potential for vehicle conflicts. A related function of speed limits is to provide the basis for enforcement and sanctions for those who drive at speeds excessive for conditions and endanger others.

In setting speed limits, decision makers attempt to establish a reasonable balance between risk (safety) and travel time (mobility) for a road class or specific highway section. Thus, the posted speed limit should inform motorists of maximum driving speeds under favorable conditions that decision makers consider reasonable and safe for a road class or highway section.

EFFECTIVENESS OF SPEED LIMITS

The principal objective of speed limits is improved safety, but simply posting a speed limit does not guarantee the desired change in driving speeds or a reduction in crashes or crash severity. Recent changes in speed limits in the United States provide an opportunity to study these effects. In 1987 Congress allowed states to raise speed limits from 55 to 65 mph (89 to 105 km/h) on qualifying sections of rural Interstate highways. In the immediately following years, most states that raised limits observed increases on the order of 4 mph (6 km/h) in average speeds and 85th percentile speeds, and increases in speed dispersion of about 1 mph (2 km/h). These speed changes were generally associated with statistically significant increases in fatalities and fatal crashes on the affected highways—a plausible finding because of the strong link between even modest increases in speed at higher speeds and increased crash severity. Although they provided compelling evidence of higher fatalities on Interstate highways, most studies did not examine the issue of broader network effects, such as potential effects on safety from any traffic diversion or redeployment of enforcement personnel. A more limited number of studies that attempted to look at such system effects reported mixed results. One study that examined effects on non-Interstate rural highways found evidence of spillover effects in higher fatalities on these roads. Two other studies that examined system effects on a county- and statewide basis reported evidence of offsetting reductions in fatalities that resulted in neutral and even positive systemwide net safety outcomes. Additional research and analysis are needed to determine the extent and size of such systemwide effects.

Studies have been conducted following repeal of federal maximum speed limits in 1995; many of them focused on Interstate highways. Most found results similar to the speed limit changes in 1987: modest increases in average speeds and 85th percentile speeds and, in some cases, speed dispersion on highways on which speed limits were raised. Although not consistent across all states, most studies indicated an increase in fatalities on highways on which speed limits were raised. Most studies did not explore any possible system effects, and the results should be considered preliminary because they are generally based on 1 year of data or less.

Most of the recent U.S. literature has focused on the effects of raising speed limits on Interstate highways. In the future, however, circumstances could warrant reductions in speed limits on some Interstates and other major highways. An earlier Transportation Research Board study (1984) of the effects of the national 55-mph (89-km/h) speed limit found that the lower limit reduced both travel speeds and fatalities, although driver speed compliance gradually eroded. The report provides a comprehensive review of studies that examined the effects of lowering speed limits on major highways.

In contrast to the extensive analysis of speed and safety changes on Interstate highways, few studies have examined the effects of changing speed limits on lower-speed, nonlimited-access highways. Those that were identified found little effect on driving speeds or crash rates when speed limits were raised to near the 85th percentile speed or lowered to near the 35th percentile speed in selected speed zones on rural roads and on urban and suburban arterials. The results, however, cannot be generalized to speed zones on all nonlimited-access highways. Further, the lack of observed changes in driving speeds may be explained to the extent that changes in posted speed limits simply legalized existing driver behavior, that is, changed compliance levels rather than speed behavior. Nevertheless, the findings suggest the difficulty of altering behavior merely by changing the sign.

ROLE OF ENFORCEMENT AND SANCTIONS

Managing speeds through speed limits requires a system of speed laws and a process for establishing reasonable speed limits as well as enforcement, sanctions, and public education, ideally all working together. Enforcement is an integral part of such a system. Even if reasonable speed limits are established through legislation or engineering studies and most drivers comply within a small tolerance, enforcement is still necessary to ensure the conformity of a minority of drivers who will obey traffic regulations only if they perceive a credible threat of detection and punishment for noncompliance.

The main difficulty with the traditional approach to speed enforcement—radar enforcement using a mobile or stationary police vehicle—is its short-lived temporal and spatial effect on deterring speeding. Maintaining the deterrence effect requires a level of enforcement intensity and expense that has proven difficult to sustain because of competing enforcement priorities and limited resources available for speed enforcement.

Targeted enforcement combined with focused publicity campaigns can boost the effectiveness of traditional enforcement methods. Automated enforcement, particularly photo radar, has been shown to be efficient and effective where it has been used for speed control, particularly on high-volume arterials. Photo radar could also be coupled with variable speed limit systems on urban Interstate highways where high traffic volumes can make traditional enforcement methods hazardous. Alternatives to enforcement to achieve desired driving speeds on local roads include physical measures known as "traffic calming" (e.g., speed humps, roundabouts, and raised intersections). Redesigning roads to achieve greater congruity between driver perceptions of appropriate travel speeds and the cues provided by the road itself (e.g., narrowing lanes) may also influence motorists' speeds. A proper mix of these approaches can enable police to leverage their resources and deploy them efficiently.

Traffic court judges are also important participants in effective speed enforcement. They may overturn speeding violations if they think the speed limits are unreasonable or reduce fines if they believe the sanctions are too harsh. If judges are lenient in their treatment of speeding offenses and routinely dismiss speeding citations, the incentive for the police to enforce the speed limits may be reduced. Thus it is important that traffic court judges—as well as the police and motorists—perceive that speed limits are reasonable and enforceable.

GUIDANCE

On the basis of its review of the purpose and methods of setting and enforcing speed limits, the committee offers the following guidance to responsible decision makers. Its primary focus is on the effects of speed limit policies on safety rather than on travel time, energy consumption, or environmental pollution. The committee attempted to be as specific as possible, but the relevant studies and the data on which the guidance is based fall short of providing sufficient support for quantifying with much precision the effects of changes in speed limits on driving speeds and safety.

General Framework for Establishing Speed Limits

The current general approach—legislated speed limits and administratively established speed zones—is sound. It balances the desirability of uniform speed limits (legislated limits for broad road classes) with the need for exceptions (speed zones) to reflect local differences. The practice of establishing speed limits to reflect a reasonable balance between travel speeds and risks under favorable operating conditions is also sensible.

Making Decisions About Appropriate Speed Limits

Decisions about legislated speed limits reflect trade-offs and judgments about the relative importance of safety, travel time, and feasibility of enforcement. Legislators should consult with traffic engineers, law enforcement officials, judges, public health officials, and the general public in their deliberations. Consultation, however, cannot ensure that all parties will reach consensus, particularly where multiple interests are involved, such as residents and commuters on residential streets. In addition to safety, final selection of a speed limit should meet the requirements of enforceability and acceptance by the community at large. Provision should also be made to monitor driving speeds and crash experience, and the decision should be reviewed periodically because road conditions, vehicle safety features, driving attitudes, and behavior change over time.

Determination of appropriate speed limits in speed zones should be made on the basis of an engineering study. Traffic engineers normally conduct the study; consultation with law enforcement officials should be standard practice. Elected officials and citizen groups may also become involved when community concerns have been raised about driving speeds. Speed zones should be reviewed periodically—with greater frequency where conditions are changing rapidly, such as developing suburban areas—to determine whether a change in speed limits or boundaries of the speed zone is warranted.

Methods of Setting Speed Limits

Legislated Speed Limits

The strong link between speed and crash severity supports the need for setting maximum speed limits on high-speed roads (e.g., Interstate highways, freeways, high-speed rural multi- or two-lane roads) to place an upper bound on travel speeds to reduce crash probability and severity. The committee refrained from recommending a specific numeric limit, however. Road conditions vary too widely to justify a "one-size-fits-all" approach. Roads, even those in the same class, are not all built to the same design standards, nor are traffic volumes uniform.

In determining appropriate speed limits for each road type, decision makers should be guided by both the likely risks imposed on others by individual driver speed choices and the availability of information to enable drivers to make appropriate speed choices. They should take enforcement practicality into consideration. Decision makers should also request technical information on the following four factors to help guide their determination of appropriate legislated speed limits for a specific road class:

- Design speed, that is, the design speed of a major portion of the road, not of its most critical design features (e.g., a sharp curve);
- Vehicle operating speed, measured as a range of 85th percentile speeds taken from spot-speed surveys of free-flowing vehicles at representative locations along the highway;
- Safety experience, that is, crash frequencies and outcomes; and
- Enforcement experience, that is, existing speed tolerance (i.e., allowance for driving above the posted speed limit) and level of enforcement.

The weight given to these factors, particularly those related to speed, depends on the type of road. For example, on many rural Interstate highways, vehicle operating speeds should be a major factor in setting speed limits. Design speeds provide little additional information because restrictive design features are not generally present on these highways; typically drivers can anticipate conditions and determine appropriate driving speeds. In addition, risks to other road users are small compared with other highways. Finally, maintaining high levels of enforcement is difficult on long stretches of rural Interstate. In contrast, design speeds should carry greater weight in the determination of speed limits on nonlimited-access rural roads where restrictive roadway geometry is likely to play an important role in defining an appropriate driving speed. Poor safety records on these roads support lower speed limits, but the limits must be reasonable for conditions; enforcement is limited because of extensive rural road mileage.

Safety and enforcement considerations should be given higher priority than design speeds or vehicle operating speeds on many urban roads, particularly residential streets. Intersections and traffic signals play a more critical role than design in limiting speed. Driver misjudgment about appropriate driving speeds poses high risks to vulnerable road users (e.g., pedestrians and bicyclists) on many urban roads. Neighborhood pressures may result in setting very low speed limits on residential streets, but often they are not enforced—or enforcement tolerances are large—and compliance is poor even by some neighborhood residents. Thus, where low speeds are desirable, speed limits must be enforced, or alternatives such as traffic calming should be considered for certain residential streets. More detailed guidance for each of seven road classes plus one category for special speed zones (e.g., school and work zones) is provided in Chapter 6.

Speed Limits in Speed Zones

Determination of appropriate speed limits in speed zones should be made on the basis of an engineering study. The most common factor considered in setting speed zone limits is the 85th percentile traffic speed. Setting the speed limit at or near this level can be desirable on some roads because it (*a*) enables the police to focus their enforcement efforts on the most dangerous speed outliers and (*b*) is generally at the upper bound of a speed range where crash involvement rates are lowest on certain road types, according to some studies that have examined the relationship between speed and crash probability.

Setting the speed limit primarily on the basis of the 85th percentile speed is not always appropriate. Potential safety benefits may not be realized on roads with a wide range of speeds (i.e., the spread between the slowest and fastest drivers). Basing the speed limit on a measure of unconstrained free-flowing travel speed is not appropriate for urban roads with a mix of road users and high traffic volumes and levels of roadside activity. Traffic engineers should consider an expert-system approach, discussed in Chapter 3, which offers a systematic and consistent method of determining speed limits in these speed zones.

Differential Speed Limits

No conclusive evidence could be found to support or reject the use of differential speed limits for passenger cars and heavy trucks. More research and evaluation of the effects of differential speed limits on driving speeds and safety outcomes are needed in states that have adopted them.

Motorists do not appear to decrease speed at night when lower nighttime speed limits are in effect. However, compelling evidence could not be found to support the elimination of nighttime speed limits in states that have adopted them.

Variable Speed Limits

Technology is available to support speed limits that change with conditions, but more experimentation and evaluation are needed to determine the effectiveness of these systems from a safety and traffic efficiency perspective and to learn where variable speed limits can be deployed most usefully. The current high cost of variable speed limit systems restricts their use to Interstate highways and freeways with high traffic volumes or to selected segments of major roads where weather (e.g., fog, visibility) is a frequent problem. Once their effectiveness is more clearly established, broader application of variable speed limit systems should be considered on urban Interstate highways in the United States because they are well suited to addressing temporal changes in traffic volumes, speed, and density on these highways.

Enforcement and Other Speed Management Strategies

Policy makers can affect the level of enforcement through resource allocation, but they must recognize that if drivers believe that a speed limit is unreasonable, enforcement will be difficult and expensive. If a low speed limit is posted on a road designed for higher speeds, enforcement problems will be considerable. This occurred on many Interstate highways under the NMSL. When speed limits were raised by 10 mph (16 km/h) on sections of qualified rural Interstate highways in 1987, average traffic speeds increased much less than the change in the speed limit immediately following the change. Apparently many drivers were already exceeding the old speed limits because speeds had crept up since the NMSL went into effect.

Strategic deployment of traditional enforcement methods on roads and at times when speed-related incidents are most common or where road conditions are most hazardous can help focus resources on potential problems. The relative infrequency of crashes, however, can make it difficult to show systematic safety improvements from targeted enforcement strategies. Planned patrols at varying times and locations can extend deterrence effects temporally and spatially from particular locations, but only after an initial period of continuous enforcement. Patrols must be visible and sufficiently frequent to create a credible deterrent. Police can improve compliance by combining enforcement initiatives with high-profile public information campaigns. Publicity must be followed up by enforcement actions, however, if the approach is to successfully deter speeding. Changing fundamental attitudes about speeding requires a long-term sustained effort.

Automated enforcement, particularly photo radar, can be used to complement traditional enforcement methods, particularly where roadway geometrics or traffic volume makes traditional methods difficult or hazardous. Photo radar is controversial. Its successful introduction requires adoption of legal changes (e.g., resolution of constitutional privacy issues, vehicle owner versus driver liability), funding, and public education. It should be deployed selectively at first—at locations that are hazardous and difficult to patrol with traditional methods and where speeding is a problem—to ensure essential public support. In the near term, speed limits should be set at levels that are largely self-enforcing or at the lowest speed the police are able to enforce.

Speed limits alone will not be effective in all situations. Keeping driving speeds at desired levels in urban areas poses a particular challenge. Traffic calming can be used judiciously on residential streets, but community as well as resident support is important for its success. Systemwide effects must also be considered so that the traffic and safety problems will not simply migrate to other streets. Road redesign has the potential to achieve greater consistency between desired and actual operating speeds. Unfortunately, strict application of current roadway design procedures does not ensure speed consistency. Because of the size of the U.S. road network and the pace of rehabilitation, road redesign is a long-term strategy, and more understanding concerning the overall safety benefits of alternative designs is needed. The approach can yield satisfactory solutions, but additional study of the relationships between operating speeds and roadway geometric elements is necessary.

CONCLUDING COMMENT

Most states chose to raise speed limits on major highways following repeal of the NMSL. The effects of their decisions on driving speeds and safety outcomes, in particular, should be closely monitored. Efforts to mitigate any adverse safety effects through enforcement should be redoubled, and initiatives to promote safety belt use and reduce driving while intoxicated—measures with large and proven safety benefits—should be continued.

Technological advances may offer additional techniques for controlling driving speeds on all types of roads. For example, technology can help establish limits that are more sensitive to actual changes in road conditions and thus provide drivers with better information. Such technology can be installed in the vehicles and highways of the future to monitor and control speed. Finally, it can help improve the efficiency and effectiveness of enforcement. Further development, experimentation, and evaluation are needed for many technologies to realize their potential.

The issue of appropriate driving speeds, however, will persist as long as there are individual drivers making choices about risk and time efficiency. Ultimately, decisions about appropriate speed limits depend on judgments about society's tolerance for risk, valuation of time, and willingness to police itself. These judgments, in turn, should be reviewed periodically in the light of changes in vehicles and highway conditions and shifts in public perceptions of safety and attitudes toward risk.

REFERENCE

ABBREVIATION

TRB Transportation Research Board

TRB. 1984. *Special Report 204: 55: A Decade of Experience.* National Research Council, Washington, D.C., 262 pp.

1

Introduction

In 1995 Congress rescinded the National Maximum Speed Limit (NMSL) of 55 mph (89 km/h), which had been in effect since 1974 following the oil shortages experienced in the preceding year.[1] The National Highway System Designation Act of 1995 returned to the states the prerogative of setting speed limits on major highways.

Following repeal of the NMSL, 49 state legislatures have raised statutory speed limits, often to levels that were in effect before passage of the NMSL (Figure 1-1, Table 1-1). The 55-mph (89-km/h) speed limit was retained only in the predominately urban District of Columbia and Hawaii. The highest speed limits are in western states where congestion is relatively low and the highway infrastructure of more recent construction than in many eastern states. One state—Montana—advocated that drivers themselves determine the safe speed at which to travel. Consequently, Montana does not post day-

[1] In 1987 Congress had relaxed the 55-mph (89-km/h) speed limit, allowing states to raise the limit to 65 mph (105 km/h) on qualified sections of rural Interstate highways.

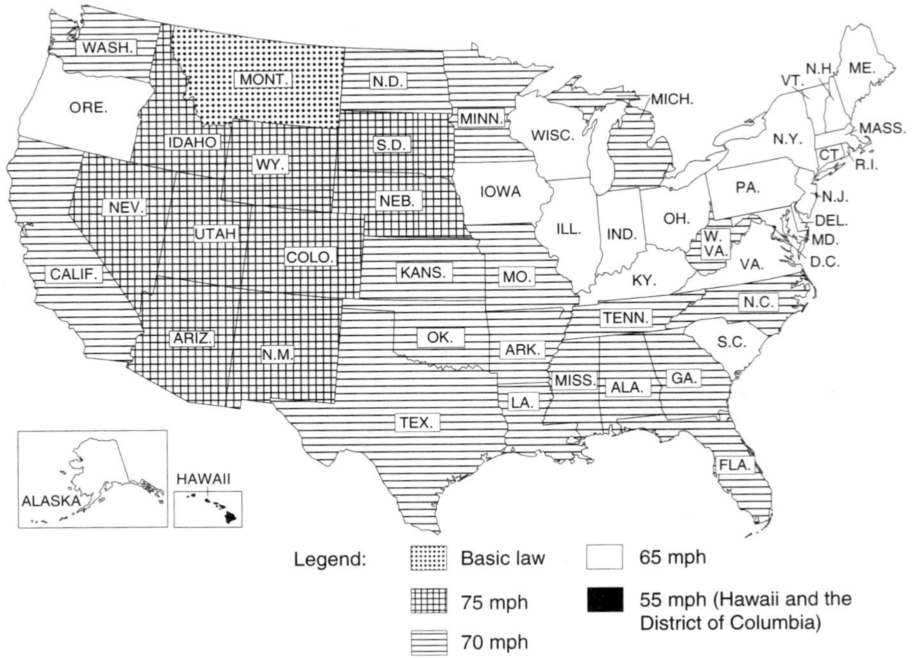

Figure 1-1 Maximum speed limits on Interstate highways as of June 10, 1998 (data from National Highway Traffic Safety Administration and Federal Highway Administration regional offices, state legislatures, and other sources).

Table 1-1 Maximum Speed Limits by State as of June 10, 1998 (Data from National Highway Traffic Safety Administration and Federal Highway Administration Regional Offices, State Legislatures, and Other Sources)

State	Pre-NMSL Maximum (mph)	Current Maximum Speed Limit (mph) Interstate Highway	Primary Highway
Alabama	70	70	55
Alaska	70	65	55
Arizona	75	75[a]	55
Arkansas	75	70 (65)	55
California	70	70[b] (55)	65 (55)
Colorado	70	75	55
Connecticut	60	65[c]	55
Delaware	60	65[d]	50
District of Columbia	60	55[e] (50)	50
Florida	70	70[d] (65)	55
Georgia	70	70[f]	55
Hawaii	70	55	55
Idaho	70	75	65
Illinois	70	65[g] (55)	55
Indiana	70	65 (60)	55
Iowa	75	65[b]	55
Kansas	75	70	70
Kentucky	70	65	55
Louisiana	70	70	65
Maine	70	65	55
Maryland	70	65	55
Massachusetts	65	65	55
Michigan	70	70 (55)	55
Minnesota	65	70	65[h]
Mississippi	70	70	65
Missouri	70	70[i]	65
Montana	Basic Law[j]	Basic Law[j,k] (65)	Basic Law[j,l] (60)
Nebraska	75	75[l]	60
Nevada	Basic Law[j]	75	70 (55)
New Hampshire	70	65	55
New Jersey	70	65[m]	55[m]
New Mexico	70	75[a]	60[n]
New York	55	65	55

(continued on next page)

Table 1-1 *(continued)*

State	Pre-NMSL Maximum (mph)	Current Maximum Speed Limit (mph) Interstate Highway	Primary Highway
North Carolina	70	70[o]	55
North Dakota	75	70	65[p]
Ohio	70	65 (55)	55
Oklahoma	70	70[q]	65 (55)
Oregon	75	65 (55)	55
Pennsylvania	65	65	65[d]
Rhode Island	60	65[d]	55
South Carolina	70	65	55
South Dakota	75	75	65[r]
Tennessee	75	70	65
Texas	70	70 (65)[s]	70 (60)[s]
Utah	70	75	55
Vermont	65	65	50
Virginia	70	65	55
Washington	70	70 (60)	60 (55)
West Virginia	70	70	65
Wisconsin	70	65	55
Wyoming	75	75[t]	65

Note: Figures in parentheses are speed limits for heavy trucks. Primary highways are part of the federal-aid highway system—highways that are eligible for federal highway funds. The Federal-Aid Primary System comprises interconnecting main roads important to interstate, statewide, and regional travel, consisting of rural arterial routes and their extensions into or through urban areas (see text box). NMSL = National Maximum Speed Limit. 1 mi = 1.609 km.

[a] Urban Interstates remain 55 mph (89 km/h).

[b] Rural freeways and expressways only. Other freeways and expressways are at 65 mph (105 km/h). Other city, county, and state roads may go to 65 mph on the basis of engineering and traffic surveys.

[c] Speed limit increases on suitable multilane limited-access highways will be implemented by Oct. 1, 1998. Differential speed limits may be enacted.

[d] Only certain segments.

[e] Only part of Woodrow Wilson Bridge eligible for 55 mph (89 km/h).

[f] Urban Interstates are 65 mph (105 km/h). Speed limits of some divided highways without controlled access are 65 mph based on engineering and traffic studies.

[g] Only some urban Interstates are at 65 mph (105 km/h).

[h] Approximately 120 mi (193 km) of non-Interstate freeways and expressways will remain at 55 mph (89 km/h) as well as all two-lane state highways.
[i] State can raise any road to 70 mph (113 km/h) with safety study.
[j] A speed that is reasonable and prudent for conditions but with no numeric limit.
[k] No maximum numeric posted daytime limit for passenger vehicles; daytime speed is "reasonable and proper" for conditions. Nighttime speeds for passenger vehicles are 65 mph (105 km/h) on the Interstate and 55 mph (89 km/h) on all other roads. Speed limits for heavy trucks are 65 mph day and night on the Interstate, and 60 mph (97 km/h) day and night on all other roads except for triple truck combinations, which are limited to 55 mph day and night on all roads.
[l] Urban Interstates remain at 60 mph (97 km/h). Speed limits on four-lane expressways are 65 mph (105 km/h) with some exceptions.
[m] In January 1998, state legislation was passed raising speed limits to 65 mph (105 km/h) on approximately 400 mi (640 km) of limited-access highways for an 18-month trial period.
[n] 70 mph (113 km/h) on four-lane roads with shoulders; 65 mph (105 km/h) on two-lane roads with shoulders; and 60 mph (97 km/h) on two-lane roads without shoulders.
[o] An additional 340 mi (550 km) of non-Interstate controlled access are 70 mph (113 km/h).
[p] 55 mph (89 km/h) on two-lane highway at night, and 55 mph (89 km/h) on gravel roads, day and night.
[q] 75 mph (121 km/h) on rural segments of turnpike [50 mph (80 km/h) minimum], 65 mph (105 km/h) on urban segments [40 mph (64 km/h) minimum], 60 mph (97 km/h) on urban Interstates, and 55 mph (89 km/h) on state roads and other highways at night.
[r] 65 mph (105 km/h) on major two-lane highways. Forty counties have decided to retain 55 mph (89 km/h).
[s] For cars, 70 mph (113 km/h) in the daytime, 65 mph (105 km/h) at night. For trucks, 65 mph on Interstates in daytime, 60 mph (97 km/h) on primary roads in the daytime, 55 mph (89 km/h) at night. The Texas Transportation Commission approved speed limits lower than the state maximum of 70 mph on about half of the state's farm-to-market system.
[t] 60 mph (97 km/h) on urban Interstates; 65 mph (105 km/h) on four- and two-lane roads; some secondary and mountain roads remain at 55 mph (89 km/h).

time speed limits for passenger vehicles on major highways, but drivers must travel at a reasonable and proper speed for conditions. In many states where speed limits were raised, public officials are closely monitoring related changes in vehicle speeds and safety outcomes.

SCOPE OF STUDY AND CHARGE

With such a major policy shift, this study was conceived as an opportunity to review current practice in setting speed limits on all roads, not just major highways, and to provide guidance to state and local governments on both appropriate speed limit and enforcement policies. Of course, speed limits are only one strategy for managing vehicle speeds. Redesigning roads to achieve desired operating speeds[2] and retrofitting neighborhood streets with speed humps and traffic circles are alternative approaches to reducing traffic speeds. These strategies are often considered on streets where compliance with local speed limits is poor. This study touches briefly on such strategies, but they have been widely covered elsewhere.

The primary focus here, in response to the study charge, is on regulating speed through speed limits and enforcement. More specifically, the interdisciplinary committee of experts convened to conduct the study has, in response to the charge,

- Reviewed research to establish what is known about various methods of setting speed limits; the role of speed in safety; the role of road design and function in setting and enforcing speed limits; the effectiveness of speed limits, particularly with regard to safety; enforcement of and compliance with speed limits; and social benefits and costs of speed limits (i.e., trade-offs among safety, travel efficiency, and other factors that affect driver speed choices);
- Considered the effects of new and emerging technologies for speed management and speed enforcement and expected changes in the highway environment (e.g., growing numbers of older drivers); and
- Provided its judgment concerning appropriate changes to current practice on the basis of its findings.

[2] Technical terms are defined in a glossary, which can be found in Appendix E.

Setting speed limits is complex and frequently controversial. The process is often viewed as a technical exercise, but the decision involves value judgments and trade-offs that are frequently handled through the political process by state legislatures and city councils. Speed limits represent implicit trade-offs among safety, efficiency of travel, and feasibility of enforcement. These trade-offs, in turn, reflect societal norms about appropriate driver behavior, tolerable levels of risk,[3] and acceptable levels of enforcement. In this study alternative methods of establishing speed limits (e.g., legislated mandates, engineering studies) are considered in terms of what is known about the trade-offs among safety, efficiency, and enforceability. What is known and what is not known from available studies and data concerning the effects of changes in speed limits on driving speeds, safety, and travel times are also reviewed.

RESPONSIBILITY FOR SETTING SPEED LIMITS

With two exceptions—during World War II and more recently with the NMSL of 55 mph (89 km/h)—setting speed limits in the United States has been a responsibility of state and local governments. Every state has a basic speed statute, which requires drivers to operate their vehicles at a speed that is reasonable and prudent for existing conditions and hazards.[4] State statutes authorize maximum speed limits that may vary by highway type (e.g., Interstate highways) or location (e.g., urban district) (NHTSA 1997a, vi).[5] Generally, statutory limits apply throughout a political jurisdiction (ITE 1992, 347).

[3] The term "risk" as it is used in this report includes both the probability of being in a crash and the severity of the crash.

[4] This basic structure is contained in the most recent version of the Uniform Vehicle Code, which provides a model set of motor vehicle laws to encourage uniformity in state traffic regulation (National Committee on Uniform Traffic Laws and Ordinances 1992, 82).

[5] There are two types of maximum speed limits: (*a*) absolute limits and (*b*) prima facie limits. An absolute speed limit is a limit above which it is unlawful to drive regardless of roadway conditions, the amount of traffic, or other influencing factors. A prima facie speed limit is one above which drivers are presumed to be driving unlawfully but where, if charged with a violation, they may contend that their speed

States and, in most cases, local governments have the authority to establish speed zones where statutory limits do not fit specific road or traffic conditions. Alternative maximum legal speed limits are established by administrative action in the speed zone, typically on the basis of an engineering study, and become effective when the limits are posted and properly recorded (ITE 1992, 347). Speed limits are set to inform motorists of appropriate driving speeds under favorable conditions. Drivers are expected to reduce speeds if conditions deteriorate (e.g., poor visibility, adverse weather, congestion, warning signs, or presence of bicyclists and pedestrians), and many state statutes reflect this requirement.

Speed control regulations—both legislated and administratively established maximum speed limits—provide the legal basis for adjudication and sanctions for violations of the law. State and local officials may also post advisory speed signs, which do not have the force of law but warn motorists of suggested safe speeds for specific conditions at a particular location (e.g., turn, intersection approach) (ITE 1992, 347).

PURPOSE OF SETTING SPEED LIMITS

The primary reason for setting speed limits is safety. In setting speed limits, decision makers attempt to strike an appropriate societal balance between travel time and risk for a road class or specific highway section. Thus, the posted legal limit informs motorists of maximum driving speeds that decision makers consider reasonable and safe for a road class or highway section under favorable conditions. In addition, speed limits provide the basis for enforcement. Well-conceived speed limits provide law enforcement officers and courts with an indication of appropriate speeds for favorable conditions and thus help target enforcement and sanctions on those who drive at speeds that are excessive for conditions and likely to endanger others. Speed

was safe for conditions existing on the roadway at that time and, therefore, that they are not guilty of a speed limit violation. Approximately two-thirds of the states have absolute speed limits and one-third have prima facie limits or limits of each type (ITE 1992, 347).

limits have also been established for fuel conservation, as they were following the oil crisis in 1973. Finally, speed limits could be enacted to improve air quality—motor vehicles emit more pollutants at high speeds—but speed limits are very rarely established solely for environmental goals.

The broad objectives of speed limits are not always easy to achieve in practice. For example, the basic premise of a speed limit—that it communicates information about a driving speed that decision makers have determined appropriately balances risk and travel efficiency for a particular road section—assumes both that a safe and reasonable speed can be defined and that there is a cause-and-effect relationship between speed limits (as opposed to speed) and safety (ITE 1993, 1). Neither of these assumptions is self-evident.

Drivers, neighborhood residents, traffic engineers, law enforcement officials, and legislators may differ as to what constitutes a reasonable balance between risk and travel efficiency. For example, local governments frequently receive requests to lower speed limits from neighborhood residents who seek to reduce speeding on local streets. Traffic engineers may not find the reduction to be justified by an engineering study. Drivers themselves—depending on their age, risk tolerance, trip purpose, and familiarity with particular roads—may not agree on what speed best balances risk with travel efficiency. However, without some consensus concerning appropriate driving speeds among drivers, the law enforcement community, and the courts, the imposition of speed limits alone is not likely to have much effect on driver speeding behavior.

Moreover, as the experience with the 55-mph (89-km/h) NMSL shows, even when there is a high degree of driver compliance, public attitudes can change over time. Initially there were high levels of support for the 55-mph speed limit, reflecting the national sense of crisis because of fuel shortages. Support eroded, however, as the crisis eased and fuel became more plentiful. In 1986, the year before Congress relaxed the 55-mph limit on rural Interstates, the Federal Highway Administration reported that 76 percent of vehicles exceeded 55 mph on these highways (FHWA 1987, p. 183). Attitudes toward appropriate speed limit levels could change again. For example, as the driving population ages or if aggressive driving incidents, of which speeding is a component, become more pervasive,[6] some segments of the population could favor lower limits. Or, if vehicles and roads become safer, motorists could favor higher limits, at least on the safest roads.

OVERVIEW OF ISSUES RELATED TO SETTING SPEED LIMITS

Safety

Safety is the most important reason for managing speed through the imposition of speed limits. Traffic safety has significantly improved on U.S. highways over the last several decades. In 1996, the most recent year for which data are available, the fatality rate per 100 million vehicle-mi (100 million vehicle-km) of travel remained at its historic low of 1.7 (1.1) as compared with 2.5 (1.6) in 1986 and 3.2 (2.0) in 1976 (NHTSA 1997b, 15). Since 1992, however, the numbers of fatalities and injuries have slowly crept up, although the fatality rate has remained constant (NHTSA 1997b, 15). Speeding contributes to motor vehicle crashes, but many other driver-related factors affect traffic safety: driving under the influence of alcohol or other drugs, safety belt use, age and attitudes toward risk, and experience of the driver.

The relationship among speed limits, driver speed choice, and safety on a given road is complex. Setting appropriate speed limits and related enforcement strategies is the first step in a chain of events that may affect crash probability and crash severity (Figure 1-2). Presumably, well-conceived speed limit and enforcement policies will

---

[6] According to Ricardo Martinez, administrator of the National Highway Traffic Safety Administration (NHTSA), aggressive driving is defined as driving behavior that endangers or is likely to endanger people or property (*AASHTO Journal* 1997, 8). It includes such driving behaviors as honking, gesturing and screaming, tailgating, running lights, weaving through traffic, improper lane changes, speeding, shoulder running, and even shooting (*Highway and Vehicle Safety Report* 1997, 3). Incidents of aggressive driving are linked with irresponsible driving behavior, reduced levels of traffic enforcement, and increased congestion and travel, especially in urban areas (*AASHTO Journal* 1997, 8).

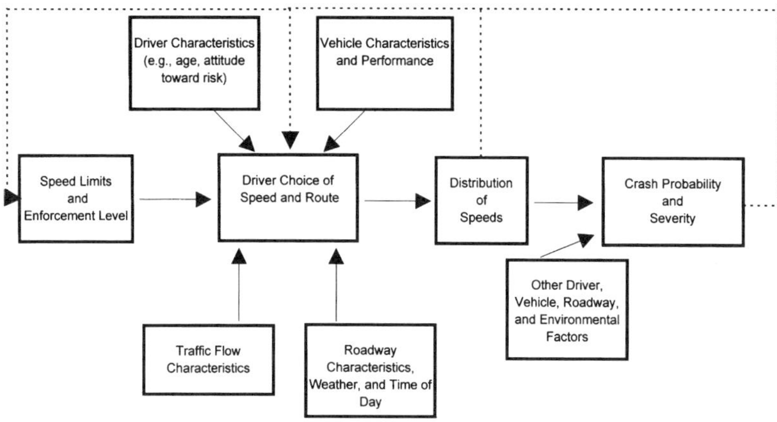

Figure 1-2 Systems view of relationships among speed limits, enforcement levels, and safety.

affect a driver's choice of speed. They may also influence route selection. For example, a driver may divert to a road with a higher speed limit if such an alternative is available. However, driver decisions about speeds and route choice are influenced by many other factors including the characteristics of the driver, the vehicle, the road, and traffic flow; weather; and time of day (Figure 1-2). Speed choices made by individual drivers determine the aggregate distribution of traffic speeds on a particular road section, which in turn affects both the probability and severity of crashes.[7] Finally, over time the safety record of a particular road may influence drivers' speeds and, in the long term, could result in a change in the speed limit or in enforcement strategies.

A cause-and-effect relationship between speed limits and safety is not straightforward. In this study, what is known about the relationships among speed, crash probability, and crash severity is examined first to help identify the importance and role of speed in traffic safety. Then, the effects of speed limits and changes in these limits as a

[7] Of course, in those situations in which there is only one vehicle on the road, then it is the speed level alone—not the distribution of speeds—that affects crash probability and severity.

strategy for managing driving speed are reviewed to help determine the effect on driver behavior and safety outcomes. Finally, the implications of these reviews for methods of setting speed limits as they relate to safety are discussed.

Road Class

The relationships among speed limits, speed, and safety differ by road class (see text box). Congested traffic on city streets with low posted speed limits creates numerous opportunities for vehicle conflicts (e.g., stopped and turning vehicles, traffic entering the street). Numerous crashes may result, but typically they are not severe unless a pedestrian or a cyclist is struck. Driving on divided, limited-access highways with substantially higher speed limits under free-flowing traffic conditions offers an environment with less potential for vehicle conflicts. When crashes do occur, however, they are more likely to involve injuries or fatalities. If crashes are aggregated over both road types, speeds appear to be inversely related to crashes (i.e., as speed increases, crashes decline). However, if crash type and road type are separated, the true relationships are revealed (i.e., driving slowly on congested urban roads is associated with large numbers of crashes that often involve minor injury or property damage only, whereas driving on high-speed freeways is associated with fewer but more severe crashes). Where possible in this study, the relationships between speed limits, speed, and safety are analyzed by road type, and the methods of setting speed limits for different road classes are discussed.

Driver Perception of Risk

The willingness of drivers to heed and comply with speed limits is influenced by their perception of the riskiness of driving in general and of speeding in particular. According to a nationwide survey conducted for *Prevention Magazine* by Princeton Survey Research Associates, nearly 57 percent of drivers surveyed say they do not observe the speed limit, that is, they do not always drive at or below the speed limit (1996, 7). Notwithstanding the limitations of self-reported behavior, one could legitimately ask why so many drivers exceed posted speed limits.

U.S. Highways by Road Class (AASHTO 1994, 10–15; TRB 1984, 20–22)

Interstate highways and freeways are a type of principal arterial highway characterized by multiple lanes with traffic separated by direction, controlled access (i.e., limited access), and grade separation (rather than intersections). These highways, which can accommodate the highest travel speeds, generally provide direct service between cities and larger towns either between or within states and generate a large proportion of longer trips. Most long-distance commercial and recreational travel occurs on the rural portions of this system. The urban segments also serve local traffic in and around major metropolitan areas.

Other arterial highways serve as traffic "arteries" by carrying traffic to and from urbanized areas. These highways also carry large traffic volumes at relatively high speeds, but access is not controlled (i.e., nonlimited access), most intersections are at grade, and access to abutting property is permitted. In rural areas, arterial highways provide for through-travel movement between and within counties. Arterial highways provide for major circulation within metropolitan areas.

Collector highways collect and disperse traffic between rural and urban arterial highways and lower-level roads. These highways have at-grade intersections, limited sight distance, and other design limitations. They carry lower traffic volumes at lower speeds.

Local roads and neighborhood and residential streets account for the vast majority of road mileage but carry the smallest traffic volumes at low speeds. The primary function of these roads is to provide access to residential arcas, individual farms, and businesses; through traffic is discouraged. Pedestrians, bicyclists, and parked vehicles may use these facilities.

In general, motorists do not perceive driving as a life-threatening activity. Millions of Americans drive each day and most complete their trips safely, thus reinforcing the individual driver's perception that the risks involved in driving are low. With about 180 million licensed drivers, each driving an average of 13,800 mi (22 200 km) per year, driver involvement in a crash,[8] on the average, is one every 131,300 driver-mi (211 300 driver-km), or once every 9.5 years of driving. Driver involvement in a fatal crash is considerably less—one every 44 million driver-mi (71 million driver-km), or about once every 3,200 years of driving.[9]

Motorists have different tolerances for risk, and they travel under a variety of conditions, some of which are more conducive to serious crashes. For example, the probability of driver involvement in a fatal crash is considerably higher on two-lane rural roads, on weekend nights when alcohol consumption is a key factor, and for young (under 25) and older (65 or over) drivers and vehicle occupants. Nevertheless, the common perception, even among drivers who have been in a crash, is that such incidents are rare, unpredictable events largely outside reasonable human control—a view reinforced by the frequent direct feedback of crash-free motor vehicle trips (Evans 1991, 311).

Many motorists believe not only that the personal risk of driving is low but also that they themselves are less likely than others to experience a crash. Most drivers rank their own driving skills and safe driving practices as better than average (Evans 1991, 322–324; Williams et al. 1995, 119; Svenson 1981, 146).

Drivers may perceive their driving capabilities to be above average, but their actual judgments may not be as good as they believe. Drivers often underestimate the risks of traveling at high speeds. Younger drivers, for example, frequently say "I can handle the speed; my reflexes are good." In addition, drivers often misjudge the speed

---

[8] Estimates of driver involvement in motor vehicle crashes provided by the National Safety Council—18,900,000 driver involvements in 1996—were used for this calculation (National Safety Council 1997, 78). Driver involvements in police-reported crashes, estimated at 12,185,000, are considerably lower (NHTSA 1997b, 94).

[9] NHTSA is the primary source for the figures on driver involvements in fatal crashes and vehicle miles traveled (NHTSA 1997b, 15, 94).

at which they are traveling. They have limited capacity to estimate the relative speeds of vehicles in both car-following and car-overtaking situations, and after prolonged travel at higher speeds they are apt to perceive moderate speeds to be even lower than they really are (Várhelyi 1996, 38–39; Recarte and Nunes 1996, 291). Given the tendency of drivers to underestimate or misjudge the effects of speed in driving, it is not surprising that speeding is often ranked by motorists as less serious than other traffic offenses, such as driving while intoxicated or running red lights (Várhelyi 1996, 33–36).

In part because of driver underestimation or misjudgment of the effects of speed in driving, most drivers in the United States do not interpret speed limits as rigid thresholds that must be observed. In addition, drivers do not always concur that speed limits are reasonable for conditions. Thus, they have come to expect enforcement "tolerances" of up to 10 mph (16 km/h), and even greater on roads on which posted speed limits are well below average traffic speeds (TRB 1984, 149). For all these reasons, many drivers appear more concerned with "going with the flow," or going below the enforcement threshold, than with the risk of a crash or of detection for exceeding the speed limit.

If consistently applied and enforced, speed limits can be an important means of conveying useful information to drivers about appropriate driving speeds. However, as with most information, drivers will heed the message to the extent that it is perceived as important, relevant, and consistent with their prior beliefs (Bettman et al. 1991, 18–19). Of course, speed limits have the force of law and, if enforced, can influence behavior. The more drivers perceive speed limits to be credible and reasonable for conditions, and enforced, the more likely they will be obeyed.

FACTORS AFFECTING DETERMINATION OF APPROPRIATE SPEED LIMITS

Those responsible for determining appropriate speed limits—state and local legislators and traffic engineers, often with input from law enforcement officials and community groups—must define limits that are appropriate for different road classes and users.

Roadway Function and Use

Different vehicle speeds and speed limits are appropriate for different road classes. New highways are planned with a speed in mind, known as the design speed, to accommodate the intended function of a particular facility and its expected level of service, subject to the constraints of terrain, development, and other environmental factors (Krammes et al. 1996, 8).[10] Once selected, the design speed influences many critical design decisions, such as the amount of banking on horizontal curves and the length of vertical curves. The design criteria recommended for these critical features by the American Association of State Highway and Transportation Officials (AASHTO) have considerable built-in safety margins; they are often based on worst-case scenarios and performance characteristics of older vehicles (e.g., locked-wheel braking on wet pavements) (Krammes et al. 1996, 14).

Speed limits are often set on the basis of operating speeds determined by spot speed surveys of a sample of free-flowing vehicles traveling under favorable weather and visibility conditions at a particular location on a highway.[11] This speed can exceed design speeds. The disparity, however, is not necessarily cause for concern because of the built-in safety margins in the design values.[12] In addition, many highway features are constructed with more than minimum design values so that the design speed may actually apply to only a small number of critical features on a road segment. As a result, the design speed of a highway is likely to underestimate the "maximum safe speed" over much of its length (Krammes et al. 1996, 14).

---

[10] See glossary for definitions used in this section.

[11] The speed limit is often set at the 85th percentile of the speed distribution, that is, the speed at or below which 85 percent of drivers are operating their vehicles. (See glossary and Chapter 3 for a more detailed discussion.)

[12] Concerns about liability when posted speed limits based on vehicle operating speeds exceed the design speed of a highway segment, however, may lead to a redefinition of terms to bring about greater consistency among posted speed limits, operating speeds, and design speeds (Fitzpatrick et al. 1997, 59). A recently initiated multiyear study conducted under the auspices of the National Cooperative Highway Research Program will examine the relationships among design speeds, operating speeds, and posted speeds, and will develop appropriate alternatives to speed-based geometric criteria for use in project design.

According to AASHTO-recommended design criteria, the highest-level roads—new freeways and expressways built to expedite through traffic—should be designed for vehicular speeds of 68 to 75 mph (110 to 120 km/h) where environmental conditions are good and traffic volumes are light (AASHTO 1994, 63). Speed limits for these roads are as high as 75 mph in some states (Table 1-1) and may exceed design speeds at certain locations.

At the other end of the spectrum, AASHTO-recommended criteria for local streets serving residential areas suggest designs that accommodate speeds between 19 and 31 mph (30 and 50 km/h), and speed limits are typically established in this range (AASHTO 1994, 429). Certain factors, such as development and street grid patterns with numerous intersections, have a greater influence on actual vehicle speeds than design speed, which has limited practical significance on these streets (AASHTO 1994, 429).

Differences in speed limits by road class also reflect differing objectives with respect to road users. Travel efficiency is a priority on rural Interstate highways and freeways, which are restricted to motorized vehicles, have limited access, and are intended primarily for through traffic. Thus, speed limits are set at the higher end of the traffic speed distribution on these highways. By comparison, access is the primary consideration for motor vehicles on residential streets. Motorists share local streets with pedestrians and bicyclists, who are more vulnerable than vehicle occupants in a collision. Thus, travel efficiency is not the primary consideration in neighborhood travel, and speed limits often correspond to speeds at the lower end of the speed distribution.[13]

These distinctions may not be as clear on other road classes. For example, travel efficiency is still an important goal on urban Interstate highways, but in many metropolitan areas congestion limits travel speeds for several hours of the day. Through traffic must share urban Interstates with local traffic, whose frequent entries and exits at closely spaced interchanges can interrupt traffic flow, creating

---

[13] Speed limits in many urban areas actually correspond to the 30th percentile speed in the speed distribution (Tignor and Warren 1989, 2).

the potential for vehicle conflicts. Thus these highways may be posted with speed limits lower than design considerations alone would warrant. Nonlimited-access, two-lane rural roads and suburban arterials are examples of other road types that have multiple objectives and multiple road users. Many two-lane rural roads can accommodate through travel at high speeds. However, the potential for conflict at intersections and driveways, and between motor vehicles and farm equipment on the road, often requires setting speed limits lower than if travel efficiency were the primary objective. Similarly, the exposure of pedestrians and cross-street traffic to through traffic operating at high speeds on arterials in rapidly developing suburban areas may also warrant lowering speed limits on these roads.

Vehicle and Driver Characteristics

In some states, differential speed limits are established for major vehicle classes with different operating characteristics—primarily heavy trucks and vehicles towing trailers (Table 1-1).[14] Differential speed limits reflect longer stopping distances for such vehicles than for passenger vehicles. Some analysts argue that differential speed limits exacerbate actual speed differences among vehicles, creating the potential for conflict by encouraging passing and overtaking maneuvers, thereby degrading safety. State experience with differential speed limits is reviewed in this study.

Drivers have different capabilities to operate vehicles safely at higher speeds. For example, speeding appears to be a factor in the high fatality rate of the youngest segment of the driving population. Drivers aged 15 to 20 years old are involved in more speeding-related fatal crashes than any other age group (NHTSA 1997c, 2). Numerous studies have documented the high risk-taking behavior of young drivers, which involves tailgating and driving at speeds well in excess of the speed limit (Jonah 1986; Evans and Wasielewski 1983; Wasielewski 1984 in Evans 1991, 104, 137). Driving inexperience

[14] A variation of this approach is differential speed limits for day and night. Historically, crash probability was higher at night than during the day.

may also play a role (Evans 1991, 104). However, without knowing the incidence of speeding by age group in the general population of drivers, it is not possible to determine the extent to which speeding contributes to the probability of fatal crashes for the youngest drivers.

Speeding is not a major factor in the high fatality rates of older drivers. As a group, drivers 65 years of age and older have the second-highest fatality rates of all driver groups but the lowest involvement in speeding-related fatal crashes (NHTSA 1997c, 2). Many older drivers have reduced capacity to handle speed, though, which increases their probability of having a crash. For example, on the average, they have longer reaction times and lessened visual acuity (TRB 1989, 72–73). Their tendency to misjudge the speed of oncoming vehicles when turning at intersections and to drive at lower speeds than the prevailing traffic, in addition to their frailty, contributes to their high fatality and injury rates (NHTSA 1997b, 21).

These and other differences in the behavior and abilities of different driver population groups that relate to speed are difficult to manage through speed limit policies. Highways and speed limits must accommodate a broad spectrum of drivers. Minimum speed limits have been established on some high-speed roads that may deter slow drivers as well as vehicles that cannot maintain adequate speed levels. In certain communities speed limits have been reduced in areas where large concentrations of the elderly reside. Speed limits alone, however, are insufficient to address the highway safety problems of these special populations. Other strategies for addressing their speed-related problems are briefly discussed in the report.

ORGANIZATION OF REPORT

Many of the issues raised in this introductory section are addressed in detail in the following chapters. In Chapter 2 the relationship between speed and safety is investigated in more depth to help identify the role of speed in crash causation and injury severity. The relationship of speed to travel time and vehicle operating costs is also considered because drivers make trade-offs among safety, travel time, and other trip-related costs in deciding what speed to travel. Having laid the groundwork for the importance of speed on traffic safety and travel efficiency, Chapter 3 is focused on speed limits—the primary method for managing speed addressed in this study. The theoretical justification for speed limits is elaborated, the strengths and weaknesses of the primary methods of setting speed limits are described, and what is known about the effects of speed limits on driving speeds and safety is summarized. Speed enforcement and adjudication issues are examined in Chapter 4, including the relevance of deterrence theory for speed enforcement and the potential for application of automated enforcement technologies to augment traditional enforcement methods. In Chapter 5, other speed management strategies are discussed briefly, including highway design and infrastructure approaches, highway- and vehicle-related technologies, and interventions for special driver populations. Finally, the committee's guidance on appropriate strategies for both setting and enforcing speed limits is provided in Chapter 6.

REFERENCES

ABBREVIATIONS

AASHTO	American Association of State Highway and Transportation Officials
FHWA	Federal Highway Administration
ITE	Institute of Transportation Engineers
NHTSA	National Highway Traffic Safety Administration
TRB	Transportation Research Board

AASHTO. 1994. *A Policy on Geometric Design of Highways and Streets*. Washington, D.C.

AASHTO Journal. 1997. Hearing Addresses Aggressive Driving. Vol. 97, No. 29, July 18, pp. 7–9.

Bettman, J.R., E.J. Johnson, and J.W. Payne. 1991. Consumer Decision Making. In *Handbook of Consumer Behavior* (T.S. Robertson and H.H. Kassarjian, eds.), Prentice-Hall, Englewood Cliffs, N.J., pp. 50–84.

Evans, L., and P. Wasielewski. 1983. Risky Driving Related to Driver and Vehicle Characteristics. *Accident Analysis and Prevention*, Vol. 15, No. 3, pp. 121–136.

Evans, L. 1991. *Traffic Safety and the Driver*. Van Nostrand Reinhold, New York, 405 pp.

FHWA. 1987. *Highway Statistics 1986*. FHWA-PL-89-002. U.S. Department of Transportation.

Fitzpatrick, K., R.A. Krammes, and D.B. Fambro. 1997. Design Speed, Operating Speed and Posted Speed Relationships. *ITE Journal*, Vol. 67, No. 2, Feb., pp. 52–59.

Highway and Vehicle Safety Report. 1997. Officials, Experts Testify Before House Panel on "Road Rage." Vol. 23, No. 2, Aug. 4.

ITE. 1992. *Traffic Engineering Handbook: Fourth Edition* (J.L. Pline, ed.). Prentice-Hall, Englewood Cliffs, N.J.

ITE. 1993. *Speed Zone Guidelines: A Proposed Recommended Practice.* Washington, D.C., 5 pp.

Jonah, B.A. 1986. Accident Risk and Risk-Taking Behaviour Among Young Drivers. *Accident Analysis and Prevention,* Vol. 18, No. 4, pp. 255–271.

Krammes, R.A., K. Fitzpatrick, J.D. Blaschke, and D.B. Fambro. 1996. *Speed: Understanding Design, Operating, and Posted Speed.* Report 1465-1. Texas Transportation Institute, College Station, March, 16 pp.

National Committee on Uniform Traffic Laws and Ordinances. 1992. *Uniform Vehicle Code and Model Traffic Ordinance.* Evanston, Ill.

National Safety Council. 1997. *Accident Facts, 1997 Edition.* Itasca, Ill.

NHTSA. 1997a. *Summary of State Speed Laws.* DOT HS 808-510. U.S. Department of Transportation, Jan., 280 pp.

NHTSA. 1997b. *Traffic Safety Facts 1996.* DOT-HS-808-649. U.S. Department of Transportation, Dec., 192 pp.

NHTSA. 1997c. *Traffic Safety Facts 1995: Speeding.* U.S. Department of Transportation, 6 pp.

Prevention Magazine. 1996. Auto Safety in America 1996: Special Report. Rodale Press, Inc., Emmaus, Pa., May.

Recarte, M.A., and L.M. Nunes. 1996. Perception of Speed in an Automobile: Estimation and Production. *Journal of Experimental Psychology: Applied,* Vol. 2, No. 4, pp. 291–304.

Svenson, O. 1981. Are We All Less Risky and More Skillful Than Our Fellow Drivers? *Acta Psychologica,* No. 47, pp. 143-148.

Tignor, S.C., and D.L. Warren. 1989. *Speed Zoning in America: Some Preliminary Research Results.* Federal Highway Administration, June.

TRB. 1984. *Special Report 204: 55: A Decade of Experience.* National Research Council, Washington, D.C., 262 pp.

TRB. 1989. *Special Report 218: Transportation in an Aging Society.* Vol. 1, National Research Council, Washington, D.C., 125 pp.

Várhelyi, A. 1996. *Dynamic Speed Adaptation Based on Information Technology—A Theoretical Background.* Bulletin 142. Lund University, Lund Institute of Technology, Sweden, 220 pp.

Wasielewski, P. 1984. Speed as a Measure of Driver Risk: Observed Speeds Versus Driver and Vehicle Characteristics. *Accident Analysis and Prevention,* Vol. 16, No. 2, pp. 89–103.

Williams, A.F., N.N. Paek, and A.K. Lund. 1995. Factors That Drivers Say Motivate Safe Driving Practices. *Journal of Safety Research,* Vol. 26, No. 2, pp. 119–124.

2

Effects of Speed

The minutes
Some folks
Save through speed
They never even
Live to need
Burma Shave (Rowsome 1965)

The major reason for managing traffic speeds is safety. In this chapter, what is known about the relationships among speed, crash incidence, and crash severity is reviewed. Individual driver decisions about appropriate travel speeds, however, are guided by more than safety considerations. Thus, the relationship of speed to travel time, fuel use, and other vehicle operating costs is also examined. In addition, driver decisions about speed affect other costs, such as vehicle emissions, which contribute to air pollution in metropolitan areas and to atmospheric changes that may increase the risk of global climate change. These costs, which are briefly reviewed, are borne largely by society as a whole rather than by individual drivers, at least in the United States. The chapter concludes with an assessment of the effects of speed on safety, travel time, and other related costs, and their implications for managing speed.

DETERMINATION OF APPROPRIATE DRIVING SPEEDS—MAKING TRADE-OFFS

How do people decide how fast to drive? Many factors come into play including the characteristics of the road; the amount of traffic on the road; weather conditions and time of day; the speed limit and its enforcement; the length and purpose of the trip; the vehicle's operating characteristics, such as handling and stopping as well as fuel consumption and emissions; and driver-related factors, such as the propensity to take risks and the pleasure associated with driving fast. Taking these and other factors into consideration, drivers face an important trade-off between travel time and safety. By driving faster, travel time is reduced and the destination is reached sooner if the trip is safely completed. However, as discussed later in this chapter, a driver who chooses to drive very fast relative to other traffic or very fast for existing road conditions may increase the probability of being involved in a crash as well as the severity of the crash. A driver can reduce crash probability and severity by driving more slowly, although driving too slowly relative to other traffic may also increase the probability of crash involvement.

The theory underlying the trade-off between travel time and safety is discussed in more detail in Appendix A. Conceptually the trade-off is straightforward, but practically one could question whether drivers really trade off safety and travel time when making their trips. Some drivers indicate that this trade-off is not foremost in their mind while traveling; others claim that they are not conscious of making this trade-off.

For some drivers in many situations, the choice of driving speed is heavily influenced by speed limits and their enforcement so that the trade-off is, in a sense, made for them. But even in situations where there is little or no speed limit enforcement and many drivers exceed the posted speed limit, few motorists will drive as fast as their vehicles are capable of going. Something other than the fear of speed limit enforcement causes drivers to drive at less than the maximum possible speed. Similarly, when weather conditions such as fog, rain, or snow cause visibility to deteriorate and traction to be reduced, drivers may slow down, often to speeds well below the posted limits. For many drivers faced with these conditions, their choice of a lower speed and increased travel time is almost certainly made with safety in mind. There is reason to believe, therefore, that where speed choice is not constrained by speed limits and their enforcement, the driver does trade off travel time and safety.

Even when visibility and weather conditions are good, drivers may still make trade-offs. Rather than making them continuously, however, they may rely on rules of thumb based on driving experience. For example, motorists may well rely on experience with particular roads or types of roads to select a driving speed that has proven to be a reasonable trade-off for them in the past. Only when they encounter new conditions or conditions they face infrequently would they be conscious of explicitly making such a trade-off. In this chapter what is known about the key factors affecting drivers' choice of speeds is reviewed.

RELATION OF SPEED TO SAFETY

The relation of driving speed to safety is investigated first because of the importance that most drivers place on completing their trips safely. The link between speed and safety is complex. Thus an in-depth review of the literature on this topic was commissioned to help shed light on the relationship of speed to crash causation and injury severity. The results of that review, which can be found in its entirety as Appendix B, are summarized in the following sections.[1]

---

[1] These sections also draw on a second review, discussed more extensively in Chapter 3 and presented in its entirety as Appendix C.

Speed and the Probability of Crash Involvement

One of the more widely cited sources of statistics on speed and crashes is the Fatal Analysis Reporting System (FARS) administered by the National Highway Traffic Safety Administration (NHTSA), the federal agency charged with regulating automotive safety. In 1996 NHTSA reported that speeding was a contributing factor in 30 percent of all fatal crashes on U.S. highways in that year (NHTSA 1997a, 1). In addition to the 13,000 lives lost in these speeding-related crashes, 41,000 people were reported critically injured at an estimated economic cost to society of nearly $29 billion (NHTSA 1997a, 1).[2] Thus speeding is singled out as "one of the most prevalent factors contributing to traffic crashes" (NHTSA 1997a, 1).

These figures must be interpreted with caution. The definition of speeding is broad; for the purposes of coding crash-related information, speeding is defined as "exceeding the posted speed limit or driving too fast for conditions" (NHTSA 1997a, 1). The determination of whether speeding was involved in a fatal crash is based on the judgment of the investigating police officer; fatal crashes receive a thorough investigation.[3] Even if speeding is listed as a contributing factor in a crash, it may not have been the primary cause. Furthermore, and perhaps most important, without knowledge of the incidence of speeding in the driving population, the fatal crash data

---

[2] Economic costs include productivity losses, property damage, medical costs, rehabilitation costs, travel delay, legal and court costs, emergency service costs, insurance administration costs, premature funeral costs, and costs to employers. They do not include any estimate of the value of lost quality of life associated with deaths and injuries, that is, what society is willing to pay to prevent them.

[3] To ensure reporting consistency, FARS analysts, who are state employees contracted and trained by NHTSA, retrieve information about the crash from the police crash report and other sources and put it in a standardized coding format. For each crash, information is recorded at four levels—by crash, vehicle, driver, and person. Speed appears in two places—(*a*) on the crash-level coding sheet where the speed limit is recorded, and (*b*) on the driver-level coding sheet where speed-related violations are recorded. Typical violations, noted in the 1996 FARS Coding Manual, include driving at a speed greater than reasonable or prudent or in excess of the posted maximum, towing a house trailer at more than 45 mph (72 km/h), or driving too slowly so as to impede traffic.

cannot be properly interpreted. For example, a recent study suggests that driver compliance with posted speed limits is poor, particularly for limits less than 45 mph (72 km/h) on nonlimited-access highways (Parker 1997, 43). The proportion of those driving above the posted speed limit—hence "speeding" by NHTSA's definition—typically exceeds the share of speeding drivers (approximately 20 percent according to FARS) involved in fatal crashes.[4] The literature review attempts to examine the evidence that speeding is linked to the probability of being involved in a crash.

Theoretical Issues

At least three theoretical approaches link speed with crash involvement: (*a*) the information processing approach, (*b*) the traffic conflict approach, and (*c*) the risk-homeostasis motivational approach.

The first approach views the driver as an information processor with a limited capacity to process information. As driving speed increases, the rate at which the driver must process information about the highway and its environment increases directly, even though the total amount of information the driver has to process may stay constant. At higher speeds there is less time for the driver to process information, decide, and act between the time the information is presented to the driver (e.g., a child is running into the road) and the time when action must be taken to avoid a crash.[5] A crash is likely to occur when the information processing demands exceed the attentional or information processing capabilities of the driver (Shinar 1978).[6] Unexpected events dramatically increase information pro-

---

[4] Note that the 20 percent figure refers to the share of drivers involved in speeding-related fatal crashes as a percentage of drivers involved in all fatal crashes, whereas the 30 percent figure cited earlier refers to the share of speeding-related fatal crashes as a percentage of all fatal crashes.

[5] More specifically, as speed increases, the distance covered during the driver's perception-reaction time and the minimum distance required for braking both increase. For a vehicle on a level roadway, minimum braking distance increases with the square of the speed (see glossary definition of braking distance).

[6] Although drivers can increase their level of attention and concentration with increasing speed, a heightened level of attention cannot be maintained for long periods because it is fatiguing.

cessing requirements and hence the probability of a crash. This approach leads to the conclusion that "speed kills"; as more drivers increase their speed, the probability of information overload increases along with the potential for crashes.

The second approach—the traffic conflict approach—assumes that crash probability is related to the potential for conflict among vehicles traveling in traffic. More specifically, the probability of an individual driver being involved in a multiple-vehicle crash increases as a function of the deviation of that individual driver's speed from the speeds of other drivers. Drivers with speeds much faster or much slower than the median traffic speed are likely to encounter more conflicts (Hauer 1971).[7] This relationship leads to the conclusion that "speed deviation kills" and the prediction that on roads with equivalent average traffic speeds, crash rates will be higher on roads with wider ranges of speed. The theory, as formulated, relates only to two-lane rural roads (Hauer 1971, 1).

A third approach—the risk-homeostasis motivational approach—looks at speed and crash involvement from the perspective of driver perception of risk. From this point of view, drivers are neither passive information processors nor reactors to potential traffic conflicts. Rather they adjust their speed according to the risks they perceive (Taylor 1964) to maintain a subjectively acceptable level of risk (Wilde et al. 1985).[8] The issue is not the link between speed and crash probability but between actual and perceived risk. Thus, driving

[7] The number of conflicts between vehicle pairs is represented by the number of passing maneuvers. The number of passing maneuvers a driver must make increases with his driving speed; the number of times a driver is passed by other vehicles increases as he reduces speed. Hauer (1971) showed that the distributions of the two functions (i.e., the number of times passing and the number of times being passed) have a minimum at the median traffic speed. The findings relate only to rural roads between intersections (Hauer 1971, 1).

[8] There is mixed empirical support for Wilde's risk-homeostasis theory. For example, Mackay (1985) found that British drivers of newer and heavier cars drove faster than drivers of older and lighter cars (with the exception of sport cars), and Rumar et al. (1976) found that drivers with studded tires drove faster than those without such tires on curves in icy but not in dry conditions. O'Day and Flora (1982), however, found that restrained occupants actually had lower impact speeds in tow-away crashes than unrestrained occupants, suggesting that drivers have different risk tolerances.

at high speeds per se is not dangerous. Rather, the danger comes from driving at a speed inappropriate for conditions, stemming from a misperception of the situational demands or a misestimation of the vehicle's handling capabilities or the driver's skills. This approach would predict that, under most circumstances, drivers who increase speed do not necessarily increase the risk of their crash involvement.

Review of Empirical Data

Several studies reviewed in this section (Table 2-1), many dating back to the 1960s, have tested the theories about the relationship between driving speed and crash involvement by analyzing actual vehicle speeds and crash data on different classes of roads. Speed is defined in several ways in these studies. It can relate to the speed of a single vehicle or to the distribution of speeds in a traffic stream. In the former case, the term speed deviation is used when referring to the deviation of an individual driver's speed from the average speed of traffic. In the latter case, when referring to the distribution of speeds in a traffic stream, three measures of speed are typically considered: the average speed, the 85th percentile of the speed distribution, and the dispersion in travel speeds. Speed dispersion, in turn, can be quantified by the variance, standard deviation, 10-mph pace, or range (high minus low) of a sample of speed measurements.[9] In many studies, the standard deviation is approximated as the 85th percentile speed less the average speed.[10]

With several measures of speed, interpreting the results of these studies is often difficult. Validity of the speed measures can also be a problem. For example, it is nearly impossible to obtain a reliable measure of true precrash speeds for crash-involved vehicles because crashes are not planned events. Thus, precrash speeds must be estimated, but there is no way of validating their accuracy. In attempting to isolate the effect of speed, many studies assume that everything else remains equal. Of course, crash occurrence and injury severity are

[9] See definitions in glossary.

[10] The 85th percentile minus the average speed roughly corresponds to one standard deviation (S), which is the positive square root of the variance (S^2).

Table 2-1 Selected Studies of the Relationship Between Speed and Crash Probability

Authorship and Date of Study	Road Class and Speed Limit Levels	Analysis	Major Findings
Solomon (1964)	Main rural roads, U.S.; three-fourths were two-lane rural roads with speed limits of 55 to 70 mph (89 to 113 km/h) on 28 out of 35 sections	Compared speeds of crash-involved vehicles with speeds of non-crash-involved vehicles	Found U-shaped relationship between crash involvement and travel speeds. Lowest crash involvement rates at speeds slightly above average travel speeds. Highest crash involvement rates at speeds well above and well below average traffic speeds
Cirillo (1968)	Rural and urban Interstate highways, U.S.; no speed limits given	Compared speeds of crash-involved vehicles with speeds of non-crash-involved vehicles; limited to daytime travel and certain multiple-vehicle crash types (i.e., rear-end and angle collisions and same-direction sideswipe crashes)	Same finding as Solomon, but crash involvement rates were lower for all travel speeds suggesting importance of roadway geometry to crash probability (i.e., higher design standards on Interstate highways than on rural two-lane roads)
RTI (1970); West and Dunn (1971)	State and county highways in Indiana with speed limits greater than or equal to 40 mph (64 km/h)	Compared speeds of crash-involved vehicles with speeds of non-crash-involved vehicles; separated out crashes involving turning vehicles	Found same U-shaped relationship between travel speed and crash involvement, but the relationship was less extreme, particularly at low speeds, when crashes involving turning vehicles were removed from the analysis

(continued on next page)

Table 2-1 *(continued)*

Authorship and Date of Study	Road Class and Speed Limit Levels	Analysis	Major Findings
Lave (1985)	Six U.S. highway types—rural and urban Interstates, arterials, and collectors; data from 50 states	Analyzed relationship between average traffic speed, speed dispersion (measured as 85th percentile speed minus 50th percentile speed), and two nonspeed measures—traffic citations per driver and access to medical care—on fatality rates	Speed dispersion significantly related to fatality rates for rural Interstates and rural and urban arterials. After controlling for speed dispersion, average traffic speed not significantly related to fatality rates for any road type
Garber and Gadiraju (1988)	Higher-speed roads [i.e., with average traffic speeds of 45 mph (72 km/h) or above], including rural and urban Interstates, expressways and freeways, rural and urban arterials, and rural collectors in Virginia	Analyzed relationship between crash rates and average traffic speed, speed variance, design speed, and posted speed limits	Crash rates increased with increasing speed variance on all road classes. No correlation between crash rates and average traffic speeds when data were disaggregated by road class

Harkey et al. (1990)	Rural and urban roads with posted speed limits of between 25 and 55 mph (40 and 89 km/h) in North Carolina and Colorado	Compared speeds of crash-involved vehicles with speeds of non-crash-involved vehicles	Found same U-shaped curve as Solomon and Cirillo; crashes limited to weekday, nonalcohol, nonintersection involvements
Fildes et al. (1991)	Two urban arterials with speed limits of 37 mph (60 km/h) and two rural undivided roads with speed limits of 62 mph (100 km/h), Australia	Compared free-flowing travel speeds and self-reported crash histories of drivers who participated in a road safety survey	Found no evidence of Solomon's U-shaped relationship. Those traveling at very fast speeds were more likely to report previous crash involvement than those traveling at slower speeds. Self-reported crash involvements were lowest for those traveling at speeds below average traffic speeds and highest at speeds above the average with no advantage at the average
Baruya and Finch (1994)	Urban roads with average traffic speeds ranging from 21 mph (33 km/h) to 33 mph (53 km/h), Great Britain	Analyzed relationship between personal injury crashes, speed levels, and speed dispersion, defined as the coefficient of variation of the speed distribution	Both speed level and speed dispersion affected crashes. Increased crashes were associated with increasing average traffic speeds. Decreased crashes were associated with reductions in speed dispersion at increasing speeds. The net effect, however, was an increase in personal injury crashes with increasing speeds
Kloeden et al. (1997)	Speed zones with 37-mph (60-km/h) speed limits in metropolitan Adelaide, Australia	Compared speeds of casualty crash-involved vehicles with speeds of control vehicles traveling in the same direction, at the same location, time of day, day of week, and time of year under free-flowing traffic in daylight and good weather	Found statistically significant increase in probability of involvement in a casualty crash with increasing travel speed above, but not below, the speed limit. Probability of crash involvement at speeds below the speed limit was not statistically different from traveling at the speed limit

influenced by other driver behaviors (e.g., drinking, not using safety belts) and characteristics (e.g., age), vehicle characteristics (e.g., size and weight), and road design (e.g., limited- or nonlimited-access highways). To the extent that these contributory variables are not taken into account, results of the studies must remain highly qualified.

Correlational Studies

This category of studies attempts to determine whether there is a link between speed and crash probability. In the benchmark study conducted by Solomon (1964), travel speeds of crash-involved vehicles obtained from police reports were compared with the average speed of free-flowing traffic on two- and four-lane, nonlimited-access rural highways. Solomon found that crash-involved vehicles were overrepresented in the high- and low-speed areas of the traffic speed distribution. His well-known U-shaped curve (Figure 2-1) showed that crash involvement rates are lowest at speeds slightly above average traffic speeds. The greater the deviation between a motorist's speed and the average speed of traffic—both above and below the average speed—the greater the chance of involvement in a crash. The correlation between crash involvement rates and deviations from average traffic speed gave rise to the often-cited hypothesis that it is speed deviation, not speed per se, that increases the probability of driver involvement in a crash. Hauer's subsequent theory of traffic conflict (1971) provided a theoretical basis for Solomon's findings.[11]

Solomon's U-shaped relationship was replicated by Munden (1967) using a different analytic method on main rural roads in the United Kingdom, by Cirillo (1968) on U.S. Interstate highways

[11] Some have interpreted these results to suggest that it is as unsafe to drive below as above the average traffic speed. This ignores the fact that drivers involved in a crash at higher speeds are at greater risk of injury than those driving at lower speeds, a relationship that Solomon confirms in his analysis of the relation between speed and crash severity (see subsequent section).

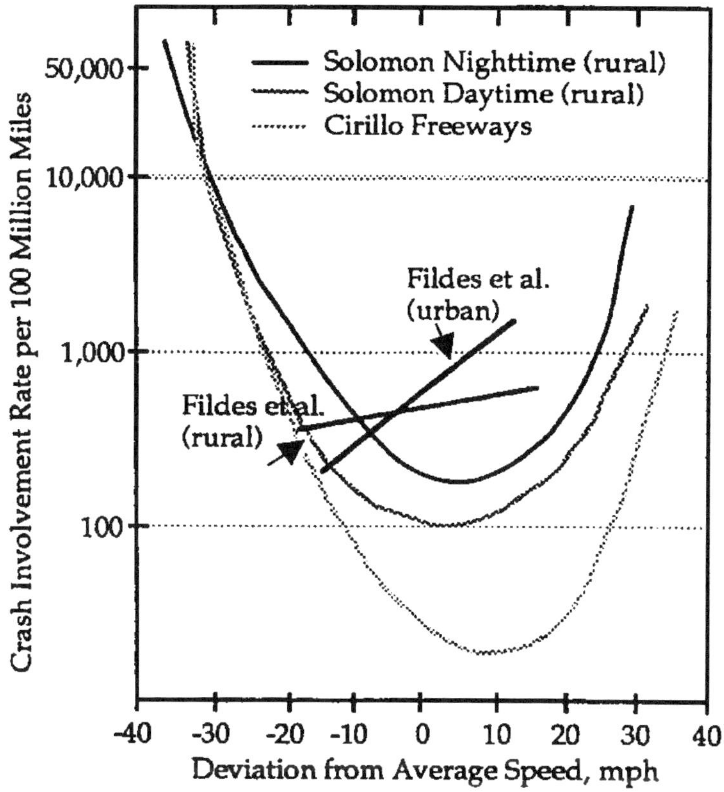

Figure 2-1 Vehicle crash involvement rates as a function of deviation from average traffic speeds (Solomon 1964; Cirillo 1968; Fildes et al. 1991 in Stuster and Coffman 1997, 6). 1 mph = 1.609 km/h.

(Figure 2-1),[12] and most recently by Harkey et al. (1990) on rural and urban roads posted at speeds ranging from 25 to 55 mph (40 to 89 km/h) in two U.S. states.[13] All of the U.S. studies, but most par-

[12] Cirillo limited her study to rear-end and angle collisions and same-direction sideswipe crashes involving two or more vehicles traveling between 9 a.m. and 4 p.m. on the assumption that the effect of deviation from average traffic speeds on crash involvement could best be determined by examining crashes involving vehicles traveling in the same direction (Cirillo 1968, 71). Thus, head-on, single-vehicle, and pedestrian crashes were not included.

[13] Unfortunately, Harkey et al.'s results cannot be compared with Solomon's results because the former excluded intersection involvements.

ticularly Solomon's, have been criticized for their dependence on crash reports[14] for the precrash speeds of the crash-involved vehicles, which could bias the results (White and Nelson 1970, 67).[15] Solomon's study has also been criticized for unrepresentative comparative traffic speed data,[16] lack of consistency between the crash and speed data,[17] and mixing of crashes of free-flowing with slowing vehicles, which could explain high crash involvement rates at low speeds.[18]

The Research Triangle Institute (RTI) together with Indiana University (RTI 1970) addressed several of these issues by using speed data based, in part, on traffic speeds recorded at the time of the crash.[19] They examined crashes on highways and county roads with speed limits of 40 mph (64 km/h) and above and found a similar but less pronounced U-shaped relationship between crash involvement

[14] Solomon's study relied on estimates by the crash-involved driver or by the police or other third parties contained in police reports (Solomon 1964), which are frequently criticized as unreliable.

[15] The authors demonstrated mathematically that errors in estimating speeds of the crash-involved vehicles could result in overestimates at the extreme speed deviations and underestimates in the middle speed interval, resulting in the U shape (White and Nelson 1970, 70–71).

[16] Spot speed surveys were taken at one location for each highway section, which state highway department engineers selected as being representative of the average traffic speed for the entire section. Crashes, however, occurred at many different locations along a section where average traffic speeds may or may not have been comparable with those at the speed survey location (Kloeden et al. 1997, 10).

[17] The speed observations were made over a 12-month period ending in 1958, whereas the crash data were gathered over a 4-year period, also ending in 1958 (Solomon 1964, 7). Although expansion procedures were used and cross checks made to extend the speed data, the data collection issues remain troubling.

[18] It was argued that if slowing or turning vehicles had been removed, the crash-involvement rates for vehicles moving at slow but free-flow speeds would have been lower (*Accident Reconstruction Journal* 1991, 16).

[19] A system of on-line digital computer and magnetic loop detectors was installed in the pavement of an Indiana highway, which computed vehicle headways, speeds, lengths, and volumes (West and Dunn 1971, 52). By tracing vehicle trajectories and speeds between detectors, changes in speed fluctuations resulting from a crash could be identified and the crash-involved vehicles pinpointed (West and Dunn 1971, 53). The data from this instrumented highway comprised about half of the sample of crash involvements investigated in the study (Cowley 1987, 11).

and speed. Thus, the RTI study appears to confirm the critical role of deviation from average traffic speeds for crash-involved vehicles.

Deviation from average traffic speeds, however, is not the only factor linking speed with crash involvement. It does not explain, for example, the significant fraction of speeding-related driver involvements in fatal crashes involving only one vehicle—nearly 50 percent in 1996.[20] In fact, when Solomon's data are disaggregated by crash type, the U-shaped relationship is only fully replicated for one crash type—nighttime head-on collisions (Cowley 1980 in Cowley 1987, 9) (Figure 2-2).

Several studies have provided alternative explanations for the high crash involvement rates found by Solomon at the low end of the speed distribution, whereas others have simply not found the association. For example, West and Dunn (1971) investigated the relationship between speed and crash involvement, replicating Solomon's U-shaped relationship. However, when crashes involving turning vehicles were removed from the sample, the U-shaped relationship was considerably weakened—the curve became flatter—and the elevated crash involvement rates that Solomon had found at the low end of the speed distribution disappeared; crash involvement rates were more symmetric above and below mean traffic speeds (Figure 2-3).[21] West and Dunn's analysis supports the conclusion that the characteristics of the road—numerous intersections or driveways on undivided highways, for example—are as responsible for creating the potential for vehicle conflicts and crashes as the motorist's driving too slowly for conditions.[22]

---

[20] According to FARS 1996 data, nearly 70 percent of speeding-related fatal crashes involved a single vehicle. The lower driver involvement figure is used here to be consistent with Solomon's definition of crash involvement.

[21] Solomon, too, found that rear-end and angle collisions accounted for a substantial proportion of total crash involvements at lower speed ranges, suggesting the presence of stopping and turning vehicles, even though the study sections had been selected so that crossroads and driveways were at a minimum (Solomon 1964, 36).

[22] The one exception to this finding is the analysis conducted by Harkey et al. (1990) relating crash involvement to deviation from average traffic speeds on lower-speed rural and urban roads. Crash involvements were limited to weekday, nonalcohol, and nonintersection crashes. The analysis shows the same U-shaped curve as Solomon's even though intersection involvements were excluded (Harkey et al. 1990, 48). This study, however, suffered from the precrash speed measurement problems mentioned earlier.

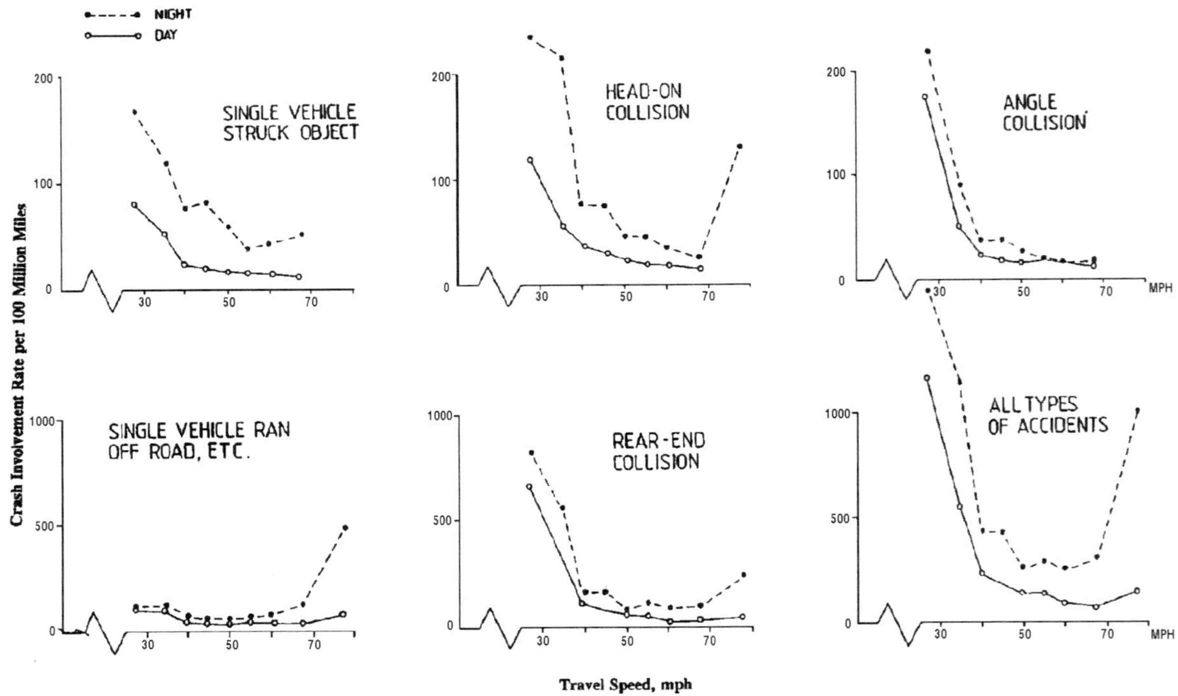

Figure 2-2 Vehicle crash involvement rates by crash type (Cowley 1980 in Cowley 1987). Disaggregation of Solomon data for nonlimited-access rural highways. 1 mph = 1.609 km/h.

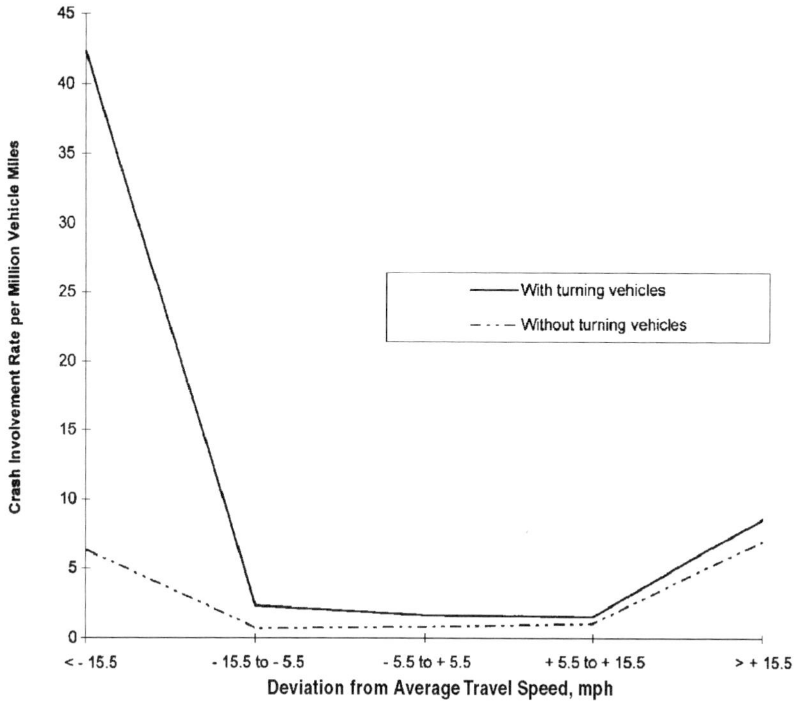

Figure 2-3 Vehicle crash involvement rates including and excluding turning vehicles (West and Dunn 1971, 53–54). 1 mph = 1.609 km/h.

A more recent Australian study (Fildes et al. 1991), which examined crash involvement rates as a function of speed on urban arterials as well as on two-lane rural roads,[23] found no evidence of the U-shaped relationship. Crash involvement rates rose linearly as a function of speed; crash involvements were lowest at speeds below average traffic speeds and highest at speeds above the average with no advantage at the average (Fildes et al. 1991, 60) (Figure 2-1). Furthermore, the researchers did not find evidence of very low-speed driving that had been apparent in both the Solomon and Cirillo data (Fildes et al. 1991, 60). The results are based on small sample sizes

[23] Posted speed limits were 37 mph (60 km/h) on the urban arterials and 62 mph (100 km/h) on the rural roads (Fildes et al. 1991, 5–6).

and self-reported crash involvement, although Shinar notes that there is little reason to believe that slow-moving drivers would underreport their crashes.[24] The findings point to a linear and positive association between crash probability and the speed of crash-involved vehicles.

A very recent Australian study (Kloeden et al. 1997) that examined the relationship between speed and the probability of involvement in a casualty crash lends support for some of the results reported earlier by Fildes et al., at least for speeds above the average speed of traffic. Using a case control approach, the authors compared the speeds of cars involved in casualty crashes[25] (the case vehicles) with the free-flowing speeds of cars not involved in crashes but traveling in the same direction at the same location, time of day, day of week, and time of year (the control vehicles) (Kloeden et al. 1997, i). Data collection was focused on weekday, daylight crashes—to exclude most alcohol-related crashes—in speed zones with a 37-mph (60-km/h) speed limit in the Adelaide metropolitan area (Kloeden et al. 1997, i). Precrash speeds were determined using crash reconstruction techniques (Kloeden et al. 1997, 30). The data showed a steady and statistically significant increase in the probability of involvement of the case vehicles in a casualty crash with increasing speed above, but not below, the 37-mph speed limit, which roughly approximated the average traffic speed. The risk approximately doubled with each 3-mph (5-km/h) increase in speed above the limit (Kloeden et al. 1997, 38).[26] The probability of casualty crash involvement at speeds below 37 mph was not statistically different from the probability at the speed limit (Kloeden et al. 1997, 38). The absence of a significant association between speed and crash involvement at speeds below the average traffic speed may well be the result of the study design. The analysis excluded all but injury crashes; crashes at lower speeds tend to be less severe. In addition, case vehicles were confined to those

[24] See discussion of this report in Appendix B.

[25] Casualty crashes are defined as crashes that involve transport of at least one person from the crash scene by an ambulance.

[26] In contrast to the results reported by Fildes et al., the relationship between speed and crash involvement above the speed limit is nonlinear.

with free-flow speeds prior to the crash, thus excluding the speeds of slowing vehicles that may have "caused the crash."

Several studies have attempted to analyze the relationship between crash involvement and measures of the distribution of speeds in a traffic stream, thereby avoiding the problem of estimating the pre-crash speeds of individual vehicles. On the basis of data from 48 states, Lave (1985) developed models for a range of road classes (e.g., Interstates, arterials, collectors) to investigate the relationship between average traffic speed, speed dispersion, and fatality rates, attempting to hold constant some of the other factors that affect highway fatality rates using standard statistical techniques.[27] He found that speed dispersion was significantly related (in a statistical sense) to fatality rates for rural Interstates and rural and urban arterials (Lave 1985, 1162).[28] After controlling for speed dispersion, average traffic speed was not found to be significantly related to fatality rates for any road type (Lave 1985, 1162). A series of analyses spawned by Lave's study, many of which contained a larger set of explanatory variables (e.g., driver age, alcohol use), confirmed the importance of speed dispersion to fatality rates but also found that average traffic speed is an important determinant.[29] None of the studies discussed in this paragraph examined differences in roadway design features or traffic levels within road class, which could affect traffic speeds and crash rates.

---

[27] Lave defined speed dispersion as the difference between the 85th percentile speed and the average traffic speed. These measures are aggregated over the period used to collect the speed data and thus may not reflect the distribution of traffic speeds at the time of the crashes. The other variables included a measure of enforcement—traffic citations per driver—and access to medical care.

[28] Speed dispersion, measured as the difference between the 85th percentile and average traffic speed, was statistically significant at the 5 percent level of confidence for the models for these road classes but not for the others. With the exception of rural Interstates, where the variables in the models explained 62 percent of the variation in fatality rates for 1981 and 52 percent for 1982, the variables in the models for the other road classes explained one quarter or less of the variation in the fatality rate (Lave 1985, 1161).

[29] The relevant studies are those by Levy and Asch (1989), Fowles and Loeb (1989), Snyder (1989), Lave (1989), and Rodriguez (1990).

A related study by Garber and Gadiraju (1988) found, as Lave had, that average traffic speeds are not significantly related to fatality rates. Garber and Gadiraju examined the relationship between crash rates, speed dispersion,[30] average traffic speed, and other measures that influence speed—design speed and posted speed limits—on several different classes of roads in Virginia.[31] They found that crash rates declined with an increase in average traffic speeds when data for all road classes were combined (Garber and Gadiraju 1988, 26). The correlation disappeared when the data were disaggregated by road class, suggesting that the aggregated analysis simply reflected the effects of the different design characteristics of the roads being studied (e.g., lower crash rates on high-speed Interstates). When crash rates were modeled as a function of speed dispersion for each road class, however, crash rates increased with increasing speed dispersion (Garber and Gadiraju 1988, 28).[32] The minimum speed dispersion occurred when the difference between the design speed of the highway, which reflects its function and geometric characteristics, and the posted speed limit was small [i.e., ≤ 10 mph (16 km/h)] (Garber and Gadiraju 1988, 23–25).

Evidence by Road Class

The studies just reviewed suggest that the type of road may play an important role in determining driver travel speeds and crash proba-

---

[30] Garber and Gadiraju quantified speed dispersion using speed variance as the measure. Similar to Lave's treatment, this measure is based on aggregate data, which may or may not correspond to the distribution of traffic speeds and speed variance at the time of the crashes.

[31] They examined higher-speed roads [i.e., average traffic speeds of 45 mph (72 km/h) or above], including rural and urban Interstate highways, expressways and freeways, rural and urban arterials, and rural collectors (Garber and Gadiraju 1988, 15).

[32] Kloeden et al. (1997) point out, however, that the relationship between crash rates and speed dispersion could also reflect different design features of the roads being studied. For example, better-designed roads have lower crash rates because provision is made for overtaking and turning vehicles (or is not an issue on Interstate highways and freeways), thereby mitigating the circumstances that lead to speed dispersion (e.g., platoons forming behind slow-moving vehicles) (p. 23).

bility. Thus, what is known about speed and crash probability by road class was also examined.

Limited-Access Highways

Most studies have focused on high-speed roads. By design, limited-access highways provide the least opportunity for vehicle conflicts and thus should have the lowest crash rates of all road classes. Cirillo's study (1968)—the only study focused specifically on limited-access Interstate highways—bears out this judgment. Crash involvement rates were lower across the board than those reported for other road types, except at very low speeds (Figure 2-1). Cirillo found, as Solomon had before, an association between crash involvement rates and deviation from average traffic speeds even on Interstate highways. More specifically, crash involvement rates were higher in the vicinity of interchanges where differences in vehicle speeds were greatest and, thus, the potential for vehicle conflicts was highest (Cirillo 1968, 75). Not surprisingly, the effect was greater near interchanges on urban Interstate highways because of higher traffic volumes, making merging and diverging more difficult, and because of more complex and less adequate design of some urban interchanges (Cirillo 1968, 75). This finding points to the effect of traffic density as well as speed dispersion on crash rates.

Two other studies reinforce the importance of traffic speed dispersion to crash involvement on Interstate highways. Lave (1985, 1162) found a statistically significant relationship between increasing traffic speed dispersion and fatality rates on rural but not on urban Interstate highways. Garber and Gadiraju (1988, 28–29) found that crash rates increased as traffic speed dispersion increased on both rural and urban Interstate highways.

Nonlimited-Access Rural Highways

The potential for vehicle conflicts is considerably greater on undivided highways, particularly high-speed nonlimited-access highways. Vehicles entering and exiting the highway at intersections and driveways, and passing maneuvers on two-lane undivided highways, increase the occurrence of conflicts between vehicles with large speed differences and hence increase crash probability. Solomon's study

(1964) provides strong evidence for these effects on two- and four-lane rural nonlimited-access highways. High crash involvement rates are associated with vehicles traveling well above or below the average traffic speed; at low speeds, the most common crash types are rear-end and angle collisions, typical of conflicts at intersections and driveways (Solomon 1964, 36). West and Dunn's analysis (1971) pinpointed the important contribution of turning vehicles to crash probability on these highways. When turning vehicles were excluded from the analysis, crash involvement rates at low speeds were not as high as those found by Solomon (Figure 2-1); they were more symmetric with crash involvement rates at high speeds (Figure 2-3). The study by Fildes et al. (1991) showed a gradual increase in crash probability for vehicles traveling above, but not below, average traffic speeds on two-lane rural roads (Figure 2-1).

The previously cited studies by Garber and Gadiraju (1988) and Lave (1985) provide additional support for the contribution of speed dispersion to traffic conflicts and crash involvements on rural nonlimited-access highways. Garber and Gadiraju (1988, 28–30) found a high correlation between increasing speed dispersion and crash rates on rural arterial roads, but the model included only these two variables. Lave's rural arterial model, which attempted to control for more variables, found a weak but statistically significant relationship between traffic speed dispersion and fatality rates for only 1 year of data (wider dispersions were associated with higher fatality rates) (Lave 1985, 24). Neither study found any significant relationships between average traffic speeds and crash or fatality rates for this road class.

Solomon's study provides some support for the role of speed per se in crash involvement on high-speed, nonlimited-access rural highways. He found that the percentage of single-vehicle crashes, which are more common on high-speed roads generally (NHTSA 1997b, 51), increased sharply as a function of the speed of the crash-involved vehicles (Solomon 1964, 36).[33]

[33] Single-vehicle involvements represented a small proportion of all crash involvements at lower speeds, but they increased sharply at speeds in excess of 50 mph (80 km/h). At speeds exceeding 70 mph (113 km/h), they accounted for up to half of all crash involvements (Solomon 1964, 36).

Together, these studies suggest that speed dispersion, created in part by the characteristics of rural nonlimited-access highways, contributes significantly to increased crash probability for this road class. The level of speed also appears to affect crash probability for certain crash types, such as single-vehicle crashes.

Urban Roads and Residential Streets

This category encompasses a wide variety of situations, from high-speed urban arterials to low-speed local streets. In theory, traffic speed dispersion and the potential for vehicle conflicts are likely to be high on urban roads, particularly on heavily traveled urban arterials. The highest levels of driver noncompliance with speed limits are in urban areas where an average of 7 out of 10 motorists exceed posted speed limits (Tignor and Warren 1990, 84). Numerous intersections, high levels of roadside activity, high traffic volumes, and insufficient following distances in congested traffic all contribute to increased crash probability. Offsetting these effects to some extent is the fact that congestion tends to reduce driving speeds, thus lessening the severity of the crashes that do occur.

Some studies of the relationship between speed and crash probability on urban arterials found a link between speed deviation and crash involvement for vehicles that travel at speeds well above average traffic speeds. The primary evidence comes from the two Australian studies—Kloeden et al. (1997) and Fildes et al. (1991). Neither study, however, found that crash probability increased for those traveling below average traffic speeds. In fact, Fildes et al. found that crash involvement rates were lower for vehicles traveling below average traffic speeds, providing support for the importance of speed itself to crash probability.

Lave found a low correlation between his measure of speed dispersion and fatality rates in his model for urban arterials and reported that the correlation was statistically significant for only 1 of 2 years of data (Lave 1985, 1162).[34] A small study of vehicle-pedestrian

[34] The model only explained about 17 to 18 percent of the variation in fatality rates (Lave 1985, 1162).

crashes at an urban intersection in Helsinki, for which vehicle speeds were actually videotaped, found that the majority of crash-involved drivers (8 of 11) were driving faster (30 mph or 48 km/h) than the average traffic speed (24 mph or 39 km/h) or the speed limit (25 mph or 40 km/h), thus also providing some confirmation of the role of speed deviation in urban crashes (Pasanen and Salmivaara 1993). Finally, a recent study of traffic speeds and personal injury crashes on urban roads in Great Britain, which classified roads by speed-related variables, found that measures of speed dispersion and speed levels have counterbalancing effects (Baruya and Finch 1994, 228).[35] Crashes increase with the average speed of traffic,[36] but at higher speeds, the dispersion in speeds is less, thereby reducing crash involvements. The net effect, however, is negative; the effect of increasing crash involvement with higher speeds appears to overwhelm any reduction in crash involvement from more uniform travel speeds (Baruya and Finch 1994, 229).

The results of these studies suggest but do not prove that speed dispersion plays a role in crash probability on urban streets, particularly on urban arterials, and that many other factors, including speed itself, affect crash occurrence.

Unfortunately, no studies that examine the relationship between speed and crash probability on residential streets could be found.

Causal Studies

The correlational studies are useful for identifying speed-related variables associated with crash probability. However, they fail to establish a cause-and-effect relationship. In another type of study, generally referred to as clinical studies, detailed analyses of individual crashes

[35] The roads were categorized using nonhierarchical cluster analysis into four groups with average traffic speeds ranging from 21 to 33 mph (34 to 53 km/h). Unfortunately the speed data were collected in 1992 and 1993, whereas the crash data were collected from 1983 to 1988 (Baruya and Finch 1994, 220–221).

[36] Geometric design differences among the different roads studied did not appear to play a significant role in the model as a correlate of crash frequency (Baruya and Finch 1994, 228).

are conducted to determine the contribution of causal factors, such as speed, to crash occurrence. These studies enable more definitive statements to be made about the contribution of speeding to crash involvement. Their primary failing is the absence of any adjustment for exposure, that is, for any measure of the incidence of speeding in the general driving population relative to the crash-involved driver. Without such a measure, it is difficult to gain perspective on the relative importance of speeding as a highway safety problem.

Results of Clinical Studies

The role of speeding as a crash cause was probably first analyzed in a detailed and comprehensive manner in Indiana University's Tri-Level Study (Treat et al. 1977). Speed was defined as causal if it met two conditions: (*a*) it deviated from the "normal" or "expected" speed of the average driver for the site conditions, and (*b*) it "caused" the crash, that is, the crash would not have occurred had the speed been as expected. On the basis of this definition, the study estimated "excessive speed" to be a definite cause in 7 to 8 percent of the crashes and a probable cause in an additional 13 to 16 percent of the crashes.[37] Speed was identified as the second most common factor contributing to crash occurrence, second only to "improper lookout" (i.e., inattention) (Treat et al. 1977 in Bowie and Walz 1994, 32).

Bowie and Walz (1994) integrated three large data files to obtain more reliable estimates of the role of speed in crash causation.[38] Although they were based on different data sets and methodologies, the three sources yielded similar estimates, with "excessive speed" reported as being involved in approximately 12 percent of all crashes and more than 30 percent of fatal crashes (Bowie and Walz 1994, 31).

[37] The crashes dated from 1970 to 1975 and were confined to state, county, and municipal roads in Monroe County, Indiana (Treat et al. 1977).

[38] These files included the census of all fatal crashes from FARS; 1 year of data from all police-reported crashes from six states in NHTSA's Crash Avoidance Research Data File (CARDfile), which had been specifically developed to analyze the factors involved in crash causation; and a subset of the crashes analyzed in depth from the Tri-Level Study. The full range of road classes was represented.

A more recent study of fatal crashes,[39] analyzed for crash causation and crash avoidance opportunities, found that aggressive driving, excessive speed, and loss of control were involved in 19 percent of those crashes (Viano and Ridella 1996, 132). The second most frequently cited crash cause—responsible for 11 percent of the fatal crashes—was labeled "rocket-ship." It involved single-vehicle, frontal-impact crashes with the "vehicle leaving the road at a very high speed." Because the analysis was confined to fatal crashes of belted occupants—and unbelted occupants are more highly represented in fatal crashes—the percentage of speeding-related fatal crashes in the population at large is certain to be higher.

Crash data from police crash reports from 1991 to 1995 were examined in a recent Canadian study (Liu 1997) to determine the role of speed in crashes. A speed-related crash was defined as one in which the driver was reported by the investigating officer to be both "exceeding the speed limit and driving too fast for conditions" (Liu 1997, 67). Although the definition is conservative, it is appropriate because police reports are not as reliable as professional, in-depth crash investigations. On the basis of this definition, Liu found that speed was a causal factor in 9 to 11 percent of all crashes and 12 to 15 percent of all casualty crashes (Liu 1997, 67).

Despite different data files, different definitions of speeding and excessive speed, and different and often subjective techniques for making judgments about crash causation, the studies consistently found that speeding or excessive speed contributes to a relatively small but significant percentage of all crashes and a higher percentage of more severe crashes.

Behavioral Data on Speeding

Relatively little is known about the behavioral aspects of speeding, at least in the United States. Some data are available from FARS about

[39] The crashes actually occurred during an 18-month period from 1985 to 1986 throughout the United States, during which time the insurance industry undertook an incentive program to increase safety belt use by providing a $10,000 insurance policy in case of death while restrained in a crash. The cases were well documented by insurance adjusters and safety engineers (Viano and Ridella 1996, 125).

a subset of the driving population: those involved in fatal speeding-related crashes. Speeding appears to be linked with other driver characteristics and behaviors. For example, young drivers (ages 15 to 20) are overinvolved[40] in speeding-related fatal crashes (NHTSA 1997a, 2). Moreover, a high percentage of youthful drivers involved in speeding-related fatal crashes were also intoxicated and not wearing their safety belts at the time of the crash (NHTSA 1997a, 2, 5).

Speeding-related fatal crashes also appear to be largely a phenomenon of single-vehicle crashes. In 1996 single-vehicle fatal crashes represented 68 percent of all speeding-related fatal crashes according to FARS data. The next highest percentages were head-on (12 percent) and angle (10 percent) crashes. Single-vehicle fatal crashes are also highly associated with alcohol use, unbelted drivers, and nighttime driving (NHTSA 1997b, 56).

Speeding-related fatal crashes are also linked with road class. In 1996, for example, 17 percent of all speeding-related fatal crashes occurred on Interstate highways and freeways, according to FARS data. Fifty-four percent occurred on non-Interstate rural roads—approximately equally divided between primary arterials and major collectors and other rural roads. The remaining 29 percent occurred on non-Interstate urban roads, the majority on local urban streets. Road design appears to play a role in the link between speed and fatal crash involvement, but making a definitive connection depends on knowing the incidence of speeding by road class, data for which are unavailable.

Summary

Although the evidence is not conclusive, speed appears to contribute to crash occurrence. Theory, empirical data drawn from correlational studies, and causal analyses of crashes provide evidence that both speed and speed dispersion are associated with crash involvement. Crash involvement rates rise as a function of speed for certain crash

[40] Overinvolvement is based on the percentage of young drivers in the population, not on the exposure of young drivers.

types, such as single-vehicle crashes. Deviation from the average traffic speed is also associated with crash involvement. At high speeds, deviation from average traffic speeds not only increases crash probability but also the risk of a severe crash because of the close link between speed and injury severity discussed in the following section. At lower speeds, roadway characteristics—the presence of intersections, turning vehicles, and the presence of pedestrians and bicyclists—create the potential for conflict and crash involvement, but crashes may be less severe.

Limited data are available to analyze speed-safety relationships by road class. Deviation from average traffic speeds appears to play a role in crash involvement on Interstate highways, particularly near interchanges on urban Interstates, and to a greater extent on rural non-limited-access highways where high vehicular speeds and poorer road design combine to increase crash probability. Less is known about the role of speed and speed dispersion on urban roads. Given the character of many urban streets—numerous intersections, roadside activity, and the presence of pedestrians and bicyclists—the potential for conflict is great, but congestion often restrains speed and lessens crash severity. The studies that have examined these relationships suggest that speed dispersion does indeed play a role in crash probability on urban streets, particularly on urban arterials, but that many other factors, including speed itself, are likely to affect crash probability. Very little is known about the role of speed and speed dispersion on residential streets.

The clinical studies are unanimous in their finding that "excessive speed," that is, driving too fast for conditions, contributes to a significant share of all crashes and a higher share of severe crashes. As the following section shows, the evidence for the effect of speed on crash severity is far more conclusive.

Speed and Crash Severity

The relationship between speed and crash severity is more straightforward than the link between speed and crash probability. Once a crash has occurred—a vehicle has hit another vehicle or a stationary object—the vehicle undergoes a rapid change in speed. The vehicle decelerates rapidly but vehicle occupants continue to move at the vehicle's speed prior to impact until they are stopped in a second collision by striking the interior of the vehicle, by impact with objects external to the vehicle if ejected, or by being restrained by a safety belt or an airbag that deploys (Evans 1991, 247). The greater the speed at which occupants must absorb the energy released by the vehicle at impact, the greater the probability and severity of injury.

The vehicle's rapid velocity change in a crash, which is often referred to as Delta-V, is thus an important measure of crash severity. The probability that a crash will result in an occupant injury increases nonlinearly with impact speed. The energy released at impact, in turn, is determined by the speed at which the vehicle was traveling at the time of the crash. The power relationship between impact speed and the energy released in a crash—the energy release is proportional to the square of the impact speed—is responsible for the sharp rise in injury probability for the vehicle occupants.[41] For example, an 18 percent increase in impact speed in a collision—from 55 to 65 mph (89 to 105 km/h)—results in nearly a 40 percent increase in the energy that must be absorbed by the vehicle occupants. Actual effects may differ because several factors can mitigate the duration and rate of the deceleration and hence the injury to the vehicle occupants. These measures include vehicle mass (the greater the vehicle weight relative to the weight of the other vehicle involved in a collision, the less the energy that must be absorbed and the injury to the occupants of the heavier vehicle),[42] the energy-absorbing characteristics of the vehicle other than the mass, and the restraints on the vehicle occupants—safety belts and airbags—which enable them to "ride down" the impact forces (Evans 1991, 221).

Solomon's 1964 study investigated the relationship between speed and crash severity in real-world crashes. Using three measures of crash severity—deaths, injuries, and property damage per involvement—the study showed that the higher the speed, the greater the

---

[41] The equation that describes the release of kinetic energy as it relates to vehicle mass and speed is as follows: kinetic energy = 0.5 × mass × $(\text{velocity})^2$.

[42] Vehicle mass, however, is less relevant when the vehicle strikes a fixed object.

fatalities, injuries, and property damage (Solomon 1964, 11–14). Injury severity levels at high speeds were much greater than at lower speeds. For example, up to about 45 mph (72 km/h), 20 to 30 persons were injured and about 1 person killed per 100 crash-involved vehicles (Solomon 1964, 12). At 65 mph (105 km/h), 70 persons were injured and 6 persons killed per 100 crash-involved vehicles. The rate increased dramatically at very high speeds.[43] Of course, Solomon's study was conducted before federal safety standards were introduced for motor vehicles. Consequently, fatality and injury rates are lower in absolute terms today. However, the association between higher speeds and higher crash severity levels that Solomon found has been borne out in subsequent studies.

Several other researchers have confirmed the consistent relationship between speed and injury severity in crashes. Using data from the National Crash Severity Study, an intensive investigation of approximately 10,000 crashes from 1977 to 1979, O'Day and Flora (1982) found that the probability of a fatality increased dramatically with Delta-V. A driver crashing with an impact speed of 50 mph (80 km/h) was twice as likely to be killed as one crashing with an impact speed of 40 mph (64 km/h) (O'Day and Flora 1982 in TRB 1984, 39). At impact speeds above 50 mph, the probability of death exceeded 50 percent.

Using NHTSA's National Analysis Sampling System (NASS), which contains data on a nationally representative sample of police-reported crashes of all severity levels, Joksch (1993) also found a very consistent relationship between Delta-V and the probability of death for drivers involved in car-to-car collisions. Fitting curves to crash data from 1980 to 1986 with known and estimated Delta-Vs, he obtained very similar functions: the probability of a fatality is related to Delta-V to the fourth power (Joksch 1993, 104).

[43] For example, at speeds of 73 mph (117 km/h) and greater, nearly 130 persons were injured and 22 persons were killed per 100 crash-involved vehicles (Solomon 1964, 12). The fatality estimates should be interpreted with care because of the small numbers of crash involvements. However, the same trend is evident for the injury data, where the sample is larger.

Bowie and Walz (1994) examined the crash severity relationship for nonfatal injuries using somewhat more recent NASS data (from 1982 to 1989) and the Abbreviated Injury Scale (AIS). The AIS system rates injury levels from 1 (for a minor injury) to 6 (for an injury that is not currently survivable). The results (Figure 2-4) showed a dramatic increase in injury severity as Delta-V increased, confirming that real-world crash experience follows the laws of physics (Bowie and Walz 1994, 34). Combining several different crash files, the authors also compared injury severity levels with the distribution of injuries in speeding-related crashes. They found that the share of speeding-related crashes increased with increasing injury level. Ten percent of

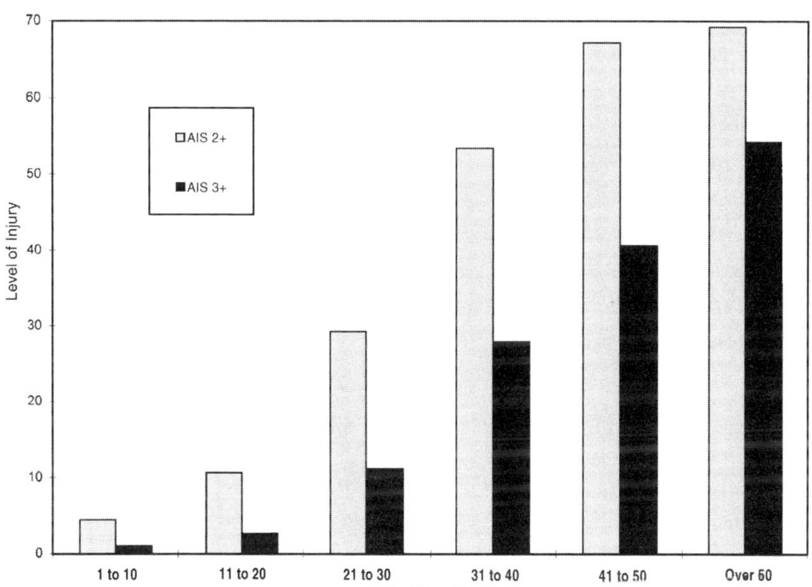

Figure 2-4 Injury rates by crash severity, NASS (1982–1986) and Crashworthiness Data System (1988–1989) (Bowie and Walz 1994, 33). Rates are based on the number of vehicle occupants at a known Delta-V level injured at a specific AIS level divided by the total number of vehicle occupants involved in crashes at that level of Delta-V times 100. AIS 2+ injuries range from moderate to fatal; AIS 3+ injuries range from serious to fatal. Data are limited to tow-away crashes involving passenger cars and light-duty trucks. 1 mph = 1.609 km/h.

noninjured vehicle occupants, 17 percent of occupants sustaining incapacitating injuries, and 34 percent of fatally injured occupants were involved in speeding-related crashes (Bowie and Walz 1994, 34).

The relationship between speed and crash severity is perhaps most dramatically demonstrated for vehicle crashes with pedestrians, the most vulnerable road users. The study of vehicle-pedestrian crashes in Helsinki (Pasanen and Salmivaara 1993) showed that the risk of death for a pedestrian increased rapidly from very low speeds (15 mph or 24 km/h) to about 50 mph (80 km/h), where death was almost certain (Pasanen and Salmivaara 1993, 308). A European review of several studies of vehicle-pedestrian crashes confirmed these results. It concluded that 5 percent of pedestrians are likely to die if they are struck by a vehicle traveling at 20 mph (32 km/h) and that risk levels rise sharply with speed—to a 45 percent probability of fatality for the pedestrian at 30 mph (48 km/h) and an 85 percent probability of fatality at 40 mph (64 km/h) (ETSC 1995, 11).

In summary, all of the studies that have investigated the link between vehicle speed and injury severity have found a consistent relationship. As driving speed increases, so does the impact speed of a vehicle in a collision. Increased impact speed, in turn, results in a sharp increase in injury severity because of the power relationship between impact speed and the energy released in a crash.

RELATIONSHIP OF SPEED TO TRAVEL TIME

In addition to safety, travel time is a major factor affected by speed that influences drivers' choice of an appropriate driving speed. The importance and cost of travel time as a function of speed were amply illustrated by the recent experience of the 55-mph (89-km/h) National Maximum Speed Limit (NMSL). A review of the NMSL (TRB 1984) estimated that in 1982 motorists were spending about 1 billion extra hours on highways posted at 55 mph because of slower driving speeds compared with speeds on these highways in 1973, the year before the NMSL was enacted (TRB 1984, 120). Most of this additional travel time was expended by passengers in personal vehicles (TRB 1984, 119). Frequently it involved small increments in travel time for individual trips.

Of course, any analysis of the time cost of travel has to take into account the cost savings from reduced crashes and averted fatalities and serious injuries from driving at lower speeds. When travel time costs were compared with estimated lives saved and serious injuries averted by the 55-mph (89-km/h) travel speed, the time cost worked out to about 40 years of additional driving time per life saved and serious injury avoided (TRB 1984, 120). The average remaining life expectancy of motor vehicle crash victims in 1982 was about 41 years. Thus, the number of years of extra driving time closely approximated the number of years of life saved.[44] Although the study committee concluded that making a comparison between the value of a year of life and the value of a year of driving time was not meaningful, it did provide one framework for assessing the central trade-off between travel time and safety involved in the decision to retain or relax the 55-mph speed limit (TRB 1984, 120).

Travel time costs are not equally distributed either by road type or road user. For example, the 55-mph (89-km/h) NMSL exacted the highest travel time costs for users of rural Interstate highways. At the time of the introduction of the NMSL, these highways had the highest speeds, among the lowest crash rates, and carried the majority of long-distance travel, particularly commercial travel. Lowering speeds on these roads was estimated to cost motorists and truckers alike 100 years of additional driving per life saved—about four times as much as on all other affected roads (TRB 1984, 123). The travel time costs to motorists on other road classes were estimated to have much smaller effects, in part a reflection of the role of congestion and roadway geometry in limiting travel speeds on these nonlimited-access highways.[45] Given these results, it was not surprising that the relaxation of the NMSL first occurred on rural Interstate highways.

---

[44] A more recent analysis of the time-safety trade-off of raising speed limits on qualified sections of rural Interstate highways in 1987 found that the 65-mph (105-km/h) limit cost at least as much time as it saved when the years lost to deaths, injuries, and travel delays were compared with the travel time saved (Miller 1989, 73).

[45] The comparable figures were 31 years of driving per life saved on urban Interstate highways and freeways, 28 years on rural arterials, and 14 years on rural collectors (TRB 1984, 123).

Travel time costs also tend to be unevenly distributed by road user. Most of the additional travel time attributed to the NMSL, for example, was borne by motorists engaged in personal travel. However, the value of this travel depends on trip purpose and length. For example, more highly valued work-related travel is relatively insensitive to changes in speed limits and accounts for a sizeable share of all local personal vehicle travel—most recently estimated at 32 percent in 1990 (FHWA 1992). However, commuting trips typically are short—the average trip length is about 11 mi (18 km)—and average trip time is about 22 min (VNTSC 1994). Thus, slower speeds generally result in adding small time increments. For many work trips, congestion is likely to have more effect on driving speeds and travel time than are reductions in speed limits.

Most personal travel (68 percent in 1990) is for shopping, family and other personal business, and social and recreational purposes. Because many of these trips are discretionary and do not have the same economic purpose as work travel, the time value of these trips is lower than for work travel, and, by extension, the incremental cost of reduced driving speeds from lower speed limits is also lower. Fortunately, most of these trips are short.

Particular groups of road users—commercial truckers and other business travelers—may be more adversely affected by reduced driving speeds attributable to lower speed limits. These groups drive more miles than the average motorist and often use high-speed roads. The economic cost of increased travel time for these user groups, particularly from lost productivity, can be substantial.[46]

RELATION OF SPEED TO FUEL USE AND OTHER VEHICLE OPERATING COSTS

The primary motivation for the NMSL was to conserve energy by reducing driving speeds. Today, because of low fuel prices, driver concern for fuel economy plays a much smaller role in determining appropriate driving speeds.

---

[46] In the case of the NMSL, however, the lower speed limit did have some benefits for truckers, such as lower fuel and maintenance costs.

The most recent study of fuel efficiency (West et al. 1997 in Davis 1997, 3-50), based on a small sample of 1988 to 1995 model year automobiles and light-duty trucks, shows a clear relationship between fuel economy and driving speed. Under steady-state, cruise-type driving conditions, fuel economy peaks at about 55 mph (89 km/h) and then declines at higher speeds, reflecting primarily the effect of aerodynamic drag on fuel efficiency (Figure 2-5).[47] At lower speeds, engine friction, tires, and accessories (e.g., power steering) reduce fuel efficiency (TRB 1995, 63).

Fuel efficiency also varies as a function of vehicle class. Sport utility vehicles, minivans, and pickup trucks—which represent a growing share of the U.S. passenger vehicle fleet—have poorer fuel economy, on

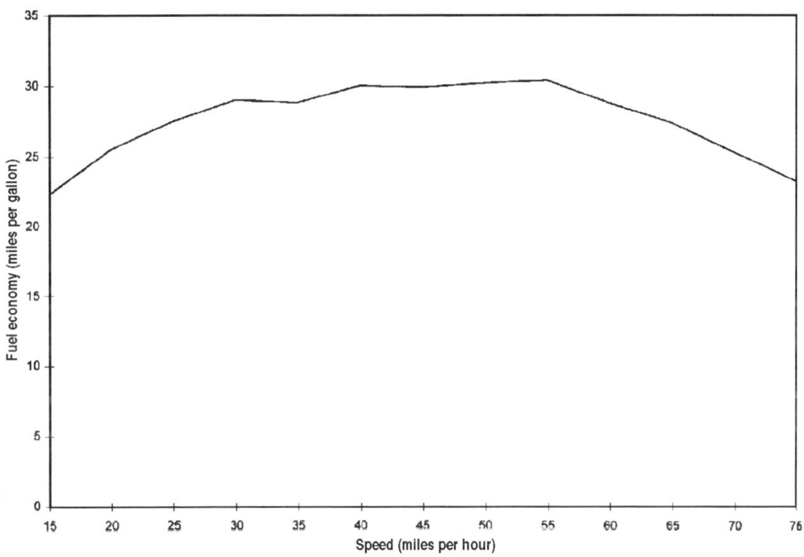

Figure 2-5 Fuel economy as a function of speed, model year 1988–1995 automobiles and light-duty trucks (Davis 1997, 3-51). 1 mph = 1.609 km/h; 1 gal = 3.8 L.

[47] Data on fuel economy as a function of speed for heavy trucks are older and more sparse. The available information suggests that fuel economy for heavy-duty diesel trucks declines sharply at speeds above about 50 mph (80 km/h), largely because of the effect of aerodynamic drag (TRB 1995, 125).

the average, than all but the heaviest automobiles for a wide range of speeds (Davis 1997, 3-52). Similarly, their fuel economy peaks at lower speeds, on the average, than does that of most passenger vehicles.

Other vehicle operating costs, such as tire wear, are also likely to increase as a function of speed. Relative to fuel costs, however, these other operating costs are small; speed-related changes in their costs are not readily discernible by the average driver. Thus, they are not likely to affect motorists' choice of appropriate driving speeds.

RELATION OF SPEED TO EMISSIONS

Speed is clearly linked with vehicle emissions that contribute to pollution of the atmosphere, particularly to the degradation of metropolitan air quality. According to current models, volatile organic compounds (VOCs)—an ozone precursor—and carbon monoxide (CO) are highest at very low speeds associated with heavily congested stop-and-go traffic and rise again with high-speed, free-flow highway driving (TRB 1995, 49–52). At high speeds, increased power demands on the engine cause CO and VOC emissions to increase, but at exactly what speed this occurs and by how much emissions are increased are unclear (TRB 1995, 122). Emissions of oxides of nitrogen (NO_x), another ozone precursor, are thought to increase gradually at speeds well below free-flow highway driving, but again there is considerable uncertainty about the speeds at which this increase begins and the rate of increase (TRB 1995, 122).

Data on emissions of heavy trucks as a function of speed are far more limited. The available data suggest that exhaust emissions of VOC and NO_x from heavy-duty diesel vehicles rise at high speeds (TRB 1995, 122). Detailed data on diesel particulate emissions as a function of speed are unavailable. This is particularly troubling because particulate concentrations pose a significant health risk, and heavy-duty diesel vehicles are the primary source of highway vehicle particulate emissions (TRB 1995, 129).

In addition to being a source of pollutants that degrade metropolitan air quality, transportation in general and motor vehicles in particular are the largest source of carbon dioxide (CO_2) emissions, one of the principal greenhouse gases associated with global warming.[48] In 1994, motor vehicles accounted for about one-quarter of all U.S. CO_2 emissions (TRB 1997, 83). The United States, in turn, is the largest emitter of CO_2, accounting for one-quarter of global emissions (TRB 1997, 84).

CO_2 emissions—a by-product of any engine that burns fossil fuels—are closely linked with fuel economy and thus speed. At high speeds, where fuel economy is poor, vehicles emit more CO_2.

Vehicle speeds are also associated with noise; noise levels rise at higher vehicle speeds. Sonic pollution is of greatest concern to those living near freeways and on residential streets with higher-speed traffic.

Despite the link between driving speeds and adverse environmental effects, U.S. drivers do not directly pay for the costs that this pollution imposes on society.[49] Thus they are not apt to consider environmental costs in their choice of an appropriate driving speed.

SUMMARY

In this chapter, the role of speed has been considered as it relates to the major factors motorists take into account in determining appropriate driving speeds. The relation of speed to safety—a major concern for most drivers—is complex. Driving speed is clearly linked with crash severity. Injury severity in a crash rises sharply with the speed of the vehicle in a collision, reflecting the laws of physics. At equivalent impact speeds, injury severity for pedestrians, the most vulnerable of road users, is dramatically greater than for vehicle occupants. Furthermore, the incidence of speeding as a contributing factor in crashes is higher the more severe the crash. The strength of the relationship between speed and crash severity alone is sufficient grounds for managing speed.

[48] Unlike most other vehicle emissions, CO_2 is not toxic. Along with other greenhouse gases, its effect in the upper atmosphere is to trap heat and warm the earth; hence the term greenhouse effect.

[49] Drivers do pay for the cost of pollution controls on vehicles, emission inspections, and improved fuels.

Speed is also related to the probability of being in a crash, although the evidence is not as compelling. Theory, the results of empirical studies, and clinical analyses of crash causation all link speed with crash probability. However, crashes are complex events, and isolating the effect of speed from all the other factors that contribute to crash probability to establish causality unequivocally is not practicable. Moreover, the concept of speed itself is complex. Crash involvement has been associated with the dispersion in traffic speeds—in particular, with the deviation of an individual driver's speed from the average speed of traffic at both higher and lower speeds than the average. Those who drive at high speeds, well above the average speed of traffic, pose the greatest safety concern to themselves and others because of the clear link between speed and crash severity. Crash involvement has also been associated with a driver's speed of travel. For example, single-vehicle crash involvement rates have been shown to rise with travel speed.

The relationships among speed, speed dispersion, and crash probability also appear to vary by road class. However, data are limited for many road types, and thus the observations that can be drawn are suggestive rather than conclusive. Speed dispersion poses an important safety concern on high-speed, nonlimited-access highways, such as rural, two-lane, undivided highways; wider speed dispersions are associated with higher crash involvement rates. Crash probability is also associated with speed dispersion on Interstate highways, particularly on urban Interstates near interchanges. The potential for vehicle conflict is high on most urban streets, where pedestrians and parked vehicles augment normal vehicle conflicts. On these roads, however, lower driving speeds reduce injury severity if a collision occurs. Vehicle-pedestrian crashes are an exception, because pedestrian injuries tend to be severe even at low impact speeds. Both speed and speed dispersion appear to play a role in crash likelihood on urban arterials; speed deviation above average traffic speeds and higher speeds in general are closely linked with crash probability on these roads. Little is known about the relationship between safety and speed on residential streets.

Crash probability also varies by crash type. Speed dispersion is a contributing factor in the occurrence of multiple-vehicle rear-end and angle collisions, particularly for those driving well below average traffic speeds. Driving at high speeds is associated with a greater incidence of single-vehicle crashes.

Travel time is another major factor affected by speed that influences motorists' selection of an appropriate driving speed. However, travel time costs are not equally distributed either by road class or by road user. The highest travel-time costs occur on high-speed roads, particularly Interstate highways and freeways, where speed regulation, if enforced, can increase driving time under free-flowing traffic conditions. Commercial truckers and business travelers are heavy users of these types of roads and typically drive more miles than the average motorist. Consequently, the economic cost of increased travel time and lost productivity from speed reduction measures can be substantial for these road users.

Currently, fuel and other vehicle operating costs play a relatively minor role in motorists' selection of an appropriate driving speed. The relationship between speed and fuel use is unambiguous—fuel economy is inversely related to driving speeds above about 55 mph (89 km/h) for passenger vehicles, on the average, and at somewhat lower speeds for light and heavy trucks. After more than a decade of low fuel costs, however, drivers have little incentive to consider fuel costs in their choice of speed.

Driving speed is clearly linked with vehicle emissions that contribute to metropolitan air pollution and emissions of CO_2, a greenhouse gas closely associated with global warming. High driving speeds are also associated with noise pollution. U.S. drivers, however, have never directly paid for these costs. Thus, at present, the choice of an appropriate driving speed is not affected by consideration of environmental costs.

These findings have several implications for managing speed. First, the unambiguous relationship between speed and crash severity alone is sufficient justification for controlling driving speeds. Second, if they are enforced, speed limits—the most common method of managing speed—can help restrict travel speeds, particularly at the very high speeds where the injury consequences of crashes are the greatest. Third, deviation of driving speeds from the average speed of traffic is associated with crash involvement. Thus, speed limit policies should attempt to minimize speed dispersion.

REFERENCES

ABBREVIATIONS

ETSC	European Transport Safety Council
FHWA	Federal Highway Administration
NHTSA	National Highway Traffic Safety Administration
RTI	Research Triangle Institute
TRB	Transportation Research Board
VNTSC	Volpe National Transportation Systems Center

Accident Reconstruction Journal. 1991. Is Speed Variation, Not Speed Itself, the Real Problem? Vol. 3, No. 6, Nov.–Dec.

Baruya, A., and D.J. Finch. 1994. Investigation of Traffic Speeds and Accidents on Urban Roads. *Proc., Seminar J, PTRC European Transport Forum,* University of Warwick, England, pp. 219–230.

Bowie, N.N., and M. Walz. 1994. Data Analysis of the Speed-Related Crash Issue. *Auto and Traffic Safety,* Vol. 1, No. 2, Winter, NHTSA, U.S. Department of Transportation, pp. 31–38.

Cirillo, J.A. 1968. Interstate System Accident Research—Study II—Interim Report II. *Public Roads,* Vol. 35, No. 3.

Cowley, J.E. 1980. *A Review of Rural Speed Limits in Australia.* Report CR 20. J.E. Cowley & Associates, Melbourne, Australia.

Cowley, J.E. 1987. *The Relationship Between Speed and Accidents: A Literature Review.* J.E. Cowley & Associates, Melbourne, Australia, March.

Davis, S.C. 1997. *Transportation Energy Data Book: Edition 17.* ORNL-6919. Oak Ridge National Laboratory, Oak Ridge, Tenn., Aug.

ETSC. 1995. *Reducing Traffic Injuries Resulting from Excess and Inappropriate Speed.* Brussels, Belgium, Jan., 35 pp.

Evans, L. 1991. *Traffic Safety and the Driver.* Van Nostrand Reinhold, New York, 405 pp.

FHWA. 1992. *1990 Nationwide Personal Transportation Survey: Summary of Travel Trends.* FHWA-PL-92-027. U.S. Department of Transportation, March.

Fildes, B.N., G. Rumbold, and A. Leening. 1991. *Speed Behavior and Drivers' Attitude to Speeding.* Report 16. Monash University Accident Research Center, Monash, Victoria, Australia, June.

Fowles, R., and P.D. Loeb. 1989. Speeding, Coordination, and the 55-mph Speed Limit: Comment. *The American Economic Review,* Vol. 79, pp. 916–922.

Garber, N.J., and R. Gadiraju. 1988. *Speed Variance and Its Influence on Accidents.* University of Virginia, Charlottesville, July, 56 pp.

Harkey, D.L., H.D. Robertson, and S.E. Davis. 1990. Assessment of Current Speed Zoning Criteria. In *Transportation Research Record 1281,* Transportation Research Board, National Research Council, Washington, D.C., pp. 40–51.

Hauer, E. 1971. Accidents, Overtaking and Speed Control. *Accident Analysis and Prevention,* Vol. 3, pp. 1–13.

Joksch, H.C. 1993. Velocity Change and Fatality Risk in a Crash. *Accident Analysis and Prevention,* Vol. 25, pp. 103–104.

Kloeden, C.N., A.J. McLean, V.M. Moore, and G. Ponte. 1997. *Travelling Speed and the Risk of Crash Involvement. Vol. I—Findings.* NHMRC Road Accident Research Unit, The University of Adelaide, Australia, Nov., 60 pp.

Lave, C. 1985. Speeding, Coordination, and the 55-mph Limit. *The American Economic Review,* Vol. 75, pp. 1159–1164.

Lave, C. 1989. Speeding, Coordination, and the 55-mph Limit: Reply. *The American Economic Review,* Vol. 79, pp. 926–931.

Levy, D.T., and P. Asch. 1989. Speeding, Coordination, and the 55-mph Speed Limit: Comment. *The American Economic Review,* Vol. 79, pp. 913–915.

Liu, G.X. 1997. Identification and Analysis of Speed Related Accidents on Highways. *Proc., Canadian Multidisciplinary Road Safety Conference X,* Toronto, Ontario, Canada, June 8–11, pp. 65–74.

Mackay, M. 1985. Seat Belt Use Under Voluntary and Mandatory Conditions and Its Effects on Casualties. In *Human Behavior and Traffic Safety* (L. Evans and R.C. Schwing, eds.), Plenum Press, New York, pp. 259–277.

Miller, T.R. 1989. *65 MPH: Does It Save Time?* The Urban Institute, Washington, D.C. In *33rd Annual Proc., Association for the Advancement of Automotive Medicine,* Baltimore, Md., Oct. 2–4, pp. 73–90.

Munden, J.W. 1967. *The Relation Between a Driver's Speed and His Accident Rate.* Report LR 88. Road Research Laboratory, Crowthorne, England.

NHTSA. 1997a. *Traffic Safety Facts 1996: Speeding.* U.S. Department of Transportation, 6 pp.

NHTSA. 1997b. *Traffic Safety Facts 1996.* DOT-HS-808-649. U.S. Department of Transportation, Dec., 192 pp.

O'Day, J., and J. Flora. 1982. *Alternative Measures of Restraint System Effectiveness: Interaction with Crash Severity Factors.* SAE Technical Paper Series No. 820798. Warrendale, Pa.

Parker, M.R., Jr. 1997. *Effects of Raising and Lowering Speed Limits on Selected Roadway Sections.* FHWA-RD-92-084. Martin R. Parker & Associates, Inc., Wayne, Mich., Jan., 175 pp.

Pasanen, E., and H. Salmivaara. 1993. Driving Speeds and Pedestrian Safety in the City of Helsinki. *Traffic Engineering and Control,* Vol. 34, No. 6, pp. 308–310.

Rodriguez, R.J. 1990. Speed, Speed Dispersion, and the Highway Fatality Rate. *Southern Economic Journal,* Oct., pp. 349–356.

Rowsome, F., Jr. 1965. *The Verse by the Side of the Road.* The Penguin Group.

RTI. 1970. *Speed and Accidents, Vol. II.* Final Report, Summary and Conclusions, May.

Rumar, K., U. Bergrund, P. Jernberg, and U. Ytterbom. 1976. Driver Reaction to a Technical Safety Measure. *Human Factors,* Vol. 18, pp. 443–454.

Shinar, D. 1978. *Psychology on the Road: The Human Factor in Traffic Safety.* Wiley, New York.

Snyder, D. 1989. Speeding, Coordination, and the 55-mph Limit: Comment. *The American Economic Review,* Vol. 79, pp. 922–925.

Solomon, D. 1964. *Accidents on Main Rural Highways Related to Speed, Driver, and Vehicle.* Bureau of Public Roads, U.S. Department of Commerce, July, 44 pp.

Stuster, J., and Z. Coffman. 1997. *Synthesis of Safety Research Related to Speed and Speed Management* (unpublished draft). Anacapa Sciences, Inc. Santa Barbara, Calif., FHWA, U.S. Department of Transportation, 56 pp.

Taylor, D.H. 1964. Drivers' Galvanic Skin Response and the Risk of Accidents. *Ergonomics*, Vol. 7, pp. 439–451.

Tignor, S.C., and D.L. Warren. 1990. Driver Speed Behavior on U.S. Streets and Highways. *ITE Compendium of Technical Papers, 60th Annual Meeting*, Orlando, Fla., Aug. 5-8, pp. 83–86.

TRB. 1984. *Special Report 204: 55: A Decade of Experience.* National Research Council, Washington, D.C., 262 pp.

TRB. 1995. *Special Report 245: Expanding Metropolitan Highways: Implications for Air Quality and Energy Use.* National Research Council, Washington, D.C., 387 pp.

TRB. 1997. *Special Report 251: Toward a Sustainable Future.* National Research Council, Washington, D.C., 261 pp.

Treat, J.R., N.S. Tumbas, S.T. McDonald, D. Shinar, R.D. Hume, R.E. Mayer, R.L. Stansifer, and H.J. Castellan. 1977. *Tri-Level Study of the Causes of Traffic Accidents. Volume I: Causal Factor Tabulations and Assessment.* DOT-HS-805-085. National Highway Traffic Safety Administration, U.S. Department of Transportation.

Viano, D.C., and S. Ridella. 1996. Crash Causation: A Case Study of Fatal Accident Circumstances and Configurations. No. 960458. Society of Automotive Engineers, International Congress and Exposition, Detroit, Mich., Feb. 26–29, pp. 123–134.

VNTSC. 1994. *Journey-to-Work Trends in the United States and Its Major Metropolitan Areas, 1960–1990.* FHWA-PL-94-012. U.S. Department of Transportation.

West, B.H., R.N. McGill, J.W. Hodgson, S.S. Sluder, and D.E. Smith. 1997. *Development and Verification of Light-Duty Modal Emissions and Fuel Consumption Values for Traffic Models.* Federal Highway Administration, U.S. Department of Transportation, April.

West, L.B., Jr., and J.W. Dunn. 1971. Accidents, Speed Deviation and Speed Limits. *Traffic Engineering*, Vol. 41, No. 10, pp. 52–55.

White, S.B., Jr., and A.C. Nelson, Jr. 1970. Some Effects of Measurement Errors in Estimating Involvement Rate as a Function of Deviation from Mean Traffic Speed. *Journal of Safety Research*, Vol. 2, No. 2, June, pp. 67–72.

Wilde, G.J.S., S.P. Claxton-Oldfield, and P.H. Platenius. 1985. Risk Homeostasis in an Experimental Context. In *Human Behavior and Traffic Safety* (L. Evans and R.C. Schwing, eds.), Plenum Press, New York, pp. 119–149.

3

Managing Speeds: Speed Limits

Angels
Who guard you
When you drive
Usually
Retire at 65
Burma Shave (Rowsome 1965)

The preceding chapter provided evidence of a close link between speed and safety. Speed is directly related to injury severity in a crash, reflecting the laws of physics. The link between speed and the probability of being in a crash is weaker, reflecting the fact that motor vehicle crashes are complex events that can seldom be attributed to a single factor.

The evidence presented, however, is sufficiently strong to reaffirm the need for managing speed. In this chapter, one of the primary methods of managing drivers' choice of speed—the imposition of speed limits—is discussed. Speed limits are part of a speed management system, which involves laws and a process for setting reasonable speed limits as well as enforcement, sanctions, and publicity. The chapter begins with an explanation of why regulatory intervention is justified. After a brief history of speed regulation, the major methods of establishing speed limits are introduced and their strengths and weaknesses summarized. The application of speed limits to different road classes and roadway environments is considered next. A review of what is known about the effect of speed limits on driver behavior and safety follows, drawing heavily on studies of recent changes in speed limits both in the United States and abroad. The chapter ends with a discussion of the implications of these findings for speed limit policies.

REGULATING SPEED—A THEORETICAL JUSTIFICATION

Drivers continually make choices about appropriate driving speeds, making their own assessment concerning the amount of risk they are willing to bear. Because drivers have a strong incentive to complete their trips safely, one could ask why they should not be left to choose their own travel speeds. There are three principal reasons for regulating drivers' speed choices: (*a*) externalities,[1] that is, the imposition of risks and uncompensated costs on others because of inappropriate speed choices made by individual drivers; (*b*) inadequate information that limits a motorist's ability to determine an appropriate driving speed; and (*c*) driver misjudgment of the effects of speed on crash probability and severity.

The strongest case for regulatory intervention can be made on the grounds of externalities. Drivers may not take into account the risks imposed on others by their choice of an appropriate driving speed.

[1] Externalities are defined as the "effect that occurs when the activity of one entity (a person or a firm) directly affects the welfare of another in a way that is not transmitted by market prices" (Rosen 1995, 91).

For example, drivers who choose to drive very fast relative to other traffic or very fast for existing road conditions in exchange for a shorter trip time may accept the higher risk of death or injury for themselves, but their choice almost certainly increases the risk of death and injury for other road users. Even a single-occupant, single-vehicle crash imposes medical and property damage costs that are not entirely paid for by the driver. Other externalities in the form of higher fuel consumption or higher emissions resulting from higher driving speeds are not directly paid for from current fuel or vehicle operating taxes. Such externalities are the major theoretical justification for the imposition of speed limits. (Speed limits, of course, are not the only possible regulatory response.) The externalities—particularly the risks to others—may be relatively small on lightly traveled Interstate highways but quite large on streets adjacent to schools or in highly congested areas. The differences in the effects of the externalities are important to consider in setting appropriate speed limits on different types of roads.

Regulatory intervention is also justified if drivers are systematically making "wrong" choices because of a lack of information or an inability to understand the information presented to them. (A wrong choice is defined as a choice that is different from the choice drivers would make if they had and understood all the relevant information.) For example, some drivers may not correctly judge the capabilities of their vehicles (e.g., stopping, handling) or anticipate roadway geometry and roadside conditions sufficiently to determine appropriate driving speeds. These circumstances may not be as relevant for experienced drivers driving under familiar circumstances, although these drivers can make inappropriate decisions because of fatigue or other factors. Inexperienced drivers, or experienced drivers operating in unfamiliar surroundings, are more likely to underestimate risk and make inappropriate speed choices. For example, even experienced drivers may not make informed choices when faced with entirely new driving circumstances, such as the southerner confronting snow or the easterner confronting a winding mountain road with no shoulders.

Another reason for regulatory intervention, which is related to the issues of information adequacy and judgment, is the tendency of some drivers to underestimate or misjudge the effects of speed on crash probability and severity. For example, drivers may have a good sense of the relationship between driving speed and travel time, but they may not have as good an appreciation of the effect of speed on crash probability and crash severity. As noted in Chapter 1, there is some evidence that drivers systematically overestimate their driving skills and underestimate the risks of driving, particularly at higher speeds. Other drivers may simply be indifferent to speed regulations and will drive as fast as they can, ignoring the risks their speed choices impose on others. The justification for imposing speed limits, however, still leaves open the question of how the limits should be set, the topic of the following section.

METHODS OF SETTING SPEED LIMITS

Brief History of Speed Regulation

The idea of regulating the speed of motor vehicle travel has a long history. In fact, the first speed regulations predated the invention of the automobile by some 200 years. The town of Newport, Rhode Island, prohibited the galloping of horses on major thoroughfares in an effort to prevent pedestrian deaths; Boston, Massachusetts, limited horsedrawn carriages to a "foot pace" on Sundays to protect churchgoers (Ladd 1959). In 1901 Connecticut was the first state to impose a maximum speed limit of 8 mph (13 km/h) in cities (Labatut and Lane 1950).

A review of early speed legislation suggests that the primary purpose of regulating speed was to improve public safety (Parker 1997, 1); another goal was uniformity in state speed regulations (UVC 1967, 436). The Uniform Vehicle Code (UVC), first published in 1926, provided the framework for speed control as it is known today. The original code contained (*a*) a basic rule requiring motorists to operate at speeds reasonable and prudent for conditions and (*b*) maximum general speed limits[2] in business and residential districts and other specific situations (e.g., grade crossings, in the vicinity of

[2] These maximum limits were established as prima facie limits (UVC 1967, 437).

schools) (UVC 1967, 428, 437–438). The 1934 version of the UVC broadened the maximum speed limits to cover more general situations (e.g., urban districts) and introduced the concept of speed zones, wherein state agencies would determine alternative maximum speed limits at particular highway locations on the basis of engineering and traffic investigations (UVC 1967, 437, 446).[3]

With the rise of the traffic safety movement during the 1930s, the National Safety Council organized a Committee on Speed Regulation in 1936 to study the speed problem. Its report (NSC 1941) reiterated the framework laid out by the UVC—a basic rule, maximum general speed limits, and authority for establishing speed zones on the basis of a traffic engineering study. The committee recommended that state legislatures adopt uniform speed legislation based on this framework (NSC 1941, 5, 15). Above all it recommended a balanced approach toward speed control, directed at speed "too fast for conditions" rather than at speed in excess of some arbitrary general limit (NSC 1941, 4). At the time the committee was conducting its work, cars were capable of reaching speeds of 80 to 100 mph (129 to 161 km/h), but the general statewide speed limit in many states was 35 to 45 mph (56 to 72 km/h) (Joscelyn and Elston 1970, 32).

With the tremendous growth in motor vehicle travel and further improvements in the highway system and the automobile during the 1930s and 1940s, the motoring public clamored for speeds higher than the maximum posted limits, which were frequently ignored because they were considered below those deemed reasonable by motorists (*The American City* 1950). In response, traffic engineers began to advocate an approach to setting speed limits (described subsequently) that is based on operating speeds as well as other factors. This method attempts to define a safe speed but also accommodates drivers' desire for a reasonable speed

[3] The 1926 UVC had previously recommended that local authorities be empowered to increase speed limits on through highways under their jurisdiction (UVC 1967, 450).

Considerations in Establishing Speed Limits

General Speed Limits Versus Speed Zones

In any discussion of speed limits, it is important to distinguish between general limits, which apply statewide or even nationwide, and limits in speed zones, which apply to a particular section of road. The former are set by legislation—by state statute, municipal ordinance, or Congress (ITE 1992, 347). Typically, general or legislated limits apply to a category of highway (see glossary)—a freeway or an arterial, for example—and reflect the design characteristics of the particular road class. They also differ by area, distinguishing rural from urban or local roads. By definition, general speed limits represent a compromise; they may be well suited for some roads but are either "too high" or "too low" for others (Harwood 1995, 89).

Speed limits in speed zones, on the other hand, are established by administrative action and are intended to be determined on the basis of an engineering study (ITE 1992, 347). The limits are tailored for a specific length of road where the general limit is deemed to be inappropriate. Guidance is abundant on how to conduct the requisite engineering assessment of the traffic, road, and land use conditions that should be considered in establishing an appropriate speed limit in a speed zone (Harwood 1995, 89).

Uniformity

One might ask why speed zones are not established for every road segment, thereby tailoring speeds to the particular characteristics of the road and the location. Besides creating obvious resource problems because of the requirement to both undertake the necessary engineering studies and post signs on each highway section, a system of frequently changing speed limits would create confusion for the driver (Harwood 1995, 90). It could encourage a patchwork of different speed limits that may or may not be consistent across road classes and locations (Figure 3-1). The current system of statutory limits with speed zones as exceptions has the merit of encouraging uniformity and consistency of speed limits across a broad range of highways.

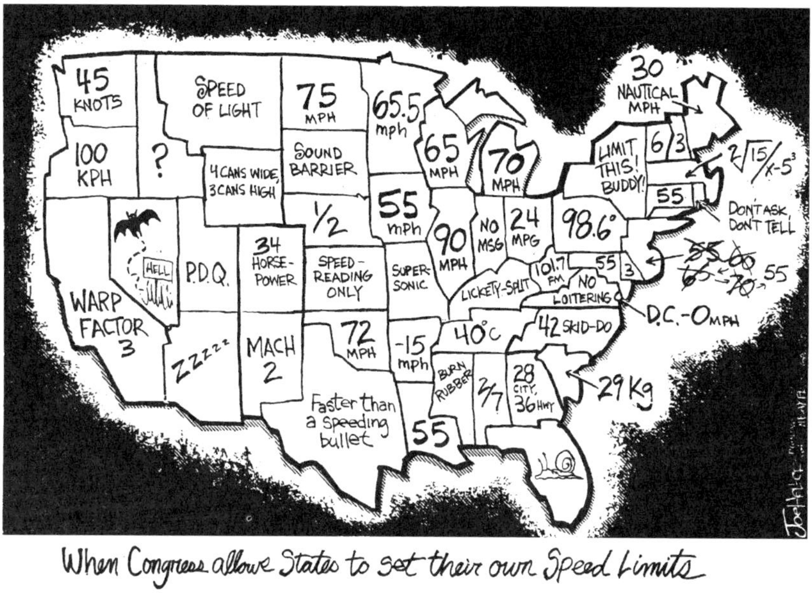

Figure 3-1 Parody of state response to repeal of 55-mph (89-km/h) National Maximum Speed Limit (reprinted with permission of Joe Heller, *Green Bay Press-Gazette*).

Objectives of Speed Limits

The primary purpose of speed limits is to enhance safety by reducing the risks imposed by drivers' speed choices. Speed limits enhance safety in two ways. They have a limiting function. By establishing an upper bound on speeds, the objective is to reduce both the probability and severity of crashes. Speed limits also have a coordinating function—to reduce dispersion in driving speeds (Lave 1985); more uniform speeds are associated with fewer vehicle conflicts. Another function of speed limits, which is related to their coordinating function, is to achieve an orderly flow of traffic and improve traffic flow efficiency. Once established, well-conceived speed limits help determine a reasonable standard for enforcement. Historically, speed limits have also been established for energy conservation purposes during times of national crisis.

Those who set speed limits attempt to balance road user safety and travel efficiency, among the many other factors that determine drivers' speed choice. Determining the optimal trade-off between these objectives depends, in part, on the function of the road. On limited-access facilities built to move traffic efficiently, greater emphasis may be placed on minimizing travel time without compromising safety. On local roads, where the primary function is access to abutting property, speed limits may be set to accommodate access rather than the efficient movement of traffic (Harwood 1995, 90).

Informational Content and Reasonableness

Whatever trade-offs are made between safety and travel time in establishing speed limits, posted limits ought to convey information to drivers. According to current practice, the numerical value on the sign advises the motorist of the maximum speed at which a driver can lawfully proceed under favorable conditions (e.g., good weather, daylight, and free-flowing traffic). Drivers are expected to reduce their speeds as these conditions change. The maximum speed limit should be related to the actual risk characteristics of the road (e.g., curvature, lane width) if drivers are to perceive the speed limit as credible and if adequate levels of voluntary compliance are to be achieved (Fildes and Lee 1993, 22). State and local governments do not have the resources—nor do they perceive it as a good use of resources—to apprehend and penalize large numbers of out-of-compliance drivers. Routine violation of speed limits by the majority of drivers may breed contempt not only for speed limits but also for other traffic regulations. As a general proposition, then, speed limits should be set at levels that are largely self-enforcing so that law enforcement officials can concentrate their efforts on the worst offenders. This goal, however, may not be achievable on all road classes (e.g., local streets) where lower driving speeds are desirable but speed compliance is poor. These roads may be candidates for other speed management strategies, such as traffic calming.

Primary Methods of Setting Speed Limits

The process of setting speed limits is often viewed as a technical exercise. However, the decisions concerning appropriate limits require value judgments and trade-offs that are appropriately handled by the political process—by Congress in the case of setting national speed limits and by state legislatures and city councils in determining general limits for highways under their respective jurisdictions. In this section, the major methods of determining speed limits are described. The section begins with a description of the methods most appropriate for setting statutory or legislated speed limits and continues with a discussion of the methods appropriate for setting speed limits in speed zones (Table 3-1).

Statutory Limits

Statutory national speed limits were imposed twice in U.S. history, both during times of national crisis. A federal speed limit of 35 mph (56 km/h) was imposed during World War II. More recently, Congress established the NMSL of 55 mph (89 km/h) during the energy crisis of 1973 to reduce reliance on imported oil. In both cases, the objective was to reduce energy costs rather than transportation costs. Safety benefits and travel time costs were a by-product rather than an intrinsic part of the initial determination of an appropriate speed limit.[4]

Following repeal of the NMSL in 1995, most state legislatures acted to raise speed limits on highways subject to the 55-mph (89-km/h) speed limit. Many states reverted to the maximum general speed limits in effect for these highways before the NMSL was enacted. Other states established new speed limits on these highways. Legislative decisions typically were accompanied by public input and technical support provided by state departments of transportation (DOTs). Before posting speed limit increases, many state

[4] Benefit-cost considerations, particularly the trade-offs between loss of life, injury costs, and time savings, were more directly considered and debated when Congress decided to allow states to raise speed limits on rural Interstates in 1987.

Table 3-1 Characteristics of the Primary Methods of Setting Speed Limits

Speed Limit Method	Most Common Application	Relation to Safety	Appropriateness by Road Class	Ease of Implementation	Relation to Enforcement
Statutory limits	General limits	Trade-offs among safety, travel time, and other objectives are politically determined	Statutory limits typically are established by road class and sometimes by location (e.g., rural)	Difficult to achieve consensus on national limits except during times of crisis—easier to establish at state and local level	Can be difficult to enforce if limits are set arbitrarily
Optimum speed limits	General limits or speed zones	Safety is balanced with other objectives (e.g., travel time) to minimize social highway transport costs	Theoretically, should be adaptable for any road class	No known practical application—difficult to quantify key variables	If implemented, could be difficult to enforce because socially optimal speed limits are typically lower than what individual drivers would select
Engineering study method with speed limits set near the 85th percentile speed	Speed zones	Not necessarily a safe speed for all road classes; it depends, for example, on the dispersion of speeds between the slowest and fastest drivers	May not be as appropriate for urban roads, particularly residential streets, with greater mix of road users and functions than major arterials and freeways	Well-established methodology for determining 85th percentile speed	Helps establish a reasonable target of out-of-compliance drivers for enforcement

Expert system–based approach	Speed zones	Helps identify many factors, in addition to vehicle operating speeds, that may affect safety	Probably most useful and appropriate for roads in urban areas where speed limits based solely on 85th percentile speed may be inappropriate	Complex system to develop, requiring knowledgeable experts and computer capability	System has been used to target photo enforcement (i.e., where recommended program limit is substantially below drivers' preferred operating speeds)
Variable speed limits	Freeways	Not fully demonstrated—some indication that more uniform speeds reduce crashes	Because of expense, most appropriate for highest-class roads with large traffic volumes	Limited experience in United States—new technologies are being introduced	Systems are often combined with photo radar enforcement

DOTs conducted engineering surveys of candidate state highways for speed limit increases, examining design speeds, pavement condition, traffic congestion, crash data, and existing travel speeds, among other factors, to determine where the limits could be safely raised. Many states are monitoring driving speeds and crash experience to determine whether further changes in speed limits should be legislated. At least one state, New Jersey, has raised speed limits on a trial basis pending the results of a study of the overall effect of the legislated increases.[5]

Statutory speed limits also have a long history at the local level. Many local governments have set speeds by statute or ordinance on local roads. In recent years, citizen concerns about speeding, particularly on neighborhood streets, have led to lower speed limits and other measures to manage driver speeds in residential areas.

The concept of legislated speed limits has appeal from a policy perspective. The trade-offs between safety, travel time, and other costs implicit in setting speed limits involve value judgments that are often best resolved by the political process. On the other hand, legislated speed limits can be arbitrary. The recent NMSL, for example, had been criticized for not appropriately reflecting differences in geography and local traffic conditions.

Optimum Speed Limits

In the early 1960s Oppenlander proposed a scientifically based procedure for regulating vehicle operating speeds to set speed limits at an optimal level from a societal perspective (Oppenlander 1962). The

[5] The legislation, enacted Jan. 19, 1998, raised speed limits to 65 mph (105 km/h) on 400 mi (644 km) of highways but requires the Commissioner of Transportation in consultation with the Attorney General and the authorities (i.e., New Jersey Highway Authority, New Jersey Turnpike Authority, and South Jersey Transportation Authority) to conduct an 18-month study of speeds, crash rates, fatalities, enforcement, air quality, and other issues to evaluate fully the effect of the 65-mph speed limit. They are requested to submit recommendations to the legislature as to whether the number of miles of highways eligible for 65 mph should increase, decrease, or remain the same [P.L. 1997, Chapter 415 (3)].

method recognized that individual drivers do not always select driving speeds that take into account the risks imposed on others by their choice. For example, driving at high speeds can increase the likelihood of a severe crash, which may involve other road users; it also results in added fuel consumption and higher emission levels, costs that are not entirely borne by the individual driver or even other highway users (MacRae and Wilde 1979, 136–137). Because of these external costs, the optimum speed for an individual driver is different from the socially optimum speed.

Oppenlander's approach attempted to define costs per mile of travel as a function of speed for four cost categories: (*a*) vehicle operation, (*b*) travel time, (*c*) crashes, and (*d*) service (i.e., comfort and convenience) (Oppenlander 1962, 78). The cost curves were developed from studies of vehicular travel on various types of highways for different traffic situations, travel conditions, and types of motor vehicles (Oppenlander 1962, 78). The "optimal speed" was determined by solving for the minimum point on the total cost curve, which represented the minimum social cost of highway transport for a particular set of conditions (Oppenlander 1962, 78). The approach is most appropriate for establishing general speed limits for different road classes. However, it can also be used for setting speed limits in speed zones by adjusting optimal speeds to reflect the specific physical and environmental features of a given highway segment.

Marcellis (1962) attempted to apply Oppenlander's theory for different types of travel (rural and urban), for different types of roads (two- and four-lane), and for different types of vehicles (passenger cars and commercial vehicles) during daytime and nighttime travel. He found an optimal speed that minimized the cost of traffic movement for each of these conditions.[6] The recommended application of his results was the establishment of general speed limits (Marcellis 1962, 1).

---

[6] For example, he found large differences, up to 11 mph (18 km/h), between the optimal speeds of passenger cars and commercial vehicles. There were also large differences in optimal speeds by area. In rural areas, the optimal speed for passenger cars was 50 mph (80 km/h); in urban areas optimal speeds decreased with an increase in the number of stops per mile from 41 to 29 mph (66 to 47 km/h). Lesser differences were found for optimal speeds on two- versus four-lane rural highways, and even smaller differences were found between daytime and nighttime optimal speeds (Marcellis 1962, 1, 59).

A more recent variant of this approach (Jondrow et al. 1982) determines the socially optimum speed by starting with the private optimum speed and then adjusting it to account for external costs. The potential benefit of this approach is that it is based on the driver's judgment about the values of trip time, gasoline costs, and, most important, the value of life. It does not impose externally derived valuations of these parameters. The shortcoming is that it assumes a single representative driver, which implies that all drivers have the same preferred optimum speed.

Although conceptually appealing, optimum speed limits have never been used in practice. One problem, which is typical of most benefit-cost analyses, is the difficulty of quantifying key variables. Considerable work has been done on valuation of travel time as well as on the costs of injury and mortality, but there is no clear consensus on these estimates. Another issue is implementation. In their analysis, MacRae and Wilde (1979) attempted to estimate an optimum national speed limit—a preliminary estimate was between 55 and 60 mph (89 and 97 km/h). However, when consideration was given to recommending such a limit, it was not clear that the optimum limit would achieve its goal. Successful implementation of the approach depends on driver compliance and perception that the speed limit is reasonable and on the level of enforcement activity.

Engineering Study Method

The most common method for determining speed limits in a speed zone sets the limit on the basis of an engineering study. The study requires data collection and analysis in the determination of an appropriate limit. The data include measurement of prevailing traffic speeds, crash data, and information on highway, traffic, and roadside conditions not readily apparent to drivers.[7]

---

[7] Many roadside and roadway features are readily apparent to drivers and have already been taken into account in the speed they choose to drive. The factors that are not so readily apparent and that may warrant a lower speed limit include hidden intersections or driveways, lane drops, and other unexpected conditions.

A recent survey of state and local governments (Fitzpatrick et al. 1997) found that the 85th percentile speed is the most widely used factor for determining the level at which to set the limit. Other frequently considered factors included crash experience, roadside development, roadway geometry, and maximum speed limits set by state statute or local ordinance (Fitzpatrick et al. 1997, 52). Typically, the speed data—more specifically the 85th percentile speed—provide the first approximation of the speed zone limit (ITE 1992, 348). The limit may be adjusted from this value on the basis of the other factors.

Setting the speed limit near the 85th percentile, that is, the speed at or below which 85 percent of drivers operate their vehicles, assumes that most drivers are capable of judging the speed at which they can safely operate (Krammes et al. 1996, 7, 12). The 85th percentile speed is determined through spot speed studies of free-flowing traffic (i.e., traffic unimpeded by other vehicles), which yield a distribution of speeds from which the 85th percentile is calculated (Krammes et al. 1996, 7) (Figure 3-2).[8] The implication for enforcement is that no more than 15 percent of motorists will be out of compliance. In practice, typical enforcement tolerances of between 5 and 10 mph (8 and 16 km/h) above posted limits further narrow the enforcement band.

As early as 1941, the report of the Committee on Speed Regulation (NSC 1941, 13) advocated determining critical or maximum safe speeds by observing the operating speeds at or below which 80 or 90 percent of drivers travel under normal weather and daylight conditions. Although the method was recommended for establishing

[8] At least two additional measures of speed dispersion are available for calculating operating speed as a basis for setting speed limits. The first is the pace speed, which is defined as the 10-mph (16-km/h) range encompassing the greatest percentage of all the speed observations at a particular site. It is described by both the speed value at the lower end of the range and the percentage of all vehicles that are within the range and thus is an alternative indicator of speed dispersion (see glossary). The second is the skewness of the speed distribution. Research by Taylor (1965) found a strong relationship between the rate of occurrence of crashes and a skewed (i.e., nonnormal) speed distribution on rural state highways. Hence, he argued that the appropriate speed for a speed zone should be based on changing the speed distribution from a nonnormal to a normal distribution by a "before" and "after" analysis of the actual speed distribution within the zone (Taylor 1965, 51).

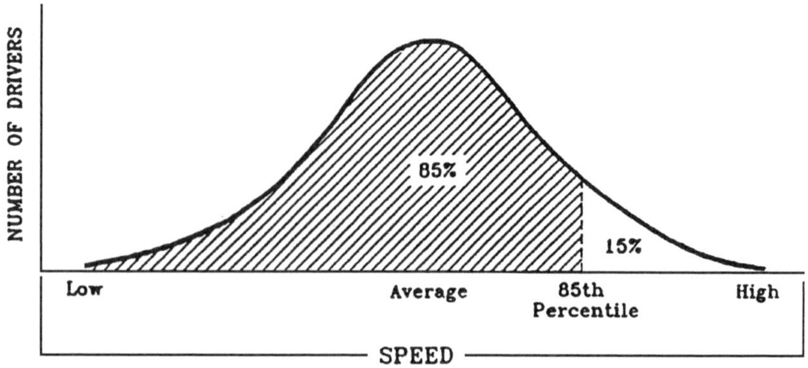

Figure 3-2 Speed distribution showing the 85th percentile speed (Krammes et al. 1996).

appropriate speed limits in speed zones, it was also advocated as a way of determining proper values for general speed limits, particularly on rural highways.[9] A 1960 survey of the member departments of the American Association of State Highway Officials found that the majority set speed limits in speed zones primarily on the basis of the 85th percentile speed, although a few departments used the 90th percentile speed; such factors as design speed, geometric characteristics, crash experience, traffic volumes, and development were secondary considerations (Sub-Committee on Speed Zoning 1969 in Joscelyn and Elston 1970, 99). The 85th percentile speed was accepted because traffic engineers often found that this was the upper limit of the 10-mph (16-km/h) pace (Carter 1949 in Joscelyn and Elston 1970, 94). Setting the speed limit near this point would encourage most drivers to travel at more uniform speeds, thus minimizing opportunities for vehicle conflict (Baerwald 1953 in Joscelyn

[9] Speed limits on rural highways in some midwestern states were set at 50 mph (80 km/h), which the committee thought could be raised somewhat for daytime travel. Other states had not posted numerical limits for rural highways because of concerns about the adequacy of enforcement efforts. Speed limits based on operating speeds were perceived to be useful both in determining reasonable speed limits and for enforcement (NSC 1941, 14, 16).

and Elston 1970, 105). In addition, experience indicated that the 85th percentile speed appeared to be reasonable from a law enforcement standpoint (Tennessee Department of Highways 1968 in Joscelyn and Elston 1970, 99).

Analytic support for setting speed limits near the 85th percentile speed came from a series of traffic safety studies (Solomon 1964; Cirillo 1968; RTI 1970) whose strengths and weaknesses were discussed in the preceding chapter. The studies found that crash involvement rates on certain road classes were lowest for vehicles traveling in a speed range whose upper bound was about one standard deviation above average traffic speeds, or approximately at the 85th percentile speed.[10] Thus, the 85th percentile speed not only represents the upper bound of the preferred driving speed of most drivers, but, according to some studies, for some roads it also corresponds to the upper bound of a speed range where crash involvement rates are lowest.[11]

Setting the speed limit near the 85th percentile speed has great appeal from a behavioral and an enforcement perspective. However, it is less clear that the 85th percentile speed necessarily corresponds to the lowest crash involvement rates on all road classes. The safety benefits may well depend on the range of speeds. The narrower the speed dispersion—the less the spread between the average speed and the 85th percentile speed—the greater the safety benefits. This principle was illustrated with the imposition of the NMSL in 1973. The lower speed limit resulted in a considerable narrowing of the spread between the slowest and fastest drivers in 1974, contributing to the substantial reduction in fatalities in that year (Figure 3-3) (Godwin 1988, 25).[12]

---

[10] The relationship between crash involvement rates and deviation from average traffic speeds can also be used to establish minimum speed limits, particularly on limited-access highways designed for high-speed driving. Some states have set minimum speed limits on these highways at one standard deviation below the average traffic speed, or approximately at the 15th percentile speed.

[11] According to most of these studies, crash involvement rates are lowest from about the 50th to the 85th percentile speed (Figures 2-1, 2-3).

[12] In addition, the fuel shortages of the time caused people to travel less, and, because of high levels of motorist compliance, average speeds declined. Reduced travel and reduced speeds both affected safety.

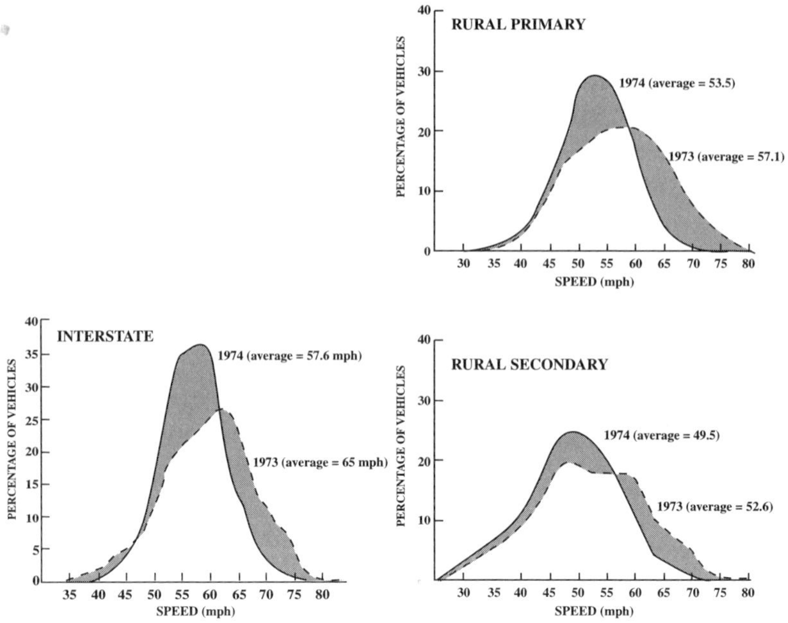

Figure 3-3 Change in vehicle speed distribution by various road classes, 1973-1974 (TRB 1984, 26–27). 1 mph = 1.609 km/h.

Also, the 85th percentile speed is not stationary. Monitoring data collected on speeds, including the 85th percentile speed, following the relaxation of speed limits on some rural Interstates in 1987 showed an increase in 85th percentile speeds both for states that raised and states that retained the 55-mph (89-km/h) speed limit (Godwin 1992, 4).[13] Data collected by the Insurance Institute for

[13] Between 1986 and 1988, 85th percentile speeds changed by 1.7 mph (2.7 km/h) in 55-mph (89-km/h) states and by 3.2 mph (5.1 km/h) in 65-mph (105-km/h) states for which reliable data were available (Godwin 1992, 4). The increase in 85th percentile speeds in 55-mph states was attributed to higher-speed driving by motorists from other states accustomed to the 65-mph limit (Godwin 1992, 7). It could also have reflected a general relaxation in driver compliance with and enforcement of the 55-mph speed limit. However, because average speeds did not change as much in 55-mph states as 85th percentile speeds, speed dispersion [measured by the estimated standard deviation (85th percentile speed minus average speed)] was larger in these states than in 65-mph states (Godwin 1992, 4).

Highway Safety (Retting and Greene 1997) suggest that a similar "speed creep" phenomenon may be occurring in the wake of the repeal of the NMSL in 1995. Both 85th percentile speeds and speed dispersion (measured as the speed standard deviation) have increased (Retting and Greene 1997). The key issues of concern from a safety perspective are whether speeds will continue to increase with driver expectations of an enforcement tolerance and what effect these changes will have on crash frequency and crash severity. The findings from a review of studies on this topic are reported later in the chapter.

A final concern with setting the speed limit at the 85th percentile speed is that it may not be appropriate for all classes of roads. For example, property access, community concerns, and pedestrian safety are important factors in setting appropriate speed limits on many urban roads, particularly residential streets. Thus, basing speed limits on the 85th percentile speed—a measure of unconstrained free-flowing travel speed—will not be as appropriate on these streets as on major arterial highways where travel efficiency is the primary road function (Harwood 1995, 90). However, compliance with speed limits on urban roads is already poor,[14] suggesting that setting the limits too low may create a greater enforcement burden or demand a greater tolerance for noncompliance. Lowering travel speeds, particularly on residential streets, may require other speed management strategies.

Expert System–Based Approach

Several states in Australia have developed an expert system–based approach to setting speed limits in speed zones. Victoria was the first state to embark on this approach in 1987 as the result of its comprehensive review of all aspects of speed management. The goal was to

[14] Research on driver speed behavior on a sample of U.S. roads found that, on the average, 7 out of 10 motorists exceeded the posted speed limit in urban areas. Many of the current speed limits in these areas correspond to the 30th percentile speed (Tignor and Warren 1989, 2).

develop a more uniform and consistent approach to setting speed limits within speed zones (Donald 1994, 284).[15]

The decisions and judgments required to establish speed limits were thought to be particularly amenable to an expert system approach. Expert systems are computer programs that mimic an expert's thought processes to solve complex problems in a given field (Donald 1994, 287). The problem must have a well-defined knowledge base, "experts" must be able to verbalize their knowledge and experience in the form of tasks to be undertaken and decisions to be made, and outcomes must be limited in number and clearly defined (Donald 1994, 287).

Development of the Victoria expert system VLIMITS, which was undertaken by the Australian Road Research Board (ARRB), began with field measurements at over 60 sites. Experts then reviewed the field data to elicit decision rules for determining appropriate speed limits for various road classes and traffic conditions. This "expert judgment" was reduced to a personal computer program, which leads the user through a series of question-answer menus that ultimately results in a recommended speed limit for a particular road section. VLIMITS was revised and updated in 1992. At the same time, development of related versions of the program—NLIMITS and QLIMITS—was begun for use in New South Wales and Queensland, respectively (Donald 1994, 293).[16] The ultimate objective is to develop a single countrywide speed zone program.

The most recent version of the system takes the user through a five-step process (Figure 3-4), which includes (*a*) environmental characterization of the area (e.g., urban, rural), (*b*) roadway and roadside factors (e.g., divided highway, number of lanes), (*c*) a first approximation of a speed limit based on a and b, (*d*) special activities (e.g., school zone) or other factors that might modify the final zoning (e.g., zone length, adjacent zone speed limits), and (*e*) 85th per-

[15] Similar to the United States, Australia uses general speed limits supplemented by speed zones where the general speed limits are not considered suitable for the particular road and traffic conditions.

[16] Development costs for NLIMITS, the more recent system, were $51,800 U.S. (Coleman et al. 1996, 48).

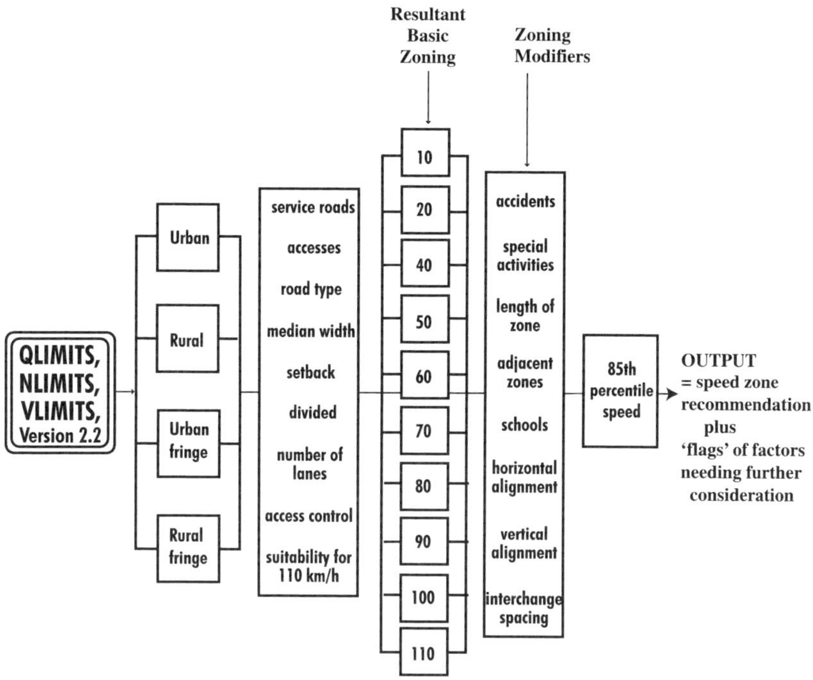

Figure 3-4 Overview of the structure of the Australian computer-based speed limit advisor (Donald 1994, 292). 1 km/h = 0.621 mph.

centile speed. The output of this process is a recommended speed zone value; specific factors may also be flagged for further consideration. The system is programmed not to allow a value higher than the general speed limit established for the particular road class under consideration (Coleman et al. 1996, 48).

The expert system approach includes all the factors covered in the engineering study method. The main difference is the process. The expert system approach makes the factors and the decision rules involved in determining an appropriate speed limit more explicit.

The computer-based advisor[17] is used primarily to assist regional road authorities to determine appropriate speed limits in speed

[17] System developers have moved away from calling the program an expert system, because it does not "learn" from its previous experience. Rather, the current system

zones. Program results are not intended to be automatically adopted but to provide advice to those who must make the final decision. The system is also used by Local Council Authorities to respond to neighborhood requests, generally for lowering speed limits. Two additional uses in Victoria are by the Royal Automobile Club, primarily to respond to member complaints about unreasonable speed limits, and by the Victoria Police Department, who use it as a guide in selecting locations for speed cameras (personal communication, D. Donald, ARRB, Sept. 4, 1997).

In practice, on higher-speed roads, the computer advisory system recommends a speed limit that is close to the 85th percentile speed in most cases (Coleman et al. 1996, 48). The system appears to be most useful on roads where the 85th percentile speed is seen as an inappropriate basis for setting speed limits. Heavily trafficked urban areas with a mix of road users, including bicyclists and pedestrians, and heavy roadside activity (e.g., parking, access to businesses) fall into this category, and here the system—using a common set of criteria—is likely to recommend a lower speed limit more compatible with the needs of all road users. However, lower speed limits require high levels of enforcement to ensure compliance. In Victoria, as in other Australian states, photo radar is heavily used to enforce lower limits (personal communication with D. Donald, ARRB, Sept. 11, 1997).

Other Methods of Setting Speed Limits

Basic Law Limits

Another approach to setting speed limits is to leave it up to the driver to determine a reasonable and prudent travel speed. This is the current policy for passenger vehicles in Montana on Interstate highways during daylight hours.[18] With the repeal of the NMSL, the

---

is hard-coded so that any changes require computer programming input (personal communication with D. Donald, ARRB, Sept. 11, 1997).

[18] There are nighttime speed limits for passenger vehicles of 65 mph (105 km/h) on Interstate highways and 55 mph (89 km/h) on all other roads. Heavy trucks must obey 65-mph speed limits day and night on Interstate highways, and 60-mph (97-km/h) speed limits during the day and 55-mph speed limits at night on all other roads.

state reverted to its former law or "basic rule," which affirms that "vehicles shall be driven in a careful and prudent manner, depending on the conditions at the time and place of operation."[19] The issue, of course, is how drivers and law enforcement officials interpret "careful" and "prudent" (Figure 3-5).

Variable Speed Limits[20]

Even when speed limits are made explicit, drivers are expected to adjust their speeds on the basis of actual conditions. Variable speed limits offer drivers guidance on appropriate maximum and minimum speed limits on the basis of real-time monitoring of prevailing traffic and roadway conditions, using dynamic information displays to inform motorists of the appropriate limits (Parker and Tsuchiyama 1985). Variable message signs, which provide information to motorists about speeds for specific conditions (fog, high crosswinds, work zones), have been in use for some time. Development of a new generation of technologies as part of the Intelligent Transportation Systems program[21] has given new impetus to implementation of variable speed limit systems. Variable speed limits are now being used more widely, particularly on motorway systems in some European countries. For example, the Germans have an extensive system of variable speed limits, primarily to manage traffic flow under adverse environmental conditions on the autobahns. The systems have reportedly been successful in reducing crash rates (Coleman et al. 1996, 24). The Dutch (Van den Hoogen and

---

[19] Minimum fines for violation of the basic rule were increased to $70, and the level of enforcement was increased. The number of fines for violations of the basic rule increased by 88 percent to more than 5,700 for the first 9 months of 1996 compared with the same period in 1995 (Montana Department of Transportation and Montana Highway Patrol 1996, 19, 41).

[20] Variable speed limits and other speed management approaches are reviewed in detail in Appendix D in the section entitled "Automated Speed Management."

[21] The highway-related part of this program, whose primary objective is more efficient use of the existing roads, is focused on equipping both vehicles and highways with electronic controls to provide the driver with more real-time information on traffic conditions, among other objectives.

Figure 3-5 Defining a careful and prudent speed. (Reprinted with permission of Martin Kozlowski.)

Smulders 1994) and, more recently, the British (TRL 1997)[22] have introduced variable speed limits on a pilot basis on major motorways. Their primary purpose is to improve traffic flow in congested conditions by equalizing speeds in all lanes.[23] Preliminary results indicate that, when the variable speed limits are in effect, traffic speeds are

---

[22] Finland has also installed and is in the process of monitoring the effectiveness of a system of variable speed limit signs and message boards on a 9-mi (14-km) experimental section of a motorway to warn drivers of ice and other hazardous conditions (Pilli-Sihvola and Taskula 1996).

[23] Variable speed limits are most effective, however, before traffic becomes heavily congested. Under heavily congested conditions, the limits are unable to affect stop-and-start driving (TRL 1997).

more uniform and—in the British pilot—automobile crashes are reduced (Van den Hoogen and Smulders 1994; TRL 1997). The results are promising, but more time is needed to determine whether these improvements can be sustained. Variable speed limit systems are not yet widely in use in the United States, but limited applications are being developed as part of the Intelligent Transportation Systems program.[24]

Special Situations

Speed limits are also developed for special situations.

Advisory Speeds

Engineers post advisory speeds to help drivers select safe speeds at hazardous locations, such as horizontal curves, intersections, exit ramps, or steep downgrades. The hazardous location warrants a lower speed than the general or posted speed limit, but rather than lowering the limit at each such location, traffic engineers post an advisory speed sign instead. Advisory speeds are not legally enforceable except under the basic speed law, which states that motorists must operate at speeds that are reasonable and prudent for conditions. Research suggests that advisory speeds have modest to little effect on driver speeds, particularly for drivers who are familiar with the road (Graham-Migletz Enterprises, Inc. 1996, 5). One reason for poor compliance is that posted advisory speeds are often set unrealistically low; the current criteria for setting advisory speeds on curves, for example, are based on vehicles and tests from the 1930s (Chowdhury et al. 1998, 32).

---

[24] For example, the Nevada Department of Transportation in conjunction with the U.S. Department of Transportation is developing a variable speed limit system that reflects actual traffic speeds and weather conditions on a section of Interstate highway that is frequently subject to adverse weather. Deployment of the system will be accompanied by a monitoring effort to assess effects on driving speeds and crash experience. A similar system, called Travel Aid, was recently installed at Snoqualmie Pass near Seattle, Washington, to display weather-appropriate speed limits for motorists in an effort to reduce the large number of crashes on this stretch of road (*Highway and Vehicle Safety Report* 1998, 8).

Nighttime Speed Limits

At least four states—Montana, North Dakota, Oklahoma, and Texas—have different nighttime speed limits on certain classes of highways. The report of the Committee on Speed Regulation (NSC 1941) strongly advocated the imposition of nighttime speed limits from a public education perspective to impress on motorists the need to drive more slowly because of poorer visibility (NSC 1941, 18). The higher incidence and severity of crashes at night have also been used to support lower night speed limits (Solomon 1964, 10, 13). Today, more crashes of all types occur during daylight hours—or in dark but lighted conditions—than at night under unlighted conditions or at dawn or dusk (NHTSA 1997, 47). Thus, special nighttime limits are much less common. Moreover, such limits are considered difficult to enforce. Drivers show little inclination to decrease speeds in nighttime conditions.[25] Finally, lighting of highways, vehicles, and signs has improved.

School and Work Zone Speed Limits

Special regulatory speed limits are often used in school and work zones. Many jurisdictions establish special speed limits for streets in the vicinity of schools during certain hours of the day in response to the public perception that lower speeds improve safety (Graham-Migletz Enterprises, Inc. 1996, 5). Studies of the effectiveness of school zone limits, however, have generally found poor driver compliance, particularly when the limits are set very low, and no relationship between pedestrian crashes and the special limits (Graham-Migletz Enterprises, Inc. 1996, 5).

In recent years transportation departments have begun to use regulatory speed limits, rather than advisory speed warnings, in work zones. Similar to school zone limits, however, work zone speed limits alone[26] have not proved very effective in reducing vehicle speeds

[25] Data collected on free-flow average and 85th percentile speeds at six sites with speed limits ranging from 25 to 55 mph (40 to 89 km/h) found a 0- to 3-mph (5-km/h) difference for daytime, nighttime, and dawn and dusk driving (Harkey et al. 1990, 44).

[26] Several studies found that the presence of law enforcement officers in work zones was effective in reducing motorist speeds (Graham-Migletz Enterprises, Inc. 1996, 6).

in work zones, and only limited evaluations of their effects on safety have been conducted (Graham-Migletz Enterprises, Inc. 1996, 5–7).

APPLICATION OF SPEED LIMITS

Establishing appropriate speed limits depends to a great extent on the class of road involved and its design features, traffic density, geographic location and land use, and to a lesser extent on the type of vehicles using the road. In this section, what is known about each of these factors and their effect on establishing suitable speed limits to encourage appropriate driving speeds is discussed.

Roadway Functional Class and Geometric Characteristics

Roadway functional class and geometric design features are among the characteristics with the greatest effect on driving speeds and the determination of appropriate speed limits. Research has shown that drivers tend to travel at higher speeds on highways with better geometric design characteristics regardless of posted speed limits (Garber and Gadiraju 1988, 20–21). Moreover, speed dispersion was shown to decrease when the difference between design speed—a surrogate for geometric design characteristics—and posted speed limits is low; the lower the speed dispersion, the lower the crash rates, controlling for type of highway (Garber and Gadiraju 1988, 23, 28).

Hence, one approach to establishing appropriate speed limits is to design or redesign roads so that their function and design characteristics are more apparent to drivers and more closely aligned with desired motorist driving speeds. The Dutch Government has officially adopted a policy and implementation program known as sustainable road safety, one of whose primary goals is prevention of traffic crashes by rationalizing the road system. A long-term approach, the program attempts to distinguish roads more clearly by their primary function (e.g., traffic flow, traffic distribution, access) and to encourage more homogeneous use of each road, preventing large differences in vehicle speed and even separating different types of traffic where necessary (Transport Research Centre 1996, 6). The theory is that a more uniform and predictable traffic system should enhance motorists' ability to determine appropriate driving speeds, thereby reducing the incidence of speeding and other traffic conflicts that may lead to crashes.

Similar efforts to bring road design more closely in line with desired vehicle speeds are under consideration in the United States, although the extent of mileage and the diversity of conditions on U.S. highways will likely preclude as comprehensive an approach as in the Netherlands. Specifically, efforts to identify geometric design characteristics that influence motorists' speeds on low-speed urban streets [i.e., below 40 mph (64 km/h)] and on two-lane rural highways—roads with some of the highest crash rates—are being pursued.[27]

Traffic Density

Traffic density is also a key factor affecting drivers' choice of speeds and the determination of appropriate speed limits. On freeways, for example, speed-flow analyses show that average traffic speeds are relatively constant for a wide range of traffic volumes, slowing modestly until conditions reach breakdown levels (TRB 1998, 3-10). On two-lane rural highways, which have more limited capacity and more restricted geometric design features, travel speeds tend to deteriorate more rapidly with increasing traffic volumes.

In its report, the Committee on Speed Regulation of the National Safety Council advocated setting speed limits for average traffic conditions where the speed limit is prima facie, thereby allowing some leeway for higher speeds when traffic is light and other conditions are favorable (NSC 1941, 15). Where a maximum speed limit is used, however, the recommendation was to set the speed limit for light traffic conditions to avoid an unreasonably low limit (NSC 1941, 15). Today, most speed limits are set for favorable conditions—light traffic, dry pavement, and daylight.[28] Drivers are expected to exercise

[27] These approaches are discussed at greater length in Chapter 5.

[28] In fact, policy guides for setting speed limits in speed zones require that speed studies be conducted during off-peak traffic hours during the day in fair weather conditions when traffic speeds are unimpeded.

judgment and slow down when high traffic volumes, poor weather and visibility, or other adverse conditions are present.

By using variable speed limit systems, speed limits can be adapted on a real-time basis to different traffic and environmental conditions (e.g., wet weather, reduced visibility). Although drivers already adapt their speeds to different traffic conditions, variable speed limits can provide more uniform guidance on appropriate speeds for conditions and fine-tune this guidance even on a lane-by-lane basis. Currently, the high cost of variable speed limit systems—between $0.6 million and $1.6 million U.S. per mi ($0.4 million and $1 million U.S. per km)—limits their use to high-volume or high-crash locations where environmental or traffic conditions create large fluctuations in desired speeds (Coleman et al. 1996, 57).

Geographic Location and Land Use

Determination of the appropriate balance between risk and travel time in setting speed limits will vary by land use as well as road class. For example, on many rural freeways and on some nonlimited-access rural roads, vehicles can travel long distances largely under free-flowing traffic conditions, where the opportunities for vehicle conflict (e.g., intersections, restricted sight distance) are limited and enforcement is difficult. These conditions suggest that vehicle operating speeds and travel efficiency should be more important in the determination of speed limits for these highways than for other road classes.

Urban freeways have many of the characteristics just described. However, peak-period traffic congestion, more entering and exiting traffic, and generally more frequent interchanges suggest the need for somewhat lower speed limits than on rural freeways. Variable speed limits would be appropriate for this road class to manage temporal changes in traffic demands and speeds.

Many nonlimited-access rural roads, particularly two-lane roads, have restrictive roadway geometry (e.g., sharp curves). Moreover, drivers may not always be able to anticipate appropriate speeds. Speed limits should reflect these poorer conditions. Appropriate use of speed zones and advisory speed warnings can alert the driver to problem areas or to particularly hazardous locations.

Determining appropriate speed limits on nonlimited-access roads in urban areas poses a more complex problem. Urban roads often have more than one function—access as well as traffic flow. Potential for vehicle conflicts is high because of roadside development and activities, intersecting streets and driveways, parking, traffic signals, and general traffic density. Urban roads also serve a broad range of users, including pedestrians and bicyclists in addition to motor vehicles. Thus, speed limits must meet the objectives of this broader group of road users. Speed limits that give priority to travel efficiency will not be valid for all urban streets.

As a solution, many European countries have adopted blanket urban speed limits for built-up city areas where access is the primary objective [e.g., 19-mph (30-km/h) zones in the Netherlands, Denmark, and Germany], sometimes in combination with car-free zones in central cities. These speed limit zones appear to have successfully reduced speeds and crashes within the zones,[29] at least when implemented with complementary policies, such as publicity campaigns, engineering measures, and increased enforcement. With some exceptions, U.S. cities do not have the density of European town centers. Moreover, compliance with urban speed limits in the United States is already poor (Tignor and Warren 1989). Adoption of blanket limits would be difficult without more enforcement effort or a large enforcement tolerance.

Another approach, which was recommended by the 1941 report of the NSC Committee on Speed Regulation, is to establish special higher speed zones for arterial roads whose primary function is the distribution of traffic through a metropolitan area with lower general limits for specific core business and residential areas (pp. 49–50). However, this approach does not resolve the difficulty of enforcing low urban speed limits. Slowing traffic by engineering and traffic measures (e.g., speed humps, lane narrowing, turn prohibi-

[29] There is some evidence, however, that part of the decrease in crashes is due to the decrease in traffic volumes in the zones and diversion of traffic outside the zones. This diversionary effect needs to be studied further to assess the net safety effects of urban speed zones. See the discussion in Appendix C.

tions), known as traffic calming, has been advocated as an alternative approach to managing speed, particularly in residential areas.[30]

Setting appropriate speed limits on roads in rapidly developing urban fringe areas presents a special problem. The driving environment in these areas is complex; traffic volumes and roadside development create the potential for vehicle conflicts and conditions that frequently approximate more congested inner-city roads. Several studies have shown that drivers—particularly motorists exiting freeways who had been driving at highway speeds—have difficulty adapting to the more complex environment and reducing their speed (Várhelyi 1996, 25–26; Casey and Lund 1992, 135). However, lowering speed limits in fringe areas to reflect this environment appears to have little effect on average speeds or the uniformity of speeds; rather, it increases the percentage of out-of-compliance drivers (Ullman and Dudek 1987, 45; Thornton and Lyles 1996, 70).[31]

Vehicle Characteristics

Several states have adopted differential speed limits on highways with heavy-truck traffic[32] to reflect the different operating characteristics of heavy trucks and passenger vehicles (Table 1-1). Differential speed limits are widely used in Europe, where speed governors have been required on all heavy vehicles since January 1994 (ECMT 1996, 32).[33]

Contrary to the perception of many motorists, passenger vehicles travel, on the average, 1 to 5 mph (2 to 8 km/h) faster than trucks on U.S. roads representing a range of different conditions and speed lim-

[30] This approach is discussed in more detail in Chapter 5.

[31] As Ullman and Dudek point out, lower speed limits were not accompanied by any increased enforcement or public notification, which could have changed driver compliance levels (p. 49).

[32] Heavy trucks typically are defined as those weighing at least 26,000 lb (12 000 kg).

[33] As of January 1, 1994, heavy goods vehicles over 12 tonnes entering into circulation in European Union member states must be fitted with a device that limits speed to 56 mph (90 km/h) and that limits passenger transport vehicles over 10 tonnes to 62 mph (100 km/h) (ECMT 1996, 32).

its (Harkey et al. 1990, 43–44). In urban areas, truck speeds are consistently about 3 mph (5 km/h) slower than car speeds (Tignor and Warren 1989, 2). Differential speed limits recognize the different performance characteristics of these vehicles by establishing lower speed limits for heavy trucks, although in many cases the speed limit differential is 10 to 15 mph (16 to 24 km/h) (Table 1-1).

Advocates of lower speed limits for heavy trucks point to their lower acceleration, more limited maneuverability, and longer stopping distances from a given speed[34] relative to passenger vehicles. At higher speeds, these features in combination with the heavy weight of large trucks may increase crash probability and most certainly increase the severity of crashes that do occur. Opponents of differential speed limits maintain that the speed differences introduced by lower limits for trucks are likely to increase the potential for vehicle conflicts from lane changes and passing maneuvers and thus increase crash probability.

Several studies have been conducted on the effects of differential speed limits on speed and safety on U.S. highways, particularly since 1987 when Congress allowed states to raise the maximum speed limit to 65 mph (105 km/h) on qualifying sections of rural Interstate highways.[35] States that raised speed limits were faced with the decision of whether to set the limits uniformly for all vehicles.

Several studies reported that average truck speeds were lower in states with differential speed limits (Baum et al. 1991a, 6; Harkey and Mera 1994, 54). More important, speed dispersion increased for vehicles of all types on roads with differential speed limits, and these speed differences resulted in more interaction among vehicles and thus greater potential for conflict (Harkey and Mera 1994, 55; Garber

[34] An offsetting factor in some situations, however, is the higher position of the truck driver's eyes because of the higher position of the seat in the vehicle, enabling the driver to see farther and thus to begin to brake sooner if needed.

[35] On a recent Federal Highway Administration Study Tour for Speed Management and Enforcement Technology, no studies could be found of the effect of differential speed limits on speed and safety in the countries visited, which included the Netherlands, Germany, Sweden, and Australia (Coleman et al. 1996, ix).

and Gadiraju 1991, 38).[36] Changes in speeds associated with differential speed limits, including average speeds and measures of speed dispersion, were statistically significant only for speed limit differentials of at least 10 mph (16 km/h). Interestingly, greater speed differences on highways with differential limits of 10 mph were also associated with a significant reduction in the number of trucks traveling at very high speeds [i.e., greater than 70 mph (113 km/h)] (Baum et al. 1991a, 6; Harkey and Mera 1994, 55). On balance, however, the evidence supports the hypothesis that differential speed limits of 10 mph or greater tend to increase speed differences in the traffic stream.

The effects of less uniform driving speeds on safety are inconclusive. The studies that examined crash data (Garber and Gadiraju 1991; Harkey and Mera 1994) found that a greater percentage of crashes were rear-end and two-car collisions on roads with differential speed limits.[37] But differences between highways with differential speed limits and highways with uniform speed limits in the total number, rate, and severity of crashes were not statistically significant, suggesting no safety advantage to the former (Garber and Gadiraju 1991, 36–39; Harkey and Mera 1994, 57). The results are not robust because of methodological shortcomings in study design (e.g., problems with site selection and representativeness, matching of speed with crash data).[38] Thus, a strong case cannot be made on empirical grounds in support of or in opposition to differential speed limits.

---

[36] Harkey and Mera measured speed dispersion by calculating the standard deviation of speed and the coefficient of variation [i.e., standard deviation divided by the average and expressed as a percentage (pp. 12, 22)]. Garber and Gadiraju measured speed dispersion using speed variance—the square of the standard deviation in speed (p. 19). Baum et al. (1991a) measured speed dispersion by observing differences in vehicle speeds at different percentiles—85th, 90th, and 95th—for states with and without differential speed limits. They did not find a statistically significant increase in speed dispersion in states with differential speed limits (p. 6).

[37] Garber and Gadiraju (1991) only found significant differences (i.e., at the 95 percent confidence level) for two-vehicle, nontruck-nontruck crashes (pp. 34–35).

[38] For example, Harkey and Mera collected detailed speed data on matched pairs of highways with and without differential speed limits, but the crash data were drawn from a single broad road category—mainline rural Interstates.

EFFECTIVENESS OF SPEED LIMITS

How effective are speed limits at managing traffic speeds? Two important indicators of effectiveness are traffic flow efficiency and safety (Joscelyn and Elston 1970, 106).

The effect of speed limits on traffic flow efficiency can be estimated by examining speed distributions and flow rates before and after speed limits have been established or changed. For example, a major objective of variable speed limits is to smooth traffic flows as traffic becomes more congested. The effectiveness of variable speed limits could be demonstrated by more uniform traffic flows and more even lane use, and such effects have been found (refer to preceding discussion of variable speed limits). It has not been demonstrated, however, that the changes have resulted in increased capacity. In heavily congested traffic, speed limits probably have little effect on traffic efficiency because most vehicles are traveling below the speed limit.

Most effort has been focused on assessing the effect of changes in speed limits on safety; a large body of literature exists on this topic.[39] However, empirically establishing a relationship (or the absence of one) presents a difficult task. Studies of behavior change in real-world conditions are inherently messy, and the studies of driver responses to speed limit changes are no exception. The studies must disentangle numerous factors that contribute to driver choice of speed, using data that are often imprecise and general. For example, study data on speed distributions are often highly aggregated. Ideally, speed distribution data must be closely linked with crash data to understand both whether and how actual speed changes—as opposed to changes in speed limits—have affected crash probability and outcomes. Even when speed data are good, isolating the effect of the speed change from all the other factors that affect traffic safety (e.g., changes in traffic volume, alcohol use) to establish a causal link between changes in speed limits, speeds, and crashes is extremely dif-

[39] This section draws heavily on a literature survey of the effect of changes in speed limits on speed distributions and highway safety especially commissioned for the study committee, which is presented in its entirety as Appendix C.

ficult. In addition, few studies have analyzed the effects of alternative enforcement levels in combination with speed limit changes (Finch et al. 1994, 5) to assess how a key determinant of driver speed choice—enforcement—may interact with a change in the speed limit. Finally, coverage can be a problem. Many studies simply examine the direct effects of speed limit changes on those highways where the limits have changed. However, because highways form a network, where a change on one part of the system is likely to affect other system links, a comprehensive analysis should take into consideration traffic diversion and spillover effects to obtain a complete understanding of the net safety effects (McCarthy 1994, 355–356).[40] Recognizing these limitations, the following discussion focuses on the most methodologically sound studies of recent changes in speed limits both in the United States and abroad.

Review of U.S. Studies of Changes in Speed Limits

Numerous studies of the effects of the imposition of the NMSL on speed and safety were conducted in 1974. These studies are not included here because they were extensively reviewed in an earlier assessment of the effects of lowering speed limits on major highways (TRB 1984). The TRB study of the effects of the 55-mph (89-km/h) speed limit found that the lower limit reduced both travel speeds and fatalities, although driver speed compliance gradually eroded.

In recent years, there have been two major changes in speed limits in the United States. In 1987 Congress allowed states to raise the NMSL on qualifying sections of rural Interstate highways to 65 mph (105 km/h) from 55 mph (89 km/h). Forty states raised their limits accordingly and numerous studies were conducted, nationally and at

[40] The diversion effect refers to shifts in travel to roads where speed limits have been raised. The spillover effect refers to the adjustments resulting from the diversion effects. For example, if increased speed limits on rural Interstates have diverted traffic from roads with lower speed limits, then the remaining traffic on these lower-speed roads may be able to travel faster. The net effect on safety is ambiguous, however; the reduced traffic on the lower-speed road improves safety, but the higher speed may not.

the state level, to determine the effects of this change on traffic safety. In 1995 Congress repealed the NMSL entirely. As of the writing of this report, 49 states have raised maximum speed limits and many are monitoring the effects on speed and safety.

Review of Studies of 1987 Change in NMSL on Rural Interstate Highways

This review included both national and state studies of the effect of the speed limit changes. For the most part, it concentrated on studies that examined at least 2 years of postchange experience.

Effect of Speed Limit Changes on Driver Speeds

Most studies that examined the effect of speed limit changes on speed distributions provided information on several key speed measures, including average traffic speeds, 85th percentile speeds, and speed dispersion (typically defined in these studies as the difference between 85th percentile speeds and average traffic speeds).[41] Some of the key national studies reviewed for this report (Table 3-2) found that raising rural Interstate speed limits resulted in higher average and 85th percentile speeds on the affected highways and an increase in speed dispersion of about 1 mph (2 km/h).[42] Figure 3-6 shows the National Highway Traffic Safety Administration's (NHTSA's) estimate of the change in the distribution of travel speeds on rural Interstate highways between 1986 and 1990 for the 18 states that raised speed limits and continued to monitor speed data (NHTSA

[41] This definition of speed dispersion can be traced to the 1970 Research Triangle Institute study, one of the most careful efforts to examine the relationship between crash involvement rates and speed deviations from the average traffic speed by relating the speed of vehicles involved in crashes to the actual distribution of speeds in the traffic stream at the time of the crash. Analysis of the speed data collected for that study found that one standard deviation was approximately ±7 mph (11 km/h) from the average traffic speed, following a normal distribution, the same as the 85th and 15th percentile speeds, respectively (West and Dunn 1971, 54–55).

[42] Average speeds increased on the order of 4 mph (6 km/h) or less for a 10-mph (16-km/h) increase in the speed limit. Eighty-fifth percentile speeds increased by roughly the same magnitude (see Appendix C).

Table 3-2 Summary of Selected National Studies on Speed and Safety Effects of 1987 Speed Limit Changes on Rural Interstate Highways

Authorship and Date of Study	Data and Analysis Method	Major Findings—Speed	Major Findings—Safety
Garber and Graham 1989	40 states that raised speed limits by mid-1988 Pooled time series regression (1976–1988)	No speed data	In 65-mph states, 15 percent median increase in fatalities on rural Interstates among the 40 states, controlling for exposure and other variables; 5 percent median increase in fatalities on rural non-Interstates
McKnight et al. 1989	Twenty 65-mph states; eight 55-mph states[a] Quasi-experimental ARIMA models Before/after analysis (1982–1988)	65-mph states: 48 percent increase in speed (measured as speeds > 65 mph) on rural Interstates; 9 percent increase in speed on other 55-mph roads 55-mph states: 18 percent increase in speed on rural Interstates; 37 percent increase in speed on other 55-mph roads	65-mph states: 22 percent increase in fatal crashes on rural Interstates; 1 percent increase in fatal crashes on other 55-mph roads 55-mph states: 10 percent increase in fatal crashes on rural Interstates; 13 percent increase in fatal crashes on other 55-mph roads

(continued on next page)

Table 3-2 *(continued)*

Authorship and Date of Study	Data and Analysis Method	Major Findings—Speed	Major Findings—Safety
Baum et al. 1991b	Forty 65-mph states; eight 55-mph states Before/after odds ratio (1982–1986 versus 1989)	No speed data	65-mph states: 19 percent increase in fatalities on rural Interstates relative to other rural roads, taking into account changes in exposure and vehicle occupancy 55-mph states: no effect on odds ratio (changes on rural Interstates relative to changes on other rural roads)
NHTSA 1989	Thirty-eight 65-mph states; ten 55-mph states[b] Before/after (1986–1988) Regression trend analysis (1975–1988)	3.0-mph increase in average speeds in 65-mph states 3.5-mph increase in 85th percentile speeds in 65-mph states 0.7-mph increase in estimated speed standard deviation (85th percentile minus average speed) in 65-mph states	65-mph states: 35 percent increase in fatalities between 1986 and 1988; 18 percent increase in fatality rates on rural Interstates 55-mph states: 9 percent increase in fatalities between 1986 and 1988; 0 percent increase in fatality rates on rural Interstates

NHTSA 1992	Thirty-eight 65-mph states; ten 55-mph states[b] Before/after (1986–1990) Regression analysis with comparison series (1975–1990)	3.4-mph increase in average speeds in 65-mph states 4.1-mph increase in 85th percentile speeds in 65-mph states 0.7-mph increase in estimated speed standard deviation (85th percentile minus average speed) in 65-mph states	65-mph states: 27 percent increase in fatalities between 1986 and 1990; 0 percent increase in fatality rates on rural Interstates 55-mph states: 3 percent increase in fatalities between 1986 and 1990; 12 percent decline in fatality rates on rural Interstates
Lave and Elias 1994	Thirty-eight 65-mph states; eight 55-mph states Before/after analysis, 1986 versus 1988 Regression analysis, 1976–1990, using and extending Garber and Graham's data	No speed data	65-mph states: 3 to 5 percent reduction in statewide fatality rates on average, controlling for the effects of long-term trends, exposure, safety belt laws, and economic factors

(continued on next page)

Table 3-2 *(continued)*

Note: ARIMA = Autoregressive Integrated Moving Average. See Appendix C for discussion of methodology and more detailed discussion of study results. Equivalences between miles per hour mentioned in the table and kilometers per hour are as follows:

mph	*km/h*
0.7	1.1
3.0	4.8
3.4	5.5
3.5	5.6
4.1	6.6
55	89
65	105

[a] Speed analysis based on nine 65-mph states and seven 55-mph states.
[b] Speed analysis based on eighteen 65-mph states and eight 55-mph states.

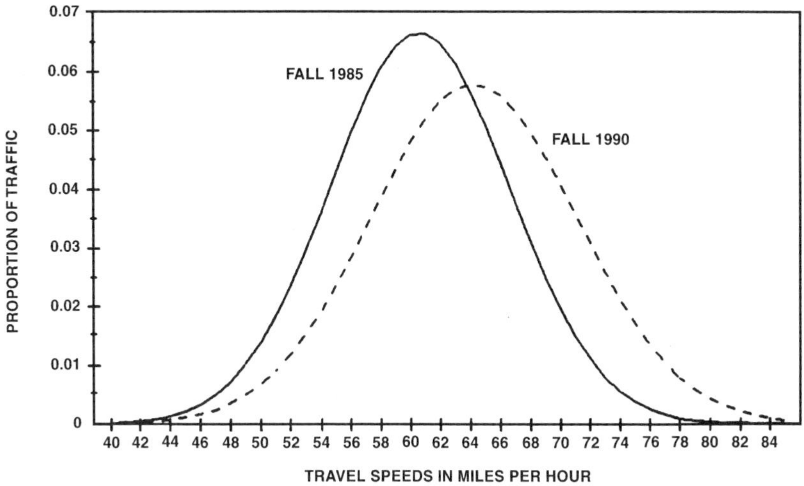

Figure 3-6 Estimated changes in the distribution of rural Interstate travel speeds between the fourth quarter of 1986 and the fourth quarter of 1990 in the 18 states that raised speed limits in 1987 (NHTSA 1992, 13). 1 mph = 1.609 km/h.

1992, 12).[43] It shows a shift toward higher average traffic speeds and a wider speed dispersion, with more vehicles traveling at higher speeds. Actual speed effects, however, differed widely by state, suggesting the need for better control of other factors (e.g., weather) that may have affected driver speed changes.

The studies manifested two additional limitations. First, those that used comparison groups to examine the speed effects in states that raised the speed limit [65-mph (105-km/h) states] versus those

[43] Changes were approximated using average and 85th percentile speed data provided by the 18 states, assuming a normal distribution of travel speeds on rural Interstates (NHTSA 1992, 12). From 1986 to 1990, reported average speeds for the 18-state group increased from 60.6 to 64 mph (98 to 103 km/h); 85th percentile speeds increased from 66.6 to 70.7 mph (107 to 114 km/h); and standard deviations, measured as the difference between 85th percentile and average speeds, increased from 6.0 to 6.7 mph (9.7 to 10.8 km/h).

that did not [55-mph (89-km/h) states] made the critical assumption that the only difference between the two groups of states was the speed limit change. However, an examination of states that retained the lower 55-mph limit shows that the majority (the exceptions are Alaska and Hawaii) are located in the eastern United States, where population density, levels of congestion, and traffic volumes are different from those of the states that raised speed limits. Second, to the extent that the studies examined the effects of raising the speed limit on speed distributions on other roads (i.e., the spillover effects on 55-mph highways in 65-mph states and on speed distributions on Interstate and non-Interstate highways in 55-mph states), the results are mixed.[44]

Effect of Speed Limit Changes on Safety

Conceptually, increased average traffic speeds are associated with greater crash severity. These findings appear to be borne out by national (Table 3-2) and state studies of the safety effects of raising speed limits to 65 mph (105 km/h) on rural Interstate highways. The studies generally found that raising the speed limit led to an increase in both rural Interstate fatalities and fatal crashes. Increased crash severity, even from modest increases in speed levels, is plausible because of the sharp increase in injury severity associated with increased vehicle speeds at impact.

Similar to the findings concerning the effects of speed limit changes on driving speeds, the safety effects were not uniform. For example, Garber and Graham, authors of a widely cited study (1989) that attempted to control for many other variables affecting highway safety,[45] found a 15 percent overall increase in fatalities on rural Interstate highways for the 40 states that had raised speed limits.

---

[44] For example, McKnight et al. (1989) found that in 55-mph (89-km/h) states, the percentage of drivers exceeding 65 mph (105 km/h) on rural Interstates increased by 18 percent and increased on other 55-mph highways by 37 percent. In 65-mph states, however, there were 48 and 9 percent increases, respectively. Traffic diversion could explain the large difference in the 65-mph states but not the difference in the 55-mph states.

[45] The other variables included data on economic performance, seasonal effects, weekend travel, safety belt laws, and a time trend to capture the effect of changes in vehicle miles traveled.

However, the data for individual states showed that fatalities increased in 28 states and either decreased or were unchanged in 12 states.[46] Similar cross-state heterogeneity was found in other studies.[47] In addition, the studies reported mixed effects for fatalities and fatal crashes on non-Interstate roads in 65-mph (105-km/h) states.

These results, particularly the differences among states, are not surprising given the many differences in state geographic and traffic conditions and the difficulties in modeling the effects in small states with relatively few fatalities. Garber and Graham conclude that the preponderance of the statistical evidence supports a finding of increased fatalities on rural Interstate highways in most states but acknowledge the need to identify and control for other factors that may explain the heterogeneity of effects (Garber and Graham 1989, 15–16, 18).

The importance of controlling for factors that could affect highway safety other than speed limits was well illustrated by a series of follow-up studies conducted by Baum et al. (1991b) on the fatality consequences of the 65-mph (105-km/h) speed limits. Their study controlled for changes in vehicle miles traveled and vehicle occupancy. Without these adjustments, the study indicated that the odds of a fatality on a rural Interstate in 65-mph states in 1989 increased 29 percent over a base period (1982 to 1986). With the adjustments, the fatality risk increased by 19 percent (Baum et al. 1991b, 171). Similarly, estimates by NHTSA of increased fatalities for states that raised rural Interstate speed limits in 1987 dropped by one-third after travel increases were taken into account (NHTSA 1989, 1). The results illustrate the potential for biased estimates of speed limit effects when significant causal variables are omitted from the analysis.

The effects of a change in speed limits may spill over to other roads. Some studies have suggested that these network effects result

[46] The increase was statistically significant in 10 states and the decrease in 2 states (Garber and Graham 1989, 15).

[47] For example, Baum et al. (1989) found an overall 18 percent increase in fatalities on rural Interstates in 65-mph (105-km/h) states. However, a state-by-state analysis showed that fatality levels decreased in 14 of the 38 states analyzed.

in increased fatalities even on roads where speed limits are not changed (Garber and Graham 1989). Others suggest that network effects can offset the adverse effects of higher Interstate speed limits and result in a neutral (McCarthy 1994) or even positive (Lave and Elias 1994) systemwide net safety effect. Lave and Elias suggest two reasons for offsetting effects. First, when speed limits were raised on qualifying rural Interstate highways in 1987, state highway patrols were able to shift their resources from monitoring these highways, as the NMSL had required, to patrolling other less safe roads. Second, some traffic may have diverted from less safe, nonlimited-access roads to the safer, but now higher-speed, rural Interstate highways.

Lave and Elias (1994) looked for evidence of these effects. They found general support for increased flexibility in deployment of enforcement resources in police testimony (p. 50) and for the occurrence of traffic diversion in comparative data on traffic growth by road type in states that had raised or retained rural Interstate speed limits (pp. 52–53). Using Garber and Graham's data set and model but substituting statewide fatality rates for Interstate fatalities as the dependent variable, Lave and Elias estimated that the new speed limits reduced statewide fatality rates by 3.4 to 5.1 percent (p. 61). Two subsequent comments—Griffith (1995) and Lund and Rauch (1992)[48]—took issue with the use of statewide data as too broad a measure of network effects and questioned the validity of the traffic volume data. Garber and Graham's analysis had found evidence that spillover effects from higher rural Interstate speed limits on rural non-Interstate highways offset traffic diversion effects in most states. They reported a net median 5 percent increase in rural non-Interstate fatalities in those states in which speed limits had been raised (Garber and Graham 1989, 18).

McCarthy (1994) used county-level data to examine diversion and spillover effects as well as direct effects of raising speed limits to 65 mph (105 km/h) on selected rural Interstate highways in California. The author found statistically significant increases in total, fatal, and

[48] This comment critiqued an earlier version of the Lave and Elias (1994) article.

injury crashes in counties where the speed limits had been raised (McCarthy 1994, 362). In counties where speed limits had not been raised, there was no evidence of spillover effects and some evidence of improving highway safety. The net effect across all counties showed no safety decrement. The author concluded that overall safety on California roads had not been compromised by the speed limit increase, but negative effects were experienced in the counties with rural Interstate highways where speed limits had been raised (McCarthy 1994, 362–363).

The issue of systemwide effects, particularly the selection of an appropriate analysis unit, is an important topic that requires further research and analysis.

Review of Studies Following Repeal of the NMSL in 1995

With repeal of the NMSL in 1995, the federal government no longer requires that states monitor driving speeds. However, several states that raised speed limits voluntarily collect speed and crash data on highways where the limits were raised. Reports based on these data have been released in several states and are focused primarily on Interstate highways where speed limits were raised first. NHTSA provided a report to Congress on the effects of the changes in the first year following repeal of the NMSL (NHTSA 1998).[49] Finally, the Insurance Institute for Highway Safety (IIHS) released an assessment of the effects of speed limit increases on motor vehicle occupant fatalities during 1996 (Farmer et al. 1997).[50]

[49] The NHTSA study addresses the effects of higher speeds on fatalities (not fatality rates) for three groups of states: (*a*) 11 states (Arizona, California, Delaware, Illinois, Massachusetts, Montana, Nevada, Oklahoma, Pennsylvania, Texas, and Wyoming) that raised speed limits in late 1995 and early in the first quarter of 1996, (*b*) 21 states that raised speed limits through the remainder of 1996, and (*c*) 18 states plus the District of Columbia that did not raise speed limits (NHTSA 1998, v).

[50] The IIHS study is focused on 12 states that raised maximum speed limits to at least 70 mph (113 km/h) between Dec. 8, 1995, and April 1, 1996: Arizona, California, Kansas, Mississippi, Missouri, Montana, Nevada, Oklahoma, South Dakota, Texas, Washington, and Wyoming. The comparison group included 18 states that either did not raise maximum speed limits in 1996 or raised them on less than 10 percent of urban Interstate mileage (Farmer et al. 1997, 3).

All of the studies are preliminary. At the time this report was written, most studies had accumulated only 1 year of data. Crash data, in particular, are limited; information on crash rates are often missing or preliminary, and with only 1 year of data, it is difficult to know whether the reported changes in crashes, crash rates, fatalities, and injuries represent a new trend or simply reflect normal year-to-year variations. Thus, drawing definitive conclusions from these studies is premature. However, the data they provide are provocative and worth a brief discussion here.

Effect of Speed Limit Changes on Driver Speeds

Most studies of speed limit changes in individual states tracked data on changes in speed, including average speeds and 85th percentile speeds, before and after the new speed limits came into effect.[51] A few studies (Retting and Greene 1997; Pezoldt et al. 1997; Davis 1998; Montana Department of Transportation and Montana Highway Patrol 1996) also provided data on speed changes at the high end of the speed distribution [i.e., greater than 70, 75, and 80 mph (113, 121, and 129 km/h)]. Some state studies compared speed parameters on highways on which speed limits had been raised with those that had not.

Average speeds typically increased 1 to 3 mph (2 to 5 km/h) despite larger increases in the speed limit—a minimum of 5 mph (8 km/h). The relatively small changes in average speeds compared with the change in the speed limit may reflect poor driver compliance levels with the lower limit in effect before the change.

Eighty-fifth percentile speeds also generally increased by 1 to 3 mph (2 to 5 km/h). Thus, speed dispersion—at least as measured by the aggregate difference between the 85th percentile and the average speed—remained relatively unchanged 1 year after repeal of the NMSL. Retting and Greene (1997) found somewhat larger increases in speed standard deviations at selected locations (i.e., Riverside,

[51] The NHTSA study (1998) did not report speed data. IIHS tracked speed data for selected locations in a separate study (Retting and Greene 1997).

California, and Houston, Texas) where careful "before" and "after" speed monitoring was conducted.[52]

A few studies found a large percentage of drivers violating the new speed limits. This suggests that some drivers expect the same enforcement tolerances of 5 to 10 mph (8 to 16 km/h) at the higher speed limits. For example, speed measurements taken on three urban freeways and one urban Interstate in Riverside, California, found that, 1 year after the speed limit was raised to 65 mph (105 km/h), 41 percent of drivers exceeded 70 mph (113 km/h)—up from 29 percent immediately before the change (Retting and Greene 1997, 43).[53] Thus, there is some evidence that, when speed limits are raised, the distribution of traffic speeds not only shifts rightward with higher average speeds but also outward with a greater dispersion in speeds, at least at the high end of the speed distribution. Data from Montana on speed distributions on Interstate highways before and up to 9 months after the change in speed limits, although preliminary, provide a good illustration of the shifts for the full range of speeds (Figure 3-7). Following the speed limit change, the range in driving speeds widened initially, and average and 85th percentile speeds reportedly increased (Montana Department of Transportation

[52] Retting and Greene (1997) found that speed standard deviation had increased from 6.2 to 6.5 mph (10 to 10.5 km/h) on three urban freeways (non-Interstate) and one urban Interstate highway in Riverside immediately before and 12 months after the speed limit was raised to 65 mph (105 km/h) for cars; the limit remained at 55 mph (89 km/h) for trucks (p. 43). The increase was larger for the same time comparison on urban freeways in Houston. Speed standard deviation increased from 5.9 to 6.8 mph (9.5 to 10.9 km/h) on four urban freeways (non-Interstate) and one urban Interstate highway where the speed limit was raised to 70 mph (113 km/h) for cars and to 60 mph (97 km/h) for trucks; lower nighttime speed limits—65 mph for cars and 55 mph for trucks—were in effect (pp. 43–44).

[53] Retting and Greene (1997) also found that 14 percent of the drivers in Riverside exceeded 75 mph (121 km/h) 1 year after the speed limit was changed, up from 8 percent before the change (p. 43). Fifty percent of drivers on urban Interstates and freeways in the Houston metropolitan area were traveling faster than 70 mph (113 km/h) 1 year after the speed limit was raised to that level, compared with 15 percent immediately before the new maximum speed limit took effect (Retting and Greene 1997, 44); 17 percent exceeded 75 mph 1 year after the speed limit change compared with 4 percent immediately before (Retting and Greene 1997, 44).

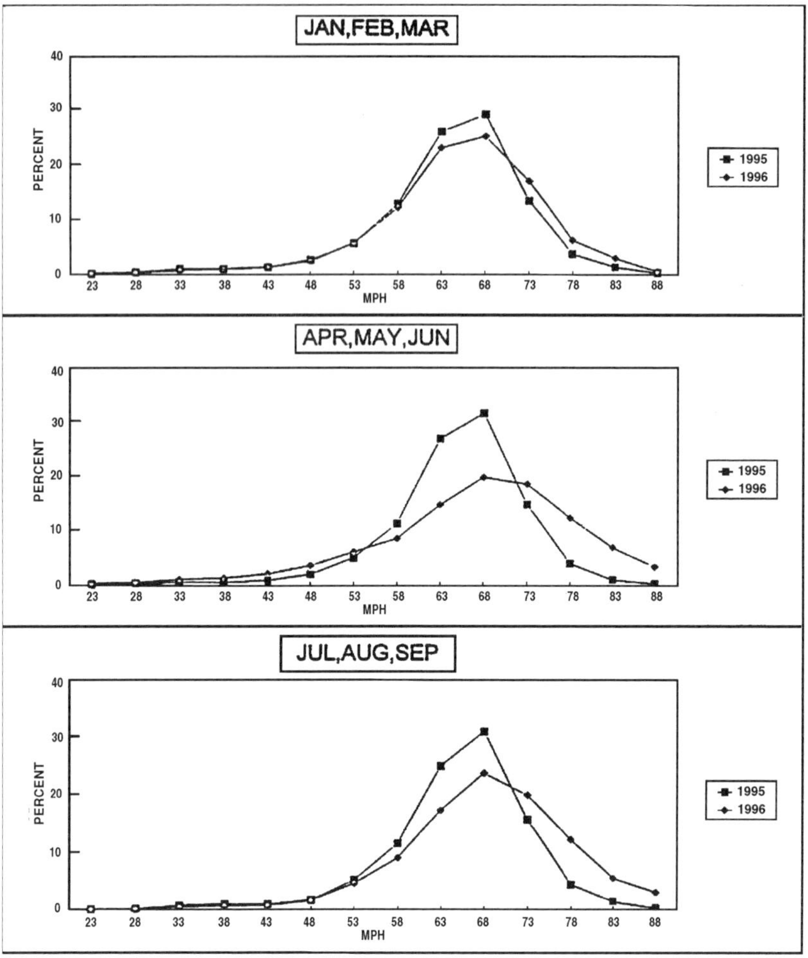

Figure 3-7 Daytime traffic speed distribution on Interstate highways, Montana, 1995 versus 1996 (Montana Department of Transportation and Montana Highway Patrol 1996, 13). 1 mph = 1.609 km/h.

and Montana Highway Patrol 1996, 10, 15). Increased skewness or dispersion in speed distributions has been associated with a higher risk of crash involvement (Solomon 1964; Taylor 1965; Cirillo 1968; Harkey et al. 1990). Higher average speeds and 85th percentile speeds are clearly associated with greater crash severity.

Effects of Speed Limit Changes on Safety

Unfortunately, data to confirm or refute changes in safety attributable to changes in speed limits are presently limited. According to NHTSA, in the first year of experience with higher speed limits, states that increased speed limits experienced approximately 350 more fatalities on Interstate facilities than would have been expected on the basis of historical trends, or about 9 percent above expectations (NHTSA 1998, v).[54] NHTSA regards the 9 percent increase as a lower bound.[55] The agency noted that the estimated fatality increase follows historical patterns of similar increases associated with raising the speed limit, although the increase was not as large as in 1987 (NHTSA 1998, iii). All states that had increased speed limits in 1996 had statistically significant increases in Interstate fatalities compared with those states that had not increased speed limits (NHTSA 1998, 22). Only the "early change" group showed a statistically significant upward trend relative to historical trends (NHTSA 1998, 27). NHTSA concluded that without information on increased travel on higher-speed roads, shifts in travel, changes in average and top vehicle speeds, and other traffic safety factors, it was unable to determine how these other factors may have contributed to the increase in Interstate fatalities (NHTSA 1998, v). It is not clear that travel data can ever be collected that would allow changes in exposure to be separated from changes in risk.[56] The NHTSA study did not address the issues of diversion and spillover effects to determine net safety effects because the data were preliminary and limited.

---

[54] The study compared fatalities in 1996 with historical trends since 1991 for the three analysis groups (NHTSA 1998, v).

[55] The current calculations use total Interstate fatalities for estimating absolute and percentage changes. However, if much less than 100 percent of Interstate mileage was affected by increased speed limits, then the baseline number of fatalities used in the denominator for computing the percentage change would be too large, and the percentage change would be too small. Also, the current analysis did not include any spillover effects on non-Interstate roads (i.e., higher speeds and crashes on these roads), which, if found and linked to raising speed limits, would increase the fatality effect (NHTSA 1998, 30).

[56] Estimates of vehicle miles traveled are not tabulated according to posted speed limits. Thus, it is impossible to identify a suitable baseline of highways and travel

IIHS researchers found a larger safety decrement in their analysis of the initial experience with speed limit increases. They reported a statistically significant 16 percent increase in occupant fatalities and nearly a 17 percent increase in fatality rates for a 9-month period in 1996 on Interstate highways and freeways in 12 states that had raised maximum speed limits to 70 mph (113 km/h) by March 1996 (Farmer et al. 1997, 5, 9).[57] In contrast, occupant fatalities had increased 4 percent on Interstate highways and freeways in the 18-state comparison group. (Comparable data were not reported for fatality rates.) Spillover effects, however, were small; no statistically significant differences were reported for occupant fatalities on roads other than Interstates and freeways for the two groups (Farmer et al. 1997, 10). This finding is not surprising, because many states raised speed limits on limited-access highways first. Thus, the net safety effect that was attributed to the speed limit increase was a 6 percent increase in total occupant fatalities on all roads combined (Farmer et al. 1997, 10).

The IIHS study is limited to a short period. The data were insufficient to analyze the effects of speed limit changes separately for each state. In addition, the comparison group approach assumes comparability between the two study groups, and, without controls for other factors that may have affected fatality rates, the estimates may be biased.

Studies from individual states were limited by data availability. NHTSA's review of findings from 10 states[58] that provided data concluded that there is some evidence of a link between higher speed limits and increases in crashes, but the effects did not follow a consistent pattern in all states (NHTSA 1998, 52). In many states, the

---

data on road sections where speed limits were raised as a basis on which to compare fatality outcomes (NHTSA 1998, 11–12).

[57] A comparison of the effect of speed limit increases on rural and urban Interstate highways and freeways yielded mixed results. Speed limit increases on rural Interstates were associated with a statistically significant 11 percent increase in occupant fatalities; no statistically significant changes were found for speed limit increases on urban Interstates and freeways (Farmer et al. 1997, 9).

[58] California, Idaho, Iowa, Michigan, Missouri, Montana, Nebraska, New Mexico, Texas, and Virginia.

data appeared to confirm IIHS's finding of a significant increase in crash severity on roads where speed limits were raised. In California, for example, fatal crashes and fatal crash rates increased on freeways where speed limits had been raised to 65 and 70 mph (105 and 113 km/h).[59] In Texas the effect was confined to fatal and serious injury crashes on urban Interstates where the speed limit was raised from 65 to 70 mph.[60] Idaho had sharp increases in speed-related crash rates on urban Interstates where speed limits were raised to 70 mph but no corresponding increase on rural Interstates where they were raised to 75 mph (121 km/h) (Idaho Department of Transportation 1997).

Data from New Mexico are interesting for what they reveal about the importance of enforcement to driver compliance with speed limits. On two rural Interstate highways where speed limits were raised from 65 to 75 mph (105 to 121 km/h), speeds [i.e., average speeds, 85th percentile speeds, and the percentage of drivers exceeding 80 mph (129 km/h)] increased and so did crash frequency and severity.[61] The increase in incapacitating injuries in multiple-vehicle crashes—mainly rear-end and sideswipe crashes—was linked to increases in

[59] Fatal crash rates on California freeways increased 22 percent [from 0.4 to 0.5 per 100 million vehicle-mi (100 MVM) (0.2 to 0.3 per 100 million vehicle-km); from 330 to 403 fatal crashes] 11 months after speed limits had been raised from 55 to 65 mph (89 to 105 km/h) compared with the same 11 months before the new limits were introduced. Similarly, fatal crash rates on freeways increased 12 percent [from 1.5 to 1.7 per 100 MVM (0.93 to 1.1 per 100 million vehicle-km); from 165 to 185 fatal crashes] 11 months after speed limits had been raised from 65 to 70 mph (105 to 113 km/h) compared with the same 11 months before the new limits were introduced (California Department of Transportation, provisional data as of Dec. 31, 1996).

[60] Average monthly serious crash frequencies (defined as crashes in which at least one person was killed or suffered an incapacitating or nonincapacitating injury) increased from 36 (Jan.–Sept. 1995) to 52 (Jan.–Sept. 1996). Serious crash rates increased from 13.6 to 18.8 per 100 MVM (8.5 to 11.7 per 100 million vehicle-km) for the same periods (Pezoldt et al. 1997, 21). Increases in serious crash frequencies and rates were statistically significant. A subsequent review by the Texas Department of Transportation (unpublished data, May 16, 1997), however, attributed most of the increases to severe winter weather and other factors (e.g., drunk driving, fatigue), largely unrelated to the higher speed limit.

[61] Tow-away crashes increased by 29 percent, injuries by 31 percent, incapacitating injuries by 44 percent, and fatalities by 50 percent. All of the increases are statistically significant (Davis 1998, 1).

speed dispersion (Davis 1998, 2, 16–17). This experience was in sharp contrast to another rural Interstate—I-10—where speed limits had also been raised but where speeds remained relatively constant and injury crashes and crash severity showed a slight decline (Davis 1998, 1). The major differences were attributed to rigorous enforcement and the high percentage of heavy-truck traffic on I-10, which tended to keep all vehicle speeds lower.[62]

Review of Studies of Changes in Speed Limits on Nonlimited-Access Highways

Most U.S. studies have focused on changes in speed limits on limited-access highways. A recent study (Parker 1997), however, examined the effect of changes in speed limits—both increases and decreases—in short speed zones [typically less than 2 mi (3 km)] on rural and urban nonlimited-access highways. Changes in driving speeds and crash experience at these sites were compared with closely matched comparison sites where speed limits remained constant.[63]

The study found that changing posted speed limits had little effect on driving speeds. Specifically, a review of before and after speed data at the selected sites revealed that differences in average speeds, standard deviations of speeds, and 85th percentile speeds were generally less than 2 mph (3 km/h) and were not related to the amount the posted speed limit was changed (Parker 1997, 85).[64] Part of the explanation may lie in the fact that the speed limit changes—at least increases in the speed limit—simply rationalized the speeds that drivers were already driving. In fact, where speed limits were raised

---

[62] The Doña Ana County Sherriff's Office issued more than 1,000 citations for speeding under a grant from the Traffic Safety Bureau during the time the speed data were being recorded on I-10 (Davis 1996, 7).

[63] The comparison sites could not be randomly drawn from the same population or source, but every effort was made to match as closely as possible the geometric, volume, and speed characteristics of the sites where the speed limits had been changed (Parker 1997, 9).

[64] The researchers noted that the changes were statistically significant, primarily because of large sample sizes, but "not sufficiently large to be of practical significance" (Parker 1997, 87).

by 10 to 15 mph (16 to 24 km/h),[65] there was a fourfold increase in driver compliance levels (Parker 1997, 46). Conversely, where speed limits were lowered, compliance levels declined sharply; drivers appeared to ignore the new, lower speed limits at these sites (Parker 1997, 46). The author concluded that changing posted speed limits alone—without additional enforcement, educational programs, or other engineering measures—has only a minor effect on driver behavior (Parker 1997, 87).

Not surprisingly, with such small speed changes, Parker found no evidence of changes in total crashes or fatal and injury crashes when posted speed limits were raised or lowered (Parker 1997, 86). The study findings, however, cannot be generalized to all nonlimited-access roads because the site selection process was not random.[66] The lack of observed changes in driver behavior raises the concern that, if the planned speed limit changes simply legalized existing behavior, the results could be significantly biased in favor of the finding that the speed limit changes had little effect on driver behavior and thus offer little insight into the independent effect of a change in speed limits on the distribution of driving speeds.[67]

Nevertheless, Parker's results were confirmed in another recent study of speed limit changes for a range of road types, mainly nonlimited-access state highways (Agent et al. 1997). Data were collected on speeds and crashes at more than 100 speed zones in Kentucky where speed limits had been changed. In most cases, the speed limit was lowered to near 35th percentile speeds; the predominant change was from 55 to 45 mph (89 to 72 km/h). The study found modest changes in 85th percentile speeds—less than the change in the speed limit itself—whether the speed limit was raised or lowered (Agent et al. 1997, 12). Where 85th percentile speeds before the change were high relative to the new limit, modest

[65] "Before" speed limit levels ranged from 20 to 50 mph (32 to 80 km/h) (Parker 1997, 91–92).

[66] It should be noted that safety issues and legal concerns are likely to preclude any experimental design that involves random site selection for speed limit changes.

[67] For a more detailed discussion of the Parker study, see the section on Posted Speed Limits and Speeding Behavior in Appendix C.

reductions in speed were recorded but were accompanied by a high rate of noncompliance (Agent et al. 1997, 12–13). The authors concluded that motorists will drive at what they consider an appropriate speed regardless of the speed limit (Agent et al. 1997, iii). Not surprisingly, given the small changes in speed, no statistically significant changes were observed in the total number of crashes or fatal or injury crashes (Agent et al. 1997, 16).

The study exhibits many of the same limitations of the Parker study, mainly nonrandom selection of sites, that limit generalization of results. In addition, variability in data collection techniques for speed measurement may have affected the reliability of results. However, both studies suggest the need for reasonable speed limits and the difficulty of changing driver behavior where drivers perceive that an appropriate speed is other than the posted speed limit.

Review of International Experience on the Effects of Changes in Speed Limits

In addition to the U.S. research on the relationship between changes in speed limits and highway safety, a number of international studies have examined this issue.[68] International studies of the effects of changes in speed limits on low-speed roads are numerous and were summarized briefly earlier in the chapter. This section focuses on a more limited number of recent studies of speed limit changes on high-speed roads.

In contrast to the United States, where most studies have evaluated the speed and safety effects of raising speed limits on limited-access highways, international studies have primarily examined the effects of reductions in speed limits. Studies of speed limit reductions in Sweden (Nilsson 1990; Johansson 1996), the Netherlands (Borsje 1995), Victoria, Australia (Sliogeris 1992), and Finland (Salusjärvi 1981) all reported results that are a mirror image of those found in the United States. Lower speed limits resulted in lower average speeds, although

[68] This section also draws heavily on the review commissioned for this study, which is presented in its entirety as Appendix C.

the changes were typically less than the absolute reduction in the speed limit. Lower speed limits were also associated with reduced crash incidence and, in some cases, with reduced crash severity. Many of the studies, however, do not control for the potentially confounding effects of other policies undertaken at the same time as the speed limit change (e.g., public information campaigns, increased levels of enforcement) or other factors that may have affected highway safety (e.g., changes in amount of travel affecting exposure levels, safety belt legislation). Most studies failed to consider systemwide effects of speed limit changes to determine net safety effects. Any generalization of the results to the United States, of course, must be mindful of differences in highway networks, driving environment, and driving culture (there is more legal high-speed driving in European countries).

SUMMARY

The potential adverse consequences of speeding, particularly the risks imposed on others from an individual driver's speed choice, are sufficient reason for regulating speed. Speed limits, one of the oldest methods of managing speeds, are intended to enhance safety by establishing an upper bound on speed to reduce both the probability and the severity of crashes. They also have a coordinating function; the intent is to reduce dispersion in driving speeds and thus reduce the potential for vehicle conflicts.

Numerous methods are available for setting speed limits, ranging from legislated limits on broad road classes, to limits in speed zones determined on the basis of an engineering study, to limits established by local ordinance on residential streets. Whatever method is used, speed limits reflect implicit trade-offs among road user safety, travel efficiency, and practicality of enforcement.

The trade-offs vary by roadway functional class and environment, reflecting in part different levels of risk associated with driving on different roadway types. Setting speed limits that give priority to travel efficiency, for example, may be appropriate on rural freeways where vehicles travel long distances under free-flowing traffic conditions with little likelihood of conflict with other road users and where the ability to enforce speed on extensive road mileage is limited. A maximum speed limit is probably necessary, however, because of the cause-and-effect relationship between high speeds and crash severity.

Speed limits that give priority to travel efficiency are less likely to be appropriate in urban areas, where the roads must be shared with a broad range of users, including vulnerable pedestrians and bicyclists, and where roadside development increases opportunities for vehicle conflict and raises the probability of an unexpected event. Because driver compliance with urban speed limits has been poor, alternative methods for managing and enforcing speeds may be necessary in these areas.

Most roads and roadway conditions fall between these extremes. Appropriate use of speed zones can help establish speed limits suitable for conditions.

The effects of speed limits, particularly on safety, have been studied extensively. U.S. experience with raising speed limits on qualified sections of rural Interstate highways in 1987 suggests that higher speed limits resulted in higher average and 85th percentile speeds and modest increases in speed dispersion. Higher speeds are linked unequivocally with increased injury severity in a crash. Indeed, the most methodologically sound studies found that higher speeds led to increased fatalities and fatal crashes on rural Interstates in most states. The studies were less clear about the absolute size of the safety decrement, the extent and direction of any network effects, and the role of enforcement in encouraging driver compliance with new speed limits.

Preliminary data are available for speed and safety changes, primarily on limited-access highways, in the first year following repeal of the NMSL in 1995. Average and 85th percentile speeds rose less than increases in the posted limit, reflecting, in part, poor driver compliance with lower speed limits in effect before the change. Speed dispersion increased in some states but not in others, in part depending on what measure of speed dispersion was used. Monitoring studies show some evidence of more high-speed driving at levels that exceed the new speed limits, suggesting that at least some drivers expect the same enforcement tolerance as at the lower speed limits. Although the findings are not consistent across all states, most studies indicated an increase in fatalities on highways where speed limits were raised. Only one study examined possible system effects, finding modest spillover effects. The results of these studies must be considered preliminary because they are generally based on 1 year of data or less.

The available studies of speed limit changes in speed zones on nonlimited-access highways in the United States found little change in speeds or crashes when speed limits were raised to near the 85th percentile speed or lowered to a limit well below the 85th percentile. Although methodological problems limit the generalization of study results, the findings suggest the difficulty of changing driver behavior merely by changing the sign.

Speed limits are likely to have more effect if the majority of drivers perceive the limits as reasonable and related to the risks of driving, including risks to other road users. The increased probability of a severe crash is sufficient reason to impose maximum speed limits and direct enforcement at motorists who drive well in excess of the speed limit. Speed limits alone, without enhanced enforcement or innovative engineering measures, are insufficient to achieve compliance with posted speed limits on many roads. In most cases, enforcement is critical to ensure driver compliance. Appropriate enforcement strategies—the subject of the next chapter—can help persuade drivers that speed limits are in fact legal limits and not simply guidance on appropriate driving speeds.

REFERENCES

ABBREVIATIONS

ECMT	European Conference of Ministers of Transport
ITE	Institute of Transportation Engineers
NHTSA	National Highway Traffic Safety Administration
NSC	National Safety Council
RTI	Research Triangle Institute
TRB	Transportation Research Board
TRL	Transport Research Laboratory
UVC	Uniform Vehicle Code

Agent, K.R., J.G. Pigman, and J.M. Weber. 1997. *Evaluation of Speed Limits in Kentucky.* KTC-97-6. Kentucky Transportation Center in cooperation with the Kentucky Transportation Cabinet and the Federal Highway Administration. April, 90 pp.

Baerwald, J.E. 1953. *Indiana Traffic Speeds 1942–1952.* Joint Highway Research Project. No. 73. Purdue University, Lafayette, Ind., March.

Baum, H.M., A.K. Lund, and J.K. Wells. 1989. The Mortality Consequences of Raising the Speed Limit to 65 MPH on Rural Interstates. *American Journal of Public Health,* Vol. 79, No. 10, Oct., pp. 1392–1395.

Baum, H.M., J.R. Esterlitz, P. Zador, and M. Penny. 1991a. Different Speed Limits for Cars and Trucks: Do They Affect Vehicle Speeds? In *Transportation Research Record 1318,* Transportation Research Board, National Research Council, Washington, D.C., pp. 3–7.

Baum, H.M., J.K. Wells, and A.K. Lund. 1991b. The Fatality Consequences of the 65 MPH Speed Limits, 1989. *Journal of Safety Research,* Vol. 22, No. 4, Winter, pp. 171–177.

Borsje, J.F. 1995. The Effects of the 1988 Differentiation of Speed Limits in The Netherlands. No. 2A, Part 4. *Proc., Road Safety in Europe and Strategic Highway Research Program (SHRP),* Lille, France, Sept. 26-28, 1994, pp. 24–36.

Carter, F.M. 1949. Speed Zoning. *Proc., First California Institute on Street and Highway Problems,* Berkeley, Calif., Jan. 31-Feb. 2, pp. 151–156.

Casey, S.M., and A.K. Lund. 1992. Changes in Speed and Speed Adaptation Following an Increase in the National Maximum Speed Limit. *Journal of Safety Research,* Vol. 23, pp. 135–146.

Chowdhury, M.A., D.L. Warren, H. Bissell, and S. Taori. 1998. Are the Criteria for Setting Advisory Speeds on Curves Still Relevant? *ITE Journal,* Vol. 68, No. 2, Feb., pp. 32–45.

Cirillo, J.A. 1968. Interstate System Accident Research—Study II—Interim Report II. *Public Roads,* Vol. 35, No. 3, 1968.

Coleman, J.A., et al. 1996. *FHWA Study Tour for Speed Management and Enforcement Technology.* FHWA-PL-96-006. Federal Highway Administration, U.S. Department of Transportation, Feb., 83 pp.

Davis, J.W. 1996. *The Effects of Higher Speed Limits in New Mexico.* Draft. Grant 1-TR-97-01. University of New Mexico, Jan.

Davis, J.W. 1998. *The Effects of Higher Speed Limits in New Mexico.* Grant 98-TR-01-01. Division of Government Research, University of New Mexico, Jan., 19 pp.

Donald, D. 1994. Using Expert System Technology to Set Appropriate, Consistent Speed Limits—The Australian Experience. In *Proc., Third International Conference on Safety and the Environment in the 21st Century: Lessons from the Past, Shaping the Future,* Tel Aviv, Israel, Oct., pp. 284–295.

ECMT. 1996. *Speed Moderation.* Organisation for Economic Cooperation and Development. OECD Publications Service, Paris, 86 pp.

Farmer, C.M., R. A. Retting, and A.K. Lund. 1997. *Effect of 1996 Speed Limit Changes on Motor Vehicle Occupant Fatalities.* Insurance Institute for Highway Safety, Arlington, Va., Oct., 12 pp.

Fildes, B.N., and S.J. Lee. 1993. *The Speed Review: Road Environment, Behaviour, Speed Limits, Enforcement and Crashes.* Monash University Accident Research Centre, Victoria, Australia, Sept., 146 pp.

Finch, D.J., P. Kompfner, C.R. Lockwood, and G. Maycock. 1994. *Speed, Speed Limits and Accidents.* Project Report 58. S211G/RB. Transport Research Laboratory, Berkshire, England, 24 pp.

Fitzpatrick, K., R.A. Krammes, and D.B. Fambro. 1997. Design Speed, Operating Speed and Posted Speed Relationships. *ITE Journal,* Vol. 67, No. 2, Feb., pp. 52–59.

Garber, N.J., and R. Gadiraju. 1988. *Speed Variance and Its Influence on Accidents.* University of Virginia, Charlottesville, July, 56 pp.

Garber, N.J., and R. Gadiraju. 1991. *Impact of Differential Speed Limits on Highway Speeds and Accidents.* University of Virginia, Charlottesville, Feb., 52 pp.

Garber, S., and J.D. Graham. 1989. *The Effects of the New 65 Mile-Per-Hour Speed Limit on Rural Highway Fatalities: A State-By-State Analysis.* DOT-HS-807-452. National Highway Traffic Safety Administration, U.S. Department of Transportation, July, 34 pp.

Godwin, S.R. 1988. Implications of Raising the U.S. Maximum Speed Limit to 65 mph. VTI Rapport 332A. *Proc., Roads and Traffic Safety on Two Continents,* Gothenburg, Sweden, Sept. 9–11, 1987, pp. 21–43.

Godwin, S.R. 1992. Effect of the 65 m.p.h. Speed Limit on Highway Safety in the U.S.A. *Transport Review,* Vol. 12, No. 1, pp. 1–14.

Graham-Migletz Enterprises, Inc. 1996. Procedure for Determining Work Zone Speed Limits. *Research Results Digest,* No. 192, National Cooperative Highway Research Program, Sept., 43 pp.

Griffith, M.S. 1995. Discussion of "Did the 65 mph Speed Limit Save Lives?" (with response by C. Lave). News, Queries and Comment, *Accident Analysis and Prevention,* Vol. 27, No. 1, pp. 137–140.

Harkey, D.L., H.D. Robertson, and S.E. Davis. 1990. Assessment of Current Speed Zoning Criteria. In *Transportation Research Record 1281,* Transportation Research Board, National Research Council, Washington, D.C., pp. 40–51.

Harkey, D.L., and R. Mera. 1994. *Safety Impacts of Different Speed Limits on Cars and Trucks.* FHWA-RD-93-161. The Scientex Corporation, Charlotte, N.C., May, 67 pp.

Harwood, C.J. 1995. Criteria for Setting General Urban Speed Limits. *Road and Transport Research,* Vol. 4, No. 2, June, pp. 88–94.

Highway and Vehicle Safety Report. 1998. Speed Limits Change with Weather in Seattle. Vol. 24, No. 8, Jan.

Idaho Department of Transportation. 1997. *Speed and Accident Report for May–October, Six-Month Report Comparing May–October for 1991 Through 1996.* Jan. 8.

ITE. 1992. *Traffic Engineering Handbook: Fourth Edition* (J.L. Pline, ed.). Prentice-Hall, Englewood Cliffs, N.J.

Johansson, P. 1996. Speed Limitation and Motorway Casualties: A Time Series Count Data Regression Approach. *Accident Analysis and Prevention,* Vol. 28, No. 1, pp. 73–87.

Jondrow, J.M., M. Bowes, and R.A. Levy. 1982. Optimal Speed Limit: A New Approach. In *Transportation Research Record 887,* Transportation Research Board, National Research Council, Washington, D.C., pp. 1–2.

Joscelyn, K.B., and P.A. Elston. 1970. *Maximum Speed Limits—Volume II, The Development of Speed Limits: A Review of the Literature.* FH-11-7275. Indiana University, Bloomington, Oct., 146 pp.

Krammes, R.A., K. Fitzpatrick, J.D. Blaschke, and D.B. Fambro. 1996. *Speed: Understanding Design, Operating, and Posted Speed.* Report 1465-1. Texas Transportation Institute, College Station, March, 16 pp.

Labatut, J., and W. Lane. 1950. *Highways in Our National Life: A Symposium.* Princeton University Press.

Ladd, W.D. 1959. *Organizing for Traffic Safety in Your Community.* Charles C. Thomas, Springfield, Ill.

Lave, C. 1985. Speeding, Coordination, and the 55-mph Limit. *The American Economic Review,* Vol. 75, pp. 1159–1164.

Lave, C., and P. Elias. 1994. Did the 65 MPH Speed Limit Save Lives? *Accident Analysis and Prevention,* Vol. 26, No. 1, pp. 49–62.

Lund, A.K., and W.J. Rauch. 1992. *On the Contrary! A Comment on Lave and Elias's Question "Did the 65 mph Speed Limit Save Lives?"* Insurance Institute for Highway Safety, Arlington, Va., 5 pp.

MacRae, D., Jr., and J.A. Wilde. 1979. The Optimum Speed Limit. In *Policy Analysis for Public Decisions,* Duxbury Press, Mass., pp. 133–156.

Marcellis, J.C. 1962. *An Economic Evaluation of Traffic Movement at Various Speeds.* Vehicular Speed Regulation Research Project, Department of Civil Engineering, University of Illinois, Sept.

McCarthy, P.S. 1994. An Empirical Analysis of the Direct and Indirect Effects of Relaxed Interstate Speed Limits on Highway Safety. *Journal of Urban Economics,* Vol. 36, pp. 353–364.

McKnight, A.J., T.M. Klein, and A.S. Tippetts. 1989. *The Effect of the 65 MPH Limit on Speeds and Accidents.* DOT-HS-807-463. National Public Services Research Institute, Landover, Md., National Highway Traffic Safety Administration, U.S. Department of Transportation, Aug., 48 pp.

Montana Department of Transportation and Montana Highway Patrol. 1996. *Data Reference Related to Montana Speed Laws.* Dec.

NHTSA. 1989. *Effects of the 65 mph Speed Limit Though 1988: A Report to Congress.* U.S. Department of Transportation, Oct.

NHTSA. 1992. *Effects of the 65 mph Speed Limit Through 1990: A Report to Congress.* U.S. Department of Transportation, May.

NHTSA. 1997. *Traffic Safety Facts 1996.* DOT-HS-808-649. U.S. Department of Transportation, Dec.

NHTSA. 1998. *The Effect of Increased Speed Limits in the Post-NMSL Era.* Report to Congress. DOT-HS-808-637. NRD-31. U.S. Department of Transportation, Feb.

Nilsson, G. 1990. Reduction in the Speed Limit from 110 km/h to 90 km/h During Summer 1989. *VTI Rapport 358A,* Swedish Road and Traffic Research Institute, 36 pp.

NSC. 1941. *Speed Regulation.* Committee on Speed Regulation, Chicago, Ill., July, 62 pp.

Oppenlander, J.C. 1962. A Theory on Vehicular Speed Regulation. *Bulletin 341,* Highway Research Board, National Research Council, Washington, D.C., pp. 77–91.

Parker, M.R., Jr. 1997. *Effects of Raising and Lowering Speed Limits on Selected Roadway Sections.* FHWA-RD-92-084. Martin R. Parker & Associates, Inc., Wayne, Mich., Jan., 175 pp.

Parker, M.R., Jr., and K.H. Tsuchiyama. 1985. *Methods for Reducing Large Speed Differences in Traffic Streams, Volume 1 - Inventory of Methods.* FHWA/RD-85/103. Martin R. Parker & Associates, Inc., Canton, Mich., Aug., 124 pp.

Pezoldt, V.J., R. Q. Brackett, and D.E. Morris. 1997. *The Impact of the Change in Speed Limits on Texas Highways: A Nine-Month Evaluation.* Texas Transportation Institute, Texas A&M University System, College Station, Feb. 19.

Pilli-Sihvola, Y., and K. Taskula. 1996. Mustaa Jäätä and Finland's Weather-Controlled Road. *Traffic Technology International 1996,* UK and International Press, Surrey, United Kingdom, pp. 204–206.

Retting, R.A., and M.A. Greene. 1997. Traffic Speeds Following Repeal of the National Maximum Speed Limit. *ITE Journal,* Vol. 67, No. 5, May, pp. 42–46.

Rosen, H.S. 1995. *Public Finance (*4th edition*).* Richard D. Irwin, Inc.

Rowsome, F., Jr. 1965. *The Verse By the Side of the Road.* The Penguin Group.

RTI. 1970. *Speed and Accidents, Vol. II.* Final Report, Summary and Conclusions. May.

Salusjärvi, M. 1981. *The Speed Limit Experiments on Public Roads in Finland.* Road and Traffic Laboratory, Technical Research Centre of Finland, Dec., 133 pp.

Sliogeris, J. 1992. *110 Kilometre Per Hour Speed Limit—Evaluation of Road Safety Effects.* GR 92-8. Vic Roads, Kew, Victoria, Australia, Aug., 27 pp.

Solomon, D. 1964. *Accidents on Main Rural Highways Related to Speed, Driver, and Vehicle.* Bureau of Public Roads, U.S. Department of Commerce, July, 44 pp.

Sub-Committee on Speed Zoning. 1969. Resolution of the Annual Meeting of the American Association of State Highway Officials.

Taylor, W.C. 1965. Speed Zoning, A Theory and Its Proof. *Traffic Engineering,* Vol. 34, No. 12, Jan., pp. 17–19, 48–50.

Tennessee Department of Highways. 1968. *A Summary of Practices in Establishing Speed Zones.* Traffic Engineering Division, June.

The American City. 1950. What Do Speed Limits Mean? Vol. 65, No. 11, Jan., p. 121.

Thornton, M., and R.W. Lyles. 1996. Freeway Speed Zones: Safety and Compliance Issues. In *Transportation Research Record 1560,* Transportation Research Board, National Research Council, Washington, D.C., pp. 66–73.

Tignor, S.C., and D.L. Warren. 1989. *Speed Zoning in America: Some Preliminary Research Results.* Federal Highway Administration, U.S. Department of Transportation, June.

Transport Research Centre. 1996. *Toward Safer Roads: Opportunities for a Policy to Bring About a Sustainably Safe Traffic System.* Ministry of Transport and Public Works, The Netherlands, 16 pp.

TRB. 1984. *Special Report 204: 55: A Decade of Experience.* National Research Council, Washington, D.C., 262 pp.

TRB. 1998. *Special Report 209: Highway Capacity Manual.* Third Edition, 1997 Update. National Research Council, Washington, D.C.

TRL. 1997. *M25 Controlled Motorways Monitoring: Executive Summary.* Crowthorne, Berkshire, England, Feb., 4 pp.

Ullman, G.L., and C.L. Dudek. 1987. Effects of Reduced Speed Limits in Rapidly Developing Urban Fringe Areas. In *Transportation Research Record 1114,* Transportation Research Board, National Research Council, Washington, D.C., pp. 45–53.

UVC. 1967. *Rules of the Road with Statutory Annotations.*

Van den Hoogen, E., and S. Smulders. 1994. Control by Variable Speed Signs: Results of the Dutch Experiment. Conference Publication 391, *Road Traffic Monitoring and Control,* April 26–28, IEE, pp. 145–149.

Várhelyi, A. 1996. *Dynamic Speed Adaptation Based on Information Technology—A Theoretical Background.* Bulletin 142. Lund University, Lund Institute of Technology, Sweden, 220 pp.

West, L.B., Jr., and J.W. Dunn. 1971. Accidents, Speed Deviation and Speed Limits. *Traffic Engineering,* Vol. 41, No. 10, pp. 52–55.

4

Speed Enforcement and Adjudication

Thirty days
Hath September
April
June and the
Speed offender
Burma Shave (Rowsome 1965)

Compliance with any regulation such as a speed limit requires that it represent a reasonable constraint on behavior. In the preceding chapter, a range of methods for setting reasonable speed limits was discussed, reflecting trade-offs among safety, travel time, and enforceability on different types of roads and roadway environments. In this chapter, two additional requirements for driver compliance are considered: public support and consistent enforcement.

Public support (i.e., willingness to obey) is closely linked with and should follow from the first requirement, that is, reasonableness of speed limits. For compliance with speed limits to be at a high level, a majority of the driving public must perceive them to be legitimate and comply with them voluntarily. Otherwise, large numbers of motorists will disregard the limits. In this situation, if attempts are made to enforce them, large numbers of violations will overwhelm the law enforcement community—the police, the prosecutors, and the courts. Moreover, without strong public support, law enforcement agents themselves may be reluctant to enforce the speed limits. This response is typical of laws that are viewed as nonlegitimate in the eyes of the public (Wilson 1983; Ross 1973; Ross 1982). Of course, a combination of reasonable speed limits, sustained enforcement, and education may change driver behavior toward speed compliance, but this requires the perception that speeding is a safety problem and a long-term effort to change driver attitudes and behavior.

Even if speed limit regulations are generally viewed as legitimate by most motorists, enforcement is essential to ensure conformity of the remaining drivers who will obey the laws only if they believe they are likely to be apprehended and prosecuted for noncompliance. In this chapter, appropriate methods of speed enforcement and adjudication are considered. The chapter begins with a discussion of the role of deterrence, surveillance, and sanctions in ensuring compliance with speed limits. Then, evidence of the effectiveness and the limitations of traditional enforcement methods on speed choice and safety outcomes is considered. Next, the potential of automated technologies and public information programs to supplement traditional enforcement methods is reviewed. The role of the courts in adjudication of speeding violations is then considered. Finally, key conclusions concerning enforcement of speed limits and related judicial procedures are summarized.

LESSONS FROM DETERRENCE THEORY

Enforcement works primarily through the principle of deterrence. The fundamental idea is that credible threats of punishment deter unwanted behavior.[1] More specifically, the proscribed behavior is discouraged by the perception that legal punishment is "swift, sure, and severe" (Ross and LaFree 1986, 132).

Elements of the Deterrence Process

The effectiveness of deterrence depends on several factors. First, the proscribed behavior must be definable, understandable, and detectable, not only by the individuals to be deterred but also by those who are expected to enforce compliance and penalize those who do not comply (TRB 1987, 91). In the case of speeding, police officers must be able to reliably verify vehicle speeds and provide evidence that will hold up in court.

Second, the effectiveness of deterrence depends on the perceived risk of apprehension (TRB 1987, 91; Shinar and McKnight 1985, 387). For the risk to be credible, drivers must believe that they have a nontrivial chance of being apprehended if they engage in the proscribed behavior. Thus, some minimum level of enforcement leading to actual apprehension is necessary (Shinar and McKnight 1985, 407). A well-designed publicity campaign coupled with visible enforcement will expand the perception of risk to a large segment of the target population (Shinar and McKnight 1985, 409).

Third, the effectiveness of deterrence depends on the swiftness, certainty, and severity of the punishment (TRB 1987, 91). Empirical research suggests that the perceived certainty of punishment is a more powerful deterrent than the severity of the penalty (Shinar and McKnight 1985, 387).[2] One explanation is that, if the risk of pun-

---

[1] The approach is based on the philosophic view that human behavior is rational and that human beings behave to maximize personal pleasure and minimize pain. Thus, unwanted behavior can be deterred by increasing the costs of an undesired behavior so that it outweighs the benefits (Ross and LaFree 1986, 130).

[2] In principle, the behavior of potential scofflaws should be affected by both the certainty and severity of punishment, and illegal behavior should decline when either the certainty or the severity of the penalty is increased. However, empirical research has found that, for a series of crimes, the response depends much more on the certainty than on the severity of the penalty (Waldo and Chiricos 1972; Sellin 1967; Tittle 1969;

ishment is so low that the violator regards the threat as negligible, then the severity of the punishment is irrelevant (Ross and LaFree 1986, 144).[3] In addition, more severe penalties may actually reduce the deterrence effect by requiring more legal representation, which precludes swift punishment and may lessen the likelihood of receiving any penalty at all (Ross 1990 in Zaal 1994, 11). However, debate continues about just how immediate the penalty must be to provide an effective deterrent (Harper 1991 in Zaal 1994, 12).

Role of Police and the Courts

The effectiveness of deterrence is also influenced by actions of the police and the courts who carry out the apprehension and punishment of lawbreakers. The traditional police role in controlling vehicle speeds is to detect, apprehend, and punish the speeding driver. Like other traffic violations, penalties for speeding include fines; some states assess penalty points that can lead to license revocation. If a court hearing is involved, judges have discretion to vary the penalties.

Traditional police enforcement works in two ways: through detection and punishment of specific drivers who exceed the speed limit and through deterrence of speeding behavior in general. The first method, often referred to as specific deterrence, is based on the idea that individual drivers who are caught and punished for speeding will be deterred from committing further speeding violations. The second method, known as general deterrence, is based on the assumption that the process of apprehending individual violators can influence the behavior of a larger segment of the driving population. More specifically, police presence alerts drivers that traffic violations, including those related to speeding, are being enforced. In turn, increased

---

Teeven 1972; Chauncey 1975; Silberman 1976; Piliavin et al. 1986; Blumstein et al. 1978; Wilson 1983; Brier and Fienberg 1980; Cameron 1988).

[3] Increased severity of penalties can also produce undesired and unanticipated side effects through the discretion of legal agents who are perceived as unfairly apprehending a random sample of a much larger population who were simply lucky enough not to get caught (Ross and LaFree 1986, 144).

enforcement raises the perceived probability of being caught for speeding and thus helps deter unwanted speeding behavior.

Successful deterrence, however, may have the undesired effect of reducing the level of police surveillance and enforcement. Just as drivers increase their compliance as the perceived likelihood of apprehension rises, police may reduce their level of enforcement activity when the unwanted behavior diminishes (Tsebelis 1993, 366–367).[4] This close coupling of behavioral adaptation by the police and the driving public provides one explanation for the difficulty of sustaining the deterrence effects of traditional enforcement methods (Tsebelis 1993, 366; Bjørnskau and Elvik 1990, 139). It also suggests that random or automated surveillance methods that break this behavioral link may offer more effective ways of maintaining high levels of enforcement (Bjørnskau and Elvik 1990, 140–141); this topic is discussed in a subsequent section.

The courts can also deter speeding, but the effect on driver behavior is less direct. The lag between apprehension and punishment is likely to reduce the deterrence effect of sanctions on speeding drivers. Moreover, court discretion in assessing penalties for speeding, if viewed as arbitrary and unfair, can have the undesired effect of turning public opinion against enforcement and adjudication methods. If judges perceive speed limits to be unreasonable and routinely dismiss speeding citations, the incentive of the police to enforce the limits may be reduced.

Lessons for Enforcement

To optimize use of their limited resources, the police and the courts attempt to achieve the widest possible deterrence through enforcement and sanctions. The effectiveness of deterrence depends on creation of a widely perceived impression that noncompliers will be detected and apprehended if they engage in the proscribed behavior.

---

[4] This interpretation derives from a game theoretic approach to enforcement. The approach suggests that the public and the police are engaged in a game in which the probability of surveillance is not independent of the level of the crime (Tsebelis 1990; Tsebelis 1993; Cox 1994; Hirshleifer and Rasmusen 1992; Weissing and Ostrom 1991).

This impression, in turn, must be accompanied by swift, sure, and publicized punishment to establish a credible threat. The application of these principles to speed enforcement is discussed in the following section.

APPLICATION OF DETERRENCE THEORY TO SPEED ENFORCEMENT

Speed Enforcement Strategies

Speed enforcement using mobile patrol vehicles measuring driving speeds with radar is the most popular means of conducting speed enforcement in the United States, according to a special survey conducted for this study (Figure 4-1).[5] State police use aircraft as well as laser and VASCAR for speed detection.[6]

The mobile patrol method involves a police vehicle circulating through traffic and citing speeding drivers. Stationary patrol enforcement, where a marked or unmarked police car parked along the side of the roadway uses radar or LIDAR to measure speeds, is another common technique (Stuster 1995, A4–A8). Apprehension of speeding drivers occurs downstream of the monitoring vehicle, sometimes with another patrol officer.

The merits of mobile and stationary patrols have been a topic of study. The former is effective in detecting specific violators and slowing traffic in the immediate vicinity of the patrol car (Stuster 1995, A6). The latter is effective in deterring speeding at a particular location (Stuster 1995, A7). The advantages and disadvantages of visible and concealed enforcement have also been studied. One purpose of concealed enforcement is to increase the uncertainty of where and

---

[5] The survey of state law enforcement agencies was conducted by the Illinois State Police. Responses were received from 34 (68 percent) of the 50 state agencies responsible for traffic law enforcement.

[6] Laser speed guns use LIDAR technology, which stands for Light Distance and Ranging. VASCAR stands for Visual Average Speed Computer and Recorder (Coleman et al. 1996, xi–xii). VASCAR is a time-distance speed-measuring device that does not transmit a signal but computes vehicle travel time between two points. It can operate in a stationary or mobile mode in a patrol car, motorcycle, or airplane.

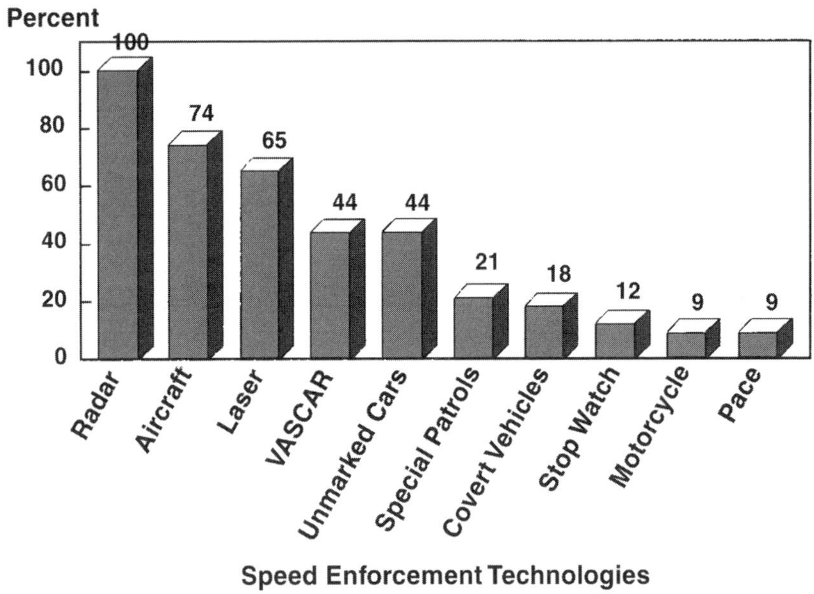

Figure 4-1 Percentage of state law enforcement agencies using the top 10 enforcement strategies, based on replies to a survey of 50 state agencies responsible for traffic law enforcement conducted for this study. Responses were received from 34 of the 50 agencies.

when enforcement will occur. As a result of its limited visibility, however, its general deterrence effect appears to be limited (Shinar and McKnight 1985, 393–394). Moreover, in jurisdictions where radar detectors are permitted, concealed police vehicles may be "seen" and their location communicated to others by CB radios, thereby compromising their concealment.

Resources for Speed Enforcement

When the 55-mph (89-km/h) National Maximum Speed Limit (NMSL) was in effect and states were required to document speed compliance levels or face penalties, only one on-duty state highway patrol officer, on the average, was available to patrol every 190 mi (306 km) of highways posted at the 55-mph limit (TRB 1984, 162). Comparable figures are not available today, but a special survey of state agencies responsible for traffic law enforcement conducted for this study provides some data on current levels of effort on speed enforcement. Data on costs of traffic enforcement, if properly collected, could provide valuable additional information. However, they are not routinely collected because of the difficulty and cost of doing so.

The percentage of law enforcement resources devoted to speed enforcement varies widely by state (Figure 4-2). More than half of the state law enforcement agencies contacted for this study reported that they spend less than 50 percent of their time in speed enforcement.[7] One-quarter of the respondents spend 50 percent or more. In addition, since repeal of the NMSL in 1995, the majority of state law enforcement agencies reported "no change" (38 percent) or reductions (24 percent) in the time expended on speed enforcement. Those who reduced effort cited budget cuts or substitution of other activities, such as community policing and investigations. Nearly one-third of the agencies (32 percent), however, reported increased time devoted to speed enforcement.[8] Given these data, if limited resources are not to be squandered, whatever speed enforcement is undertaken must be effective.

Effectiveness of Traditional Speed Enforcement

A critical difficulty in deterring speeding using traditional methods is maintaining the effect over time and space. The longevity of effects can be expressed in terms of a "halo," that is, the spatial or temporal extent of the deterrence effect from the enforcement officer. Hauer and Ahlin (1982) investigated both effects by measuring vehicle speeds before, during, and after enforcement using stationary, marked police vehicles on semirural, two-lane roads. Similar to earlier studies, the researchers found a marked reduction in average traffic speeds in the vicinity of the enforcement site to speeds close to posted speed limits (Hauer and Ahlin 1982, 277). Reduction in speed dispersion,

[7] Comparable figures could not be found for county or municipal law enforcement agencies.

[8] The remaining 6 percent were unable to offer any comparative data.

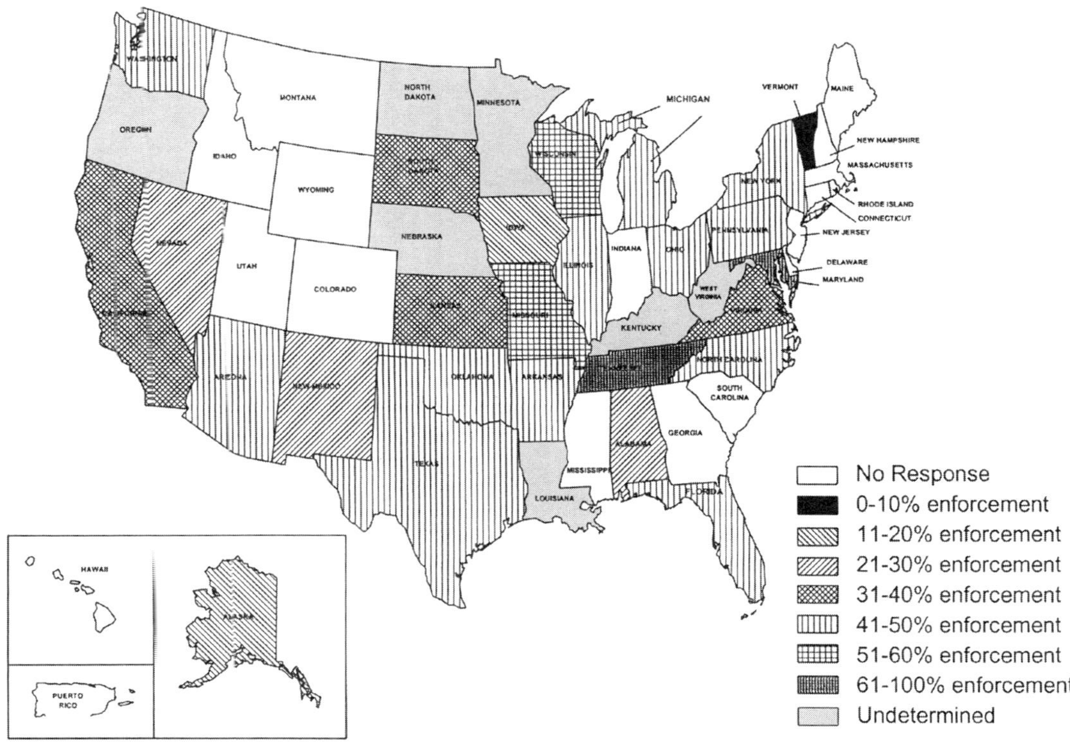

Figure 4-2 Time expended on speed enforcement as a percentage of total enforcement efforts, based on replies to a survey of 50 state agencies responsible for traffic law enforcement conducted for this study. Responses were received from 34 of the 50 agencies.

however, was less pronounced. Moreover, the distance-halo effect decayed quickly downstream of the enforcement site, following the general decay pattern of earlier studies (Hauer and Ahlin 1982, 277).[9] With regard to the time-halo effect, average traffic speeds remained depressed for 3 d following a single episode of enforcement activity and for considerably longer (up to 6 d) with repeated enforcement (Hauer and Ahlin 1982, 275). Similar results were found for the effect of police presence on urban driving speeds (Armour 1986, 45).

Increasing enforcement intensity should, according to deterrence theory, boost the deterrence effect by increasing the perceived risk of apprehension. In a review of European studies, Østvik and Elvik concluded that enforcement intensity must be increased significantly—to more than three times the initial level—before there is an appreciable effect on the perceived risk of detection or reduction in the number of speeding offenses (1991, 57).[10] Studies of experience from other enforcement campaigns that have significantly increased the certainty of apprehension, such as anti-drunk-driving programs, have found the same effect. Positive behavioral and safety effects are evident immediately after the adoption of the program. With a major initiative, the effect can last from a few months to a few years (Ross 1984, 29). However, deterrence effects of even a major program can diminish with time (Ross 1984, 29). One explanation for this effect is the previously discussed behavioral adaptation of the police to the success of the program (Tsebelis 1993, 366). Another reason is that enforcement may deter the unwanted behavior but does not necessarily change the underlying attitudes that ultimately determine the behavior (De Waard and Rooijers 1994, 764; Rothengatter 1988, 599).

There is some evidence that those who drive well in excess of the speed limit are the most impervious to the deterrence effects of traditional enforcement methods. A recent study of an intensive police

[9] Hauer and Ahlin found that the effect of enforcement was reduced by half for approximately every 2,953 ft (900 m) downstream from the enforcement site (Hauer and Ahlin 1982, 277).

[10] According to the reviewers, increasing the level of enforcement by more then five times the initial level increases the perceived risk of detection, reduces the percentage of offenders, and may reduce the number of crashes by up to 20 to 30 percent (Østvik and Elvik 1991, 57).

intervention to reduce speeding on a 40-mph (64-km/h) urban road in northern England found a greater reduction in the number of drivers breaking the speed limit by a small amount than in the number exceeding the limit by 20 mph (32 km/h) or more (Holland and Conner 1996, 595). This finding corroborates a related drivers' survey (part of the same study), which indicated that those who admitted to breaking the speed limit by a large amount in the past showed more intention to speed in the future than did those who admitted to speeding by smaller amounts (Holland and Conner 1996, 595). As discussed in Chapter 2, driving well in excess of average speeds is associated with both higher crash probability and greater crash severity. This finding is confirmed by recent evidence from British Columbia that drivers with four or more excessive speed convictions had almost twice the overall crash rate of drivers whose most serious multiple offenses were simply exceeding the posted speed limit (Cooper 1997, 94).

Roadway environment and traffic density also affect the success of traditional enforcement methods. Poor roadway geometry makes it difficult to station a patrol vehicle to take accurate speed measurements. In urban areas, high traffic volumes can hamper efforts to monitor speeding and apprehend violators (Shinar and McKnight 1985, 398). In very congested traffic, speed enforcement becomes irrelevant.

Implications for Enforcement Strategies

The foregoing evidence on the deterrence effect of traditional enforcement methods has several implications for both the uses and limitations of these methods. First, traditional enforcement "works" when the level of enforcement is sufficient to convince most drivers of the strong likelihood of detection and sanctions if they exceed the speed limit. Moreover, the level of effort must be maintained, placing a strain on most enforcement agency budgets, if the deterrence effect is to be sustained. Drivers generally revert to standard behavior once enforcement is reduced. Thus, to ensure a high level of compliance, speed limits have to be set at levels that are largely self-enforcing, or at the lowest speed the police are able to enforce.

Second, there is some evidence that enforcement does not deter those high-speed drivers who travel well in excess of the speed limit and pose a hazard to both themselves and other road users. These drivers obviously pose a special challenge for law enforcement.

Finally, traditional enforcement methods are limited in certain contexts, particularly where road geometry is poor or when traffic is congested. In the following section, alternative ways of addressing these enforcement challenges are discussed.

ALTERNATIVE METHODS FOR INCREASING EFFECTIVENESS OF SPEED ENFORCEMENT

Optimizing Traditional Enforcement Methods

The deterrence effect of enforcement clearly depends on creating the impression that road users who violate the law have a high probability of being apprehended. One way to achieve a credible level of enforcement without overstraining enforcement resources is to enforce speed regulations where and when risk-taking behaviors are most evident and traffic volumes are sufficient to justify the effort (Zaal 1994, 16–17). Planned patrols on commuter routes at varying time intervals and locations, for example, were effective in extending the time- and, to a lesser extent, the distance-halo effects of enforcement (Brackett 1977). Patrol vehicle presence was reduced without disturbing the speed suppression effect, but only after an initial minimum 6 weeks of continuous speed control activity (Brackett 1977, 48, 71). Varying the location of police patrols on commuter routes appeared to extend the distance-halo effect, but the evidence was inconclusive (Brackett 1977, 67, 72).[11]

Selective deployment strategies can also target particular types of unwanted risk-taking behavior, such as driving well in excess of the speed limit. Care must be exercised, however, that drivers do not receive the wrong message (i.e., that the de facto speed limit is well

[11] The effect could have been created by CB radio reporting or the warnings of the presence of patrol vehicles by motorists flashing the headlights of their automobiles (Brackett 1977, 67).

above the posted limit plus a small tolerance). The targeted enforcement approach should have two effects. First, police presence should reduce unwanted behavior at high-risk locations and times. Second, planned but varying deployment schedules should extend the deterrence effect to a broader segment of the driving population by increasing the expectation that enforcement may be present but leaving drivers uncertain exactly when the enforcement will occur (Zaal 1994, 17).

A review of selective enforcement programs in the United States (Jernigan 1986) found that the most successful programs are (*a*) deployed at specific localities and times when unwanted behavior is most likely to occur, (*b*) made highly visible to the public, and (*c*) maintained for more than a single year (Jernigan 1986, 2–6). Making systematic safety gains from targeted enforcement strategies is difficult, however, because of the relative infrequency of crashes.

New Speed Enforcement Technologies

Laser Speed Measurement

Several new technologies have recently been introduced that could enhance the enforcement capabilities of police officers. Radar measurements of vehicle speeds have been the primary technology used by the police to detect speeders, but their effectiveness is compromised by radar detectors. Laser speed measurement presents an attractive alternative to law enforcement agencies because it offers the ability to target individual vehicles more accurately on multilane roads and is more difficult to detect than conventional radar (Figure 4-3).[12]

A recent study of the comparative effectiveness of radar and laser speed-measuring devices (Jones and Lacey 1997) suggested that laser devices should complement rather than replace conventional radar. With its widespread and easily detected signal, radar may have a bet-

[12] The narrow laser beam width (less than 0.5 degree) provides a high level of accuracy and thus is particularly effective for use in situations in which vehicle targeting is critical, for example, on multilane roads (Jones and Lacey 1997, xi). Moreover, the narrowness of the beam reduces the probability that a radar detector can identify the beam in time for the driver to slow down and avoid apprehension (Jones and Lacey 1997, 1).

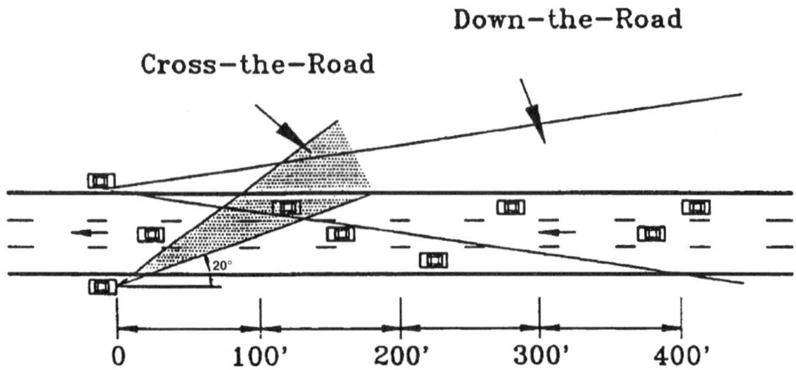

Figure 4-3 Comparison of conventional "down-the-road" radar technology with "cross-the-road" laser speed measurement (Fitzpatrick 1991, 7). 1 ft = 0.305 m.

ter general deterrence effect and thus is superior for general-purpose enforcement. Laser devices should be considered for situations where vehicle targeting is critical, such as monitoring speeders in high-traffic-volume conditions or in the left lane of a multilane facility (Jones and Lacey 1997, xi).

Automated Speed Enforcement

Automated speed enforcement (ASE) equipment has been in use for over 30 years. Recent technology improvements have enhanced its effectiveness.[13] With computer technology advances, sophisticated photographic and video equipment is now available for speed detection purposes. Most ASE systems incorporate some form of radar, which can determine vehicle speeds under most conditions; supplementary photographic equipment is used to record the speed and document information on the violator (Blackburn and Gilbert 1995, 4). The system can be mounted in a patrol car for conventional mobile

[13] This section draws heavily on a review of automated technologies for speed management and enforcement, which was commissioned for this study and appears in its entirety as Appendix D.

or stationary operation, or it can be attached to structures, such as poles or overpasses, for unattended operation (Blackburn and Gilbert 1995, 43–44).

ASE serves as a useful complement to traditional enforcement methods. It helps maintain an enforcement level that provides a meaningful deterrent to drivers by increasing the probability of detection for speeding violations. Because it can be deployed without police presence, ASE can increase the perceived level of risk to drivers and hence compliance levels without producing a reduction in police surveillance levels. It can be used in locations where patrol vehicles cannot be safely and effectively deployed. Moreover, when ASE is operated without police presence, it frees police for other traffic and law enforcement activities.

The primary ASE technology is photo radar, which combines a radar unit[14] and a computer that triggers a camera (or a video) to photograph a vehicle and its license plate if its speed exceeds some preset limit (Blackburn and Gilbert 1995, 4). The photograph records the time, date, location, and speed; the license plate is used to identify the vehicle owner. A citation is then mailed to the owner, who, depending on local laws, may be required to pay the fine or identify the offending driver. Owners can review the film at a police station and appeal the fine, but experience suggests that there are few challenges (Blackburn and Gilbert 1995, 22).

Photo radar has been used extensively abroad, and there has been some use in U.S. cities; this experience is reviewed in Appendix D. Some comprehensive efforts will be discussed here to illustrate the effect of photo radar on driving speeds and safety. One of the earliest evaluations of the effects of photo radar on speeds and crashes involved a high-crash location on a long downgrade section of the German autobahn between Cologne and Frankfurt (Lamm and Kloeckner 1984). The introduction of a 62-mph (100-km/h) speed limit, approximating the design speed for this highway segment, along with photo radar resulted in the desired reduction in driving

[14] Despite the greater precision of laser speed-measuring devices, the review of ASE technologies conducted for this study (Appendix D) did not find any examples of ASE systems that use laser technology.

speeds and a dramatic improvement in safety. Injury crash rates[15] dropped by a factor of 20 between 1971, before photo radar was introduced, and 1982, when an evaluation of the photo radar program was conducted (Lamm and Kloeckner 1984, 14).

Victoria, Australia, has perhaps the most extensive photo radar enforcement program in the world. The program was launched with a massive publicity campaign in 1989, primarily on arterial roads with 37-mph (60-km/h) speed limits in metropolitan Melbourne and rural Victoria, where there had been serious injury collisions and validated complaints of excessive speeding (Coleman et al. 1996, 43). Evaluation of the program's first 2 years found a statistically significant decline in casualty crash frequency[16] of 30 percent on arterial roads in Melbourne and 20 percent on rural roads, which corresponded to a greater level of speed camera enforcement on metropolitan Melbourne roads (Cameron et al. 1992, vi). The researchers attributed the decline to the deterrence effect of a dramatic increase in speeding offender detection and a related publicity effort (Cameron et al. 1992, ii). Speeding tickets in Victoria increased from about 20,000 per month before the program was launched to between 40,000 and 80,000 per month when photo radar was in use. Over the 2-year period, more than 20 percent of all drivers received at least one speeding ticket (Coleman et al. 1996, 42). Speed data suggest that the program was also successful in virtually eliminating very high-speed driving in the vicinity of photo radar deployment. In 5 years of operation, the percentage of vehicles exceeding the speed limit tolerance of nearly 10 mph (16 km/h) was reduced from 23 percent to 3 percent (Coleman et al. 1996, 44). A study of speed data taken near the permanent speed-monitoring sites confirmed these results for excessive speeding but found little change in average speeds and 85th percentile speeds (Rogerson et al. 1994, 33).

Norway introduced photo radar in 1988. A carefully designed before-and-after study found a statistically significant 20 percent

---

[15] Rates are measured as injury crashes per 10^6 vehicle-km.

[16] This crash reduction occurred during "low-alcohol" hours. Crash times were separated into low- and high-alcohol hours to help distinguish the effects of the speed program from a concurrent drinking/driving campaign.

reduction in injury crashes for 64 road sections with ASE (Elvik 1997, 17).[17] The largest reductions were found on sections that met two criteria that are currently used for ASE road selection: (*a*) a crash rate criterion, that is, crash rates higher than for similar road classes, and (*b*) a crash density criterion, that is, injury crash levels greater than or equal to 0.5 injury crashes per kilometer per year (Elvik 1997, 14). Nonrandom selection of study sites, however, limits generalization of the results. Data from Norway were combined with results from 15 other data sets of reported effectiveness of ASE, primarily in other European countries.[18] The combined data indicated that a statistically significant 17 percent average injury crash reduction accompanied the introduction of photo radar (Elvik 1997, 18).

Photo radar has been used sparingly in the United States. Programs are currently operating in four states—Arizona, Colorado, Oregon, and California (see Appendix D for details). Two of the best-known programs—in Paradise Valley, a small community in the Phoenix metropolitan area, and in Pasadena, California—operated for several years. Photo radar was deployed in staffed police vehicles on residential and arterial streets in both locations (Blackburn and Gilbert 1995, 34). Police data suggest that crashes were reduced, but scientifically designed studies of program effectiveness have not been conducted (Blackburn and Gilbert 1995, 37). Public opinion surveys conducted in both communities found high awareness of and support for the programs; nearly 60 percent of the respondents from both communities approved of the use of photo radar (Freedman et al. 1990, 62). However, a sizable minority (37 percent) disapproved. Since the survey was conducted, the Pasadena program has been terminated because of erosion of public support, loss of the equipment

[17] The analysis controlled for potential bias from regression to the mean. This adjustment was necessary because abnormally high crash rates are one of the criteria for using ASE; thus selection bias is potentially a serious source of error (Elvik 1997, 15).
[18] The countries are Germany, Sweden, England, the Netherlands, and Australia (Elvik 1997, 18). A statistical technique known as the logodds method of meta-analysis was used to combine the results. The method was essentially the same as combining the data from the 64 individual road sections in Norway. The results were then weighted by the crash sample size from each country to derive a weighted mean change in injury crashes (Elvik 1997, 18).

vendor, and a reduction in police personnel (for more details see Appendix D).

The primary issues regarding photo radar use in the United States are not technical but rather legal and political. Constitutional issues, such as the right to privacy and protection against illegal search and seizure, are frequently raised by opponents of photo radar use. However, state and Supreme Court decisions have ruled that driving on a public highway does not afford protections cited in the Fourth Amendment to the U.S. Constitution. It is difficult to prove that photo radar is an unreasonable exercise of police power because of its minimal intrusiveness and its legitimate public safety purpose (Gilbert 1996, 9).

Owner versus driver issues are another legal concern. Deployment of photo radar systems is simplest when the law holds vehicle owners responsible for speeding violations whether or not they were driving at the time of the infraction.[19] This reduces the burden of providing a clear frontal photograph of the driver.[20] Owner liability typically requires enabling legislation such as has been passed in Australia, the Netherlands, and some U.S. jurisdictions (Gilbert 1996, 7).[21] This legislation is easier to enact if the sanctions are civil rather than criminal. This approach treats the violation much the same as a parking ticket. In many European countries and in Australia, however, fines are graduated according to the amount of the speed violation; points can be assessed against the driver's record, and licenses can be suspended for excessive speeding—presumably with a somewhat greater deterrence effect.

Public opinion is another important issue. Surveys conducted in Paradise Valley and Pasadena found that the primary objections to photo radar were the possibility of error (i.e., the wrong person gets

---

[19] Recent research on red light running in the United States found that most drivers who were ticketed were driving their own cars (Retting et al. 1998).

[20] Of course, the owner has a clear defense if the vehicle was reported stolen prior to the time of the violation (Gilbert 1996, 7).

[21] The Paradise Valley Ordinance, for example, provides that the owner or person in whose name the vehicle is registered pursuant to Arizona state law shall be held prima facie responsible for any speeding violation. The District of Columbia, Maryland, Michigan, Oregon, California, Virginia, and Utah have similar statutes (Gilbert 1996, 7).

the ticket) and perceived fairness (e.g., entrapment, lack of personal contact to explain mitigating circumstances) (Freedman et al. 1990, 65). The efficiency of photo radar in detecting speed violations can easily turn public opinion against use of the system and has been responsible for terminating some programs (Blackburn and Gilbert 1995, 33–36). One method of addressing the fairness and "big brother" concerns is to publicize any program using photo radar at its inception, perhaps use warnings rather than fines at first, and to provide signs informing the public that ASE is in force along highways where the devices may be in use (Gilbert 1996, 9).

There are costs associated with the acquisition, deployment, operation, and maintenance of ASE equipment. However, photo radar can generate revenue, which can partially or completely offset such costs.[22] From the public perspective, one issue is who receives the revenues and for what purpose. In many U.S. communities, fines go to the jurisdiction rather than the local police department, with the result that the police are unable to cover program costs and thus drop the program. Another issue is use of the revenues; the public will not be supportive if they believe the devices are being deployed as fund-raising "speed traps."

Current experience suggests that photo radar's success depends heavily on how it is introduced. First, it is important to deploy photo radar at sites where the safety record indicates and the public perceives there is a problem, perhaps including school and construction zones, locations with high crash rates, and sites where traditional police enforcement can be dangerous (e.g., urban Interstates) (Streff and Schultz 1992). In some locations, communities have been involved in selection of these locations. To avoid any perception of entrapment, it would be wise to set high enforcement thresholds at first, targeting excessive speed limit violators [e.g., 20 mph (32 km/h)

---

[22] Most U.S. cities with ASE programs contract with a vendor to provide and support the equipment, train police officers, handle and process the film, research department of motor vehicle records, prepare citations, provide special photographic evidence for trials, and even provide expert testimony during trials (Blackburn and Gilbert 1995, 24). Depending on the penalty structure for speeding offenses, the program can be self-supporting.

or more over the speed limit].[23] Coupling the introduction of photo radar programs with high-visibility publicity campaigns can increase public awareness and inform motorists of how, where, and why the system will operate. Although these measures cannot guarantee success, they can ameliorate key obstacles to successful photo radar use.

Publicity

Whether new or conventional enforcement technologies are used, the effectiveness of speed enforcement can be enhanced by well-designed public information programs. Publicizing an enforcement program should increase driver awareness and expectation of intensified enforcement levels (Zaal 1994, 23). Of course, the publicity must be followed up with an active enforcement effort if the general deterrence effect is to be sustained. A further benefit of publicity programs is to increase public awareness of the reasons for the enforcement effort, which may help change underlying attitudes about the proscribed behavior or, at a minimum, create a more supportive climate for the enforcement program (Zaal 1994, 23).

Empirical evidence corroborates these effects. For example, experience with well-publicized anti-drunk-driving programs both abroad and in the United States suggests that sustained programs can deter drinking and driving (TRB 1987, 149–150). At least part of the decline in alcohol-related fatalities over the past decade can be attributed to a change in attitudes from greater publicity about the hazards of driving drunk and intensified enforcement.[24] Publicity campaigns in combination with primary belt use laws[25] and stepped-up enforcement have also resulted in sustained increases in safety belt use in several communities (Williams et al. 1996; Jonah et al. 1982).

[23] Again, this can be a two-edged sword if drivers perceive that the de facto speed limit is 20 mph (32 km/h) or more over the posted speed limit.

[24] The 17,126 alcohol-related fatalities in 1996 (41 percent of total traffic fatalities for the year) represents a 29 percent reduction from the 24,045 alcohol-related fatalities reported in 1986 (52 percent of the total) (NHTSA 1997, 1).

[25] Primary belt use laws enable law enforcement officers to stop and fine drivers who are not wearing safety belts.

A study of special speed enforcement programs in two California cities with extensive publicity programs to increase public awareness found statistically significant reductions in speed-related crashes (Stuster 1995, iii). Moreover, the general deterrence effect appeared to spill over and contribute to reductions in certain types of crimes (Stuster 1995, iv).

However, permanent behavior changes are not easy to achieve, as the experience with drunk driving and other public health initiatives such as antismoking campaigns has shown. A large-scale review of 87 road safety mass media campaigns for which some scientific evaluation had been performed found that, on the average, publicity campaigns can be expected to achieve about a 30 percent increase in awareness, but only a 5 percent change in attitudes and a 1 percent change in driver intentions (Elliott 1993, iv). Publicity is most effective when it is combined with enforcement in a long-term effort.

SANCTIONS AND ADJUDICATION

The courts play a key role in speed enforcement. Judges can undermine police enforcement by throwing out speeding violations or reducing fines when they believe that the limits are arbitrary or unreasonable or that the fines are too harsh. Thus the police and the traffic judges must agree that the speed limits are sensible if they are to be enforced.

Consistent treatment of speeding violations by the courts is also important to defuse any public perception that traffic regulations for speeding are arbitrary or capricious. Development of sentencing guidelines and training for traffic court judges who handle speeding violations can help ensure consistent treatment of violators. Licensing point demerit systems, which impose a system of graduated penalties for speeding and other traffic violations, have already assisted in reducing inconsistencies in penalty assessments.

The deterrence effect of sanctions for speeding violations is limited if lengthy court backlogs create a substantial lag between detection and punishment. New speed enforcement technologies, particularly photo radar, can simplify and streamline the adjudication process. For example, if speeding violations are treated as civil infractions, like parking tickets, with comparably priced fees, adjudication can be handled administratively for the most part, with a high potential for reducing court hearings and costs. Further, if legislation holds the owner of the vehicle responsible for the speeding violation as opposed to the driver, greater efficiencies can result. For example, when such vicarious liability legislation was passed in New South Wales, Australia, the cost of processing speeding offenses was reduced by approximately 50 percent (South et al. 1988 in Zaal 1994, 21).

A system that involves only civil sanctions and administrative adjudication procedures, however, is likely to have a limited deterrence effect. A fine for a speeding violation would not be reported on a driver's record; hence, no penalty would be imposed for repeated offenses. In addition, if fines are kept low to discourage costly court hearings and appeals, drivers may receive the message that the infraction is minor. Thus, efficiency may be gained at the price of effectiveness.

Some successful photo radar programs use a combined approach. For example, the Victoria, Australia, photo radar program introduced an automated traffic infringement notice (TIN) penalty system to allow efficient processing of offenses. The TIN informs the vehicle owner of the details of the offense as well as the penalties. The latter increase with the level of speeding over the posted speed limit; a combination of fines, license demerit points, or immediate license suspension may be imposed depending on the severity of the offense (Cameron et al. 1992, i). The vehicle's registered owner is liable for the penalties unless the owner identifies the driver at the time of the offense (Cameron et al. 1992, i).

The U.S. Paradise Valley photo radar program offers a similar combined approach. Drivers caught speeding 20 mph (32 km/h) or less over the posted speed limit are charged with a civil infraction. Those caught speeding more than 20 mph over the posted speed limit are charged with a misdemeanor (i.e., a criminal traffic offense) (Blackburn and Gilbert 1995, 22). If the civil infraction is ignored, a second notice is sent and the owner's driver's license is suspended until the fine is paid. If the criminal offense is ignored, the owner's driver's license is suspended and an arrest warrant is issued (Blackburn and Gilbert 1995, 22). An analysis of citations issued under the Paradise Valley ASE program in 1988 and 1989 found that most of those cited opted to pay the fine (31 percent) or attend a defensive driving class (37 percent). Fewer than 1 percent of the cases emanating from the citations went to trial, and, of these, the city prosecutor's office had an 82 percent conviction rate (Blackburn and Gilbert 1995, 22). In contrast, the Pasadena photo radar program, which did not have owner liability legislation and involved only monetary fines with limited provision for nonpayment, had large increases in speeding violators who ignored citations and declines in conviction rates as the program matured, which helped contribute to its demise (Blackburn and Gilbert 1995, 23).

SUMMARY

Enforcement and sanctions are necessary complements to speed limits. Simply posting a speed limit sign will not achieve desired driving speeds. Even if most drivers believe the limits are reasonable and comply with them, enforcement is essential to ensure conformity of the remaining drivers. Because the police have other important enforcement priorities and limited resources, their preferred strategy is to create a widely perceived impression that those who exceed the speed limits beyond some small tolerance band will be detected and apprehended. This approach is successful only if motorists perceive that they have a nontrivial chance of being apprehended if they speed.

The problem with traditional enforcement methods is their short-lived effect in deterring noncompliers. Extending the effect typically requires a level of enforcement intensity that exceeds the resources provided to the police for speed enforcement and other priorities. Policy makers can increase the resources directed toward speed enforcement, but providing adequate enforcement levels is expensive.

One approach is to stretch existing resources by increasing the effectiveness of traditional enforcement methods. Planned patrols at varying time intervals and locations on a highway section can extend the time- and, to a lesser extent, the distance-halo effects of enforcement. The effect can be sustained even with reduced patrols but only after a lengthy period of continuous initial enforcement. Some success has also been documented from selective targeting of enforcement at high hazard locations and on roads and at times when high-risk, speed-related behaviors are most common and traffic volumes are sufficient to justify the effort. Systematic safety gains from this approach are difficult to sustain because of the relative infrequency of crashes.

ASE technologies, particularly photo radar, offer an effective means of substantially increasing the intensity of enforcement and thereby the deterrence effect on speeding. Photo radar is widely used for speed control in Europe and Australia, with dramatic reductions in excessive speeding [i.e., exceeding the speed limit with a 10-mph (16-km/h) tolerance] and related reductions in casualty crash frequency. Photo radar use in the United States is limited because of legal and political, rather than technical, issues. If introduced selectively at first—at especially hazardous roads and locations with high crash rates—photo radar is likely to gain essential public support.

Whether new or traditional enforcement technologies are used, a well-designed public information program can help boost the deterrence effect. Publicity increases awareness and expectations of intensified enforcement. It can educate the public about the reasons for enforcement. To be credible, publicity must be followed up with an active enforcement effort.

Although not part of the enforcement process, the courts play a major role in ensuring motorist compliance with speed limits. Support of traffic court judges is essential to ensure that speeding violations are treated seriously and that offenders are handled consistently. Automated enforcement has the potential to reduce court backlogs and shorten the time between detection and punishment by substituting administrative adjudication procedures and civil sanctions (like parking fines) for some speeding infractions. The current system of speed limits, enforcement, and adjudication, however, is not effective for all situations. Other speed management strategies, some of which are reviewed in the next chapter, may be required.

REFERENCES

ABBREVIATIONS

NHTSA	National Highway Traffic Safety Administration
TRB	Transportation Research Board

Armour, M. 1986. The Effect of Police Presence on Urban Driving Speeds. *ITE Journal,* Feb., pp. 40–45.

Bjørnskau, T., and R. Elvik. 1990. Can Road Traffic Law Enforcement Permanently Reduce the Number of Accidents? *VTI Rapport 365A.* Institute of Transport Economics, Norway, pp. 122–145.

Blackburn, R.R., and D.T. Gilbert. 1995. *NCHRP Synthesis of Highway Practice 219: Photographic Enforcement of Traffic Laws.* Transportation Research Board, National Research Council, Washington, D.C., 67 pp.

Blumstein, A., J. Cohen, and D. Nagin. 1978. *Deterrence and Incapacitation: Estimating the Effects of Criminal Sanctions on Crime Rates.* National Academy of Sciences, Washington, D.C.

Brackett, R.Q., Jr. 1977. *Comparative Evaluation of Speed Control Strategies.* Dissertation. Texas A&M University, Dec., 99 pp.

Brier, S.S., and S.E. Fienberg. 1980. Recent Econometric Modeling of Crime and Punishment: Support for the Deterrence Hypotheses? *Evaluation Review,* Vol. 4, pp. 147–191.

Cameron, M., A. Cavallo, and A. Gilbert. 1992. *Crash-Based Evaluation of the Speed Camera Program in Victoria 1990-1991. Phase 1 and Phase 2.* Report 42. Accident Research Centre, Monash University, Victoria, Australia, Dec.

Cameron, S. 1988. The Economics of Crime and Deterrence: A Study of Theory and Evidence. *Kyklos,* Vol. 41, pp. 301–323.

Chauncey, R. 1975. Deterrence: Certainty, Severity, and Skyjacking. *Criminology,* Vol. 12, pp. 447–473.

Coleman, J.A., et al. 1996. *FHWA Study Tour for Speed Management and Enforcement Technology.* FHWA-PL-96-006. Federal Highway Administration, U.S. Department of Transportation, Feb., 83 pp.

Cooper, P.J. 1997. The Relationship Between Speeding Behaviour (as Measured by Violation Convictions) and Crash Involvement. *Accident Analysis and Prevention,* Vol. 28, No. 2, pp. 83–95.

Cox, G. 1994. A Note on Crime and Punishment. *Public Choice,* Vol. 78, Jan., pp. 115–124.

De Waard, D., and T. Rooijers. 1994. An Experimental Study To Evaluate the Effectiveness of Different Methods and Intensities of Law Enforcement on Driving Speed on Motorways. *Accident Analysis and Prevention,* Vol. 26, No. 6, pp. 751–765.

Elliott, B. 1993. *Road Safety Mass Media Campaigns: A Meta Analysis.* CR 118. Elliott & Shanahan Research, Sydney, New South Wales, Australia, Aug., 143 pp.

Elvik, R. 1997. Effects of Accidents on Automatic Speed Enforcement in Norway. In *Transportation Research Record 1595,* Transportation Research Board, National Research Council, Washington, D.C., pp. 14–19.

Fitzpatrick, K. 1991. *A Review of Automated Enforcement.* FHWA/TX-92/1232-5. Texas Transportation Institute, Texas A&M University System, College Station, Nov., 72 pp.

Freedman, M., A.F. Williams, and A.K. Lund. 1990. Public Opinion Regarding Photo Radar. In *Transportation Research Record 1270,* Transportation Research Board, National Research Council, Washington, D.C., pp. 59–65.

Gilbert, D.T. 1996. Photographic Traffic Law Enforcement. *Legal Research Digest No. 36,* National Cooperative Highway Research Program, Transportation Research Board, National Research Council, Washington, D.C., Dec.

Harper, J.G. 1991. Traffic Violation Detections and Deterrence: Implications for Automatic Policing. *Applied Ergonomics,* Vol. 23, No. 3, pp. 189–197.

Hauer, E., and F.J. Ahlin. 1982. Speed Enforcement and Speed Choice. *Accident Analysis and Prevention,* Vol. 14, No. 4, pp. 267–278.

Hirshleifer, J., and E. Rasmusen. 1992. Are Equilibrium Strategies Unaffected by Incentives? *Journal of Theoretical Politics,* Vol. 4, pp. 343–357.

Holland, C.A., and M.T. Conner. 1996. Exceeding the Speed Limit: An Evaluation of the Effectiveness of a Police Intervention. *Accident Analysis and Prevention,* Vol. 28, No. 5, pp. 587–597.

Jernigan, J. 1986. *How To Make Selective Enforcement Work: Lessons from Completed Evaluations.* VHTRC 870R15. Virginia Highway and Transportation Research Council, Charlottesville, 17 pp.

Jonah, B.A., N.E. Dawson, and G.A. Smith. 1982. Effects of a Selective Traffic Enforcement Program on Seat Belt Usage. *Journal of Applied Psychology,* Vol. 67, pp. 89–96.

Jones, R.K., and J.H. Lacey. 1997. *The Effectiveness of Laser and Radar Based Enforcement Programs for Deterrence of Speeding.* DOT-HS-808-530. Mid America Research Institute, Winchester, Mass., Feb., 70 pp.

Lamm, R., and J.H. Kloeckner. 1984. Increase in Traffic Safety by Surveillance of Speed Limits with Automatic Radar Devices on a Dangerous Section of a German Autobahn: A Long-Term Investigation. In *Transportation Research Record 974,* Transportation Research Board, National Research Council, Washington, D.C., pp. 8–16.

NHTSA. 1997. *Alcohol Traffic Safety Facts 1996.* U.S. Department of Transportation, 7 pp.

Østvik, E., and R. Elvik. 1991. The Effects of Speed Enforcement on Individual Road User Behaviour and Accidents. In *Enforcement and Rewarding: Strategies and Effects. Proc., International Road Safety Symposium* (M.J. Koornstra and J. Christensen, eds.), Copenhagen, Denmark, Sept. 19–21, 1990, pp. 56–59.

Piliavin, I., R. Gartner, C. Thornton, and R.L. Matsueda. 1986. Crime Deterrence and Choice. *American Sociological Review,* Vol. 51, pp. 128–135.

Retting, R.A., A.F. Williams, and M.A. Greene. 1998. Red Light Running and Sensible Countermeasures: Summary of Research Findings. Presented at 77th Annual Meeting of the Transportation Research Board, Washington, D.C.

Rogerson, P., S. Newstead, and M. Cameron. 1994. *Evaluation of the Speed Program in Victoria 1990–1991. Phase 3 and Phase 4.* Report 54. Accident Research Centre, Monash University, Victoria, Australia, Feb.

Ross, H.L. 1973. Law, Science and Accidents: The British Road Safety Act of 1967. *Journal of Legal Studies,* Vol. 2, pp. 1–78.

Ross, H.L. 1982. *Deterring the Drinking Driver.* Lexington Books, Lexington, Mass.

Ross, H.L. 1984. Social Control Through Deterrence: Drinking and Driving Laws. *Annual Review of Sociology,* Vol. 10, pp. 21–35.

Ross, H.L. 1990. Drunk Driving: Beyond the Criminal Approach: United States. In *Effective Strategies To Combat Drinking and Driving,* International Congress on Drinking and Driving, Edmonton, Alberta, Canada, March 28–30, pp. 217–220.

Ross, H.L., and G.D. LaFree. 1986. Deterrence in Criminology and Social Policy. In *Behavioral and Social Science, Fifty Years of Discovery* (N. J. Smelser and D.R. Gerstein, eds.), National Academy Press, Washington, D.C., pp. 129–152.

Rothengatter, J.A. 1988. Risk and the Absence of Pleasure: A Motivational Approach To Modelling Road User Behaviour. *Ergonomics,* Vol. 31, No. 4, April, pp. 599–607.

Rowsome, F., Jr. 1965. *The Verse by the Side of the Road.* The Penguin Group.

Sellin, T. 1967. Homicides in Retentionist and Abolitionist States. In *Capital Punishment* (T. Sellin, ed.), Harper and Row, New York, pp. 135–138.

Shinar, D., and A.J. McKnight. 1985. The Effects of Enforcement and Public Information on Compliance. In *Human Behavior and Traffic Safety* (L. Evans and R.C. Schwing, eds.), General Motors Research Laboratories, pp. 385–419.

Silberman, M. 1976. Toward a Theory of Criminal Deterrence. *American Sociological Review,* Vol. 41, pp. 442–461.

South, D., W.A. Harrison, and I. Portans. 1988. *Evaluation of the Red Light Camera Program and the Owner Onus Legislation.* SR/88/1. Victoria Transport, Road Traffic Authority, Hawthorn, Victoria, Australia, 35 pp.

Streff, F.M., and R.H. Schultz. 1992. *Field Test of Automated Speed Enforcement in Michigan: Effects on Speed and Public Opinion.* UMTRI-92-39. The University of Michigan Transportation Research Institute, Ann Arbor, Sept., 135 pp.

Stuster, J.W. 1995. *Experimental Evaluation of Municipal Speed Enforcement Programs.* DOT-HS-808-325. Anacapa Sciences, Inc., Santa Barbara, Calif. , Aug.

Teeven, J.J., Jr. 1972. Deterrent Effects of Punishment: The Canadian Case. *Canadian Journal of Criminology and Corrections,* Vol. 14, pp. 68–82.

Tittle, C.R. 1969. Crime Rates and Legal Sanctions. *Social Problems,* Vol. 16, pp. 409–423.

Tsebelis, G. 1990. Penalty Has No Impact on Crime: A Game Theoretic Analysis. *Rationality and Society,* Vol. 2, pp. 255–286.

Tsebelis, G. 1993. Penalty and Crime: Further Theoretical Considerations and Empirical Evidence. *Journal of Theoretical Politics,* Vol. 5, No. 3, pp. 349–374.

TRB. 1984. *Special Report 204: 55: A Decade of Experience.* National Research Council, Washington, D.C., 262 pp.

TRB. 1987. *Special Report 216: Zero Alcohol and Other Options: Limits for Truck and Bus Drivers.* National Research Council, Washington, D.C., 196 pp.

Waldo, G.P., and T.G. Chiricos. 1972. Perceived Penal Sanction and Self-Reported Criminality: A Neglected Approach to Deterrence Research. *Social Problems,* Vol. 19, pp. 522–540.

Weissing, F., and E. Ostrom. 1991. Crime and Punishment: Further Reflections on the Counterintuitive Results of Mixed Strategy Equilibria Games. *Journal of Theoretical Politics,* Vol. 3, pp. 343–350.

Williams, A.F., D. Reinfurt, and J.K. Wells. 1996. Increasing Seat Belt Use in North Carolina. *Journal of Safety Research,* Vol. 27, No. 1, pp. 33–41.

Wilson, J.Q. 1983. *Thinking About Crime* (revised edition). Vintage Books, New York.

Zaal, D. 1994. *Traffic Law Enforcement: A Review of the Literature.* Report 53. Monash University Accident Research Centre, Victoria, Australia, April, 188 pp.

5

Other Speed Management Strategies

Statistics prove
Near and far
That folks who
Drive like crazy
—Are
Burma Shave (Rowsome 1965)

Speed limits are one of the oldest strategies for controlling vehicle operating speeds, but they are not effective in all driving situations. For example, speed limits are frequently violated on local streets in urban areas, where the level of enforcement required to achieve compliance with posted speed limits using traditional enforcement methods is prohibitively expensive. In this chapter, alternative methods for controlling speeds are briefly considered. Most topics have been covered extensively elsewhere. The approaches discussed here include highway design, infrastructure improvements, and traffic control; intelligent vehicle- and highway-related technologies; and interventions for special populations, particularly older drivers and new teenage drivers.

ROADWAY DESIGN, INFRASTRUCTURE IMPROVEMENTS, AND TRAFFIC CONTROL

Approaches that fall under this category are focused on controlling driving speeds by changes in roadway design, physical changes to the roadway, and traffic operations rather than by behavioral approaches such as enforcement or public education.

Designing Roads To Manage Speed

The traditional approach to designing a new road is to define the function of a facility (e.g., through travel, distribution, access) and its expected level of service (AASHTO 1994). These characteristics, in turn, guide the choice of a design speed, which governs selection of horizontal and vertical elements of new roads—sharpness and extent of banking of horizontal curves and rate of grade change of vertical curves—as well as stopping sight distances and intersection sight distances (AASHTO 1994). In contrast, speed limits, particularly speed limits in speed zones, are often based on driver operating speeds (e.g., 85th percentile speeds), which, in turn, affect the timing of traffic signals (FHWA 1988) and other operational considerations. These different procedures can lead to inconsistencies among design speeds, speed limits, and driver operating speeds. Such differences are not necessarily cause for alarm. Design criteria have considerable built-in safety margins.[1] Hence it may be appropriate to travel at speeds

[1] Design criteria are often based on worst-case scenarios and performance characteristics of older vehicles (e.g., locked-wheel braking on wet pavements) (Krammes et al. 1996, 14). In addition, many highway features are constructed with more than minimum design values so that the design speed may actually apply to only a small number of critical features on a road segment. As a result, the design speed of a highway is likely to understate the "maximum safe speed" over much of its length (Krammes et al. 1996, 14).

higher than the design speed on a particular highway section. However, the dispersion in traffic speeds—a contributing factor to crash involvement—appears to be lowest when the difference between design speed and the posted speed limit is small (Garber and Gadiraju 1988, 23–25).

An alternative design approach that attempts to achieve greater consistency among design speeds, actual driving speeds, and posted speed limits is under development in the United States. The idea is to design roads to ensure that driver operating speeds are consistent with a target operating speed. Roadway geometry is commensurate with this target speed and, thus, is more consistent with motorists' expectations of appropriate speeds for conditions (Poe et al. 1996, 2-1). Highway geometric design procedures in Europe and Australia currently incorporate predicted vehicle operating speeds as an important determinant of highway design (Poe et al. 1996, 2-1).[2]

The key to the approach is the accurate prediction of target operating speeds. Thus, research in the United States is currently focused on development of models for predicting expected speeds as a function of roadway geometry, land use, and other traffic elements (Poe et al. 1996, xix).[3] The methodology presented by Poe et al. considers the relationship between vehicle operating speeds and roadway geometric design elements. Model development efforts are focused on higher-speed, two-lane rural highways where inadequate consistency and continuity of design contribute to wide dispersions in driving speeds and increased crash risk.[4] Models are also being developed for

---

[2] The Netherlands has embarked on a comprehensive program to rationalize its entire road system to bring road function, use, and vehicle travel speeds into greater harmony (see discussion in Chapter 3 under the section "Application of Speed Limits").

[3] The Federal Highway Administration (FHWA) is sponsoring research on a Design Consistency Evaluation Module as part of a comprehensive effort to develop an Interactive Highway Safety Design Model that would enable highway designers to consider safety systematically in developing and evaluating cost-effective highway design alternatives (Paniati and True 1996, 55).

[4] In addition to the FHWA-sponsored research to develop a computer tool, a National Cooperative Highway Research Project (15-17) is under way whose objective is to develop guidelines that designers can use to improve the geometric design consistency of roadway features on higher-speed, nonurban, two-lane roads.

low-speed urban streets where driving speeds often exceed desired levels, particularly where the roads are shared with vulnerable pedestrians and bicyclists (Poe et al. 1996; Tarris et al. 1996). Poe et al. (1996, 13-3) found that driver operating speeds on urban streets are affected by such design features as roadway alignment (i.e., how straight or curving the road is) and lane width. Thus, curving roadways and narrower lane widths on residential streets could help achieve desired lower driving speeds.

The effort to achieve greater congruence between highway design and driver expectations of appropriate operating speeds clearly has potential to improve safety. However, more research, validation of model results, and better understanding of the safety benefits of alternative designs are required before the approach can be adopted as standard design practice.

Traffic Calming

"Traffic calming" refers to a variety of physical measures to reduce vehicular speeds, primarily in residential neighborhoods. The idea originated in Europe, where the basic objective was to achieve calm, safe, and environmentally improved conditions on local streets (Pharoah and Russell 1989, 5). Some of the best-known and earliest examples of traffic calming were the Dutch "woonerf" schemes of the early 1970s, which reduced traffic speeds by the use of design treatments that aimed to give equal priority to pedestrians and other nonmotorized road users on neighborhood streets (Pharoah and Russell 1989, 4). Since that time, the concept has spread to other European countries, Australia, and the United States.

A primary reason for the approach is concern for pedestrian and bicycle safety on local streets. The risk of injury and death for pedestrians struck by a vehicle rises sharply as vehicle speed increases above very low impact speeds.[5] Thus, keeping speeds appropriately low is a priority on streets that are shared with pedestrians and other vulnerable road users. The ineffectiveness of speed limits in these sit-

[5] See relevant studies reviewed in Chapter 2 and Appendix B.

uations and the high cost of enforcement have led some communities to adopt traffic calming measures that physically constrain vehicle speeds.

Traffic calming treatments include measures to reduce vehicle speeds by narrowing the roadway and changing the path of the vehicle with roundabouts and traffic circles, widened sidewalks, raised median strips, chokers, and chicanes (Figure 5-1). Measures that make higher speeds uncomfortable—speed humps, raised intersections, and, to a lesser extent, rumble strips—are also common. Traffic calming treatments can be applied singly (e.g., speed humps on indi-

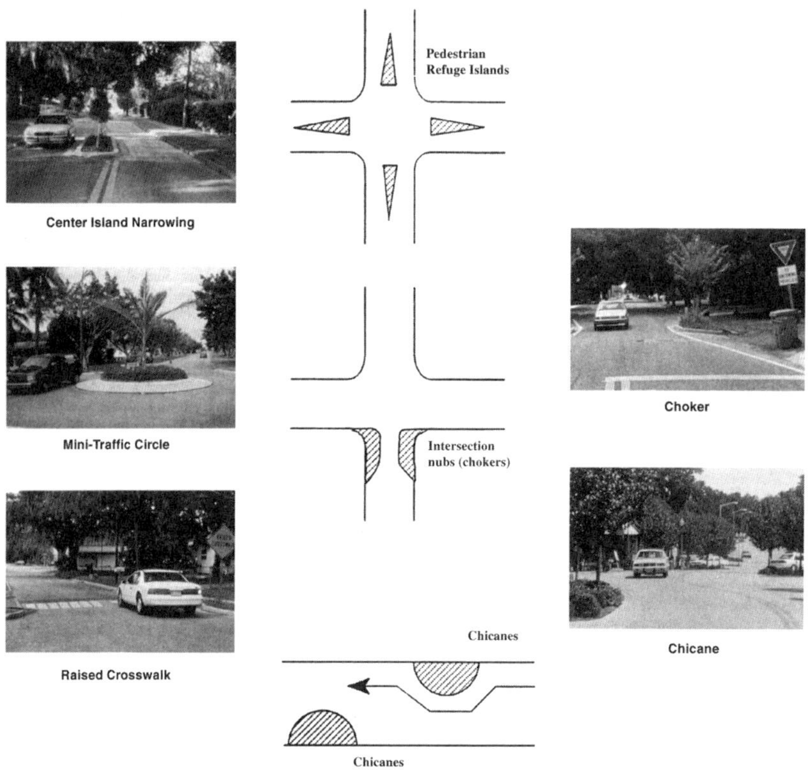

Figure 5-1 Examples of selected traffic calming techniques (Ullman 1996, 112; Ewing and Kooshian 1997, 28–33). (Photographs reprinted from *ITE Journal*, Vol. 67, No. 8, Aug. 1997, with permission.)

vidual streets) or in combination as part of an areawide strategy. They can range in expense from a speed hump, which costs $1,500 to $1,700, to traffic circles at local street intersections, which cost approximately $10,000 (Loughery and Katzman 1998, 14).

In the United States, traffic calming treatments are being adopted primarily on low-speed residential streets, although more comprehensive woonerf-type schemes have been undertaken in a few cities. Traffic calming is not considered suitable for urban arterial streets, which serve commuter and commercial traffic and carry emergency vehicles.[6] Although not widely used, traffic calming techniques are also appropriate in transition areas. For example, "gateway" treatments—a combination of road surface treatments and vertical elements, such as trees and lamp standards, to create the impression of passing through a narrowed entrance—can be used to alert drivers on rural roads to adapt their speeds as they approach villages or more built-up suburban and urban areas.[7]

Many studies have documented the speed and traffic-reducing effects of traffic calming (Pharoah and Russell 1989; Fildes and Lee 1993, 69–73; Loughery and Katzman 1998, 2–3). However, speed and traffic reduction on a treated street can divert the traffic and related speeding problems to neighboring streets. The speed hump program evaluation in Montgomery County, Maryland,[8] for exam-

---

[6] Concern has also been raised concerning response times of emergency vehicles on traffic-calmed residential streets. A recent study of the effect of an extensive speed hump program on residential streets in Montgomery County, Maryland, found that emergency response time was slowed somewhat by the presence of speed humps. Every five speed humps had the effect of increasing the distance between the station and the incident by 1/4 mi (0.4 km) compared with a response route without humps and assuming a travel speed of 25 mph (40 km/h) (Loughery and Katzman 1998, 5–6, Appendix E).

[7] Critiques of gateway schemes, particularly those aimed at reducing speed on rural roads at entrances to villages, suggest that their success depends on stringent physical measures to reduce speeds that must be applied at regular intervals to sustain speed reductions (Alink and Otten 1990 and Wheeler et al. 1994 in Comte et al. 1997, 23–24).

[8] The county has an extensive speed hump program. Since 1994, 1,150 speed humps have been installed on 300 county streets at an average cost of $1,650 per hump (Loughery and Katzman 1998, 1).

ple, found evidence of traffic diversion on parallel streets without speed humps (Loughery and Katzman 1998, 2–3). Of course, the net effect depends on the number of streets treated and the availability of parallel routes.

Many studies (Zein et al. 1997; Pharoah and Russell 1989; Brindle 1986; Fildes and Lee 1993) have also noted safety benefits of traffic calming, citing large reductions in crash frequency and injury severity, although safety is not the sole objective of neighborhood traffic calming projects. In theory, lowering vehicle speeds should reduce the severity of crashes, particularly those involving pedestrians. It is not as clear to what extent lower speeds on residential streets can reduce crash likelihood. The difficulty in studying these effects arises from the scattered pattern of crashes in residential areas and the small size of "before and after" data sets that limit statistical analysis (Pharoah and Russell 1989, 45).[9] In addition, just as traffic can migrate from treated to nontreated streets, so can crashes. Application of traffic calming techniques on an areawide basis should address traffic diversion. Reviews of low-speed zones in urban areas bear out this contention; speeds and crashes have been successfully reduced within the zones.[10] However, it is difficult to establish a direct causal link between speed reduction and crash reduction (Brindle 1986, 228) and to isolate the effects of traffic calming treatments because many of these areawide schemes have been accompanied by complementary policies, such as publicity campaigns and increased enforcement.

[9] The results of "before and after" crash data on traffic-calmed streets in Montgomery County provide some indication of the difficulty of measuring safety effects. The report noted that, of the 27 representative streets evaluated, 9 experienced a decrease in crashes after speed humps were installed and 2 experienced an increase. Where increases were reported, the number of crashes increased from zero to one. Six streets reported no change, but on five there were no crashes at all; the sixth street experienced only one crash. The 10 remaining streets had no available data (Loughery and Katzman 1998, 3–4).

[10] There is some evidence, however, that part of the decrease in crashes is due to the decrease in traffic volumes in the zones and diversion of traffic outside the zones. The diversionary effect needs to be studied further to assess the net safety effects of urban speed zones. (See discussions in Chapter 3 and Appendix C.)

Traffic Control

Operational measures can be used to slow traffic. In neighborhoods, multiway stop signs, traffic signals, turn prohibitions, and one-way streets have been used to manage speed. Because they require driver compliance, many operational measures (e.g., stop signs) are less effective than their physical counterparts in reducing driving speeds (Ullman 1996, 114).

If properly set and coordinated with posted speed limits, traffic signals can be an effective way of controlling speeds. Considerable advances have been made in designing and implementing computer-based signal control systems (GAO 1994). Improving signal timing can reduce vehicle stops and hence lessen the opportunities for rear-end collisions. It also encourages more uniform speeds. Mistimed signals can encourage speeding to avoid yellow or red lights and widen speed dispersion.

Perceptual Countermeasures

An alternative to physical changes to the road is less intrusive and lower-cost design treatments, known as perceptual countermeasures, which alter how drivers perceive the road or roadside (Fildes and Jarvis 1994, 1). A typical example is a patterned road surface (transverse road marking) that gives the appearance that one is traveling much faster than would be the case without the treatment. A range of other measures is available, including center and edge-line treatments; lane-width reductions; curvature enhancements; and delineators, guideposts, and chevrons. Most of these measures are low in cost, although some require continued maintenance to be effective. Thus, they may be appropriate in locations where more expensive treatments cannot be justified. However, their long-term effectiveness in reducing speeds is not well established and often appears to be site dependent (Fildes and Lee 1993, 77).

VEHICLE- AND HIGHWAY-RELATED TECHNOLOGIES

As vehicles have become more electronically advanced and improved technologies have enabled provision of real-time information between the highway and the vehicle, the groundwork has been laid for more sophisticated speed management strategies and more automated speed control measures. Many of these measures are encompassed under the Intelligent Transportation Systems program, whose goal is the improved safety and efficiency of highway travel. Some of these technologies are already in use. Others require more research and demonstration to ensure their reliability and public acceptance.

Vehicle-Related Technologies

Some motorists underestimate or misjudge their driving speed. With older vehicles, drivers had more physical cues about speed, including the tilting motion and sound of the tires when negotiating a sharp curve and the noise of the road when traveling at higher speeds (Comte et al. 1997, 39). Today, improved vehicle handling, high-performance tires, and air-conditioning systems mute these cues. Technologies are being developed to provide more information and feedback to the driver about driving speeds and, in the longer term, to create "intelligent" vehicle control systems.

Many such technologies are well along in development. For example, heads-up display speedometers that provide continuous speed information to drivers in their normal fields of view, rather than requiring drivers to look at the dashboard periodically to check speed, are available (Comte et al. 1997, 39). Speed checkers—electronic devices mounted on the dashboard that are activated by roadside transmitters at mileposts or on speed limit signs—have been tested for their potential to warn drivers that they are exceeding legal speed limits. Of course, user acceptance is likely to be better if the device is activated only in highly hazardous locations (Comte et al. 1997, 40). Emergency warning systems are also being developed. For example, sensors on the front of the vehicle could detect when a vehicle is closing too fast on the vehicle immediately ahead and warn the driver when the distance equals a predefined limit for the travel speed (TRB 1998, 32–33). A curve-approach warning system, using roadside communication beacons to provide information about roadway geometry, could alert drivers to sharp curves, warning them if the vehicle is approaching at excessive speed (TRB 1998, 33). This type of warning system could be particularly effective in forestalling speed-related, run-off-the-road crashes. However, commercialization and broad driver acceptance of many of these speed-related information systems depend on resolution of human factors issues, such as driver distraction and information overload.

Vehicle control technologies offer another level of sophistication in speed management. Conventional cruise-control systems, which are mainly used in freeway driving, already enable drivers to establish and maintain a fixed vehicle speed. More advanced adaptive cruise-control systems, which are under development by some automobile manufacturers and their suppliers, would use forward-looking sensors and adjust vehicle speeds automatically to maintain a safe following distance from the vehicle ahead (TRB 1998, 34). Key concerns are reliability and the pros (e.g., crash avoidance) and cons (e.g., driver inattentiveness) of automating critical driving tasks. Of course, fully developed collision avoidance systems would involve lane-departure avoidance systems as well as frontal-collision avoidance systems.

Speed governors offer a solution for limiting the maximum speed of a vehicle. Speed governors are required on heavy trucks that operate in countries that are part of the European Union (ECMT 1996, 32). Some U.S. trucking companies also use speed limiters, although increasingly sophisticated truck engines enable speeds to be controlled electronically. The primary reasons for using speed governors on heavy vehicles are fuel efficiency, safety, and equipment wear. In the United States, the speed governor or engine is usually set at the speed that provides maximum fuel efficiency, which generally falls below most current maximum speed limits on major highways. The use of speed limiters on passenger vehicles has been tested in Europe (Comte et al. 1997, 45–48), but issues of driver control, system cost—and, above all, consumer acceptance—are likely to preclude their widespread use in the foreseeable future.

Other speed-limiting approaches involve "smart cards," which combine vehicle functions with a driver's license and allow variable speed governing depending on the driver and the situation. For example, the smart card could prevent teenage drivers with provisional licenses or repeat offenders of drunk driving and speeding from exceeding certain speed thresholds. In the former case, the speed could be set by a parent; in the latter, by the courts.

Highway-Related Technologies

Road-based technologies use electronic capabilities to provide drivers with information about upcoming roadway conditions. One of the most commonly available technologies is variable message signs, which can be used for speed control. For example, a recent survey of permanently mounted changeable message sign usage in the United States and one Canadian province found the following speed-related uses: incident and traffic management, fog warnings, and warnings of other adverse weather and road conditions (Dudek 1997, 10). The effect of these signs on motorist behavior has not been studied extensively, and the studies that have been conducted tend to be out of date (Dudek 1997, 46). Use of variable message signs in Europe, particularly to display appropriate speed limits, appears to suffer from the same limited time- and distance-halo effects as traditional enforcement measures (Comte et al. 1997, 31).

Variable speed limits represent a more sophisticated use of variable message signs to convey information to drivers about appropriate speed limits. Variable speed limits are not in wide use on U.S. highways today. Where they do exist, their primary function is to provide weather advisories and appropriate speeds for hazardous conditions. Variable speed limits have been used more extensively in Europe, particularly on major motorways, for general speed management.[11] They are especially well suited to address temporal changes in traffic volumes, speed, and density on urban Interstate highways. More experience is needed concerning the efficiency gains and safety benefits of these systems. However, even if the results are highly positive, system costs are likely to limit their use to major highways.

Another road-based approach to managing speed is to provide drivers with direct feedback about their driving speeds through the use of mobile roadside speedometers. The devices usually include a speed

[11] For more detailed information on this experience, see discussions in Chapter 3 and Appendix D.

limit sign, a Doppler radar emitter and receiver to measure speeds, and a changeable message sign that displays the speed of the approaching vehicle to the driver (Casey and Lund 1993, 627). Local jurisdictions are experimenting with these devices to supplement traditional enforcement measures in problem speed locations on city streets, in neighborhoods, and in school and work zones.[12] An evaluation of the effectiveness of roadside speedometers under several controlled deployment strategies (e.g., varied, intermittent, and continuous deployment, each with and without enforcement) found that the speedometer's presence reduced average traffic speed, especially the speeds of those drivers exceeding the speed limit by at least 10 mph (16 km/h), in the vicinity of the device and short distances downstream; the device was particularly effective in school zones (Casey and Lund 1993, 627). However, the effectiveness was clearly linked with enforcement or implied enforcement, a finding of many other studies (Comte et al. 1997, 32–36). Unless coupled with periodic enforcement, roadside speedometers appear to be ignored by motorists whether the deployment is continuous or intermittent (Casey and Lund 1993, 634).

Fully Automated Vehicle and Highway Systems

Fully automated highways, which would combine many of the vehicle- and highway-related technologies described previously, would fully control speed essentially by taking the driving task away from the individual driver. To obtain the full efficiency benefits of close headways and high travel speeds, fully automated travel lanes would be required with traffic moving in coordinated platoons of fully automated vehicles (TRB 1998, 35–36.). A public demonstration of several automation technologies was held in San Diego, California, in August 1997, but prototype development, much less full deployment, of an automated highway system will not be realized any time soon.[13]

[12] Some jurisdictions are using the roadside speedometer readings to target enforcement by location and time of day.

[13] In fact, the U.S. Department of Transportation has shifted its research priorities to encourage development and deployment of nearer-term advanced vehicle control and

Even if reliability and liability issues could be resolved, the large investment costs will severely limit deployment of such a system to all but a few sections of major highways where the efficiency and safety gains might justify the expense.

SPECIAL DRIVING POPULATIONS

The problem of speeding or driving too fast for conditions is not confined to any one driving group, but certain groups of drivers—older drivers and younger drivers in particular—have special problems with speed. Aggressive drivers could also be included, but aggressive driving[14] has only recently been identified as a traffic safety problem and has not yet received much analytic review. In this section, the speed-related problems of older and younger drivers are identified and strategies to manage them are reviewed.

Older Drivers

Older drivers are one of the fastest-growing segments of the driving population. The 65 and older age group, which numbers about 34 million today, will exceed 50 million by 2020, accounting for approximately one-fifth of the driving age population in the United States (FHWA 1997, v).

Many older drivers have reduced capability to handle speed because of declining performance in visual, cognitive, and motor tasks that accompany aging (TRB 1988, 72). Vision, particularly night vision, becomes poorer and reflexes slower, so that older drivers generally have slower perception-reaction times (TRB 1988, 72). Older drivers tend to compensate for these changes by restricting their night driving and by driving slower than the prevailing traffic,

---

driver assistance features. This new Intelligent Vehicle Initiative, which deemphasizes the earlier target of fully automated driving, is focused on improving highway safety (TRB 1998, 5).

[14] Aggressive driving, or "road rage" as it is more commonly known, refers to driving behavior that endangers or is likely to endanger people or property (*AASHTO Journal* 1997, 8).

which may increase their risk of multivehicle crash involvement.[15] If a crash occurs, older persons are more likely to be injured because of their frailty (Mackay 1988).

Addressing the speed-handling capabilities of older drivers is not easy. In recent years, considerable research has been conducted on the question of whether highway design is sufficiently sensitive to assumptions about driver performance, particularly the performance of older drivers. Perception-reaction time is a key concept in models of driver behavior and highway design that underlie many highway design criteria. Current American Association of State Highway and Transportation Officials (AASHTO) design criteria assume a 2.5-s perception-reaction time for sudden stopping when the driver must brake in reaction to an unexpected obstacle (Lerner et al. 1995, 3)[16] and 2.0 s for estimating appropriate sight distances at intersections (AASHTO 1994, 704). Age differences were observed in experimental situations, with somewhat longer perception-reaction times for older drivers, but these differences are encompassed by AASHTO design criteria. No major changes in design parameters were recommended (Lerner et al. 1995, 95–97; Fambro et al. 1997).

Previously discussed technological advances in driver information systems and vehicle control technologies could enhance the ease and speed with which information is provided to the driver and simplify some driving tasks. These improvements would benefit all drivers, but could especially assist older drivers if the technologies are introduced in ways that do not distract drivers or overload their ability to process information.

Other suggestions for addressing the speed-handling capabilities of older drivers as well as their general driving skills include driver training programs especially tailored for older drivers and a graded licensing system for older drivers, which would restrict driving on the basis of the individual's capabilities. The effectiveness of training programs in improving the performance of older drivers has not been estab-

[15] See the reviews of studies linking crash involvement with deviation from average traffic speeds in Chapter 2 and Appendix B.

[16] This time consists of two components: 1 s for perceiving the situation and initiating action and 1.5 s for braking (TRB 1988, 63).

lished (McKnight 1988, 117). Technical issues, such as developing adequate licensing test procedures, and more general issues, such as age discrimination and mobility concerns, are major roadblocks to the introduction of modified licensing procedures for older drivers (TRB 1988, 73; Eberhard 1996, 36).

Younger Drivers

Although the U.S. population is aging, nearly a 20 percent increase in the population of 16- to 24-year olds is projected—from 36 million to 43 million potential drivers by 2020 (NHTSA 1997, 4). California estimates a one-third increase in its population of 15- to 19-year-olds over the next 10 years alone, the result of delayed childbearing by the Baby Boom generation, high levels of immigration, and high birth rates in parts of the population (*Highway and Vehicle Safety Report* 1998, 2–3).

In marked contrast to older drivers, younger drivers' problems with speeding are related to their propensity to take risks and their driving inexperience. Both characteristics can cause them to drive at speeds inappropriate for conditions.

Some states have enacted graduated licensing systems as one way to limit high-risk youthful driving behaviors, including speeding. The idea is to restrict the time and manner of driving in stages to allow beginning drivers to acquire on-the-road experience in lower-risk settings before obtaining a regular, unrestricted license (Status Report 1996, 1).[17] The emergence of graduated licensing systems in the United States provides an opportunity to revamp driver education programs, which, according to many studies, have fallen far short of their objective to reduce the crash experience of young drivers (Status Report 1997, 1).

Education is often recommended as a significant method of reducing risk behavior (DeJong 1991; DeJong and Atkin 1995; McMahaon 1986; Brownell et al. 1986). Many public health pro-

[17] Typical elements of a graduated licensing system include a mandatory supervised driving period, night driving curfew, limits on teenage passengers riding with a beginning driver, a freeway driving restriction, and a lower blood alcohol concentration threshold for teenagers than for adults (Status Report 1996, 1–2).

grams intended to promote healthy choices and reduce risky ones have included an education component. Efforts in smoking cessation, nutrition, exercise, pregnancy prevention, and substance abuse are examples. It is therefore likely that education should be considered as a component in working with driver groups, such as teenage drivers, who are at higher risk of speed-associated traffic injury, to increase their compliance with posted speed limits or reduce inappropriate speeding behavior. Research on education in other risk reduction situations, however, indicates that education intended to frighten individuals into changed behavior has only limited, short-term efficacy, and that education alone is almost never sufficient to achieve long-term behavior change (Job 1988; Montezeri and McEwan 1997). It must be accompanied by other approaches that increase awareness of vulnerability and provide social support, such as peer group approval for the desired behavior (Farquahar 1978).

Both younger and older drivers have special, identifiable problems handling speed. However, finding effective strategies to address their speed-related problems is difficult and represents a significant challenge.

SUMMARY

In this chapter, several alternatives to speed limits for managing driving speeds have been considered. Road redesign—and to an even greater extent traffic calming—attempt to physically constrain driving speeds to desired levels. Traffic calming can be an effective strategy for reducing speed on some residential streets, but it is not considered suitable for major urban roads. Designing roads so that the resulting roadway geometry is more consistent with motorists' expectations of appropriate driving speeds has promise for existing as well as new highways, but more research is needed to determine the safety benefits of alternative designs. Preliminary findings indicate that, on low-speed urban streets, use of an operating speed model in the design process could bring actual speeds closer to intended speeds. Even if design procedures can be modified, however, road redesign is a long-term strategy because of the extent of highway mileage in the United States and the pace and cost of rehabilitation.

Technological advances to provide more "intelligent" vehicles and highways offer another approach. New ways of communicating information to the driver about appropriate driving speeds are under development, and advances in vehicle control technologies should enable automation of some speed-related driving functions. Introduction of these technological advances awaits resolution of human factors concerns, such as driver distraction and information overload, and—with more automated systems—issues of reliability, liability, driver control, and acceptance. Some systems may become commercially available shortly, but it will be several years before they become standard equipment on all motor vehicles.

The most challenging approaches are those that attempt to change driver behaviors and attitudes toward speeding. Special populations, particularly older drivers and young drivers, have been identified as having particular, though different, problems with speeding. As the experience with other risky behaviors such as drinking and driving or smoking has shown, attitudinal changes are possible. They require awareness and understanding of risk and a long time frame. In the case of speeding, aging of the population and continued or more frequent aggressive driving could result in more negative attitudes toward speeding and greater compliance with speed limits than are evident today. Of course, if vehicles and roads become safer, motorists could favor higher limits, at least on the safest roads.

The approaches identified in this chapter offer a range of methods for controlling driving speeds. Their use is often limited to certain types of roads or settings (e.g., residential streets). For the foreseeable future, their most likely application is to complement and enhance rather than to supplant speed limits. For the longer term, they represent important areas of innovation and opportunity that bear watching and evaluation.

REFERENCES

ABBREVIATIONS

AASHTO	American Association of State Highway and Transportation Officials
ECMT	European Conference of Ministers of Transport

FHWA	Federal Highway Administration
GAO	General Accounting Office
NCHRP	National Cooperative Highway Research Program
NHTSA	National Highway Traffic Safety Administration
TRB	Transportation Research Board

AASHTO. 1994. *A Policy on Geometric Design of Highways and Streets.* Washington, D.C.

AASHTO Journal. 1997. Hearing Addresses Aggressive Driving. Vol. 97, No. 29, July 18, pp. 7–9.

Alink, G.M.M., and N. Otten. 1990. Das Fahrverhalten an Ortseinfahrten—eine Validitätsstudie. Im: Forschungsinstrument Fahrsimulator, Report 11, Schriftenreihe der Daimler-Benz AG.

Brindle, R. 1986. The Relationship Between Traffic Management, Speed and Safety in Neighborhoods. In *Living With Traffic,* Special Report 53, Australian Road Research Board, Victoria, pp. 217–231.

Brownell, K., G. Marlatt, et al. 1986. Understanding and Preventing Relapse. *American Psychologist,* Vol. 41, pp. 765–782.

Casey, S.M., and A.K. Lund. 1993. The Effects of Mobile Roadside Speedometers on Traffic Speeds. *Accident Analysis and Prevention,* Vol. 25, No. 5, pp. 627–634.

Comte, S., A.Várhelyi, and J. Santos. 1997. *The Effects of ATT and Non-ATT Systems and Treatments on Driver Speed Behaviour.* MASTER Working Paper R. 3.1.1. Managing Speeds of Traffic on European Roads, Aug.

DeJong, W. 1991. On the Use of Mass Communications To Promote the Public Health. In *Surgeon General's Workshop on Organ Donation: Background Papers.* Office of the Surgeon General, U.S. Department of Health and Human Services, Rockville, Md.

DeJong, W., and C.K. Atkin. 1995. Review of National Television PSA Campaigns for Preventing Alcohol Impaired Driving, 1987–1992. *Journal of Public Health Policy,* Vol. 16, No. 1, Spring, pp. 59–80.

Dudek, C.L. 1997. *NCHRP Synthesis of Highway Practice 237: Changeable Message Signs.* Transportation Research Board, National Research Council, Washington, D.C., 47 pp.

Eberhard, J.W. 1996. Safe Mobility for Senior Citizens. *IATSS Research,* Vol. 20, No. 1, pp. 29–37.

ECMT. 1996. *Speed Moderation.* Organisation for Economic Cooperation and Development. OECD Publications Service, Paris, 86 pp.

Ewing, R., and C. Kooshian. 1997. U.S. Experience with Traffic Calming. *ITE Journal,* Vol 67, No. 8, Aug., pp. 28–33.

Fambro, D.B., K. Fitzpatrick, and R.J. Koppa. 1997. *NCHRP Report 400: Determination of Stopping Sight Distances.* Transportation Research Board, National Research Council, Washington, D.C.

Farquahar, J.W. 1978. The Community-Based Model of Life-Style Intervention Trials. *American Journal of Epidemiology,* Vol. 108, pp. 103–111.

FHWA. 1988. *Manual on Uniform Traffic Control Devices.* U.S. Department of Transportation.

FHWA. 1997. *Older Driver Highway Design Handbook.* Draft. U.S. Department of Transportation, March, 249 pp.
Fildes, B.N., and J.R. Jarvis. 1994. *Perceptual Countermeasures: Literature Review.* Research Report CR4/94. Monash University Accident Research Centre and Australian Road Research Board Ltd., Nov., 52 pp.
Fildes, B.N., and S.J. Lee. 1993. *The Speed Review: Road Environment, Behaviour, Speed Limits, Enforcement and Crashes.* Monash University Accident Research Centre, Victoria, Australia, Sept., 146 pp.
Garber, N.J., and R. Gadiraju. 1988. *Speed Variance and Its Influence on Accidents.* University of Virginia, Charlottesville, July, 56 pp.
GAO. 1994. *Transportation Infrastructure: Benefits of Traffic Control Signal Systems Are Not Being Fully Realized.* GAO/RCED-94-105. Washington, D.C., March.
Highway and Vehicle Safety Report. 1998. California Office of Traffic Safety Warns of "Youthquake." Vol. 24, No. 8, Jan. 5, pp. 2–3.
Job, R.F.S. 1988. Effective and Ineffective Use of Fear in Health Promotion Campaigns. *American Journal of Public Health*, Vol. 78, pp. 163–167.
Krammes, R.A., K. Fitzpatrick, J.D. Blaschke, and D.B. Fambro. 1996. *Speed: Understanding Design, Operating, and Posted Speed.* Report 1465-1. Texas Transportation Institute, College Station, March, 16 pp.
Lerner, N.D., R.W. Huey, H.W. McGee, and A. Sullivan. 1995. *Older Driver Perception-Reaction Time for Intersection Sight Distance and Object Detection. Final Report. Vol. I.* FHWA-RD-93-168. COMSIS Corporation, Silver Spring, Md., Jan., 116 pp.
Loughery, D.A., and M. Katzman. 1998. *Speed Hump Program Evaluation Report.* Montgomery County, Md., Jan.
Mackay, M. 1988. Crash Protection for Older Persons. In *Special Report 218: Transportation in an Aging Society, Vol. 2,* Transportation Research Board, National Research Council, Washington, D.C., pp. 158–193.
McKnight, A.J. 1988. Driver and Pedestrian Training. In *Special Report 218: Transportation in an Aging Society, Vol. 2,* Transportation Research Board, National Research Council, Washington, D.C., pp. 101–133.
McMahaon, J.D. 1986. Lewin's Force Field Theory Applied to Behavior Change. *Journal of School Health*, Vol. 53, No. 3, March, pp. 109–110.
Montezeri, A., and J. McEwan. 1997. Effective Communication. *Patient Education and Counselling*, Vol. 30, No. 6, Jan., pp. 29–35.
NHTSA. 1997. *NHTSA 2020 Report.* U.S. Department of Transportation, Sept., 13 pp.
Paniati, J.F., and J. True. 1996. Interactive Highway Safety Design Model (IHSDM): Designing Highways with Safety in Mind. In *Transportation Research Circular 453,* Transportation Research Board, National Research Council, Washington, D.C., Feb., pp. 55–60.
Pharoah, T.M., and J.R.E. Russell. 1989. *Traffic Calming: Policy and Evaluations in Three European Countries.* Occasional Paper. South Bank Polytechnic, London, Oct., 67 pp.

Poe, C.M., J.P. Tarris, and J.M. Mason, Jr. 1996. *Relationship of Operating Speeds to Roadway Geometric Design Speeds.* FHWA-RD-96-024. Pennsylvania Transportation Institute, The Pennsylvania State University, University Park, Dec., 268 pp.

Rowsome, F., Jr. 1965. *The Verse by the Side of the Road.* The Penguin Group.

Status Report. 1996. Race on Among the States. Vol. 31, No. 7, Insurance Institute for Highway Safety, Aug. 10, pp. 1–3.

Status Report. 1997. Driver Education Does Not Equal Safe Drivers. Vol. 32, No. 1, Insurance Institute for Highway Safety, Jan. 11, pp. 1–6.

Tarris, J.P., C.M. Poe, J.M. Mason, Jr., and K.G. Goulias. 1996. Predicting Operating Speed on Low-Speed Urban Streets: Regression and Panel Analysis Approaches. In *Transportation Research Record 1532,* Transportation Research Board, National Research Council, Washington, D.C., pp. 46–54.

TRB. 1988. *Special Report 218: Transportation in an Aging Society. Vol. 1.* National Research Council, Washington, D.C., 125 pp.

TRB. 1998. *Special Report 253: National Automated Highway System Research Program: A Review.* National Research Council, Washington, D.C.

Ullman, G.L. 1996. Neighborhood Speed Control—U.S. Practices. *Compendium of Technical Papers for the 66th ITE Annual Meeting,* Minneapolis, Minn., Sept. 15–18, 115 pp.

Wheeler, A., M. Taylor, and J. Barker. 1994. *Speed Reduction in 24 Villages: Details from the VISP Study.* Project Report 85. Transport Research Laboratory, Crowthorne, United Kingdom.

Zein, S.R., E. Geddes, S. Hemsing, and M. Johnson. 1997. Safety Benefits of Traffic Calming. In *Transportation Research Record 1587,* Transportation Research Board, National Research Council, Washington, D.C., pp. 3–10.

6

Guidance on Setting and Enforcing Speed Limits

In this chapter the committee offers its guidance on appropriate methods of setting and enforcing speed limits. Speed limits represent trade-offs between risk and travel time for a road class or specific highway section that reflect the decision makers' attempt to achieve an appropriate balance between the societal goals of safety and mobility. The process of setting speed limits is often viewed as a technical exercise, but the decision involves value judgments and trade-offs that are frequently handled through the political process in state legislatures and city councils. Thus, the guidance offered here is directed toward a broad audience of those involved in decisions about setting and enforcing speed limits: state and local legislators, traffic engineers, law enforcement and judicial officials, and the interested general public.

The guidance attempts to be as specific as possible, recognizing that decision makers are looking for practical advice. However, it stops short of recommending numeric speed limits. Road conditions vary too widely to justify a "one-size-fits-all" approach. There is no single "right" answer in setting appropriate speed limits because policy makers in different communities may legitimately disagree on the priority given to the factors—safety, travel time, enforcement expenditures, community concerns—that affect decisions about speed limits. Moreover, the available studies and data fall short of providing decision makers with an adequate basis on which to quantify with much precision the effects of changes in speed limits on such critical factors as driving speeds, safety, and travel time by road class. Technical input on how these factors should be weighed in different situations, however, can help guide the decision. Thus, the focus here is to identify the critical decision factors, elaborate what is known and what is not known about their importance by road class, and comment on the decision-making process itself. The primary focus is on the effects of speed limit policies on safety, rather than on travel time, energy consumption, or environmental pollution.

The chapter is organized as a series of questions and answers. It begins with a general discussion of the rationale, purpose, and current methods of setting speed limits both for broad road classes (legislated limits) and specific road sections (speed zones). The decision process for determining speed limits is then discussed. Next, a roadway classification scheme is offered, which distinguishes seven different road classes and a category for special zones (i.e., school and work zones); advice is provided on the key factors for consideration in determining appropriate speed limits for each category. The role and limits of current enforcement and adjudication methods in regulating driving speeds are then discussed. Finally, the potential for technology to improve methods of determining and enforcing speed limits is considered. Key points are highlighted in bold in the text that follows.

WHY REGULATE DRIVING SPEEDS?

The argument can be made that most motorists drive in a reasonable and prudent manner, selecting their driving speeds so as to arrive at their destinations safely. If this is so, why not leave it up to the individual driver to determine an appropriate speed? **There are three principal reasons for regulating drivers' individual speed choices: (*a*) externalities, that is, the risks and uncompensated costs imposed**

on others because of individual driver choices about appropriate driving speeds; (*b*) inadequate information that limits a motorist's ability to determine an appropriate driving speed; and (*c*) driver misjudgment of the effects of speed on crash probability and severity.

The first reason derives from differences in drivers' risk tolerances. For example, in selecting an appropriate driving speed, an older driver is apt to assign more weight to the risks of mortality and injury to himself and others than to travel time; other drivers might assign greater weight to travel time. Even the same driver may make different trade-offs between travel time and safety depending on trip urgency, trip length, and familiarity with the road. The problem arises because individual drivers' decisions about speed may be made without adequate consideration of the effect of their choices on the safety of other road users. Even a driver traveling alone who is involved in a single-vehicle crash may impose medical and property damage costs on society that are not fully reimbursed by the driver. The potential costs imposed on others is a primary reason for regulating speed.

The second reason for regulating speed is the inability of drivers to judge vehicle capabilities (e.g., stopping, handling) and to adequately anticipate roadway geometry and roadside conditions to determine appropriate driving speeds. Drivers are generally able to modify their driving speeds appropriately as traffic volumes increase and weather conditions deteriorate. Unless they are familiar with conditions, however, they may not be as aware of appropriate speeds on roads with poor geometrics or high levels of roadside activity.

A final reason for regulating speed, which is related to the issues of information adequacy and judgment, is the tendency of some drivers to underestimate or misjudge the effects of speed on crash probability and severity. This problem is often manifested by young and inexperienced drivers and may be a problem for other drivers.

The effects of externalities and the availability of information enabling motorists to anticipate conditions and select appropriate driving speeds differ significantly by road class. For example, the risks imposed on others by individual driver speed choices are likely to be relatively small on rural Interstate highways where free-flowing traffic creates fewer opportunities for conflict with other road users.

In addition, under normal conditions drivers tend to have adequate information to determine appropriate driving speeds, because these highways are usually built to the highest design standards, access is limited, and roadside activity is minimal.[1] In contrast, the risks imposed on others by individual driver speed choices may be large on urban arterials where traffic volumes are high for extended periods of the day, roadside activities are numerous, and potential for conflict with entering vehicles and with vulnerable bicyclists and pedestrians is great. These differences are important factors for consideration in setting appropriate speed limits on different types of roads.

WHAT IS THE PURPOSE OF SPEED LIMITS?

The primary purpose of speed limits is to regulate driving speeds to achieve an appropriate balance between travel time and risk for a road class or specific highway section. Speed limits have also been imposed for fuel conservation when national maximum speed limits were established on major highways during World War II and again in 1974 following the oil crisis of the preceding year.[2]

Safety—more specifically, avoidance of crashes and mitigation of crash outcomes—is the most important reason for imposing speed limits. Many factors besides speed affect traffic safety—driving under the influence of alcohol or other drugs, safety belt use, roadway geometry, and weather—but speed has been shown to play an important role.

Speed is directly related to injury severity in a crash through the change in velocity (Delta-V) that occurs in a crash. The probability of severe injury increases sharply with the impact speed through its relation with Delta-V. The energy release is proportional to the

---

[1] Not all rural Interstate highways are constructed to the highest design standards, however. Some predate the Interstate construction program and were upgraded to minimum Interstate standards.

[2] The conservation effects, however, were not large. For example, Bloomquist (1984) estimated that the 1974 National Maximum Speed Limit (NMSL) reduced fuel consumption by 0.2 to 1.0 percent. Originally enacted as a temporary fuel conservation measure, Congress made the 55-mph (89-km/h) speed limit permanent because of the apparent safety benefits (TRB 1984, 15).

square of the impact speed; the higher the impact speed, the greater the potential Delta-V. The risk of severe injury is even greater when a vehicle strikes a pedestrian, the most vulnerable of road users; mortality risk for the pedestrian rises rapidly as impact speeds increase, with the rapid rise beginning at very low speeds. The strength of the relationship between speed and crash severity alone is sufficient reason for managing speed.

Speed is also linked to the probability of being in a crash, although the evidence[3] is not as compelling because crashes are complex events that seldom can be attributed to a single factor. In addition, the association between speed and crash probability varies by road type. Crash involvement has been associated with the deviation of a driver's speed from the average speed of traffic regardless of whether the deviation is above or below the average traffic speed. Evidence of increased crash probability from traveling above the average speed is found on many different road types, including Interstate highways, nonlimited-access rural roads, and urban arterials. Evidence of increased crash probability from traveling below the average speed is found primarily on Interstate highways near interchanges where traffic slows to merge or exit and on rural roads where vehicles slow at intersections or when negotiating turns. Crash involvement has also been associated with a driver's selection of speed on certain road types. For example, on nonlimited-access rural roads, single-vehicle crash involvement rates have been shown to rise with travel speed.

Speed limits are intended to enhance safety in at least two ways. They have a limiting function. By establishing an upper bound on speed, their purpose is to reduce both the probability and the severity of crashes. They also have a coordinating function; here the intent is to reduce dispersion in driving speeds (i.e., lessen differences in speed among drivers using the same road at the same time) and thus reduce the potential for vehicle conflicts.

---

[3] The reader is directed to Chapter 2 for a more complete review of the studies that link speed and crash probability. In the interest of brevity, the specific references to these studies are not repeated here. This protocol is also followed in other places in the text where the reader is directed to specific chapters for more detailed information.

Speed limits are also established to provide motorists with a common set of rules about appropriate driving speeds. The purpose is to encourage uniform driving behavior and an orderly flow of traffic.

Setting speed limits requires making implicit trade-offs among road user safety, travel time, practicality of enforcement, and other factors that may affect motorists' decisions about appropriate driving speeds. Research can help inform the decision maker who must determine an appropriate speed limit, but the decision ultimately reflects value judgments about acceptable levels of risk, the value of time, and acceptable levels of enforcement.

WHAT INFORMATION SHOULD SPEED LIMITS CONVEY TO THE DRIVER?

A speed limit sign should convey two basic messages: (*a*) the maximum speed for a reasonable and prudent driver traveling in free-flowing traffic with good visibility and under fair weather conditions, and (*b*) the speed that will be enforced within some tolerance for minor measurement error.

Traditionally, speed limits have been set to inform motorists of appropriate driving speeds under favorable conditions. Drivers are expected to reduce speed if conditions deteriorate (e.g., poor visibility, adverse weather, congestion, warning signs, or presence of bicyclists and pedestrians). In the future, variable speed limits may make possible posted speed limits that vary with conditions.[4] However, until the technology becomes more widely available and less costly, speed limits should inform the driver of the maximum appropriate driving speed under favorable conditions. Minimum speed limits have also been established on some high-speed roads to reduce dispersion in speeds. In this case, the speed limit informs the driver of the minimum appropriate speed under favorable conditions.

---

[4] Another alternative is to use prima facie limits more widely. Prima facie limits enable drivers charged with a violation for exceeding the speed limit to contend that their speed was safe for conditions existing at the time. Prima facie limits provide greater flexibility to drivers to determine an appropriate speed for conditions and place a greater burden of proof on the enforcement community that a violation has occurred.

Speed limits should also inform drivers who exceed the maximum (or fall below the minimum) limit that, with some tolerance for minor measurement error, they can expect a citation. In other words, speed limits should mean what they say.

HOW SHOULD SPEED LIMITS BE SET?

The approach currently in wide use to set speed limits is sound, that is, speed limits are legislated by broad road class (e.g., Interstate highway) and geographic area (e.g., urban district). Where statutory limits do not fit specific road or traffic conditions, speed zones may be established administratively, and speed limits for that highway section may be reduced from or raised above the statutory limit.[5] The system appropriately balances the desirability of uniform speed limits (legislated limits for broad road classes) with the need for exceptions (speed zones) to reflect local differences.

Establishing Legislated Speed Limits by Road Class

Decision Process for Determining Legislated Speed Limits

Legislated speed limits by road class are determined by state legislatures and city councils for state and local roads, respectively. **Legislators should seek the advice of traffic engineers, law enforcement officials, judges, public health officials, and the general public in determining appropriate speed limits, and provision should be made to monitor and enforce whatever decision is reached.** Consultation, however, does not ensure that all parties will reach consensus or that tensions will be resolved between different interests, such as between commuters and residents on appropriate speed limits on residential streets. The decision process requires trade-offs and judgments concerning the relative importance of safety and travel time and the feasibility of enforcement. **There is no single "right" speed limit, but, in addition to satisfying safety, the final**

[5] In those states with absolute speed limits, speed zone limits cannot be raised above the maximum absolute limit for that road class.

selection of a speed limit should meet the requirements of enforceability and acceptance by the community at large.

Nor should the process stop there. Roadway conditions, vehicle safety features, driving behavior, and attitudes change over time. The change in driver attitudes toward and compliance with the 55-mph (89-km/h) NMSL is an example of how driver support for a legislated speed limit can erode over time. **Legislated speed limits should be reviewed periodically and revised when necessary on the basis of monitoring data on actual driving speeds and safety outcomes.**

Roadway Classification Scheme

The committee identified seven road classes plus a category of special zones (e.g., school zones, work zones) as the basis on which to differentiate speed limits by road type. The categorization scheme covers most major road classes and is expressed in terminology appropriate for the general reader. The committee's classification scheme differs from the more technical highway functional classification system developed by the American Association of State Highway and Transportation Officials (AASHTO), a classification well known to the engineering community (Table 6-1). Data on mileage, travel volume, and safety, which are useful in making decisions about appropriate speed limits by road class, are only available by the AASHTO functional classification scheme. Thus they are provided here, although there is not always a one-to-one correspondence between the AASHTO and the committee road classification systems.

Guidance on Setting Legislated Speed Limits by Specific Road Class

In determining appropriate speed limits by road class, decision makers should be guided by both the likely risks imposed on others by individual driver speed choices and by the adequacy of cues provided by the roadway to help drivers anticipate conditions and make appropriate speed choices. They should also take enforcement practicality into consideration. Table 6-2 summarizes differences between road classes on the basis of these general considerations.

Table 6-1 Road Class Categories and Characteristics (FHWA 1997)

Road Class (Committee Definition)	Road Class (AASHTO Definition)	Mileage (Percent of Total)	Annual Travel in 100 MVM (Percent of Total)	Fatal Crashes (Percent of Total)	Fatalities[a] (Percent of Total)	Fatality Rate[b]	Injuries[c] (Percent of Total)	Injury Rate[b]
Rural Interstate	Rural Interstate	32,818 (0.8)	2,324.5 (9.4)	2,388 (6.4)	2,850 (6.8)	1.23	91,200 (2.4)	39
Urban Interstate	Urban Interstate Other freeway and expressway[d]	22,240 (0.6)	5,093.5 (20.5)	3,701 (9.9)	4,137 (9.9)	0.81	444,600 (12.0)	87
Rural multilane/high-speed two-lane	Other principal arterial, rural Minor arterial, rural[e]	235,490 (6.0)	3,788.1 (15.3)	8,450 (22.6)	9,801 (23.4)	2.59	392,700 (10.5)	104
Urban/suburban multilane	Other principal arterial, urban[f]	52,973 (1.3)	3,777.2 (15.2)	4,977 (13.3)	5,434 (13.0)	1.44	731,900 (19.6)	194
Rural lower-speed two-lane	Major collector, rural Minor collector, rural[g]	705,311 (18.0)	2,410.4 (9.7)	6,477 (17.4)	7,234 (17.3)	3.0	395,000 (10.6)	164
Not defined[h]	Minor arterial, urban Collector, urban	176,940 (4.5)	4,269.9 (17.2)	4,557 (12.2)	5,092 (12.1)	1.19	778,000 (20.8)	182
Not defined[h]	Local roads, rural	2,119,154 (54.1)	1,077.7 (4.3)	3,956 (10.6)	4,280 (10.2)	3.97	253,800 (6.8)	236

Urban residential street	Local street, urban	574,524 (14.7)	2,080.8 (8.4)	2,845 (7.6)	3,079 (7.3)	1.48	646,600 (17.3)	311
Rural unpaved road	N.A.	N.A.	N.A.	N.A.	N.A.	N.A.	N.A.	N.A.

Note: Safety statistics are for 1996, the most recent year available. Year-to-year-variations by road class are small. AASHTO = American Association of State Highway and Transportation Officials; MVM = millions of vehicle miles; FHWA = Federal Highway Administration; N.A. = not applicable; 1 mi = 1.609 km.

[a] Includes vehicle occupant and nonoccupant fatalities.

[b] Fatality and injury rates are expressed as fatalities (or injuries) per 100 MVM.

[c] Includes vehicle occupant and nonoccupant injuries of all types, not just incapacitating. Estimates or 1995 data are used for 10 states plus the District of Columbia because of incomplete reporting at the time of publication.

[d] The category "other freeway and expressway" includes roads with less than full control of access.

[e] AASHTO defines this road category as serving major statewide travel. The roads are designed for relatively high-speed travel and minimum interference to through movement (AASHTO 1994, 11).

[f] This category also includes a substantial share (nearly 40 percent of the total mileage) of two-lane roads. The major purpose of these roads is traffic circulation, not access.

[g] AASHTO defines this road category as serving intracounty travel where travel distances are shorter and speeds are more moderate than on arterial routes (AASHTO 1994, 11). This category includes a small amount of four-lane divided highway mileage.

[h] The committee did not cover every possible road type. For example, the categories of "urban/suburban multilane roads" and "urban residential streets" were thought to adequately capture the major urban road types. Hence, a separate category was not defined for urban minor arterial and collector roads.

Table 6-2 Major Factors for Consideration in Setting Speed Limits by Road Class

Road Class	Effects of Externalities	Available Information for Motorist Speed Choice	Enforcement Practicality
Rural Interstates	Low—free-flowing traffic; limited access; pedestrians and bicyclists not generally pres-ent; the best safety record of all rural road classes	Good—roads usually constructed to highest design standards; drivers can generally anticipate conditions	Selective, targeted enforcement has short-term positive effects, but coverage of complete mileage is difficult
Urban Interstates	Somewhat greater than on rural Interstates because higher traffic volumes and closer interchange spacing increase potential for vehicle conflict, but still relatively low	Not as good as rural Interstates because of driver difficulties anticipating traffic bottlenecks or incidents, particularly during congested periods	Mileage is easier to cover, but apprehending speeders in high-traffic volumes on multilane seg-ments can be difficult
Rural multilane/ high-speed two-lane	Greater than on rural Interstate highways because many highways are not divided and access is not always limited, resulting in at-grade intersections with potential for vehicle con-flicts	Fair to good, depending on road-way geometry and extent of access control—speed zones can be used with lower speed limits where driver anticipation of appropriate speeds is likely to be poor	Coverage of very extensive mileage is difficult

Urban/ suburban multilane	Greater than on rural multilane roads because of more roadside activity (commercial and residential development) and presence of some vulnerable road users (e.g., bicyclists)	Wide variety of conditions. Generally poorer than for rural multilane because of greater roadside activity, access points, and cross traffic that complicate determination of appropriate speeds. Speed adaptation can be a problem traveling from rural to suburban and urban areas	Less difficult from a coverage perspective; some room to pull over violators
Rural lower-speed two-lane	Greater than on rural multilane because there are more opportunities for vehicle conflicts from limited opportunities for passing and absence of access control; poor safety record for this road class generally	Poor—lower design standards generally; motorists sometimes may have difficulty determining suitable driving speeds. Appropriate use of speed zones and warning signs and advisory speeds recommended	Adequate coverage of low-volume mileage is infeasible

(continued on next page)

Table 6-2 *(continued)*

Road Class	Effects of Externalities	Available Information for Motorist Speed Choice	Enforcement Practicality
Urban residential streets	High—high potential for vehicle conflicts at intersecting streets and driveways; many vulnerable road users (e.g., pedestrians, bicyclists) share the road	Fair—may be difficult for drivers to anticipate conditions and determine appropriate driving speeds, but speeds, in general, are sufficiently low that drivers may have time to react to unanticipated situations	Coverage is a problem because of extensive mileage
Rural unpaved roads	Low—very little traffic; roads are mostly used by local residents	Fair to good—roads are mostly used by those familiar with surroundings, although conditions can change rapidly depending on weather and amount of road maintenance	Low volume of traffic suggests minimal enforcement
Special zones (school and work zones)	High—opportunities for conflict with vulnerable road users (e.g., children on foot or on bicycles, workers)	Poor—appropriate driving speeds may not be apparent and speed adaptation nearing the work or school zone can be a problem	Adequate coverage can be a problem in areas with large numbers of school zones; difficulty of apprehending violators can be a problem in work zones depending on traffic volume

More specifically, legislators should obtain information on four key technical factors to guide their decisions:

- Design speed, that is, the design speed of a major portion of the road, not of its most critical design features;
- Vehicle operating speed, measured as a range of 85th percentile speeds taken from spot-speed surveys of free-flowing vehicles at representative locations along the highway;
- Safety experience, that is, crash frequencies and outcomes; and
- Enforcement experience, that is, existing speed tolerance and level of enforcement.

To the extent possible, a range of data should be provided for each measure at various locations along the highway. Locations with conditions that differ considerably from these ranges may be suitable for speed zones or advisory speed warnings. Examples of such locations are where crash rates are high or geometric features are particularly restrictive. As the following discussion illustrates, the weight given to the four factors, particularly those related to speed, differs by road class. Obtaining representative data on vehicle operating speeds and design speeds becomes more difficult on lower functional road classes because of greater variability of conditions and driving speeds on these roads.

Rural Interstate Highways

Roadway and traffic conditions are more uniform on rural Interstates than on any other road class. Hence, they provide a useful benchmark for comparison with lower functional road classes. Decision makers should obtain information on the four factors mentioned previously but should give greater weight to information on vehicle operating speeds and safety in determining a maximum speed limit on rural Interstates. The risks imposed on others are likely to be small, and information enabling drivers to select an appropriate speed is generally good on this road class. The risk of conflict is relatively low on many rural Interstates because traffic is generally free flowing and access is limited. Vulnerable road users (e.g., pedestrians, bicyclists) typically are not present. Rural Interstate highways have the lowest numbers of fatal crashes, fatalities, and injuries and the lowest injury rate of any road class; they have the lowest fatality rate of any rural road class (Table 6-1). Restricted geometry is generally not a problem (with the exception of some rural Interstates that pass through mountainous terrain) because rural Interstates are usually constructed to the highest geometric and roadside design standards. Thus, design speeds provide little additional information to decision makers about appropriate speed limit levels for this road class; most drivers can anticipate conditions and select an appropriate driving speed.

An appropriate maximum speed limit should be established, however, because of the link between crash severity and high travel speeds and evidence of increased probability of crash involvement for drivers who travel at speeds well above the average speed of traffic.[6] The higher fatality rate on rural than on urban Interstates—a product of higher speeds and more severe crashes—reinforces the need to limit speeds at the high end of the speed distribution (Table 6-1). The maximum speed limit, however, should be set at a level that the police can reasonably enforce and the courts adjudicate. Selective, targeted enforcement on certain highway sections can have a positive though short-lived effect, but maintaining high levels of enforcement is difficult on long stretches of rural Interstate highways. Moreover, intensive enforcement is not a desirable use of scarce resources because of the good safety record on rural Interstates compared with other rural road classes. States are also urged to review their policies for requiring slower vehicles to keep to the right on these highways as one method of reducing dispersion in driving speeds.[7]

---

[6] As discussed in Chapter 2, according to some studies, crash involvement rates are lowest in the interval between the average speed and the 85th percentile speed of the speed distribution, above which point they rise sharply. The same sources would also support establishment of minimum speed limits because crash involvement rates also rise sharply below average speeds—at about the 15th percentile. These results were found on Interstate highways and on rural nonlimited-access highways.

[7] According to NHTSA (1998), the following states reserve the left lane for passing: Arkansas, Connecticut, Hawaii, Idaho, Illinois, Indiana, Kentucky, Maine, Massachusetts, Michigan, Mississippi, Missouri, Nevada, New Jersey, Ohio, Oregon,

Despite the relatively low fatality rate of rural Interstates, decision makers are still faced with a trade-off between the level of safety and increased mobility (improved travel time) when choosing a speed limit. The committee expects that legislators grappling with the issue of which maximum limit to choose would want to do so with knowledge of changes in safety among alternative maximum limits. At the time of this writing, the most relevant information on changes in safety comes from studies of the effects of changes in the NMSL in 1987 and the repeal of the NMSL in 1995, which led to increased speed limits in most states.[8] As is often the case with studies of real-world safety effects, neither the results nor the conclusions drawn by different researchers are totally consistent across all states or all studies.

As would be expected because of the many factors affecting fatalities on rural Interstate highways, not all Interstate sections where the maximum speed limit was raised demonstrated the same effects. However, taken as a group, the studies that examined effects of the 1987 changes on Interstate sections alone indicated a relatively consistent pattern of overall increases in fatalities and fatal crashes. In short, raising the speed limit from 55 to 65 mph (89 to 105 km/h) or higher had significant adverse effects on safety on the roads where the speed limit was increased. A similar result was found on highways on which speed limits were raised after 1995. However, the latter findings should be considered preliminary because they are generally based on 1 year of data or less.

In a more limited number of studies, primarily of the 1987 change, researchers have attempted to examine "system effects" of raising the speed limit, noting that decreases in safety on the Interstates themselves might be offset by improvements in safety on other roads, perhaps through such mechanisms as diversion of traffic to the safer Interstates and better deployment of enforcement resources to the less safe (non-Interstate) roads. One study concluded that the overall effect of the changes was neutral (using counties within one state as

Rhode Island, Tennessee, Utah, Virginia, and Washington. States vary widely, however, concerning the types of roads and vehicles for which the restriction applies.

[8] Chapter 3 provides a more detailed discussion of these studies.

the system), a second concluded that increasing speed limits had a positive safety effect on the system (using entire states as the system), and one other found no offsetting effects but rather some evidence of spillovers in the form of higher fatalities on non-Interstate rural highways—although a much smaller increase than on the rural Interstates. Subsequent authors have raised the issue of how best to define the system that should be studied.

The committee found that combining such opposing findings into a consensus view of the effects of increasing limits on rural Interstates was difficult. There is agreement that speed limit increases that result in increased driving speeds—and the preponderance of the evidence suggests that increased speeds will occur—will likely result in higher fatalities and fatal crashes on Interstate sections where the limit is raised, as would be expected from studies relating speed to crash severity. There is also committee agreement that, to the extent system changes have occurred, the total safety effect could be different because most current estimates of effects are based on Interstate segments alone. Additional research on such possible system effects is clearly needed.

Urban Interstate Highways

Maximum speed limits on urban Interstate highways are often set, appropriately, at a lower level than on rural Interstates. The potential for vehicle conflicts is greater on urban Interstates because of higher traffic volumes and more interchanges, but it is still expected to be smaller than on many other road classes. In fact, the fatality rate is lower on urban than on rural Interstates, although the numbers of fatal crashes, fatalities, and injuries and the injury rate are higher (Table 6-1). Roadway geometry may be more restricted on urban Interstates, and closer interchange spacing increases the potential for disparities in speed and vehicle conflicts; hence the desirability of lower speeds to reduce speed dispersion. Maximum speed limits, however, should be set in a speed range that the police are able to enforce. Although the concentration of urban Interstate mileage and traffic volume makes enforcement easier, it can be difficult for the police to apprehend speeders in traffic. Photo radar can be a useful supplement to conventional police enforcement on urban freeways.

When conditions become congested during peak periods, drivers may have difficulty anticipating appropriate speeds, particularly as they approach traffic bottlenecks or incidents.[9] Variable speed limit systems, which indicate appropriate maximum and minimum speeds on the basis of actual traffic volume, speed, and density on specific highway sections, are well suited to address such conditions. These systems have been deployed on several high-speed European motorways, often in combination with automated speed enforcement. Variable speed limit systems are under development for limited application on U.S. highways, particularly on highway sections affected by adverse weather. Once their effectiveness is better understood, broader application of variable speed limit and related automated enforcement systems, particularly on urban Interstate highways, should be explored. Because the systems are new and unlikely to be well understood, care should be undertaken to explain the basis for setting and varying the speed limits to the courts, law enforcement officials, and motorists. Speed thresholds for enforcement should be set high at first to give drivers time to adjust to the system and to gain their support.

Rural Multilane and High-Speed Two-Lane Highways[10]

Highways in this road class range from multilane, divided highways with some access control to two-lane, undivided highways with at-grade intersections and restricted roadway geometry. Maximum speed limits should be lower than on rural Interstate highways to reflect lower design standards generally on this road class. The potential for vehicle conflicts is greater on many of these highways than on rural Interstates because vehicles can enter and exit at intersections at speeds considerably lower than the average speed of traffic. Also, many of these roads do not have median barriers, thus increasing the

[9] Drivers may have particular difficulty anticipating "shock waves"—the traffic slowdowns that build up in response to a traffic incident or bottleneck that may be created by large numbers of entering or exiting vehicles. The slowdown occurs upstream from the incident or bottleneck; the magnitude of the effect depends on the traffic volume and the duration of the incident.

[10] The committee defines "high speed" as at least 55 mph (89 km/h).

chance of head-on collisions. Roadside hazards, such as trees and utility poles, are often present on these roads. Fatal crashes and fatalities are more than three times higher—and the fatality rate is approximately twice as high—on this road class as on rural Interstates (Table 6-1).[11] Design speed should be an important consideration in setting appropriate speed limits on these highways. The cues available to motorists to select an appropriate driving speed vary depending on roadway geometry and the amount of access control. Because these highways carry a substantial amount of traffic (Table 6-1) and their function is to accommodate relatively high-speed through travel (AASHTO 1994, 11), speed zones should be used where speed limits should be appropriately lowered rather than imposing lower speed limits throughout the system. Limited enforcement coverage also supports this strategy.

Urban and Suburban Multilane Roads

This road class probably encompasses the greatest variation in roadside conditions, thus making it difficult to specify a suitable systemwide speed limit. Maximum speed limits should be set somewhat lower than for rural multilane highways, and extensive use of speed zones is recommended. The risk of vehicle conflicts is greater on urban roads because of more roadside activity, access points, and cross traffic. Bicyclists and pedestrians—the most vulnerable road users—are apt to be more common on these roads. Drivers appear to make some accommodation to these differences; fatal crashes, fatalities, and the fatality rate are considerably lower on these roads than on their rural counterparts, although injury levels and the injury rate are nearly two times higher (Table 6-1). Roadway geometrics may not differ greatly from those on rural multilane highways, but motorists are apt to have greater difficulty determining appropriate driving speeds in areas that are heavily developed. Speed adaptation can also be a problem, particularly lowering speeds appropriately as drivers travel from rural to suburban and urban areas. Enforcement is easier from a coverage perspective; there are fewer miles of urban than rural

[11] Injuries are more than four times higher and the injury rate is more than twice as high (Table 6-1).

multilane roads (Table 6-1). Also, there is often room to pull over speed limit violators. These roads may be candidates for photo radar enforcement at high-crash or highly hazardous locations.

Rural Lower-Speed Two-Lane Roads[12]
The potential for vehicle conflicts is great on this road class because of the absence of access control and limited opportunities for passing. Fatal crashes, fatalities, and the fatality rate are among the highest for all road classes; injuries and the injury rate are among the highest for all rural road classes (Table 6-1). The roads are not designed to the highest standards but rather to accommodate topography and expected traffic (AASHTO 1994, 460). Thus, motorists may sometimes have difficulty determining appropriate driving speeds for conditions. Design speed should be a key factor in establishing suitable speed limits on these roads. Appropriate use of speed zones, warning signs, and advisory speeds is recommended. Adequate coverage of extensive road mileage poses a problem for enforcement. Thus, speed limits must be reasonable for conditions and set at levels that are largely self-enforcing. Fortunately, there is some evidence to suggest that drivers do restrict their speeds on roads with lower design speeds.[13]

Urban Residential Streets
The potential for inconsistent application of speed limits is high on this road class. Neither vehicle operating speeds nor design speeds are likely to provide useful input for determining appropriate speed limits on residential streets; safety experience and enforcement practicality should be given higher priority. Neighborhood pressures may result in setting speed limits very low, but often they are not enforced and compliance is poor, even by neighborhood residents. Speed limits based on vehicle operating speeds, however, may be inappropriate because there is a high potential for vehicle conflicts, and drivers are

[12] The committee defines "lower-speed" as less than 55 mph (89 km/h).

[13] Agent et al. (1997) reported that the only roadway type in Kentucky where the 85th percentile speed was less than 5 mph (8 km/h) higher than the posted speed limit was two-lane rural roads without full-width shoulders (p. 11).

not always aware of the danger they pose to bicyclists and pedestrians with whom they share the road. The fatality rate on residential streets is the highest for all urban road classes; the injury rate is the highest for any road class (Table 6-1). Design speed also has limited practical significance for determining speed limits on residential streets; the frequency of intersections, presence of stop signs, and amount of roadside activity (e.g., parking, driveways) have a greater effect on actual vehicle speeds (AASHTO 1994, 429). The risks imposed on other road users is sufficient reason for limiting driving speeds on residential streets. However, speed limits should not be set below enforceable levels.[14] Even when there is a commitment to enforcement, there are practical limits because of the extensive mileage of residential streets. Alternative measures, such as traffic calming and other highway design techniques, should be considered to achieve desired driving speeds.

Rural Unpaved Roads

This is a road class for which posted speed limits are generally inappropriate. The basic law that drivers should adopt a reasonable and prudent speed should govern. Risks of vehicle conflict are very low on these roads; most are used by residents who are familiar with the roads and their condition. Roadway geometry varies, and roadway conditions can change rapidly depending on weather, season, and amount of road maintenance, so that establishing an appropriate speed limit is difficult even for favorable conditions. Finally, enforcement is minimal on roads with such low traffic volumes.

Special Zones

At least two situations—school zones and work zones—warrant special handling in establishing speed limits. Risks to others are likely to be great in both because of the presence of vulnerable road users—children in school zones and workers in work zones. Drivers are

[14] Another option is to use prima facie speed limits more widely, which would provide greater enforcement flexibility. This alternative would require legislative changes in the two-thirds of the states that currently have only absolute speed limits.

unlikely to anticipate appropriate driving speeds for negotiating these zones. Typically, they represent an exception to normal driving speeds, and adequate speed adaptation is a problem as drivers approach the zones. Moreover, work zones often have narrow lanes and restricted alignments at detours and lane shifts that require speed reduction. School zones are prime candidates for variable speed limit systems because lower driving speeds are generally required only for certain hours of the day. Changeable conditions in work zones as well as limited hours of operation also make them amenable to variable speed limits. Photo radar enforcement may be appropriate in those circumstances where patrolling large numbers of school zones or apprehending speeding violators in high traffic volumes in work zones proves difficult.

Setting Speed Limits in Speed Zones

Speed zones are established for highway sections where legislated limits for that road class do not fit specific road or traffic conditions. **Determination of appropriate speed limits in speed zones should be made on the basis of an engineering study. Speed zones should be reviewed periodically—with greater frequency where conditions are changing rapidly (e.g., developing suburban areas)—to determine whether changed conditions warrant an adjustment in the speed limit or in the boundaries of the zone itself.** California, for example, has established a 5-year review cycle; police will use radar enforcement in speed zones only if an engineering and traffic survey has been conducted and reviewed within the past 5 years to set an appropriate speed limit. Traffic engineers or technicians under their supervision should conduct the engineering study. Consultation with law enforcement officials is advised where this is not already accepted practice so that the proposed speed limit is enforceable. Elected officials and citizen groups may also become involved when community concerns have been expressed about driving speeds. In addition to speed data, engineering studies can provide road-specific historical data on crashes and information about hazards (e.g., pedestrian crossings, intersecting streets with restricted sight distance) not readily apparent to motorists. These data help the engineer in determining an appropriate speed limit. However, unless the decision has the support of enforcement officials and the general public, speed zoning may not result in desired driving speeds, particularly if the speed limit is set below the 85th percentile speed. On roads where enforcement is infrequent and low speeds are desirable, such as residential streets, alternatives like traffic calming should be investigated.

The most common factor considered in setting speed limits in speed zones is the 85th percentile speed, although frequently the limit is adjusted from this value on the basis of such factors as crash experience, roadside development, roadway geometry, and parking and pedestrian levels. Speeds are measured from spot-speed surveys of free-flowing vehicles taken at representative locations in the proposed speed zone. The speed limit typically is set near the speed at or below which 85 percent of motorists are driving. The advantages of setting the speed limit near the 85th percentile speed are that (*a*) police are enabled to focus their enforcement efforts on the most dangerous speed outliers, and (*b*) the 85th percentile speed is generally at the upper bound of a speed range within which crash involvement rates are lowest, at least on certain road types according to some studies that have examined the relationship between speed and crash probability.

Setting the speed limit primarily on the basis of the 85th percentile speed is not always appropriate. The potential safety benefits may not be realized on roads with a wide range of speeds. Basing the speed limit on a measure of unconstrained vehicle operating speeds is not appropriate on urban roads with a mix of road users, including bicyclists and pedestrians, and with high traffic volumes and levels of roadside activity. An expert-system approach, either formal or informal, could be developed to establish speed limits in speed zones.[15] The expert-system approach deserves consideration because it provides a systematic and consistent method of examining and weighing factors other than vehicle operating speeds in determining an appropriate speed limit.

---

[15] Details of Australia's expert system for setting speed limits are provided in Chapter 3.

Differential Speed Limits

The committee remains neutral on the desirability of differential speed limits for passenger cars and heavy trucks that have been established in some states on some road classes. It did not find compelling evidence[16] to support more widespread application of differential speed limits. Neither did it find strong evidence that differential speed limits should be eliminated where they are in use. More research on and evaluation of the effects of differential speed limits on driving speeds and safety outcomes are needed in the states that have adopted them.

The committee found little evidence to suggest that motorists decrease driving speeds at night when lower nighttime speed limits are in effect. However, it did not find compelling evidence to suggest that nighttime speed limits be eliminated in states that have adopted them.

CAN DRIVERS BE INDUCED TO OBEY SPEED LIMITS THROUGH ENFORCEMENT?

Most experts agree that enforcement is critical to achieving compliance with speed limits. Simply posting a speed limit sign will not achieve desired driving speeds. Even if most motorists believe that the speed limits are reasonable and they comply within a small tolerance, enforcement is still necessary to ensure the conformity of drivers who will obey laws only if they perceive a credible threat of detection and punishment for noncompliance.

The problem with traditional enforcement methods is their short-lived effect in deterring speeding or other unwanted behavior. Maintaining the deterrence effect requires a level of enforcement that is difficult to sustain because of limited resources provided for speed enforcement and competing enforcement priorities. Policy makers can affect the level of enforcement through resource allocation, but enforcement is expensive. Thus, the police should deploy enforce-

[16] A review of many of the key studies concerning differential speed limits can be found in Chapter 3.

ment efforts strategically on those roads and at times when speed-related incidents are most common or where road conditions are most hazardous. (The infrequent nature of crashes, however, makes targeting difficult.) There is some evidence[17] that planned patrols at varying time intervals and locations can extend the time- and distance-halo effects of enforcement at particular locations, but only after an initial period of continuous patrolling. In addition, the patrols must be visible and sufficiently frequent to convince drivers of a credible threat of detection for noncompliance. **Police can boost the longevity of the deterrence effect by combining enforcement initiatives with high-profile public information campaigns** to increase driver awareness that speed limits will be enforced. Publicity must be followed up by actual enforcement if the approach is to successfully deter speeding. Moreover, making permanent behavior changes requires a long-term sustained effort.

Automated enforcement—for example, photo radar—can be used to complement traditional enforcement methods, particularly where roadway geometry or traffic volume makes traditional methods difficult or unsafe. Photo radar has been shown to be efficient and effective where it has been used for speed control, particularly on high-volume, major arterials where compliance with speed limits is often poor. Photo radar enforcement could also be coupled with variable speed limit systems for use on urban Interstates where high traffic volumes make it difficult to apprehend speeding drivers. Photo radar is controversial. Legal issues, such as privacy and owner (versus driver) liability for speeding infractions, must be resolved. Successful introduction of automated enforcement also requires funding, public education, and careful deployment (i.e., on roads that are especially hazardous and at high-crash locations where speeding is a contributing factor or where traditional enforcement methods are hazardous) to ensure essential public support.

Other alternatives to traditional enforcement may be required in some circumstances to achieve desired driving speeds. Traffic calming has successfully reduced speeding on many residential streets, but

[17] Chapter 4 provides a more detailed discussion of studies on different enforcement strategies.

it is difficult to determine net areawide effects on safety because of the difficulty of accurately measuring traffic diversion and the small size of "before" and "after" crash data that limits statistical analysis.[18] Redesigning roads to achieve greater congruity between driver perceptions of appropriate travel speeds and cues provided by the road itself (narrowing lanes, etc.) has promise. The approach should result in more consistent vehicle operating speeds, but additional study of the relationship between operating speeds and roadway geometric elements is required. In view of the size of the U.S. road network and the cost and pace of road rehabilitation, road redesign is a long-term strategy.

In the near term, speed limits should be set at levels that are largely self-enforcing or at the lowest speed the police are able to enforce.

HOW CAN THE JUDICIAL SYSTEM ASSIST IN ACHIEVING DESIRED DRIVING SPEEDS?

Actions by law enforcement officials and the justice system can undermine the effectiveness of speed limits in achieving desired driving speeds. The police can choose not to enforce speed limits where they think the limits are unreasonable. Traffic court judges throw out speeding violations or reduce fines in cases when they believe the speed limits are inappropriate or the fines too harsh. **Thus it is important that the police and traffic court judges perceive that speed limits are reasonable and enforceable.**

When setting speed limits, care should be exercised that primary consideration is given to safety, not revenue enhancement. Driver perception of entrapment from speed limits set unreasonably low to generate income erodes the credibility of traffic regulation.

Where the courts have broad discretion in assessing penalties for speeding violations, inconsistent treatment of violations can lead to a public perception that speed limit laws are arbitrary and capricious. **Development of sentencing guidelines and training for judges who**

[18] Chapter 5 provides a lengthier discussion of traffic calming and road redesign.

handle speeding violations can help ensure consistent treatment of violators. Licensing point demerit systems have already gone a long way toward reducing inconsistencies in penalty assessments by providing a uniform system of graduated penalties for various traffic violations.

The deterrence effect of sanctions for speeding violations is often limited by lengthy backlogs of cases in courts where traffic violations are often perceived as minor infractions and not serious crimes. **Automated enforcement has the potential to relieve court backlogs through the use of administrative adjudication procedures for many speeding infractions.** Such procedures can reduce the number of court hearings as well as the cost of processing speeding violations.

WHAT POTENTIAL DOES TECHNOLOGY OFFER TO IMPROVE METHODS OF DETERMINING AND ENFORCING SPEED LIMITS?

Technology can advance the state of the art, but it does not hold the complete solution. Many applicable technologies already exist or are currently being enhanced as computing capability has grown. The difficulty in using them often lies less with the technologies themselves—although cost is an important consideration—than with political and legal hurdles to be overcome in deploying them widely. The most promising technologies for near-term adoption are discussed here.

The technology to support variable speed limits and improve traffic flow efficiency is available, but more experimentation and evaluation are needed to determine the effectiveness of these systems from a safety and traffic efficiency perspective and to learn where variable speed limits can be deployed most usefully. The current high cost of variable speed limit systems limits opportunities for their deployment to urban Interstates and freeways with large traffic volumes or to selected segments of major roads where weather (e.g., fog, visibility) is a frequent problem.

Automated enforcement, particularly photo radar, can provide an effective complement to traditional enforcement methods, particularly where police patrol vehicles cannot be deployed effectively or

safely. Successful introduction of automated enforcement may require adoption of legal changes; strong public support is essential for its success.

Intelligent Transportation System technologies that support more efficient and safer travel are being developed and demonstrated on U.S. vehicles and highways. **New techniques for communicating information to drivers about appropriate driving speeds are under development, and advances in vehicle control technologies have the potential to automate some speed-related driving functions.** Some technologies, such as "smart" cruise control, are close to commercialization. Other vehicle-related technologies, such as frontal-collision and lane-departure avoidance systems, are still in the research and development phase. Key concerns include reliability, liability, driver control, and acceptance. The technologies represent important innovations that require watching and evaluation.

CONCLUDING COMMENT

The issue of appropriate driving speeds and safety will persist as long as there are individual drivers making choices about driving speeds. Most states have recently raised speed limits on many major highways following repeal of the NMSL. Close monitoring of effects, particularly changes in driving speeds and safety outcomes, is desirable; vigilant enforcement is needed; and redoubled efforts should be taken to mitigate adverse safety outcomes by such continuing initiatives as increased safety belt use and reductions in driving while intoxicated—measures with large and proven safety benefits.

The speed-safety problem may become more acute with increased numbers of older drivers, who may not themselves speed but who have reduced capacity to handle high speeds. Congestion—which is unlikely to abate in the near term—contributes to the problem by increasing driver frustration and encouraging unsafe driving behaviors, such as speeding to avoid red lights or high-speed weaving on crowded Interstates and freeways.

Speed limits are one of the oldest and most widely used methods of controlling driving speeds, but speeds limits alone are not effective in all situations. Technology can help establish limits that are more sensitive to actual changes in conditions and thus provide drivers with better information. It can help outfit the vehicles and highways of the future with speed monitoring and control devices. Finally, technology can help improve the efficiency and effectiveness of enforcement. But the efficacy of speed limits will continue to depend largely on driver perception of the reasonableness of the limits and the willingness of the police and the courts to enforce the limits and punish violations. Where they are not present and limiting speed is desirable, alternative measures to managing driving speeds will have to be sought.

REFERENCES

ABBREVIATIONS

AASHTO	American Association of State Highway and Transportation Officials
FHWA	Federal Highway Administration
NHTSA	National Highway Traffic Safety Administration
TRB	Transportation Research Board

AASHTO. 1994. *A Policy on Geometric Design of Highways and Streets.* Washington, D.C.

Agent, K.R., J.G. Pigman, and J.M. Weber. 1997. *Evaluation of Speed Limits in Kentucky.* KTC-97-6. Kentucky Transportation Center, Kentucky Transportation Cabinet, and Federal Highway Administration, April, 90 pp.

Bloomquist, G. 1984. The 55 mph Limit and Gasoline Consumption. *Resources and Energy,* Vol. 6, March, pp. 21–39.

FHWA. 1997. *Highway Statistics 1996.* U.S. Department of Transportation, Washington, D.C.

NHTSA. 1998. *Life in the Fast Lane.* DOT-HS-808-670. U.S. Department of Transportation, Feb.

TRB. 1984. *Special Report 204: 55: A Decade of Experience.* National Research Council, Washington, D.C., 262 pp.

Appendix A

Trade-Off Decisions in Selecting Driving Speeds

In all day-to-day travel decisions, drivers are compelled to make trade-offs among the various costs and benefits associated with each trip. One of the trade-offs an automobile driver faces is between safety and travel time. At one extreme, a driver unconcerned with safety and concerned only with minimizing travel time would likely drive at the maximum speed the vehicle and the road would allow. Travel at very high speeds clearly increases the severity of any crash in which the driver becomes involved, and it may increase the probability of being in a crash. Such a driver would probably also choose a vehicle designed to maximize speed and handling, perhaps at the expense of crashworthiness. At the other extreme, a driver unconcerned with minimizing travel time and concerned only with safety would probably drive much more slowly and would likely choose a vehicle designed primarily for crashworthiness. In practice, drivers rarely, if ever, adopt such extreme positions. Instead, they balance a desire for shorter travel time with a desire for greater safety and select an intermediate speed. The purpose of this appendix is to present a more formal treatment of how drivers make these trade-offs. The role of public policy in affecting these trade-offs is also discussed.

A basic question is whether people deliberately trade off safety and travel time when making their trips. Some motorists indicate that this trade-off is not foremost in their minds while driving; others say that they are not conscious of making this trade-off at all. For drivers in many situations, the choice of driving speed is strongly influenced by speed limits and their enforcement, so the trade-off may be more one of travel time versus the likelihood and severity of penalties for exceeding the speed limit. But even in situations where there is little or no speed limit enforcement and many drivers exceed the posted speed limit, virtually no drivers are observed to drive as fast as their vehicles can go. Something other than the fear of speed limit enforcement must affect their choice of speed. Similarly, when weather and visibility are poor, drivers tend to slow down, often to speeds well below the posted limits. In many of these situations the driver's choice of a lower speed and increased travel time is almost certainly made with safety in mind. Thus, it appears that drivers do trade off travel time and safety even in the absence of speed limits and their enforcement.

Rather than making these trade-offs consciously each time they drive, however, motorists may rely on rules of thumb based on their past driving experience. When faced with the myriad of choices in day-to-day living, people often develop rules of thumb or other heuristics rather than make the considerable effort to continuously optimize over all their choices. With driving, people may well rely on their past experience with particular roads or driving situations to select a driving speed that has proven to be a reasonable trade-off for them in the past. Only when faced with unfamiliar or unusual conditions would drivers be more conscious of explicitly making such a trade-off. Since speed limit signs often convey useful information about the road, some people may base these rules of thumb on the speed limit, not necessarily adhering to the speed limit but keying the speed they choose to that limit. Reliance on past experience and rules of thumb does not mean that people are ignoring the trade-off. Rather, it means that they have used their past experience to convert that trade-off to an easy-to-follow set of internal behavioral guidelines.

How should one think about these trade-offs? In economics, such trade-offs are usually posed in terms of the benefits of one activity versus the benefits of another activity. In this case, however, the basic trade-off approach from economics is modified slightly. Safety is usually quantified in terms of probability of death or injury. Speed can just as easily be quantified for a given trip in terms of trip time. So the trade-off question is posed in terms of those two dimensions—the probability of death or injury (risk)[1] and travel time—rather than the two benefits of speed and safety.

Consider Figure A-1, in which the trip time and risk are represented.[2] What one would like, of course, is to be at the origin with zero time and zero risk, but that is not possible. Instead, a driver faces a choice among the alternatives represented in the figure, indicated by the letters A to L, which are attainable combinations of both trip time and risk. In making the actual choice, an individual need not consider all points shown in the figure. Some alternatives clearly dominate others. Point E, for example, offers both lower risk and shorter trip time than Point F, so the traveler need not even consider Point F. More generally in the example, C dominates B, D dominates F, E dominates both D and F, and J dominates both H and K. All the points that are not dominated by some other point are worthy of consideration by the decision maker; the others are not. The set of nondominated points is called the Pareto frontier.[3] Notice that along the Pareto frontier, a driver must increase risk to reduce travel time and vice versa.

[1] Risk is commonly defined as the product of probability and severity for a particular event. In this case serious injury is implicitly assumed to be equivalent to death. If degrees of severity of injury are considered, a more complex definition of risk is required.

[2] This figure represents a simplification of the major trade-offs between safety and travel time that drivers face in determining optimal driving speeds. Real-world choices are more complex. They involve continuous (as opposed to discrete) decisions about speed as motorists proceed along their trips. Factors other than safety and travel time may influence the speed choice. Finally, drivers may face a route decision (e.g., to take a higher- or lower-speed road), which in turn affects their speed choices.

[3] Named after the 19th century economist Vilfredo Pareto.

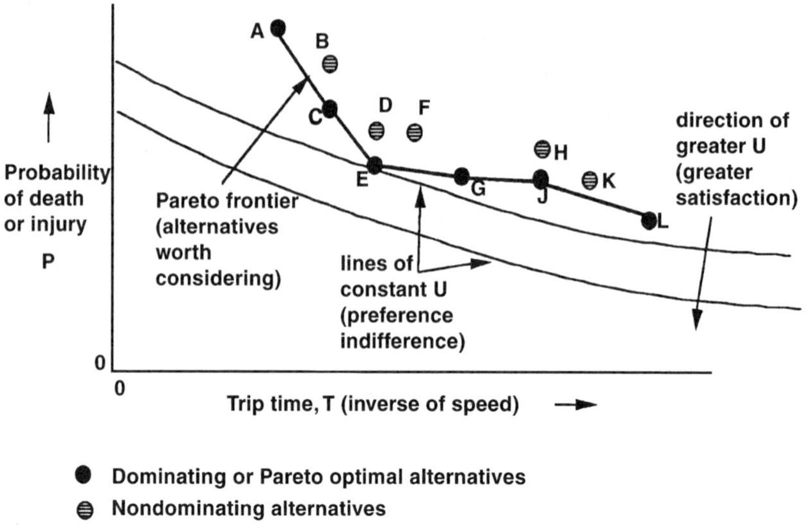

Figure A-1 Pareto optimal frontier of alternatives to be explored and optimized or satisficed.

How do the decision makers, the drivers, decide among the nondominated points? Certainly they cannot all be equally desirable to a particular individual. The choice depends on how each decision maker makes the trade-off between trip time and risk. Figure A-1 shows lines of constant utility, meaning indifference as to relative preference, with the lines of higher utility (more desirable) closer to the origin. The driver's goal, then, is to select the point on the Pareto frontier that gives the highest utility, in this case Point E. Drivers who place a very high value on their lives and are relatively indifferent to trip time will have relatively flat constant utility lines and will choose points with longer travel time and lower risk, like J or L. Alternatively, drivers who place a high value on trip time and are less concerned about safety will have steep constant-utility lines and will choose points with shorter travel time and higher risk, like A or C.

In summary, in formal decision theory the Pareto frontier specifies the "best" (nondominated) set of physically constrained trade-offs or options among which the driver must select. The Pareto frontier is independent of the driver's subjective trade-off between risk and travel time (i.e., his constant-utility or preference-indifference curve). The selection amounts to finding the point on the Pareto frontier that just touches the constant-utility curve with the highest (best) utility.

If the probability of death or injury is left on the *Y*-axis and trip time is left on the *X*-axis, the utility lines intersect the *Y*-axis at a small probability number, decrease in probability with time, and are curved, concave up. The reason why the utility lines intersect the *Y*-axis at a small number is that even if trip time were zero, no rational traveler would ever go on such a trip for a risk greater than some very small probability value. (Of course this intersection would differ with different travelers and differing trip urgency.) As trip time increased, the traveler would demand in trade some improvement in risk, such that the probability of death or injury would decrease with increasing trip time. However, adding 1 h to a very long trip time would not require the same demand for incremental improvement in risk as would adding 1 h to a very short trip time, and for that reason the curves must be shaped concave up. Further extension of the curves would require them to level off to some constant risk or else be asymptotic to the *X*-axis (zero risk) at an infinite trip time number, but this region is undefined and makes little practical sense to consider.

One critical point to observe is that, faced with the same set of alternatives, different drivers will choose different combinations of travel time and risk on the basis of how they value the trade-off. Thus, some motorists will choose to reduce their travel time by driving faster and assuming more risk, while others will choose to assume less risk and drive more slowly. The same driver may even make different trade-offs depending on the nature of the trip and the time of day or day of the week. For example, drivers may choose to travel faster on long trips where the time savings can be substantial. Thus, the variance observed in highway speeds is, in part, a natural consequence of these different choices.

The situation portrayed in Figure A-1 is further complicated because the Pareto frontier is subject to change, both by the individual and by public policy. Individuals may be able to change their risk by selection of safer vehicles. A safer vehicle may be more crashworthy or may have more features that make it easier to avoid certain kinds of crashes (e.g., antilock brakes on wet or icy roads). The risk may also be influenced by driver skill, and that skill can be enhanced by certain types of training. Thus, an individual may invest resources to alter the shape and position of the frontier. Not only do different drivers make trade-offs along the frontier differently, they may also face different frontiers.

As an example of how public policy can alter the shape of the frontier, over time safety regulations have made vehicles more crashworthy, and manufacturers have introduced new technologies (e.g., antilock brakes) to assist the driver in avoiding crashes. Some of these changes enable drivers to increase speed and decrease trip time without increasing risk, flattening the Pareto frontier. Highway design and construction can also change the frontier. Highways built to Interstate standards provide a driving environment with a lower risk for a given speed than do two-lane rural roads. Finally, through regulations such as speed limits combined with enforcement, public policy may prevent (or attempt to prevent) drivers from choosing some combinations of trip time and risk and may force them to choose others. The reason for regulation of individual driver speed choices is the effect of these choices on the risks faced not only by those drivers but also by other road users, including pedestrians and bicyclists. The transfer of risk to others is the primary rationale for policy intervention to restrict individual driver speed choice through regulation, a subject covered at greater length in the first section of Chapter 3.

Appendix B

Speed and Crashes: A Controversial Topic and an Elusive Relationship

David Shinar
Ben-Gurion University of the Negev, Israel

I was asked to write this paper on the relationship between speed and safety a few days prior to returning to the United States after a sojourn of a few months in Israel. I was returning to my home, to my car, and to my routine. On the first day back to work I drove on Washington's crash-prone I-495 beltway and had the comfortable feeling of slipping back into a familiar routine. Then I noticed I was driving at nearly 70 mph (113 km/h), way above my routine speed on the beltway. My previous typical speed on that road was 60 mph (97 km/h). I did not feel any more risk than I had felt before. In fact the feeling was one of "sameness." What I think had changed in the interim was the perceived enforced speed limit [raised from 55 to 65 mph (89 to 105 km/h)—not to be confused with the posted speed limit that has remained 55 mph] and the traffic-flow speed. What governed my chosen speed—the perceived enforced speed limit? My speed correlated with it. The prevailing speed of traffic? It correlated with that too. My risk-homeostasis level? I felt as safe as ever. My need to conform? Perhaps, since I certainly moved with the herd.

Once I realized what my speed was, my initial reaction was to ease off the gas. But I overcame this tendency (with ease) and decided to continue "with the traffic." Was I taking a greater risk by traveling at a higher speed? My recollection of the aggregate research in this area supported such a conclusion. But I did not feel that way. And, perhaps most important, I did not slow down. My behavior was consistent with my feeling of safety.

My own response and probably that of most drivers is to balance safety, pleasure, and mobility. This review focuses on safety. However, statistically significant safety benefits are not always of practical significance. What makes a statistically significant effect practically significant is its magnitude relative to the societal value of mobility and the value of the pleasure the individual derives from driving. Speeding is logically related to mobility and subjectively related, for many people at least, to pleasure. Although these issues are outside the scope of this review, they are relevant to the implications of any empirical relationship between speeding and safety.

This paper is therefore as much an attempt to synthesize the information on the relationship between speed and safety as an attempt to understand my own behavior—in the belief that it reflects that of many other motorists.

BACKGROUND

The relationship between speed and crashes is axiomatic for many people in the traffic safety community. That axiom is encapsulated in the slogan "speed kills." Speed is also listed as one of the manifestations of "aggressive driving" by the National Highway Traffic Safety Administration (NHTSA) (Martinez 1997) and safety interest groups such as Advocates of Highway and Auto Safety (Snyder 1997). Grass roots movements specifically targeting speeding are emerging (e.g., Citizens Against Speed and Aggressive Driving) (Shiekh 1997). Yet recent drops in U.S. traffic fatalities despite repeal of the National Maximum Speed Limit (NMSL) serve to raise public doubts on the relevance of speed to crashes, as reflected in the national media with front page captions like "Fewer dying despite faster speed limits" (*USA TODAY* 1997).

In the following analysis this axiom is questioned, and the causal relationship between speeding and crashes is evaluated. In referring to speed as the predictor variable and crashes as the predicted variable, it is assumed that speed is the independent variable of interest and that safety is the dependent variable of interest. Optimally, to demonstrate that speed is the independent variable behind changes in crashes, it should be under the experimenter's control (and it rarely is). For crashes to be a true dependent variable, a causal relationship has to exist, and it can never be unequivocally justified. Finally, both variables are multidimensional and need to be specifically defined.

DEFINITIONS: SPEED, SAFETY, AND INTERVENING VARIABLES

Safety is typically defined in terms of crashes or crash rates. At least two aspects of crashes should be considered as separate dependent measures of the effects of speed: crash probability (or incidence) and crash severity (given crash occurrence). In studying the effect of speed in particular, these two measures may not be highly correlated, since speed-related crashes are more commonly associated with severe injuries and fatalities and less with mild injuries and property damage. In contrast, the relationship between crash probability and speed is more complex, and speed-related crashes are not necessarily associated with high speeds.

Speed is not a singular concept in this context. First there is a need to distinguish between speed limits (prescribed speed) and travel speeds (drivers' speed). The two overlap only in the presence of at least one of the following: intense enforcement, environmental constraints (e.g., speed humps, reduced lane width, reduced visibility), or vehicle limitations (e.g., old cars) that force drivers to drive at or below the speed limit. Second, whereas speed limit is a single value, driving speed can be the speed of a single crash-involved vehicle or a statistic of the prevailing traffic speed distribution. Three such statistics are most often used in the context of safety: average travel speed, 85th percentile of the speed distribution, and some measure of the dispersion in travel speeds. Speed dispersion, in turn, can be quantified by the speed variance (the squared deviations from the mean of the speed distribution), the speed standard deviation (the square root of the variance), and sometimes by the speed range, such as the differential between the 15th and 85th percentile speed (which corresponds to approximately two standard deviations).

All the studies reviewed in this paper use some estimate of speed. In addition to the difficulty of integrating results obtained with the various speed measures mentioned above, there is a problem with the validity of the speed measures themselves. It is nearly impossible to obtain an objective measure of the true precrash speeds of crash-involved vehicles. This is because crashes are not planned, and consequently speeds must be estimated post hoc by various subjective and objective techniques, all having a limited validity. Only one study was found in which actual traffic crashes were videotaped and speed was calculated from the video frame analysis. In this study by Pasanen and Salmivaara (1993), a video camera specifically calibrated to measure speed recorded 18 intersection collisions in Helsinki, 11 of which involved pedestrians. In another study (West and Dunn 1971), precrash speeds for approximately one-fourth of the crash-involved vehicles were determined with a high degree of certainty from data obtained from speed detectors embedded in a section of an Indiana rural state highway with a 55-mph (89-km/h) speed limit. All other studies relied on drivers' estimates, police officers' estimates, or crash deformation data for calculating the speed of crash-involved vehicles. The few data that exist suggest that the relationship among the different speed measures is moderate at best (F.A. Haight, unpublished data, 1994). For studies relating traffic-flow speeds to crashes, the actual speed of the traffic stream at the place and time of the crash is usually not known; instead it is extrapolated from traffic-flow measures taken before or after the crash (e.g., Solomon 1964).

The reason drivers drive at different speeds probably affects the relationship between speed and crashes. Driving slowly in congested urban traffic is associated with many fender benders and very few severe crashes, whereas driving fast on expressways is associated with very few fender benders and a small but significant number of severe crashes. On the basis of these two situations, if all crashes are counted, it appears that speed is inversely related to crashes. However, if only severe crashes are examined, the relationship between speed and crashes is direct. In addition, driving slowly in congestion is done for a different reason than driving slowly on an open freeway. The difference may stem from the situation or from individual differences among drivers (a slow driver on a freeway may be a cognitively impaired elderly driver, whereas a slow driver on a congested urban street may be a highly capable driver hampered by traffic). For example, Solomon (1964) found that drivers at precrash speeds significantly above or below the average traffic speed have a greater likelihood of overinvolvement in crashes than do those driving just slightly above the average (Solomon 1964). But that relationship changed when turning vehicles were removed from the total driving population (Fildes and Lee 1993).

In aggregating crash data from different roads and different times to evaluate the effect of speed as a single independent variable, one assumes (at least implicitly) that "all other things remain equal." This is never the case. In real life, driving speed is highly correlated with at least the following (Bowie and Walz 1994):

1. Other crash-related driver behaviors such as drinking, not using safety belts (Evans 1991), and other types of aggressive driving (in fact, speeding is often considered as a subcategory of aggressive driving);
2. Crash-related individual differences in variables such as age and sex;
3. Road design (e.g., speed-related crashes are overrepresented on curves) and road conditions, traffic conditions, and speed limits; and
4. Vehicular variables such as type of vehicle, engine power, and steering and brake performance.

All of these factors complicate the interpretation of data. In the absence of complete data to evaluate the joint contribution of all variables, the conclusions remain qualified.

Finally, when speed data are not available, a speed management technique is often used to assess the relationship between speed and safety. It is then assumed that speed covaries with the speed assumed by the management technique. The most common management technique is the speed limit. Other techniques are speed enforcement and speed calming through traffic engineering (e.g., sequencing traffic lights) and roadway design (e.g., road humps, traffic circles, and rumble strips). It then remains to be demonstrated that these techniques affect speed.

With these caveats in mind, the literature review will be divided into three major parts: (*a*) the effect of speed management/control techniques on speed and crashes, (*b*) the effect of speed on crash incidence, and (*c*) the effect of speed on crash severity. Finally, on the basis of the literature review, conclusions concerning speed and crashes will be drawn.

SPEED REDUCTION AND SPEED MANAGEMENT TECHNIQUES

An extensive review of the relationship between speed management, especially speed limits, and crashes is outside the scope of this paper. However, since these techniques are also used as surrogate measures of travel speed, a brief review of this relationship is appropriate.

Speed Limits

The impact of speed limits on crash risk is addressed in Appendix C. However, studies measuring both speed changes and crash experience in the context of speed limit changes and enforcement are relevant to this paper. Reviews of studies that evaluated changes in crashes and injuries in conjunction with changes (or the introduction) of speed limits have generally supported the notion that increases in speed limits without other concurrent changes are associated with increases in crashes; decreases or setting of speed limits where none existed before are associated with crash and injury reductions (NHTSA 1992; Rock 1995; Summala 1985; TRB 1984). However, all of these studies suffer from the shortcomings of poor control of potentially confounding variables such as changes in traffic patterns as a consequence of speed limit changes, spillover effects of crashes to adjacent roads, changes in road service levels, and the concurrent introduction of other safety-related variables including increased enforcement, increased use of safety belts, reduction in drinking and driving, and vehicle-based safety improvements. In the context of the NMSL of 55 mph (89 km/h), a Transportation Research Board (TRB) special report on the enduring effects of this statute concluded, "Nevertheless, as improvements have been made to highways, vehicles, and medical services, the risk associated with higher speed driving has been reduced somewhat" (TRB 1984, 70). This means that comparisons across jurisdictions and over time (especially when the higher speed is the more recent) are flawed. The difficulties are so great as to yield opposite conclusions from the same data, depending on the measure of crash involvement used and the factors other than speed limits that are included in the analyses. Such disagreements have led Lave (1985; 1989; Lave and Elias 1994) to argue that, although raised speed limits increased fatalities on the affected rural roads, they have actually contributed to the observed reduction in statewide fatalities, whereas researchers of the Insurance Institute for Highway Safety (Zador and Lund 1991; Lund and Rauch 1992) have argued that the specific effects measured by Lave can be attributed to multiple other factors that have been previously linked to fatality reductions and that raising the speed limit has cost lives (NHTSA 1992).

Garber and Gadiraju (1988) suggested that the difference between the design speed and the posted speed limit accounts for differences in driving speeds, widening speed dispersion, in turn, was linked to increases in crash rates. On the Virginia highways they studied, minimum speed dispersion was obtained when the design speed was 5 to 10 mph (8 to 16 km/h) above the posted limit. This could also explain why lower speed limits sometimes increase the incidence of crashes. Parker's findings (1997) of the inconsistent effects of temporary speed limit changes on short highway sections support this conclusion. Other factors, such as traffic conditions, can also affect speed and speed dispersion. Thus, Vaa (1997) found that compliance with enforced speed limits is less during peak periods than during off-peak periods. Also, when speed limits are lowered, they are typically accompanied by increased enforcement and public information campaigns (e.g., Nilsson 1990).

Parker's analysis is relevant here because it measures the effects of changes in speed limits on driving speeds and the effects of these changes on crash involvement. Parker found small but statistically significant effects of speed limit changes on travel speed. Whereas the speed limits were changed by as much as 20 mph (32 km/h), the changes in travel speed (using either the means or percentile levels) were generally less than 2 mph (3 km/h) and were unrelated to the change in the speed limit. Also, the maximum speed limit never exceeded the 55-mph (89-km/h) NMSL that was in effect at the time of the speed limit manipulation (1985 to 1992). Finally, the relationship between speed limit and crashes in Parker's study was ambiguous. Comparisons between crashes at sites where the speed limit was changed and crashes at the control sites showed a slight increase in crashes with increases in speed limits, whereas the before-after comparisons yielded a significant decrease in crashes with increases in speed limits. Parker's study had an acknowledged major shortcoming in the site selection. The sites selected for the speed limit changes were chosen by local agencies on the basis of a predetermined need (e.g., request from the public, high incidence of crashes, compliance with local ordinances, changing land use patterns) rather than randomly. Thus it is likely that in many cases the changes actually reflected existing travel speeds. Given this severe constraint, the small number of sites, and short follow-up, Parker (1997) qualified his conclusions by stating that "the findings may apply to similar sites where the speed limits are changed for similar reasons. Generalizations to other roadways are not appropriate" (p. 85).

Under some circumstances, changes to higher speed limits may have a greater and more consistent effect. Photo-radar surveys conducted by the Insurance Institute for Highway Safety revealed that the percentage of drivers exceeding 70 mph (113 km/h) increased significantly when speed limits were raised to 65 mph (105 km/h) in California and 70 mph in Texas (Retting and Greene 1997). If speeds in excess of 70 mph are well beyond the average traffic speed on these roads (admittedly an arguable assumption), then—either because of their high speed or because of their contribution to widening the range of traffic speeds—speeding drivers are at a greater crash risk. Their increased risk is consistent with both the "speed" model and the "variance" model because the more the driver exceeds the average traffic speed, the greater the range in traffic speeds and the further the driver's position from the minimum point of the U-shaped crash involvement curve.

The issue of the role of speed dispersion is further complicated by the ambiguity of the term. Although the statistical definition of variance as a measure of dispersion is clear, the term is often misused. Different researchers have used different statistics to represent speed dispersion. Traffic engineers typically measure speed dispersion from the speeds of free-flowing vehicles over a short period. When measurements of speed dispersion are based on long durations of exposure and many of the vehicles are not free-flowing, it is not clear what the measure reflects. For example, an exposure period that covers both peak- and non-peak-period traffic can yield a wide range of traffic speeds, whereas in a short interval the range of traffic speeds may be narrower.

An intervening variable that may affect both compliance and crash involvement is the "perceived reasonableness" of the speed limit. McCoy et al. (1993) studied road sections in Nebraska and found that sites with "reasonable" speed limits were safer than those with limits 5 to 10 mph (8 to 16 km/h) below the "reasonable" levels. To ensure a good correspondence between this measure and speed choice, a recent evaluation of the relationship among safety, speed, and speed management conducted for Transport Canada suggests that the traditional rule of thumb for determination of speed limits—to use the 85th percentile for existing roads and the design speed for new roads—is still a good one (Knowles et al. 1997). Because actual speed limits are often dictated by other considerations, and given the lack of control of these variables in most studies, the researchers concluded that "changing the posted speed limit does not automatically mean that speeds and crashes will be affected by the change and that it is not clear under what conditions changing the speed limit is likely to lead to a change in safety" (p. 2-9).

Speed Enforcement

Speed enforcement is probably the most common mediator between speed limit and speed choice. There is ample evidence that drivers respond to perceived enforcement by adjusting their behavior, most notably by reducing their speed (Shinar and McKnight 1985). The effect of enforcement is typically maximal at the site of the perceived enforcement, but halo effects relating to both time and place have been demonstrated. Holland and Conner (1996) obtained a time-halo effect lasting up to 9 weeks for speed enforcement coupled with signs stating "Police Speed Check Area," and Vaa (1997) demonstrated that massive enforcement, with a daily average of police presence of 9 h, yielded speed reductions that lasted up to 8 weeks. This was done in a semirural area with a road section having speed limits of 37 and 50 mph (60 and 80 km/h). Interestingly, speed reductions varied by time of day, and morning peak-period speeders were the most resistant to change. This could have been due to pressure to get to work on time or the drivers' knowledge that enforcement is more difficult (and therefore perceived as less threatening) in high-density, peak-period traffic. Shinar and Stiebel (1986) showed that compliance was highest near police vehicles and diminished with increasing distance. The distance-halo effect was greater for a moving than a stationary police vehicle, presumably because the moving vehicle could be perceived as more threatening even when it was already out of sight.

The link between enforcement and crash reduction was evaluated by Elvik (1997), who conducted a meta-analysis of studies that evaluated automated speed enforcement in several countries including England, Germany, Sweden, Norway, Australia, and the Netherlands. He concluded that, overall, automated enforcement yielded a 17 percent reduction in injury crashes (16 to 19 percent at a confidence level of 95 percent). The difference in effectiveness at different locations suggests that it is most effective at crash "black spots" (i.e., high-crash locations). Whether the crashes migrate elsewhere, as has been argued by Lave and Elias (1994), is still an issue.

Other Speed Management Techniques

Perhaps the most cost-effective approach to speed control in the long run is through road design. This has been demonstrated with speed humps and with changes in design that are made to accommodate pedestrians in urban streets with "traffic integration." This design approach was initiated in the Netherlands (and called "woonerf") in 1968 and has spread in various forms to Germany, Denmark, England, France, Israel, and Australia (F.A. Haight, unpublished data, 1994). The integration is achieved through making roads narrow or winding or placing obstacles on the travel portion of the road so that vehicular traffic has to slow down to practically walking speeds [e.g., 9 mph (15 km/h)]. Although the effect on safety has not been the focus of evaluations of these changes, the effect on speed has been consistently reported (F.A. Haight, unpublished data, 1994).

SPEED AND CRASH INVOLVEMENT

From a very simplistic point of view it appears that as speed increases, the time to react to emerging dangers is shortened, and the likelihood of successfully coping with the imminent crash situation decreases. Also, even after a driver reacts by braking, the braking distance of the vehicle is proportional to the square of the prebraking speed. Therefore the distance traveled to a complete stop increases with speed, and the likelihood of a collision increases in a corresponding fashion. But reality is much more complicated, both theoretically and empirically. In this section an attempt is made to consider the theoretical issues involved and the empirical data that support and refute the relationship between speed and crash probability.

Some Theoretical Issues—and a Theoretical Quagmire

There are at least three theoretical approaches to relate speed to crashes, each leading to a different conclusion. Each approach views the driver and the traffic environment from a different perspective, and each has been used as a conceptual framework that relates driver behavior to highway traffic safety. Some empirical validation has been demonstrated for each of them. The three approaches are referred to as the information processing/attentional approach, the risk-homeostasis motivational approach, and the traffic conflict approach.

Information Processing Approach

This approach considers the driver as an information processor with a limited capacity. The limit is on the rate of information processing. From a theoretical perspective, if a driver is assumed to be introduced into a fixed roadway/traffic situation, then the faster that driver drives, the greater the required rate of information processing, and the greater the demands of maneuverability of the car in an imminent crash situation. A crash is likely to occur when the information processing demands exceed the attentional or information processing capabilities of the driver (Shinar 1978) or the capabilities of the car. Even if the total amount of information the driver has to process stays constant, the rate at which that information must be processed increases directly with the speed of the driver. Furthermore, even at a constant speed, the rate of information flow is not constant but changes as a function of changes in the environment. Specifically, unexpected events dramatically increase the amount of information that must be processed. Such events include a car weaving in the lane, an obstacle in the travel lane, a curve with short sight distance, merging vehicles, and so forth. Other attention-demanding factors may be unrelated to driving, such as radio broadcasts, cellular phone conversations, or distractions from within the car. Consequently, at some speed, the increase in the information load can make the driver more likely to fail to process and respond fast enough to all the information, resulting in a crash. In lay terms, the driver was surprised and unable to respond to the situation in time. This approach leads to the conclusion that "speed kills." As more and more drivers increase their speed, the likelihood of an overload increases for more and more motorists, and the probability of a crash—a situation in which the driver cannot respond appropriately in sufficient time—increases as well.

The attention factor is perhaps the most critical aspect of the information processing chain. Without exception all theories of human information processing acknowledge the limited attentional capacity of human beings; although it can vary over time, it cannot be sustained at a high level for any lengthy duration (Lindsay and Norman 1977). Furthermore, the act of paying attention is an effort (Kahneman 1973), as has been demonstrated in the driving context in sign detection and recall (Näätänen and Summala 1976; Shinar and Drory 1983). In-depth investigations of crash causes invariably point to lapses in attention (variously labeled as inattention, distraction, or improper lookout) as the most common human cause of traffic crashes. Such lapses have been implicated as a "cause" in approximately 50 percent of all crashes (Treat et al. 1977; Sabey and Staughton 1975; Shinar 1978; Evans 1991).

The implication for speed is twofold. If attention level remains constant despite increases in speed, then the crash potential due to a lapse in attention for a given duration increases as speed increases because in that duration the distance traveled increases and the safety margin decreases. If, on the other hand, the driver increases the amount of attention with increasing speed (as some drivers claim—the extreme claim being that driving slowly is boring and induces drowsiness), then the driving task becomes very fatiguing, and the heightened attention cannot be sustained for long periods. In either case, the attention factor suggests that increasing speed is tantamount to increasing crash potential. Because some highway design codes are based on assumed speed and reaction times (e.g., reading signs) and assumed sight distance to obstacles (e.g., railroad crossings), information overload and lapses in attention are more critical the faster the driver is going. Finally, as speed increases, each of the driving tasks becomes more difficult—detection of obstacles, recognition of impending danger, decision making, and response selection—and that difficulty contributes to the increase in crash risk (Kallberg and Luoma 1996).

Traffic Conflict Approach

This approach considers the traffic stream and roadway system as the source of potential conflicts to which a driver responds. The load on the driver increases as a function of increasing disparities in speed in the traffic stream because of the different behaviors and speeds of the other drivers and vehicles. If all traffic moves in unobstructed lanes on divided highways at the same speed, then there is no uncertainty about the movement of the other vehicles, differences in driving speeds approach zero, and the potential for conflicts among vehicles does not increase with increasing speeds. Unfortunately, this is not the case since most roads are not divided highways, and the traffic flow is best represented by a distribution of speeds. Thus, in reality the number of conflicts between vehicle pairs can be represented by the number of passing maneuvers. The number of passing maneuvers a driver must make increases as the driver's speed increases, and the number of times a driver is passed by other vehicles decreases as the driver increases speed. It can be shown that the distribution of the total number of overtakings (derived from the distributions of the number of times passing and number of times being passed) has a minimum at the median traffic speed. Therefore, the more the slower and faster drivers deviate from the median speed, the more conflicts they are likely to encounter (Hauer 1971). This logic leads to the conclusion that it is not speed that kills but the deviation from the median or average traffic speed that kills; the more a driver contributes to this deviation (by driving faster or slower than the median or average), the more likely the driver is to be involved in a crash. Therefore, the danger lies in the relationship between each driver and all other drivers. This can lead to the prediction that crash rates will be higher on roads with low median speeds but a wide range of speeds (e.g., two-lane rural roads) than on roads with high median speeds but a narrower range of speeds (e.g., expressways).

Risk-Homeostasis Motivational Approach

The first formulation of this approach was probably Taylor's (1964) "risk-speed compensation model," which postulated that drivers adjust their speeds in accordance with the perceived risk. Wilde et al. (1985) generalized this model to "risk homeostasis," which, in the context of driving and crash avoidance, assumes that (*a*) drivers are not passive information processors who merely react to conflicts but are active in the sense that they have needs and goals that affect their driving style, and (*b*) a primary motive of drivers is to maintain a subjectively acceptable level of risk. From this perspective, drivers do not set their speed indiscriminately; they adjust their speed according to the perceived risks. This approach has intuitive appeal since most drivers "feel" that they adjust their speed in response to the changing demands of the highway and the traffic (and thereby moderate the rate of information that must be processed). Thus, most drivers increase headways (the distance they maintain behind the cars ahead of them) at faster speeds to maintain a fixed temporal interval (Taieb and Shinar 1996), and drivers slow down on intersection approaches, on entering construction zones, in areas where the lane width is decreased, in the absence of hard shoulders, and so forth. If this adjustment is appropriate, there should be no correlation between speed and crashes. If the adjustment is insufficient, crashes should increase with speed. By the same token, if the adjustment to a perceived danger is excessive, then crash probability may actually decrease.

The question then becomes not one of the relationship between speed and crashes, but one of the correspondence between actual and perceived risk and between perceived risk and driver actions. This means that increasing speed per se is not a dangerous behavior but that an inappropriate excessive speed—stemming from misperception of the situational demands and lack of appreciation of the car and the driver's own handling capability—may be dangerous. This approach can lead to different predictions concerning the relationship between speed and crashes, but since most drivers' perceptions of the road and traffic ahead are fairly accurate, it would predict that under most circumstances the voluntary increase in speed of most drivers would not necessarily increase crash risk.

There is some empirical support for the risk-homeostasis theory. Mackay (1985) found that British drivers of newer and heavier cars drove at higher speeds than drivers of older and lighter cars (except for sports cars, which are fastest), but speeds of belted and unbelted drivers did not differ (this study was conducted in 1982, before the use of safety belts was made mandatory). Rumar et al. (1976) found that drivers with studded tires drove faster than drivers without such tires on road curves in icy conditions but not in dry conditions, indicating that drivers adjust their speed according to their perceived safety or vehicle-handling capability. On the other hand, O'Day and Flora (1982) in their analysis of National Crash Severity Study (NCSS) data for tow-away crashes found that restrained occupants had lower impact speeds than unrestrained occupants. (This finding is consistent with the notion that it is the same hard-core segment of the driving population that speed, do not use safety belts, and drink and drive.)

With these conflicting theoretical approaches, it is no wonder that the issue of the relationship between speed and safety is hotly debated and one on which the motoring public is divided. Of the three major safety issues—safety belt use, drinking and driving, and speeding—the reported tendency to obey speed limits is the lowest and has decreased over the past decade. In contrast, the reported use of safety belts and the avoidance of drinking before driving have increased continuously (Shinar and Schechtman 1998).

The remaining task is therefore to review the empirical literature to determine whether there are sufficient data to reach definitive conclusions about the nature of the relationship between speed and crashes.

Review of Empirical Data

National crash statistics from the Fatal Analysis Reporting System (FARS) indicate that "driving too fast for conditions or in excess of posted speed limit" is a "related factor" for 20.8 percent of the drivers involved in fatal crashes. This statistic is often cited as the basis for concern with speed (Martinez 1997). However, the crash data must be interpreted with caution since they do not include an exposure measure, in this case, a statistic that indicates the percentage of drivers in the traffic stream where these crashes occurred who "exceed the speed limit or drive too fast for conditions." On the basis of Parker's (1997) study on the effects of raising and lowering speed limits on selected nonlimited-access roadway sections, the percentage exceeding the posted speed limit is typically greater than 20.8 percent. For this reason, to evaluate accurately the contribution of speed to crashes, it is important to control for spurious effects through well-designed correlational analyses of crash and travel data or detailed cause-and-effect analyses of individual crashes. Unfortunately, neither type of analysis is common.

Correlational Studies: Interpreting the Evidence

Because of lack of controls, the results of the various correlational studies are often inconsistent with each other. Perhaps the best way to demonstrate the difficulty in directly testing the relationship between speed and crashes is to cite three studies that attempted to do that. The first is a comprehensive analysis of the correlation between fatality rates and speeds on various road systems in the United States during the 55-mph (89-km/h) NMSL era. The correlations of fatality rates and percentage of drivers exceeding 65 mph (105 km/h) was .33 for the expressways, .25 for rural arterial roads, and not significantly different from zero for rural collectors, urban arterials, and urban expressways. Furthermore, there were no significant correlations between fatality rates and the percentage exceeding 55 mph or 85th percentile speeds for any of the road types (TRB 1984, 66). The second analysis was detailed and focused on Virginia crashes; it failed to find any significant relationship between average speed and crash rates (Garber and Gadiraju 1988). In the most recent of the three studies, Liu and Popoff (1996) compared average speeds in seven sections of 62-mph (100-km/h) roads in Saskatchewan, Canada, between 1969–1982 and 1983–1995. Their measure of speed dispersion was the speed differential between the 15th and the 85th percentile speeds (which roughly corresponds to two standard deviations). In three sections the average speed decreased, the speed range narrowed, and the crash rate declined. In two sections the average speed remained relatively constant, the speed range narrowed, and the crash rate declined. In one section the average speed increased, the speed range narrowed, and the crash rate declined. In one section both the average speed and the speed range decreased but the crash rate increased. In contrast to these mixed results, on the basis of regressions derived from nine speed surveys on Saskatchewan provincial highways conducted since 1969, Liu and Popoff concluded that the number of casualties is linearly highly related to the average speed (with $R = 0.90$), whereas the casualty rate (relative to kilometers driven) is linearly related to their measure of speed dispersion ($R = 0.94$). The caveats in this conclusion are that the study suffered from (*a*) a small range of average speeds studied [62 to 65 mph (100 to 105 km/h)], (*b*) a small number of observations, and (*c*) no control over many other time-dependent factors. In summary, the three studies cited can be used as support for both the existence and the absence of a relationship between speed and crashes depending on the speed measures and conditions used, the study design, and the crash statistics used.

It is therefore best to address the evidence from a loose chronological perspective and attempt to integrate the data on this issue as it accumulated.

The benchmark study of the relationship between speed and crash involvement and between speed and crash severity was conducted by Solomon (1964). A critical component of Solomon's study was the inclusion of the speed of the traffic stream as a potential mediating factor. Because of the care that Solomon took in examining all three aspects of speed—average speed of the traffic stream, speed dispersion, and reported speed of crash-involved vehicles—and because Solomon's study was the first, and to date arguably the most detailed and comprehensive study of this nature, its essential design features are described before its findings and conclusions are reported.

The study analyzed the crash experience of 10,000 driver-vehicles that had been involved in crashes between 1954 and 1958 on 600 mi (1000 km) of rural two- and four-lane highways consisting of 35 sections in 11 states. Roadway characteristics varied widely [with an average of 1.33 intersections per mile (0.83 intersections per kilometer) and 0.67 entrances per mile (0.42 entrances per kilometer)], as did speed limits [45 to 70 mph (73 to 113 km/h) for passenger cars in the daytime] and design speeds [35 to 70 mph (56 to 113 km/h)]. Traffic speed measurements at each of the sites were made during 1957 and 1958. Solomon also calculated the exposure of the vehicles traveling at different speeds by multiplying the number of vehicles measured at each speed in each road section by the length of the section, and then summing the data from all 35 sections. Finally, Solomon defined crash involvement (his dependent measure) as the number of crashes per 100 million vehicle-mi (161 million vehicle-km).

Looking first at the relationship between travel speed of the crash-involved vehicles and the crash rate [number of crashes per 100 million vehicle-mi (161 million vehicle-km)], Solomon obtained the U-shaped functions reproduced in Figure B-1 for daytime and nighttime crashes. These curves show that the lowest involvement rate was at approximately 60 mph (97 km/h) and that the rate increased for both slower- and faster-moving vehicles. Note that the rate of increase relative to the minimum is plotted on a logarithmic scale. The rise would appear much steeper if the scale were linear. Figure B-1 indicates similar patterns for daytime and nighttime crashes, with overall nighttime crash rates being higher, and the minimum point for daytime crashes being approximately 5 mph (8 km/h) higher than at night. The increase in nighttime crash involvement at speeds greater than 65 mph (105 km/h) is much greater than the increase in daytime crash involvement at these speeds.

Why should speeds of 50 to 60 mph (80 to 97 km/h) yield the lowest crash rates? Solomon hypothesized that the speed with the lowest crash rates should correspond roughly to the average traffic speed. Seven years after Solomon's study was published, Hauer (1971) demonstrated mathematically that the number of vehicle encounters (in terms of passing or being passed) is a U-shaped curve with a minimum for vehicles traveling at the median traffic speed. Speeds greater than the median traffic speed involve more active passing maneuvers, and lower speeds involve more passive (being passed by others) passing maneuvers. Since most of the mileage in Solomon's study consisted of rural two lane highways, this makes perfect sense. In a detailed analysis of crash involvement on a section-by-section basis, Solomon essentially confirmed this hypothesis. Involvement rates were lowest at speeds 5 to 10 mph (8 to 16 km/h) above the average and increased as the difference between the average and the speed of the crash-involved vehicle increased. His results, summarized for all 35 sections in terms of deviation from the average traffic speed, are presented in Figure B-2. If it is assumed that the speed distribution is not symmetric around the average but is negatively skewed (with a longer tail for slower-moving vehicles), the

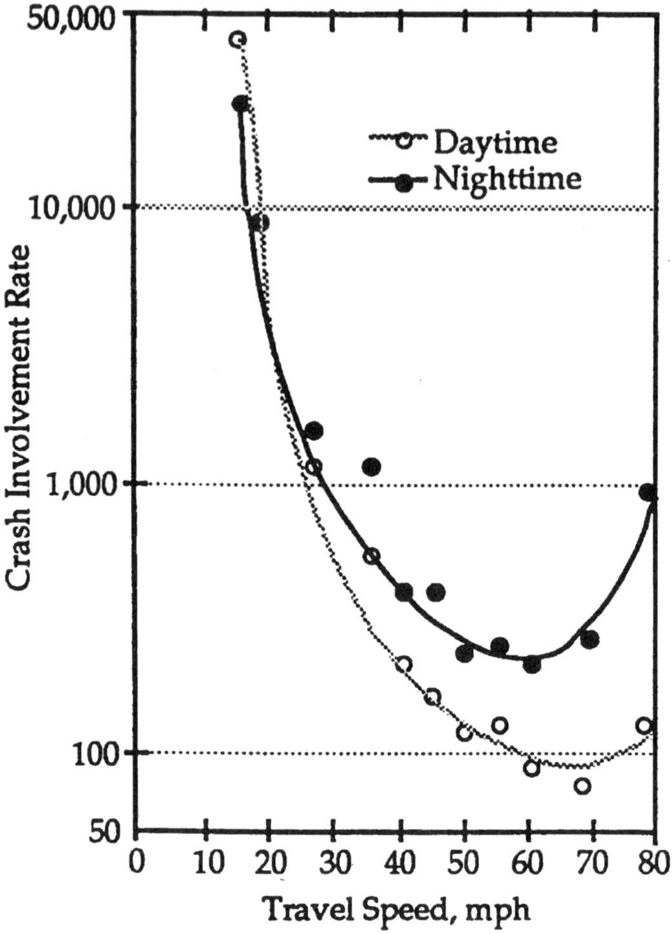

Figure B-1 Crash involvement rate by travel speed (Solomon 1964 in Stuster and Coffman 1997, 3). 1 mph = 1.609 km/h.

average traffic speed is lower than the median, and the 5- to 10-mph minimum point above the average corresponds fairly well to Hauer's (1971) theoretical derivation.

The pattern presented in Figure B-2 led Solomon to conclude that "regardless of the average speed on a main rural highway, the greater the driver's deviation from this average speed, the greater his chance of being involved in an accident" (p. 16). In light of the higher rates

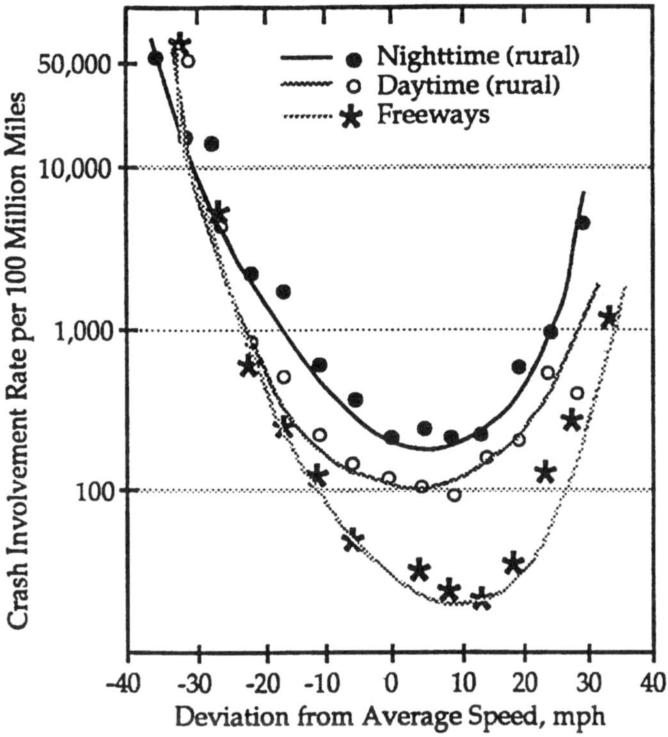

Figure B-2 Crash involvement rate by deviation from average traffic speed (Solomon 1964; Cirillo 1968 in Stuster and Coffman 1997, 4). 1 mph = 1.609 km/h.

at the negative end of the speed axis, he further concluded that "low speed drivers are more likely to be involved in accidents than relatively high speed drivers" (p. 9). Solomon's findings from the predominantly rural highways of the late 1950s were generalized to Interstate highway crashes by Cirillo (1968). Her data were limited to daytime rear-end and angle collisions and same-direction sideswipe crashes, and they are plotted alongside those of Solomon in Figure B-2.

In a related analysis, Solomon studied crash involvement of pairs of passenger vehicles involved in rear-end collisions. He found that crash-involved pairs were much more likely to travel at larger speed differences than the likelihood of such differences in the traffic stream. This analysis provided further support for his conclusion that "a reduction in the variability of speeds can be an important element in accident reduction" (p. 17).

Over the years Solomon's study has been reviewed and critiqued by many researchers (Fildes and Lee 1993; Knowles et al. 1997; Stuster and Coffman 1997). Four of the more critical shortcomings that have been mentioned are as follows:

1. The speed flow measures were not from the same times as the crashes. The speed data were collected in 1957 and 1958, whereas the crash data were distributed over 1954 to 1958.
2. The speed data from turning vehicles were eliminated from the analysis, but turning-related crashes were not.
3. The precrash speeds of the crash-involved vehicles were obtained primarily from self-reports by the drivers. They are most likely to be biased toward low speeds because "drivers tend to explain their traffic accidents by reporting circumstances of lowest culpability compatible with credibility" ["Stannard's Law" (Aronoff 1971)].
4. The roads, traffic control devices, and vehicles are all from the 1950s and may not be relevant to today's environment.

Two additional issues appear to have been overlooked in the previous critiques of Solomon's conclusions and others' interpretations of his results and should be added to the limitations. First, in arriving at his conclusion, Solomon makes the subtle substitution of a cause-and-effect relationship for the observed association between the speed deviation from the average traffic speed and crash involvement. Not only was speed deviation not manipulated in the study, but the contribution of speed deviation per se to crash involvement was never demonstrated in that study by comparing roads of similar physical geometry with different speed ranges.

Second, speed varies as a function of many factors, an important one being the design speed of the highway. In his analysis Solomon did not control for the design speed of the various road sections. Drivers tend to adjust their speed to design speed, and when different routes with different design speeds (e.g., rural collector roads and expressways) are entered into the same equation, it can be shown that crash rates decrease with increasing average speed (Garber and Gadiraju 1988). Thus, examining the effects of variability in traffic speeds across different road sections of different types can be misleading.

Munden (1967) studied the relationship between speed and crashes in the United Kingdom. His measure of speed deviation was the ratio derived from dividing the speed of the study vehicles by the speed of the four cars that preceded it and the four cars that followed it. He found that drivers observed only once during the course of the study did not yield the U-shaped curve obtained by Solomon, having little variation in crash rates despite large differences in speed ratios. On the other hand, drivers observed more than once did exhibit the U-shaped curve. Munden's explanation was that the relationship is true only for drivers who *habitually* drive at deviant—especially slow—speeds. Even if drivers observed more than once drove regularly on that route and the measurement locations were identical, it is still likely that they were involved in turning or entering the road as a part of their regular driving habit.

Still, with Solomon's and Munden's results in mind and with a decade of experience with the 55-mph (89-km/h) NMSL, TRB's *Special Report 204* stated that "if the average speed of the traffic stream could be increased without increasing the variance of the speed, then the adverse effects on safety might be comparatively small" (TRB 1984, 68). This statement was evaluated in several studies where, over time (and usually in conjunction with raising the speed limit), speeds increased. Interestingly, TRB's hypothetical scenario of increases in speed without concomitant increases in speed dispersion appears to occur. Unlike many other measures of driver performance in which the variance increases with increases in the mean, increases in speed limits typically result in smaller increases in the average speed and no consistent increases in measures of speed dispersion (Brown et al. 1990; Freedman and Williams 1992 for free-flowing vehicles on expressways; McCarthy 1991) or even a narrowing of speeds (Garber and Gadiraju 1988, who compared road sections of different road classes with different design speeds). Only a few studies reported slight increases in speed dispersion with increases in average traffic speeds (Levy and Asch 1989, using the difference between the 85th percentile and the average speed as a surrogate measure; Retting and Greene 1997, using speed standard deviation).

To focus directly on the contribution of speed dispersion to crashes, Lave (1985) analyzed the relationship between crash involvement [in the same terms as Solomon— fatalities per 100 million vehicle-mi (161 million vehicle-km)], average speed, and speed dispersion (using a surrogate measure of the speed standard deviation—the 85th percentile speed minus the average speed—which roughly corresponds to the standard deviation when the average is very close to the median speed). Using the data from 48 states as 48 data points, he showed that for most road types, speed dispersion is positively related to crash rates, and when it is held constant (statistically), the correlations of crash involvement with average speed, percentage of vehicles exceeding 55 mph (89 km/h), percentage exceeding 65 mph (105 km/h), and 85th percentile speed are all nonsignificant. Independent "comments" in reply to Lave's analysis confirmed the relevance of speed dispersion to crashes (Fowles and Loeb 1989; Levy and Asch 1989; Snyder 1989), although they all claimed that average speed is also a significant contributor. Still, in using the speed of crash-involved vehicles, none of these analyses were able to disaggregate slowing vehicles from slow-moving vehicles. Rodriguez (1990) used data from all 50 states and analyzed the contribution of average speed and speed dispersion to fatality rates [defined as number of fatal crashes per 100 million vehicle-mi (161 million vehicle-km)] separately for each year from 1981 to 1985. He also obtained a significant effect for speed dispersion (for 4 of the 5 years) and no significant effect for average speed.

Further support for the importance of speed dispersion beyond that of the average speed is the negative correlation typically obtained between the two measures: roads with higher average speeds also have narrower speed ranges (Garber and Gadiraju 1988; Lave 1985). In both of the studies that obtained this relationship, speed dispersion was defined in terms of the traffic speed distribution (and not in terms of the deviation of crash-involved vehicles from the average traffic speed). In one study, no relationship was obtained between average speed and crash involvement (Lave 1985), and in the other study (Garber and Gadiraju 1988), with recorded average speeds ranging from 42 to 59.5 mph (68 to 95.8 km/h), crash rates actually declined with increasing average speed in a logarithmic fashion.

If "variance kills," then presumably it is because it reflects the potential for intervehicle conflicts. However, accounting for Solomon's and Lave's findings and those of all the others in terms of Hauer's theoretical analysis of the potential for intervehicle conflicts is somewhat problematic. That is because maneuvers that are most likely to be involved in passing and overtaking account for less than 5 percent of all maneuvers for crash-involved vehicles in the United States [merging/changing lanes = 3.0 percent, passing other vehicle = 1.3 percent (NHTSA 1997)]. Furthermore, an analysis of the crash characteristics of speed-related fatal crashes indicates that most (nearly 70 percent based on FARS) involve a single vehicle only (Bowie and Walz 1994), casting more doubt on the role of speed deviation and slow-moving vehicles. Solomon also calculated the percentage of crash involvements for different crash types as a function of speed. He found that whereas the percentage of single-vehicle crashes increased with travel speed, the percentage of rear-end and angle crashes decreased with travel speed, peaking at 15 mph (24 km/h) for angle crashes and 0 mph for rear-end crashes. These findings also point to the likely role that being stopped or entering and leaving the highway plays in low-speed crashes.

Still, ruling out intervehicle conflict as a crash-causing factor is not so simple. Crashes are typically coded as "single vehicle" if the crash-involved vehicle does not come in actual contact with another vehicle. However, often a single-vehicle crash, such as "run off the road," may be due to an attempt to avoid a collision with another vehicle that enters its path. This information, which is often contained in crash narratives, is based primarily on the driver's (or occupants') report and is usually not available in the digitally coded crash data. In Indiana University's *Tri-Level Study of the Causes of Traffic Accidents* (Treat et al. 1977), such crashes were coded as involving a "phantom vehicle." In their representative sample of crashes, such events were relatively rare and were cited as a probable factor in 3.8 percent of *all* crashes, including multiple-vehicle crashes (Volume I,

p. 53). Their involvement may be greater in single-vehicle fatal crashes, but reports of their involvement would be rarer since most often the involved driver is killed.

Cowley (1987) recalculated Solomon's involvement rates separately for six types of collisions and replicated the complete U-shaped curves only for nighttime head-on collisions. Predictably, crash rates increased with speed for single-vehicle run-off-the-road crashes and decreased with speed for rear-end crashes. However, angle collisions, "single vehicle struck object" crashes, and daytime-only head-on collisions decreased with increasing speed, suggesting that there is something to the argument that slow or slowing vehicles are overinvolved in crashes without necessarily shedding light on why this is so.

Solomon was aware of the difference between slow-moving vehicles and vehicles that were slowing down to negotiate some maneuver. Conceptually the difference is very significant: the former suggests that slow-moving *vehicles* are dangerous, whereas the latter suggests that *situations* requiring slowing down are dangerous. A typical situation that requires slowing down is turning to enter or leave the highway. In Solomon's sample of roadways, with the exception of one segment of limited-access road, all segments had entrances and intersections. Solomon calculated that even if one-half of the crashes occurred at intersections and the data for these vehicles were eliminated from the analysis, the portion of the curve for low speeds in Figure B-1 would be reduced by a fraction of a log unit. But what if more than one-half of the crashes were at intersections? And what if some of the straight road rear-end crashes were due to vehicles suddenly slowing down in response to an emergency?

Further compounding this issue is Solomon's exclusion of vehicles that had to slow down from the traffic speed data. Thus, although turning vehicles were not excluded from the crash data, the comparison data for the traffic speed did exclude these vehicles. A partial answer to these questions was provided by Harkey et al. (1990), who replicated Solomon's U-shaped curve for nonalcohol, nonintersection, weekday accidents on non-55-mph (non-89-km/h) roads in North Carolina and Colorado. However, in this study too, the accuracy of the speed of both the crash-involved vehicles and the traffic at the time of the crashes remains questionable.

Other research has only added to the confusion about the "variance hypothesis." The Research Triangle Institute (West and Dunn 1971) collected crash and speed data on rural roads in Indiana. The researchers used the same measures as Solomon for crash involvement and for speed differences (deviation of crash vehicle from the presumed average traffic speed). They conducted separate analyses of the data for all crashes and for crashes that did not involve turning vehicles. This meant removing nearly 45 percent of all crashes. The rationale for excluding these crashes was that turning vehicles should not be considered slow-moving vehicles (since their speed prior to the crash is not typical, but rather a response to a specific situation). The difference between the two data sets is illustrated in Table B-1 and is striking. The effect of removing these vehicles was to significantly flatten the involvement rate U-shaped curve. Since turning vehicles are only a subsample of vehicles slowing (versus moving slowly) ahead, it is likely that Solomon's estimate of 50 percent of slowing vehicles is very conservative. (Other slowing vehicles are those approaching a blocked intersection, slowing in response to a vehicle ahead that is turning off or onto the road, detecting an obstacle on the road, etc.)

Cirillo (1968) studied the effect of deviations of crash-involved vehicles from the average traffic speed on freeways but also looked at crash involvement as a function of distance from an interchange. Her study was limited to same-direction and sideswipe crashes occurring

Table B-1 Relationship Between Speed and Crash Involvement (West and Dunn 1971)

	Involvement Rate per Million Vehicle Miles	
Speed Deviation from Mean Travel Speed (mph)	Including Turning Crashes	Excluding Turning Crashes
More than 15.5 below	42.3	6.3
15.5 to 5.5 below	2.3	0.7
5.5 below to 5.5 above	1.6	0.8
5.5 to 15.5 above	1.5	1.0
More than 15.5 above	8.5	6.9

Note: 1 mph = 1.609 km/h.

on weekdays between 9 a.m. and 4 p.m. These crashes were selected as the most likely to reflect the effect of speed differences in the traffic stream. Traffic speeds were also measured on weekdays between 9 a.m. and 4 p.m. As in Solomon's study, precrash speeds of crash-involved vehicles were based mainly on drivers' self-reports and therefore were probably biased toward underestimation. Cirillo found that proximity to an interchange substantially increased the crash rate, especially for urban interchanges (where the interchanges are closer to each other and the ramps may be shorter). In urban sections crash rates were highest at the entrance ramp, and in rural sections they were highest at the exit ramps. These findings provide indirect support for the role of vehicles that are forced to slow versus vehicles that move slowly, because in these locations both the traffic patterns and the roadway geometry change as a result of vehicles entering and leaving the highway from entrance and exit lanes.

Fildes et al. (1991) attempted to replicate Solomon's findings for rural highways and extend them to urban highways. They used drivers' actual measured speeds on Australian roads consisting of two rural road segments [two-lane undivided highways with a posted speed limit of 62 mph (100 km/h), and design speeds of 75 mph (120 km/h) on one and 47 mph (75 km/h) on the other] and on two urban segments [four-lane undivided arterial roads with posted speed limits of 37 mph (60 km/h)] and related them to self-reports of crash experience. Although self-reports are known to be biased (e.g., for alcohol-related crashes), there is no reason to believe that slow-moving drivers would be less inclined to report their crashes. In their study, the most recent of that kind, Fildes et al. failed to obtain a U-shaped curve at all. Their results are plotted in Figure B-3, which shows a linear rise in crashes as a function of speed, beginning with speeds well below the average. Their sample lacked any speed deviations as extreme (on the low end) as those reported by Solomon. The extreme low-speed deviations in Solomon's curve and their absence in Fildes et al.'s data further suggest that the vehicles with large deviations were those that were forced to slow down just before being struck or causing a crash.

Interpreted in this light, the U-shaped curve can be explained as follows: in a two-car following situation, slowing vehicles are more likely to be struck than fast vehicles because when they slow down,

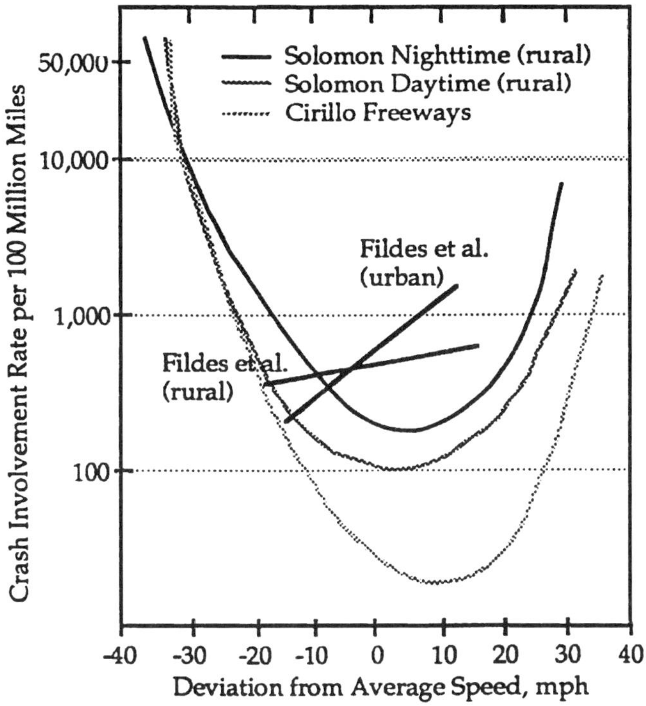

Figure B-3 Crash involvement rate by deviation from average traffic speed (Solomon 1964; Cirillo 1968; Fildes et al. 1991 in Stuster and Coffman 1997, 6). 1 mph = 1.609 km/h.

drivers behind them are often not immediately aware of the speed change, and thus slowing down reduces the headways of cars behind them. This may create imminent crash situations because of lapses in attention of following drivers, slowed responses of the following drivers, or misperception of the reduced gap by the following drivers. Lapses in attention (variously labeled as inattention, distraction, or improper lookout) are the most common human causes of traffic crashes (Treat et al. 1977; Sabey and Staughton 1975; Shinar 1978; Evans 1991). Thus, the more a driver has to slow down and the more rapid the deceleration, the more likely the driver is to be hit. Conversely, the faster the following driver is going, given momentary inattention, the more likely that driver is to fail to respond in time to the emerging collision situation.

One small study in which both precrash speeds and traffic speeds at the time of the crash were objectively measured has been reported in the literature. Pasanen and Salmivaara (1993) positioned a video camera, specifically calibrated to measure speed, above an intersection in Helsinki for more than 1 year. They recorded 18 intersection collisions, 11 of which involved pedestrians. In eight of the pedestrian crashes, the vehicles had at least a 3-s gap ahead of them (i.e., they were defined as "free-flowing"). In these cases the vehicles were traveling much faster [30 mph (48 km/h)] than the average speed of the traffic [24 mph (39 km/h)] or the speed limit [25 mph (40 km/h)] at that intersection. Thus, at least for urban intersections, there is one study with objective data demonstrating the relationship between a vehicle's speed and crash probability.

More recently, two other studies focused on the effect of speed on urban crashes, and both obtained a positive power relationship between speed and crash probability. To rule out as many nonspeed factors as possible, both studies used the case control method, in which for every injury crash the speeds of noncrashing control vehicles moving at "free travel speeds" were measured at the same sites, on the same days of the week and at the same times of day, and under the same weather conditions. In addition, drivers with nonzero alcohol or who were involved in illegal maneuvers were excluded from the studies. Although the case control method is a correlational-type study, it is a much more controlled one because every attempt is made to match crash and noncrash vehicles in terms of the driving situation. Both studies were conducted in Adelaide, Australia, in urban 37-mph (60-km/h) zones.

In the first study, Moore et al. (1995) compared the speeds of 45 crash vehicles and 450 control vehicles. With 34 to 40 mph (55 to 64 km/h) used as the reference speed, increased crash involvement was obtained only for drivers exceeding the speed limit and not for those traveling at speeds less than the speed limit. For drivers traveling at 47 to 52 mph (75 to 84 km/h), the relative risk of an injury crash was approximately 8, and at speeds greater than 53 mph (85 km/h), the relative risk was 39 (i.e., the probability of a crash was almost 40 times as high as that of a vehicle traveling at 34 to 40 mph).

The second and more extensive study by Kloeden et al. (1997) compared the speeds of 151 crash vehicles with the speeds of 604 noncrash vehicles and obtained similar results. Casualty crash rates increased exponentially above the 37-mph (60-km/h) speed limit, remaining relatively constant until that speed. For vehicles traveling at 47 mph (75 km/h), the relative risk of an injury crash was 11, for vehicles traveling at 50 mph (80 km/h) it was 32, and for those traveling at 53 mph (85 km/h) it was 57.

In summary, with the exception of one small study mentioned above, none of the observational/correlational studies that have been reviewed were able to measure or empirically or statistically control for all the potential factors that mediate speed and crash probability. Therefore, any conclusion based on these studies must rest on the bulk of the evidence rather than on the results of a single study or series of studies. On the basis of the studies reviewed, it appears that (*a*) speed is a significant contributing factor to crashes; (*b*) specific types of crashes, such as "run-off-the-road" crashes, are definitely associated with high speeds; (*c*) cars with precrash speeds that are either significantly above or below the modal or average travel speed are likely to be overinvolved in crashes; and (*d*) at least part of the overinvolvement of slow vehicles is due to forced slowing down such as for intersections, avoidance of obstacles, and so forth.

Causal Analyses

The observational data and correlational studies of the relationship between speed and crashes cannot reveal the underlying causes of this relationship. Older drivers may not be able to respond to all emerging dangers even at low speeds because of age-related and medical impairments, whereas young drivers may be able to respond in time at these speeds. In contrast, mature drivers may have a better appreciation of their limitations and adjust speed accordingly, whereas young drivers may be oblivious to their vehicle-handling limitations as well as the handling limitations of the vehicle and may therefore travel at a speed too high to respond in time to a change in the roadway or the behavior of the traffic ahead. Causal analyses of individual crashes are useful in taking all these factors into consideration. Despite their subjective nature, causal analyses performed by different investigators at different times and places consistently show that excessive speed is a factor in at least 10 percent of all crashes.

The role of speeding as a crash cause was probably first analyzed in a detailed and comprehensive manner by Treat et al. (1977). In this study, a representative sample of more than 2,000 police-reported crashes were analyzed by crash investigators at the crash sites, and 420 of them were further analyzed by multidisciplinary teams. A cause was defined as an event or action whose absence would have prevented the crash, all other things being equal. Furthermore, a human cause was cited if the causal behavior was a deviation from the normal or expected behavior of the average driver. Thus, speed would not be cited in a crash of a speeding vehicle unless the speed deviated from the speed expected at that site under the conditions that prevailed and the crash would not have occurred had the speed been as expected. With this approach to causation, the study estimated excessive speed to be a definite cause (with a subjective probability of 0.95 or higher) in 7 to 8 percent of the crashes and a probable cause (with a subjective probability of 0.80 to 0.94) in an additional 13 to 16 percent of the crashes. This approach to coding "speeding" as a causal factor is different from the FARS coding, where all causal or related factors are based on police crash reports and thus speeding as a crash cause is likely to include a mix of speeding relative to the posted speed limit and relative to prevailing conditions.

More recently, the role of speed in the causation of fatal crashes was assessed by Viano and Ridella (1996), who analyzed the data from 131 fatal crashes. The most common cause, labeled "nothing to do," involved 30 crashes. In this type of crash the vehicle driver was unable to do anything to avoid the crash. These crashes were typically caused by "an unusual sequence or recklessness by another driver." The second most frequently cited cause, responsible for 11 percent of the crashes, was labeled "rocket-ship." This type of crash involved single-vehicle frontal-impact crashes with the "vehicles leaving the road at a very high speed." No crashes were attributable to slow driving, although many of the crash scenarios involved maneuvers that presumably required drivers to slow down (e.g., yielding, 6 percent; making left turns, 4 percent; and negotiating curves, 9 percent).

Clinical post hoc causal analysis becomes much more difficult and expensive for large data files. However, it is possible to integrate several files to obtain more reliable estimates of the role of speed in crash causation. This was done by Bowie and Walz (1994), who used several independent data files. They combined (*a*) the comprehensive census of all fatal crashes in FARS, (*b*) 1 year of data from all police-reported crashes from six states that are in the Crash Avoidance Research Data file (CARDfile), and (*c*) the 420 crashes analyzed in depth by Treat et al. (1977). Although they were based on different data sets and methodologies, the three sources yielded similar estimates, with "excessive speed" being involved in approximately 12 percent of all crashes and more than 30 percent of fatal crashes.

Liu (1997) studied the Saskatchewan, Canada, crash data files for the years 1990 through 1995. He defined a speed-related crash as one in which the police crash report noted that the driver was both "exceeding the speed limit *and* driving too fast for conditions." Although this definition may appear conservative, it is appropriate since police reports are not as reliable as professional in-depth crash investigations. Liu found that speed was a causal factor in 9.2 to 10.5 percent of all crashes and in 11.9 to 15.2 percent of all casualty crashes.

In summary, in contrast to the conclusions that can be drawn from correlational analyses, studies using clinical causal assessment are unanimous in their conclusions about the contribution of speed to crashes: excessive speed (not necessarily in relation to the speed limit) definitely contributes to a small but significant percentage of all crashes and to a higher percentage of severe crashes. The various studies suggest that at least 10 percent of all crashes are speed related. However, these analyses have shortcomings: (*a*) their assessment methodology is "soft," being based on post hoc clinical judgments, and (*b*) they have no adjustment for exposure. (If the percentage of drivers speeding in the traffic stream—in the clinical sense, not relative to the speed limit—is greater than the percentage of speeders in crashes, it could be argued that speeding may be a mitigating factor in crash involvement.)

Importance of Road Type

People drive differently in different environments—on different road types, on roads with different design speeds, and [to a lesser extent

(Garber and Gadiraju 1988)] on roads with different speed limits. Consequently, it is important to consider the relevance of speed to these situations. A factorial combination of the various levels of each of the preceding three dimensions would yield many empty cells [e.g., rural expressways with a design speed of 25 mph (40 km/h) and a speed limit of 40 mph (64 km/h)]. Since average speed is closely related to design speed, and the latter is often redundant with road type, it may be best to disaggregate the findings of the studies reviewed above for specific road types. This is particularly important in light of the problem pointed out earlier concerning the validity of aggregating data across different road types. Road types that have different design speeds and different average traffic speeds, and thus for which different policy implications can be drawn, include the following:

- Limited-access highways (Interstate highways, freeways, and toll roads),
- Rural nonlimited-access arterial highways,
- Rural collector roads, and
- Urban streets.

Garber and Gadiraju (1988) analyzed the effects of road type and design speed on speed and crashes and found a strong relationship between road type and design speed and between these two variables and crash rates. Their data consisted of the average traffic speed, speed variance, and number of crashes at 36 road sections consisting of different road types with different design speeds. Limited-access highways had the highest design speeds, the highest average speeds, and the lowest crash rates. However, because of the very high correlation between design speed and driving speed ($R^2 = 0.79$), one cannot conclude that high speeds are associated with low crash rates any more than that high design speeds (i.e., good and forgiving highway design) are responsible for low crash rates. From the risk-homeostasis hypothesis, it appears that good design provides a greater safety margin than the driver compensates for. From the traffic conflict and information processing model approaches, limited-access highways minimize conflicts and information overload, enabling drivers to increase their speed without incurring the risks of information overload.

Unfortunately, few studies have limited themselves to one type of road or disaggregated their results by road type. Therefore, the following observations rest on few data. The problem is further aggravated by the fact that the studies span a period of four decades in which the density of traffic, the design of highways and control systems, and the dynamics and crashworthiness of cars changed dramatically. Nonetheless, in this section the results discussed above have been reevaluated as they apply to the specific road types. For ease of presentation, there are some redundancies with preceding reviews of the studies.

Limited-Access Highways

Only one study focused specifically on limited-access highways. Cirillo (1968) demonstrated that Solomon's U-shaped function between crash involvement and speed deviation applies to limited-access roads as well, as can be seen in Figure B-3. The main difference between Solomon's daytime crash involvement rates for rural nonlimited-access highways and Cirillo's Interstate highways is in the absolute lower level of crash rates on the latter. Otherwise, the two curves are very similar, indicating that the minimum crash involvement rate is at approximately 10 mph (16 km/h) above the average traffic speed; the rates rise above and below that point. Cirillo also found that crash involvement rates are significantly higher in the vicinity of interchanges than in straight highway segments, though an analysis by speed differences was not conducted. It is important to keep in mind that Cirillo's study suffered from the same shortcomings as Solomon's study, as mentioned earlier.

Garber and Gadiraju (1988) conducted a separate analysis on Interstate highways (rural and urban) and found a significant, positive relationship between crash involvement and speed variance. Crash rates increased as speed variance increased ($R^2 = 0.55$ in a linear regression model). Since the speeds of crash-involved vehicles were not available (unlike Solomon's and Cirillo's studies), the effect of the speed of crash-involved vehicles on crash probability could not be directly tested. Models of linear regression of the average traffic speeds on different road sections against their crash rates yielded no significant correlations.

Lave (1985) analyzed the contribution of both average speed and speed dispersion (using the difference between the 85th percentile and the average speed as a surrogate measure) separately for six road types and 2 years (1981 and 1982) using the 48 contiguous states as individual data points. For rural Interstates, he found a significant relationship between fatality rate [fatalities per 1 million vehicle-mi (1.61 million vehicle-km)] and speed dispersion, and essentially no contribution of the average traffic speed. In regression equations using both variables, $R^2 = 0.63$ for 1981, and $R^2 = 0.52$ for 1982. For all other road types (except arterial roads in 1981 as discussed later), the correlations between both variables and crash rates were statistically nonsignificant. Thus, no significant effects of average speed or speed dispersion were found for urban Interstates in either year.

Rural Nonlimited-Access Arterial Highways

Most of the road sections (27 out of 35) studied by Solomon (1964) were two-lane nonlimited-access rural roads. The remaining eight sections were four-lane divided rural highways of which only one had full access control. Thus, Solomon's data previously reviewed in detail (and shown in Figures B-1, B-2, B-4, B-5, and B-7) indicate that it is not the absolute speed of the crash-involved vehicle that is related to crash probability, but its deviation from the average traffic speed (with all the caveats listed in the section on correlational studies).

The other studies that attempted to assess the importance of speed deviation to crash involvement on nonlimited-access rural highways were less conclusive than Solomon's study. West and Dunn (1971) attempted to improve the validity of the crash-involved vehicle speed data and assess the contribution of turning maneuvers to the U-shaped curve. As can be seen in Table B-1, once turning vehicles were eliminated from the data, the U-shaped curve was greatly flattened and manifest only at very low and high speeds [i.e., 15 mph (24 km/h) above and below the average speed].

Fildes et al. (1991) conducted a speed and crash involvement study on two major rural arterial roads in Australia and were unable to replicate Solomon's (1964) findings. Their results, plotted in Figure B-3, show that there was only a simple linear association between crash rate and speed deviations of crash-involved vehicles. However, even that relationship was based on a very low correlation [as estimated from their scatterplot (p. 61)]. Furthermore, in their study the crash data were all based on self-reports, and the total number of data points was much smaller than in Solomon's study. Finally, the range of speed deviations (also noticeable from Figure B-3) was much smaller than in Solomon's study.

Garber and Gadiraju (1988) and Lave (1985) attempted to relate measures of speed dispersion to crash rates. Garber and Gadiraju obtained a significant and very high correlation (R^2 = 0.79) between speed variance and crash rates for all arterial highway sections combined. Since 12 out of the 14 arterial sections in their study were rural, it is safe to attribute the finding to rural arterial highways. Lave obtained a weak but statistically significant relationship between crash rates and a measure of traffic speed dispersion (85th percentile minus average traffic speed) on rural arterial highways for 1981 data (R^2 = 0.25 approximately), but not for 1982 data. Neither Garber and Gadiraju nor Lave obtained any significant relationships between average traffic speeds and crash rates. Speeds of the crash-involved vehicles were not available in their studies.

Rural Collector Roads

Rural collector roads form a large portion of the highway system. Their crash rates [per 100 million vehicle-mi (161 million vehicle-km)] are relatively high, but their fatality rates are lower. For example, in Virginia crash rates on rural collector roads were more than three times those of rural Interstates [169 versus 52 per 100 million vehicle-mi (105 versus 32 per 100 million vehicle-km)] but the fatality rate was the same [2.0 per 100 million vehicle-mi (1.2 per 100 million vehicle-km)] (Garber and Gadiraju 1988). Although Garber and Gadiraju collected data on seven segments of major rural collectors, they did not provide any information on the relationship between speed-related measures and crashes separately for these sections. Solomon probably also included rural collector road segments in his data, but they were not analyzed separately. Lave (1985) conducted a separate analysis of crash rates on rural collector roads, but average speed, 85th percentile speed, and his measure of speed dispersion (85th percentile speed minus the average speed) were not significantly related to crash rates.

Urban Streets

Urban streets account for the highest percentage (39 percent on "local roadway/streets and collectors") of speed-related fatal crashes among all road types (Bowie and Walz 1994). Yet only one of the studies reviewed provided data specific to these types of roads in the United States. Fildes et al. (1991), in their attempted replication and extension of Solomon's data, only obtained a positive linear relationship between crash rates and speed deviation, indicating that the higher the speed the greater the probability of crash involvement (Figure B-3). However, although the relationship appears strong, Fildes et al.'s data are based on only two sites consisting of undivided urban streets posted at 37 mph (60 km/h). More rigorous case-control studies (Kloeden et al. 1997; Moore et al. 1995) also obtained a positive power relationship between speed and crash probability. A similar conclusion, also based on a small data set, can be reached from the study of urban pedestrian crashes at a signalized intersection in Helsinki by Pasanen and Salmivaara (1993). Lave (1985) found a low correlation between his measure of speed dispersion and crash rates on U.S. urban arterial roads ($R^2 = 0.15$ approximately), but even that correlation was significant for 1982 and not for 1981.

In summary, there appears to be a limited amount of data—and with many methodological shortcomings mentioned in the preceding section—that suggest that on Interstate highways, increases in the range of traffic speeds are associated with increased crash rates; the more a vehicle deviates from the average traffic speed (or from slightly above the average traffic speed), the more likely it is to be involved in a crash. The underlying cause of the crashes of vehicles deviating from the average speed appears to be related to entering and exiting the highway, indicating that the low speed is situationally forced and not due to vehicles moving at a consistently low speed. On nonlimited-access rural arterial highways and collector roads there are more data, but they are conflicting. Consequently, it is difficult to draw any conclusions. On urban streets there appears to be a strong relationship between crash rates and the absolute speed of the crash-involved vehicles (which correlates with their deviations above average travel speeds). Although that relationship has been observed in several independent studies, with one exception (Kloeden et al. 1997), the conclusion is based on small data sets, and the majority of the studies have been conducted outside the United States.

SPEED AND CRASH SEVERITY

When his son got a driver's license, a Carnegie-Mellon University physics professor glued this reminder on the car's dashboard: $E = \frac{1}{2}mv^2$. The son got the message and remembers it to this day, 13 years later.

Crash severity can be defined in at least two ways: (*a*) the physical severity of the impact speed or Delta-V (the velocity change in the crash) and (*b*) the severity of injuries to the vehicle occupants. Over the years, the measure of physical severity has changed from the speed (or relative speed in the case of two or more vehicles) at impact to Delta-V. Injury severity is still described in various ways, such as the worst injury sustained in a crash (e.g., fatal, injury, or property-damage-only crash) or the more graduated Abbreviated Injury Scale (AIS) in which injury levels range from 1 for a minor injury to 6 for an unsurvivable one.

The relationship between speed and Delta-V is intuitively obvious. The faster a vehicle is moving prior to contact with another vehicle or a stationary object, the greater the Delta-V. Furthermore, the expected effect on injury should not be linear, because the at-crash deceleration is proportional to the square of the impact speed. Nonetheless, the actual effect on injury should be demonstrated empirically. This is because the power of the impact may be mitigated by various shock-absorbing behaviors that occupants may adopt (e.g., use of safety belts) and the various shock-absorbing design features of the various car makes and models.

In his 1964 report Solomon also studied the relationship between speed and severity using two measures of crash severity: (*a*) injury rates expressed as the number of people injured relative to the number of crash-involved vehicles and (*b*) property damage cost per crash-involved vehicle. The results of these analyses are presented in

Figures B-4 and B-5, respectively. The relationship is clear-cut: the higher the speed, the greater the cost, in both injuries and property damage. Solomon calculated fatality rates in a similar manner. With a total of 253 fatalities, Solomon found that the odds of a fatality given a crash accelerated with speed from a low of approximately 1 to 2 fatalities for every 100 crashes at speeds less than 55 mph (89 km/h) to a high of more than 20 fatalities for speeds of 70 mph (113 km/h) and above.

In an analysis of the National Analysis Sampling System (NASS) data, Joksch (1993) found a consistent relationship between the fatality risk for a driver in car-car collisions and Delta-V. On the basis of his analysis, risk is closely related to Delta-V^4 (i.e., to the fourth power). By fitting curves to crash data with known and estimated

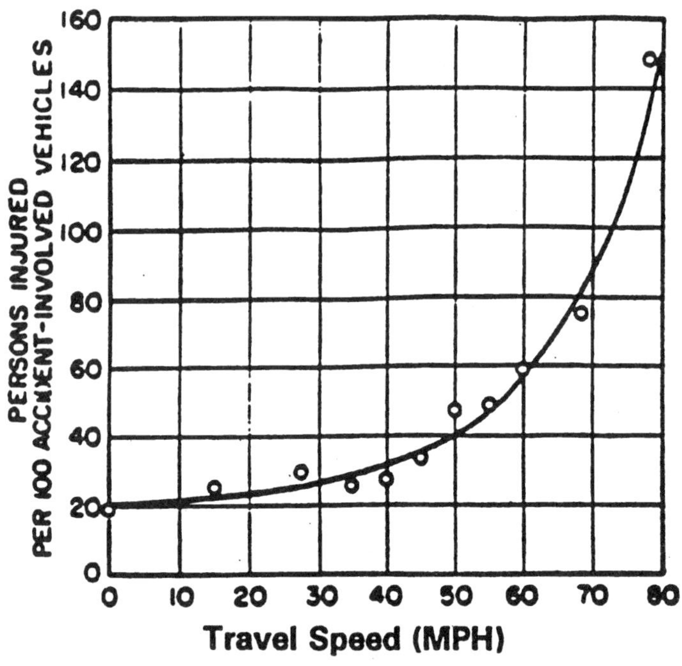

Figure B-4 Persons injured per 100 involvements versus travel speed for daytime crashes (Solomon 1964). 1 mph = 1.609 km/h.

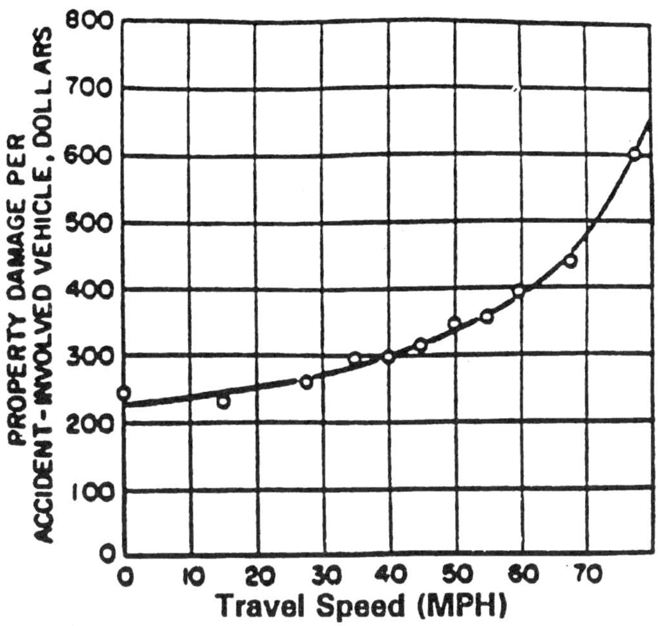

Figure B-5 Property damage per involvement versus travel speed for daytime crashes (Solomon 1964). 1 mph = 1.609 km/h.

Delta-Vs and by using different assumptions for the estimated Delta-V, Joksch obtained similar functions with exponents ranging from 3.9 to 4.1 for all types of crashes (and not just car-car). This led Joksch to conclude that "the findings are somewhat robust against changes in the assumptions" and that "the exponent 4 may reasonably reflect the relation between the fatality risk and Delta-V. Even if not precise it may be useful as a rule of thumb" (p. 104). The relationship obtained by Joksch using different assumptions about Delta-V is presented in Figure B-6. A relationship where the dependent variable is a function of the independent variable taken to some power is known as a power function. In the present analyses of the relationship between severity (the dependent variable) and speed (the independent variable), the power was always greater than 1.0, indicating not only that severity increases with speed but also that *the rate of severity* increases with speed. A similar power function was obtained in an earlier analysis of 10,000 crashes documented in the NCSS from

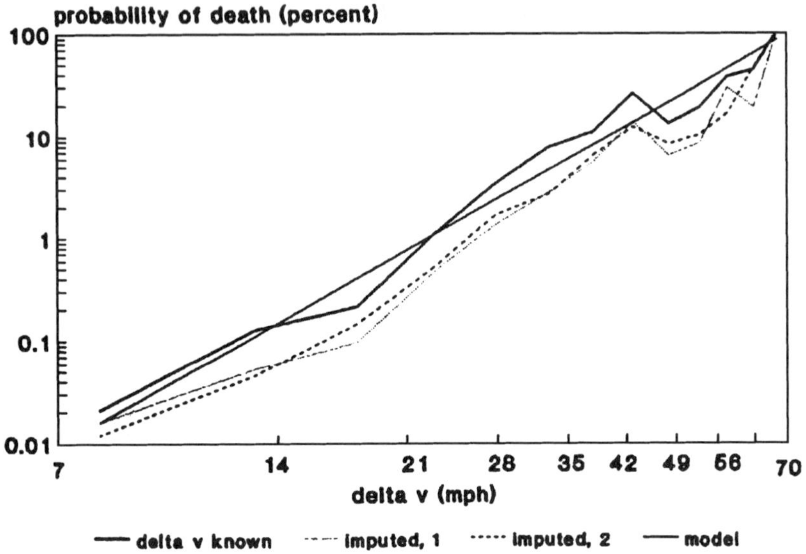

Figure B-6 Fatality risk for car drivers in relation to Delta-V, drivers of 1980 and later model-year cars involved in crashes from 1980 to 1986 (NASS data). The solid line represents only cases with known Delta-V; the straight line shows the relation $(\text{Delta-V}/71)^4$; the broken lines represent all cases. Missing Delta-Vs are imputed using different assumptions (Joksch 1993). 1 mph = 1.609 km/h.

1970 to 1979 by O'Day and Flora (1982). Their function showed that at speeds of 50 mph (80 km/h), the fatality rate—mostly for unbelted occupants—was slightly above 50 percent. Interestingly, Mackay (1988), apparently using the same U.S. NCSS data, estimated that the risk of fatality exceeded 90 percent when Delta-V exceeded 50 mph. It is next to impossible to examine the original data that both used, but it appears that O'Day and Flora's estimates are more appropriate, because 1995 NASS data (with national safety belt use rates exceeding 60 percent) indicate a fatality rate of 33 percent for Delta-Vs above 45 mph (72 km/h) (NASS 1998).

The effect of speed on pedestrian fatalities follows the same trend. The European Transport Safety Council (1995) concluded that in a 20-mph (32-km/h) collision between a vehicle and a pedestrian, the probability of pedestrian death is 0.05; at 30 mph (48 km/h) it rises to 0.45; and at 40 mph (64 km/h) it is 0.85. Pasanen and Salmivaara's (1993) data are in close agreement with these findings.

The power relationship also holds well for nonfatal injuries. Bowie and Walz (1994) calculated the relationship between Delta-V and injury rates for AIS Level 2+ injuries and AIS Level 3+ injuries and obtained the results reproduced in Table B-2. Injury rate was defined as the number of occupants injured at the Delta-V level divided by the total number of occupants involved in crashes at that Delta-V times 100. Thus the AIS 3+ injury rate increased from a range of 0.7 to 1.0 for crashes with Delta-Vs of 1 to 10 mph (1.6 to 16 km/h), to a range of 54 to 57 for Delta-Vs greater than 50 mph (80 km/h). Combining measures from FARS, CARDfile, and the General Estimates System, Bowie and Walz also showed that the percentage of speed-related crashes increases with increasing injury level: from 10.2 percent in no-injury crashes, to 17.1 percent for incapacitating-injury crashes, to 34.2 for fatal crashes.

Using an econometrics approach, O'Donnell and Connor (1996) applied models of ordered multiple choice (logit and probit) to all New South Wales 1991 crash records (totaling 28,747). They found that, relative to a benchmark crash with a 33-year old driver, a 1 percent increase in speed yielded a 0.44 to 0.56 percent increase in the probability of death. Although they mention that in econometrics models such a change of less than 1 percent is labeled "inelastic," it is a practically and statistically significant change.

In conclusion, all of the studies that have investigated the relationship between vehicle speed and crash severity have found a consistent relationship showing that as the speed increases, Delta-V and injury severity both increase.

THE COST OF SPEED: COMBINED EFFECTS OF INCIDENCE AND SEVERITY

The determination of an optimal or desirable speed is not a scientific issue but a political one. Between maximum mobility at infinite speed and maximum safety at zero speed, there is a huge range for compromise.

An appreciation of the societal costs of crashes of various severity levels is possible when crash rates are disaggregated and their inci-

Table B-2 Injury Rates by Crash Severity; Comparisons of NCSS and NASS (1982–1989) (Bowie and Walz 1994)

Total Delta-V (mph)	AIS 2+ NCSS	AIS 2+ NASS	AIS 3+ NCSS	AIS 3+ NASS
1-10	2.4	4.5	0.7	1.0
11-20	9.5	10.6	3.5	2.6
21-30	25.3	29.2	13.9	11.1
31-40	51.8	53.4	37.2	27.9
41-50	70.3	67.2	58.3	40.6
Over 50	64.7	69.3	56.9	54.3

Note: Rate equals the number of occupants at a certain Delta-V level (in 10-mph increments) injured at specific AIS levels (AIS 2+ or AIS 3+) divided by the total number of occupants involved in crashes at that level of Delta-V times 100. Rate does not include cases in which either the Delta-V level or the AIS level was unknown. AIS = Abbreviated Injury Scale; NASS = National Analysis Sampling System; NCSS = National Crash Severity Study; CDS = Crashworthiness Data System; 1 mph = 1.609 km/h.
Sources: NASS, 1982–1986 and 1988–1989 (CDS). Includes only tow-away cases. There was no statistically representative NASS file in 1987. NCSS, 1979. Data are limited to tow-away crashes involving passenger cars and light trucks. Data are not nationally representative.

dence examined separately by severity level. Speeding is typically a more common crash-related factor in the more severe crashes. In contrast, the overall crash data are heavily weighted by property-damage-only crashes, which constitute the majority of crashes. This is illustrated in Table B-3 using CARDfile data of police-reported crashes from six states (Bowie and Walz 1994, Table 5). The table indicates that, of the total crashes in the file, the percentage of speed-related crashes increases with increasing injury severity levels: from 10 percent for no-injury crashes to 34 percent for fatal-injury crashes.

A similar effect can be observed in Solomon's data. The injury rates [number of people injured per 100 million vehicle-mi (161 million vehicle-km)] in Solomon's study are shown in Figure B-7. The daytime and nighttime curves in this figure are similar to the crash rates in Figure B-1 but (*a*) have their minimum at a lower speed level [approximately 55 mph (89 km/h)] and (*b*) show a much greater rate

Table B-3 Distribution of Injuries in Speed-Related Crashes by Injury Severity Level (Bowie and Walz 1994)

Injury Severity Level	Number[a]	Speed-Related[b] (percent)	Total
No injury[c]	12,610,000	10.2	1,286,220
Possible injury	1,719,000	10.9	187,371
Nonincapacitating injury	943,000	14.6	137,678
Incapacitating injury	481,000	17.1	82,251
Fatal injury[d]	45,500	34.2	15,558

Note: GES = General Estimates System; CARDfile = Crash Avoidance Research Data File; FARS = Fatal Analysis Reporting System; 1 mph = 1.609 km/h.
[a]National totals are from 1989 GES.
[b]Speed-related percentage derived from CARDfile (1984–1986).
[c]The estimate for noninjured people is considered to be low because some states only list injured persons.
[d]Fatal crash statistics are from FARS, 1989.

of involvement at higher speeds (relative to lower speeds) than was observed for all crashes in Figure B-1. An even sharper trend (above the average speed) was noted for fatality rates. During the day, the fatality rate was relatively constant at 2 fatalities per 100 million vehicle-mi (1 fatality per 100 million vehicle-km) for speeds up to 50 mph (80 km/h), increasing to 31 fatalities per 100 million vehicle-mi (19 per 100 million vehicle-km) (i.e., by a factor of 15) for speeds higher than 72 mph (116 km/h). At night, the rate was generally higher. The rate remained under 20 per 100 million vehicle-mi (12 per 100 million vehicle-km) for speeds up to 62 mph (100 km/h). At higher speeds the fatality rate increased sharply—up to 294 per 100 million vehicle-mi (183 per 100 million vehicle-km) (also by a factor of approximately 15) for speeds higher than 72 mph.

The increased incidence of speeding with increasing injury levels was also reported by Liu (1997) on the basis of Saskatchewan crash data for 1990 through 1995. His analysis showed that excessive speed—when it was both above the speed limit and high relative to conditions—constituted:

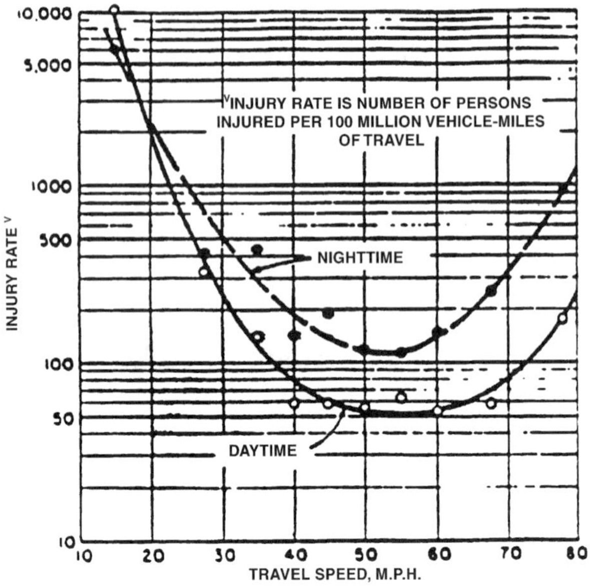

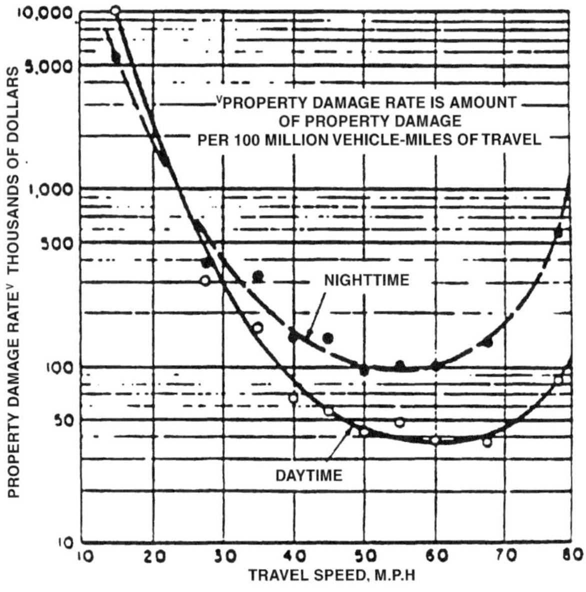

Figure B-7 Injury (above) and property damage (below) rates by travel speed, day and night (Solomon 1964). 1 mph = 1.609 km/h.

- 18 to 25 percent of all human errors in property damage crashes,
- 20 to 29 percent of all human errors in personal injury crashes, and
- 24 to 40 percent of all human errors in fatal crashes.

The most compelling demonstration of the combined effects of crash probability and crash cost as they relate to speed was recently provided in an analysis of crash data from 16 European countries. In that analysis Kallberg (unpublished data, 1997) demonstrated that disregarding the effects of speed on crash severity leads to serious underestimation of the effects of speed on crash costs. On the basis of a Swedish model of the relationship between crash probability and crash cost as a function of precrash speed, Kallberg's more conservative estimate is that an "increase from 47 to 50 km/h increases accident costs (and the number of injury accidents) by 13.2 percent, speed increases from 80 to 85 km/h by 12.9 percent, and speed increases from 90 to 100 km/h by 23.5 percent, and the effect is the same in all countries" (p. 9).

In summary, these findings indicate that because speeding is a more prominent factor in more severe crashes and because severity increases as a power function of speed, it is difficult to sustain a view that excessive speed—at least relative to the median of the prevailing traffic—is not a crash risk factor with significant societal costs in terms of injuries and fatalities as well as money.

CONCLUDING REMARKS

There is sufficient evidence to indicate that a driver's absolute speed is a correlate of crash involvement. The indications for the positive relationship between speed and crashes are derived from empirical data of single-vehicle crashes, causal crash analysis, and theoretical frameworks related to the effects of speed on information overload and reduced vehicle-handling capacity. In addition, empirical data show unequivocally that injuries and fatality rates increase as a power function of impact speed or Delta-V.

There is also ample evidence to indicate the contribution of wide disparities in speed of the traffic stream, as well as the deviation of crash-involved vehicles from the average traffic speed, to crash involvement. However, the support for these findings comes from correlational studies, and the argument for causality rests on the theoretical support for this finding. The theoretical support is not sufficient. To suggest that speed disparities in the traffic stream contribute to potential intervehicle conflicts is not sufficient, since such conflicts appear to constitute a small portion of crashes in general and an even smaller portion of the more severe crashes. So what is the source of that relationship? Liu and Popoff (1996) suggest that the "variance effect" reflects a greater vehicle mix or a greater mix of drivers with different styles and capabilities. If that is the case, the variance effect may be a spurious finding. As long as data on driver and vehicle types (both in crash samples and traffic samples) are unavailable, this remains an interesting speculation.

In a situation in which speed selection is totally at the driver's discretion, the range of speeds in the traffic stream is a function of the risk levels that different drivers are willing to tolerate, different perceptions of a "safe speed" that drivers have for a given risk level, and the handling capabilities of different cars and drivers. All of the studies reporting narrowing of speed disparities with increasing speed were conducted in the presence of speed limits, and, consequently, a threshold level of speed may have been responsible for the reduction in speed dispersion (i.e., higher speeds were due to higher speed limits on roads with higher design speeds). This is because as the speed limit is raised, fewer and fewer drivers are likely to exceed it by much, and more and more drivers tend to drive close to the limit. This also means that it is highly probable that if speed limits were strictly controlled in low-speed zones, then drivers who would otherwise exceed the limit significantly (and therefore contribute to widening speed dispersion) would refrain from doing so, and both speed dispersion and crash risk would be reduced.

The tendency of speed differences to narrow as average speed increases probably reflects drivers' tendencies to violate low speed limits (e.g., near schools) more than high speed limits [e.g., on Interstate highways with limits of 65 to 70 mph (105 to 113 km/h)]. The critical issue then is how speed limits are set. If they are realistic (e.g., 85th percentile or design speed), speed dispersion may be low, constant, and independent of average speed. Since the speed limit, the design speed, and prevailing conditions all contribute to speed choice, separating average speed from speed limits and enforcement is artificial. If speed limits are set at low levels and they are enforced, then speed dispersion would probably not decrease with increasing speed but rather would increase with it, in a manner similar to most measures of human psychomotor behaviors (where variance is positively correlated with the mean). Then what would the relationship between speed dispersion and crashes be? That is an open question. Perhaps what is needed is systematic research into the relationships between measures of speed and speed dispersion under conditions of speed control.

The importance of theory to the role of speed dispersion can be illustrated with older drivers. Older drivers are a good group to pick because the elderly are the fastest-growing age group in the population in general and on the roads in particular (Eberhard 1996). Now, if slow driving (rather than slowing down) increases crash risk, should slow drivers be advised to increase their speed? Older drivers, who tend to drive slow, do so to maintain or reduce their risk level, not to increase it. Given their slowed information processing capabilities, it would be foolhardy to recommend that these people drive faster so as to reduce speed disparities in the traffic stream. Also, removing them from high-speed roads may actually be detrimental to safety since (*a*) they already restrict their driving to safer roads and times and (*b*) their crash involvement may actually increase on other roads with lower design speeds (placing greater information processing demands on the driver) that are already associated with higher crash risks.

Given the multiple factors that coexist in the real driving environment, it is interesting to speculate if it is even possible to find or create a situation in which only speed changes. The answer is probably not. Even in a simulator study, if all that is changed is the driver's speed while the traffic speed and likelihood of emergencies stay the same, then crashes will most likely increase—but so will speed differences. If the speed of all the traffic is changed and an emergency arises, then multiple-vehicle chain crashes are likely. Chain crashes on highways with restricted view (e.g., in fog) are suggestive of the process: the faster a vehicle travels, the greater the probability of a crash—but only in the event of an obstacle ahead. However, this situation is very artificial, because drivers adjust their speed in accordance with their expectations of obstacles ahead. Thus, it is hard to think of a realistic situation, even in a simulator study, that would disaggregate the effects of the speed of a crash-involved vehicle from the disparities in speed of the traffic.

In summary, the ultimate question is not whether increasing speed increases crash probability and crash severity. Instead, there are three questions: What are the mediating factors involved? What are acceptable societal costs for increased mobility? Who should decide the levels of acceptability—elected officials, safety experts, or the motoring public through their opinion or behavior (such as the 85th percentile speed)?

With respect to mediating factors, it is impossible to hold all "other things equal" while varying speed. This is because the basis for speed choice—roadway design, traffic controls, enforcement, traffic flow, and perceived risk and comfort levels—all affect the relationship between speed and crash probability. With respect to the acceptable risk level, there is willingness at both the individual and the societal levels to accept some degree of risk to improve mobility. Thus, speed management, speed choice, crash risk, and crash severity are all intertwined and linked to the value placed on mobility.

CONCLUSIONS

1. There is ample, but not unequivocal, evidence to indicate that, on a given road, crash involvement rates of individual vehicles rise with their speed of travel.

2. There are no convincing data to demonstrate that, across all roads, crash involvement rates rise with the average speed of traffic (i.e., that roads with higher average traffic speeds have higher crash rates than roads with lower average traffic speeds). This is probably because the average traffic speed is highly correlated with the design speed of different road classes (and other conditions).

3. The absolute speed deviation of crash-involved vehicles from the average traffic speed appears to be positively related to crash

probability, especially for rural arterial highways and Interstate highways. There are insufficient data to demonstrate such a relationship for rural collector roads and urban streets.

4. The principal factor that accounts for the effects of speed deviation is the requirement to slow down to make turns and to enter and exit high-speed roads. Still, even when the effects of turning vehicles are removed from the data, some effects of speed deviation, especially at the extreme ends, remain.

5. The disparities in speed of the traffic stream may be positively related to crash probability, especially on Interstate highways. However, the data are not very consistent, and more data are needed.

6. On urban streets there appears to be a strong relationship between crash rates and the absolute speed of crash-involved vehicles. However, this conclusion is based mainly on small data sets from non-U.S. studies.

7. The data demonstrating the relevance of speed dispersion in the traffic stream and speed deviations of crash-involved vehicles are based on correlational effects and therefore cannot be used to indicate that if slow-moving drivers were to increase their speed, their crash probability would be reduced.

8. There are unequivocal data to indicate that the risk of injuries and fatalities increases as a function of precrash speed or Delta-V. This is true for all road types.

9. The overall cost of speed-related crashes is much greater than the relationship between speed and crash probability indicates. This is because high-speed crashes are associated with greater injury levels than are low-speed crashes.

ACKNOWLEDGMENTS

In preparing this report I was greatly assisted by the members of the TRB Committee for Guidance on Setting and Enforcing Speed Limits. All of them provided me with insightful comments and probing questions on a previous draft. I have tried to be responsive to all the issues raised, and I tried to incorporate all the recommended changes and additions. The responsibility for shortcomings and limitations that remain is solely my own.

I was especially assisted by the subcommittee chairperson, Forrest Council, who provided the first impetus and guidelines for this report, and by Nancy Humphrey, the TRB program manager, who provided me with most of the needed source material, acted as an intermediary between me and the committee members, spent hours on the phone with me discussing key issues, and made excellent editorial comments on the previous drafts. Finally, I would like to acknowledge the help of Richard Compton, who acted as a challenging sounding board and spent as much time as I needed to discuss the principal speed issues.

REFERENCES

ABBREVIATIONS

NASS	National Analysis Sampling System
NHTSA	National Highway Traffic Safety Administration
TRB	Transportation Research Board

Aronoff, C.J. 1971. Stannard Baker, Traffic Safety Pioneer, Retires from NU Traffic Institute. *Northwestern University News*, Aug. 27.

Bowie, N.N., and M. Walz. 1994. Data Analysis of the Speed-Related Crash Issue. *Auto and Traffic Safety*, Vol. 1, No. 2, Winter, NHTSA, U.S. Department of Transportation, pp. 31–38.

Brown, D.B., S. Maghsoodloo, and M.E. McArdle. 1990. The Safety Impact of the 65 mph Speed Limit: A Case Study Using Alabama Accident Records. *Journal of Safety Research*, Vol. 21, pp. 125–139. Cited by Rock (1995).

Cirillo, J.A. 1968. Interstate System Accident Research: Study II, Interim Report II. *Public Roads*, Vol. 35, Aug. pp. 71–75.

Cowley, J.E. 1987. *The Relationship Between Speed and Accidents: A Literature Review*. J.E. Cowley and Associates, Melborne, Australia, March.

Eberhard, J.W. 1996. Safe Mobility for Senior Citizens. *IATSS Research*, Vol. 20, pp. 29–37.

Elvik, R. 1997. Effects on Accidents of Automatic Speed Enforcement in Norway. Presented at 76th Annual Meeting of the Transportation Research Board, Washington, D.C.

European Transport Safety Council. 1995. *Reducing Traffic Injuries Resulting from Excess and Inappropriate Speed*. Brussels, Belgium.

Evans, L. 1991. *Traffic Safety and the Driver*. Van Nostrand Reinhold, New York.

Fildes, B.N., and S.J. Lee. 1993. *The Speed Review: Road Environment, Speed Limits, Enforcement, and Crashes*. CR 127 (FORS), CR 3/93 (RSB). Road and Traffic Authority of New South Wales, Australia, Sept.

Fildes, B.N., G. Rumbold, and A. Leening. 1991. *Speed Behavior and Drivers' Attitude to Speeding*. Report 16. Monash University Accident Research Center, Monash, Victoria, Australia, June.

Finch, D.J., P. Kompfner, C.R. Lockwood, and G. Maycock. 1994. *Speed, Speed Limits, and Accidents*. Project Report 58, S211G/RB. Transport and Road Research Laboratory, Crowthorne, Berkshire, England.

Fowles, R., and P.D. Loeb. 1989. Speeding, Coordination, and the 55-mph Limit: Comment. *The American Economic Review*, Vol. 79, pp. 916–922.

Freedman, M., and A.F. Williams. 1992. Speeds Associated with 55-mph and 65-mph Speed Limits in Northeastern States. *ITE Journal*, Vol. 62, No. 2, pp. 17–21.

Garber, N. J., and R. Gadiraju. 1988. *Speed Variance and Its Influence on Accidents*. University of Virginia, Charlottesville.

Harkey, D.L., H. D. Robertson, and S.E. Davis. 1990. Assessment of Current Speed Zoning Criteria. In *Transportation Research Record 1281*, Transportation Research Board, National Research Council, Washington, D.C.

Hauer, E. 1971. Accidents, Overtaking, and Speed Control. *Accident Analysis and Prevention*, Vol. 3, pp. 1–13.

Holland, C.A., and M.T. Conner. 1996. Exceeding the Speed Limit: An Evaluation of the Effectiveness of a Police Intervention. *Accident Analysis and Prevention*, Vol. 28, pp. 587–597.

Joksch, H.C. 1993. Velocity Change and Fatality Risk in a Crash. *Accident Analysis and Prevention*, Vol. 25, pp. 103–104.

Kahneman, D. 1973. *Attention and Effort*. Prentice-Hall, Englewood Cliffs, N.J.

Kallberg, V.P., and J. Luoma. 1996. Speed Kills—Or Does It and Why? *Proc., Conference of Road Safety in Europe*, Birmingham, United Kingdom, Sept. 9–11, pp. 129–149.

Kloeden, C.N., A.J. McLean, V.M. Moore, and G. Ponte. 1997. *Travelling Speed and the Risk of Crash Involvement*. Technical Report. NHMRC Road Accident Research Unit, The University of Adelaide, Australia.

Knowles, V., B. Persaud, M. Parker, and G. Wilde. 1997. *Safety, Speed and Speed Management: A Canadian Review*. Final Report, Contract T8080-5-6858. Transport Canada, March.

Lave, C. 1985. Speeding, Coordination, and the 55-mph Limit. *The American Economic Review*, Vol. 75, pp. 1159–1164.

Lave, C. 1989. Speeding, Coordination, and the 55-mph Limit: Reply. *The American Economic Review*, Vol. 79, pp. 926–931.

Lave, C., and P. Elias. 1994. Did the 65 mph Speed Limit Save Lives? *Accident Analysis and Prevention*, Vol. 26, pp. 49–62.

Levy, D.T., and P. Asch. 1989. Speeding, Coordination, and the 55-mph Speed Limit: Comment. *The American Economic Review*, Vol. 79, pp. 913–915.

Lindsay, P.H., and D.A. Norman. 1977. *Human Information Processing: An Introduction to Psychology* (2nd edition). Academic Press, New York.

Liu, G.X. 1997. Identification and Analysis of Speed Related Accidents on Highways. *Proc., Canadian Multidisciplinary Road Safety Conference X*, June 8–11, Toronto, Ontario, Canada.

Liu, G.X., and A. Popoff. 1996. *Provincial Wide Travel Speed and Traffic Safety Study in Saskatchewan*. Faculty of Engineering, University of Regina, Regina, Saskatchewan, Canada.

Lund, A.K., and W. J. Rauch. 1992. *On the Contrary! A Comment on Lave and Elias's Question, "Did the 65 mph Speed Limit Save Lives?"* Insurance Institute for Highway Safety, Arlington, Va.

Mackay, M. 1985. Seat Belt Use Under Voluntary and Mandatory Conditions and Its Effects on Casualties. In *Human Behavior and Traffic Safety* (L. Evans and R.C. Schwing, eds.), Plenum Press, New York, pp. 259–277.

Mackay, M. 1988. Crash Protection for Older Persons. In *Special Report 218: Transportation in an Aging Society*, Vol. 2, Transportation Research Board, National Research Council, Washington D.C., pp. 159–193.

Martinez, F. 1997. Statement before the Subcommittee on Surface Transportation, Committee on Transportation and Infrastructure, U.S. House of Representatives, July 17.

McCarthy, P.S. 1991. Highway Safety and the 65-mph Speed Limit. *Contemporary Policy Issues*, Vol. 9, pp. 82–92. Cited by Rock (1995).

McCoy, P.T., B.A. Moen, G. Pesti, and M. Mourssavi. 1993. *Evaluation of Lower Speed Limits on Urban Highways*. Research Report TRP-02-26-92. University of Nebraska, Lincoln. Cited by Knowles et al. (1997).

Moore, V.M., J. Dolinis, and A.J. Woodward. 1995. Vehicle Speed and Risk of a Severe Crash. *Epidemiology*, Vol. 6, pp. 258–262.

Munden, J.W. 1967. *The Relation Between a Driver's Speed and His Accident Rate*. Report LR 88. Road Research Laboratory, Crowthorne, Berkshire, England. Cited by Finch et al. (1994).

Näätänen, R., and H. Summala. 1976. *Road User Behavior and Traffic Accidents*. North-Holland, New York.

NASS. 1998. *Data from the 1995 Crashworthiness Data System*. National Highway Traffic Safety Administration, U.S. Department of Transportation.

NHTSA. 1992. *Report to Congress on the Effects of the 65 mph Speed Limit Through 1990*. U.S. Department of Transportation.

NHTSA. 1997. *Traffic Safety Facts 1996*. DOT HS 808 649. U.S. Department of Transportation.

Nilsson, G. 1990. *Reduction in the Speed Limit from 110 km/h to 90 km/h During Summer 1989: Effects on Personal Injury Accidents, Injured, and Speeds*. VTI Report 358A. Swedish Road and Traffic Research Institute, Sweden. Cited by Knowles et al. (1997).

O'Day, J., and J. Flora. 1982. *Alternative Measures of Restraint System Effectiveness: Interaction with Crash Severity Factors*. SAE Technical Paper Series No. 820798. Warrendale, Pa.

O'Donnell, C.J., and D.H. Connor. 1996. Predicting the Severity of Motor Vehicle Accident Injuries Using Models of Ordered Multiple Choice. *Accident Analysis and Prevention*, Vol. 28, pp. 739–753.

Parker, M.R., Jr. 1997. *Effects of Lowering and Raising Speed Limits on Selected Roadway Sections*. Report FHWA-RD-92-084. Federal Highway Administration, U.S. Department of Transportation.

Pasanen, E., and H. Salmivaara. 1993. Driving Speeds and Pedestrian Safety in the City of Helsinki. *Traffic Engineering and Control*, Vol. 34, No. 6, pp. 308–310.

Retting, R.A., and M.A. Greene. 1997. Traffic Speeds Following Repeal of the National Maximum Speed Limit. *ITE Journal*, May, pp. 42–46.

Rock, S.M. 1995. Impact of the 65 mph Speed Limit on Accidents, Deaths, and Injuries in Illinois. *Accident Analysis and Prevention*, Vol. 27, pp. 207–214.

Rodriguez, R.J. 1990. Speed, Speed Dispersion, and the Highway Fatality Rate. *Southern Economic Journal*. Oct., pp. 349–356.

Rumar, K., U. Bergrund, P. Jernberg, and U. Ytterbom. 1976. Driver Reaction to a Technical Safety Measure—Studded Tires. *Human Factors*, Vol. 18, pp. 443–454.

Sabey, B.E., and G.C. Staughton. 1975. Interacting Role of Road Environment, Vehicle, and Road User in Accidents. Presented at the 5th International Association for Accident and Traffic Medicine, London, Sept. 1975.

Shiekh, L. 1997. Statement before the Subcommittee on Surface Transportation, Committee on Transportation and Infrastructure, U.S. House of Representatives, July 17.

Shinar, D. 1978. *Psychology on the Road: The Human Factor in Traffic Safety*. Wiley, New York.

Shinar, D., and A. Drory. 1983. Sign Registration in Daytime and Nighttime Driving. *Human Factors*, Vol. 25, pp. 117–122.

Shinar, D. and A.J. McKnight. 1985. The Effects of Enforcement and Public Information on Compliance. In *Human Behavior and Traffic Safety* (L. Evans and R.C. Schwing, eds.), General Motors Research Laboratories, Plenum Press, New York, pp. 385–419.

Shinar, D., and E. Schechtman. 1998. *Health and Traffic Safety Behaviors in the U.S. in the Years 1985–1995*. Final Report. National Highway Traffic Safety Adminstration, U.S. Department of Transportation.

Shinar, D., and J. Stiebel. 1986. The Effectiveness of Stationary Versus Moving Police Vehicle on Compliance with Speed Limit. *Human Factors*, Vol. 28, pp. 365–371.

Snyder, D. 1989. Speeding, Coordination, and the 55-mph Limit. *The American Economic Review*, Vol. 79, pp. 922–925.

Snyder, D. 1997. Statement before the Subcommittee on Surface Transportation, Committee on Transportation and Infrastructure, U.S. House of Representatives, July 17.

Solomon, D. 1964. *Accidents on Main Rural Highways Related to Speed, Driver, and Vehicle*. Bureau of Public Roads, U.S. Department of Commerce, July.

Stuster, J., and Z. Coffman. 1997. *Synthesis of Safety Research Related to Speed and Speed Management*. Draft report. Anacapa Sciences, Inc., Santa Barbara, Calif.

Summala, H. 1985. Modeling Driver Behaviour: A Pessimistic Prediction? In *Human Behavior and Traffic Safety* (L. Evans and R.C. Schwing, eds.), General Motors Research Laboratories, Plenum Press, New York, pp. 43–65.

Taieb, M., and D. Shinar. 1996. *Maintaining Headway While Driving: Reality vs. Perception*. Paper presented at International Conference of Traffic and Transport Psychology, May, Valencia, Spain.

Taylor, D.H. 1964. Drivers' Galvanic Skin Response and the Risk of Accidents. *Ergonomics*, Vol. 7, pp. 439–451.

TRB. 1984. *Special Report 204: 55: A Decade of Experience*. National Research Council, Washington, D.C.

Treat, J.R., N.S. Tumbas, S.T. McDonald, D. Shinar, R.D. Hume, R.E. Mayer, R.L. Stansifer, and N.J. Castellan. 1977. *Tri-Level Study of the Causes of Traffic Accidents. Volume I: Causal Factor Tabulations and Assessment.* DOT-HS-805-085. NHTSA, U.S. Department of Transportation.

USA TODAY. 1997. Fewer Dying Despite Faster Speed Limits. July 14, p. 1A.

Vaa, T. 1997. Increased Police Enforcement Effects on Speed. *Accident Analysis and Prevention*, Vol. 29, pp. 373–385.

Viano, D.C., and S. Ridella. 1996. Crash Causation: A Case Study of Fatal Accident Circumstances and Configurations. No. 960458. Society of Automotive Engineers, International Congress and Exposition, Detroit, Mich., Feb. 26–29, pp. 123–134.

West, L.B., Jr., and J.W. Dunn. 1971. Accidents, Speed Deviation and Speed Limits. *Traffic Engineering*, Vol. 41, No. 10, pp. 52–55.

Wilde, G.J.S., S. P. Claxton-Oldfield, and P.H. Platenius. 1985. Risk Homeostasis in an Experimental Context. In *Human Behavior and Traffic Safety* (L. Evans and R.C. Schwing, eds.), Plenum Press, New York, pp. 119–149.

Zador, P.L. and A.K. Lund. 1991. *Comments on "Did the 65 mph Speed Limit Save 3,113 Lives?" by Charles A. Lave.* Insurance Institute for Highway Safety, Arlington, Va.

Appendix C

Effect of Speed Limits on Speed Distributions and Highway Safety: A Survey of the Literature

Patrick McCarthy
Department of Economics, Purdue University

The purpose of this review is to examine recent work on the effect of motor vehicle speed limits on highway speeds and highway safety. The review is empirical and concentrates on identifying the quantitative effects of changes in regulatory speed limit policies on the distribution of speeds and traffic safety. In general, the proposition that changes in speed limits induce observed changes in the distribution of speeds on a road network and have implications for the network's highway safety is straightforward. However, testing this proposition in a scientific inquiry to reliably answer such questions as "How will a 5-mph (8-km/h) increase in the speed limit alter the average speed of travel on a road? Will the number of fatal crashes increase if drivers, on average, travel 5 mph faster? What effect will a 5-mph increase in the speed limit have on the fatality rate?" is not straightforward.

Through local, state, and federal provision, the country's transportation system comprises a network of roads that differ by size, quality, and location. The attributes of each road's users (e.g., socioeconomic characteristics of the drivers, proportion of truck traffic) over some time period will generally differ by type, quality, and location of road. In combination with differential speed limits, traffic enforcement, and other government interventions, the nation's highways produce trips and, as a by-product, highway safety outcomes. If all roads and all road users were homogeneous, then determining the effect of alternative speed limit policies on speed distributions and highway safety would be relatively easy. However, the fact that both the individual components of a road system and its users are heterogeneous complicates the task of identifying the effects of changes in speed limit policies on highway speed distributions and safety.

Over the past 24 years, the U.S. Congress has passed three major pieces of federal legislation related to speed limits. First, responding to the oil crisis in the early 1970s, Congress passed the Emergency Highway Energy Conservation (EHEC) Act in 1974. Among its provisions, the act mandated a 55-mph (89-km/h) national maximum speed limit (NMSL) on all U.S. highways and threatened a loss of highway funds if states did not sufficiently enforce the limit. A Transportation Research Board (TRB) study (1984) concluded that implementation of the 55-mph national speed limit saved 2,000 to 4,000 lives annually.

In 1987, Congress passed the Surface Transportation Uniform Relocation Assistance (STURA) Act, which gave each state the right to increase speed limits on portions of the Interstate system lying within the least-populated areas of its boundaries. Thirty-eight states immediately responded to the legislation by raising speed limits on their rural Interstate highways, followed in 1988 by 2 additional states. Since passage of the 1987 legislation, there have been numerous national, regional, and statewide studies analyzing the effects of relaxed rural Interstate speed limits on highway safety.

Most recently, Congress passed the National Highway System Designation Act of 1995, which gave states complete freedom to set speed limits within their jurisdictional boundaries. To date, little scientific information is available on the effect this has had on speed distributions and highway safety.

By examining the empirical relationships among speed limits, speed distributions, and highway safety on nonlimited- and limited-access roads, this paper complements recent international reviews of speed limits and highway safety (Fildes and Lee 1993; Knowles et al. 1997). In general, this review covers domestic and international speed limit studies that have been conducted since the extensive 1984 TRB review. For a subset of studies, this review critically analyzes both the studies' findings and the strengths and weaknesses of their methodological approaches.

This review focuses on recent research that has analyzed the implications for highway safety as a direct result of the relaxed (rural) Interstate 65-mph (105-km/h) speed limit embodied in the STURA Act. There are three primary reasons for this focus. First, passage of the STURA Act was national in scope, affecting all roads, Interstate and non-Interstate, posted with speed limits above 55 mph (89 km/h). Of the rural and urban Interstate highways in 1990 with eligible mileage, 98 and 97 percent, respectively, had posted speed limits of 65 mph (NHTSA 1992). Moreover, although accounting for only 7.3 percent of total lane miles in the national transportation network, Interstate highways account for 26.1 percent of vehicle miles traveled (FHWA 1995). Factors that affect travel on limited-access high-speed roads have the potential for significantly affecting highway safety. Second, although it was national in scope, the 1987 STURA Act did not roll back the 1974 legislation. Rather, the act modified the structure of speed limits on limited-access roads by permitting higher speeds on sections of the system that past research had identified as the safest. This raises interesting and contentious issues concerning the law's effect on highway safety. Concentrating higher speed limits on the safest parts of the transportation network makes more plausible, for example, the controversial possibility that "fine-tuning" Interstate speed limits may have actually raised overall safety on the nation's highways. Third, a sufficient amount of time since the law's 1987 passage has elapsed for researchers to conduct longer-term studies on the law's varied effects. In contrast to short-term "impact" studies that, at times, may provide misleading information to policy makers, studies based on a longer sample of postenactment data are likely to more fully capture the traveling population's myriad adjustments to the new environment.

This paper is organized as follows. First, an overall framework within which to place existing empirical studies on the effects of speed limit laws is discussed. The methodological constructs most frequently used to empirically evaluate the effect of speed limit laws on speed distributions and highway safety are summarized. The known information on the effects of changing posted speed limits on the distribution of speeds is discussed. The effect of speed distributions on highway safety is examined. The findings of various studies examining the direct and indirect effects that relaxed speed limits on rural Interstate highways have had on the motoring public's safety are reported. International experience with speed limits is reviewed. Finally, a number of areas for further research are identified, and concluding comments are given.

SPEED LIMIT–HIGHWAY SAFETY FRAMEWORK

Figure C-1 shows the relationship between speed limits and highway safety on a given road. The basic mechanism between speed limits and highway safety is shown in the middle of the figure. Put simply, speed limits, among other factors, influence drivers' choices of optimal speeds. Solid arrows indicate a direction of direct causality. As shown by the figure, the posted speed limit is one of many objective factors that directly feed into a driver's speed decision. Other important determinants include highway and vehicle design, traffic enforcement and other highway government interventions (e.g., safety belt use laws), environmental attributes (e.g., weather conditions, topography), and characteristics of the driving population (e.g., proportion of younger drivers). At the same time, a driver has underlying preferences for risk and, in any specific driving situation, a sub-

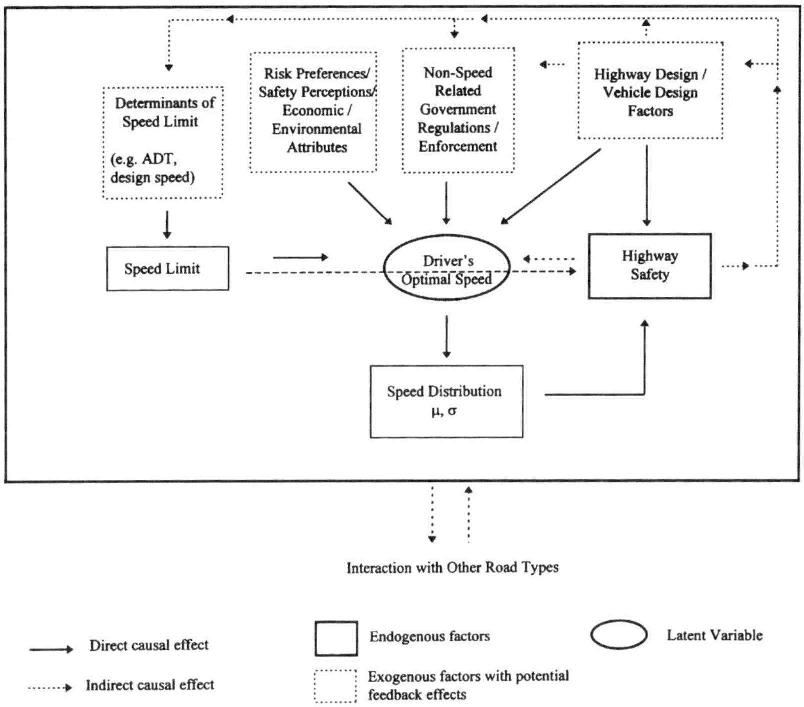

Figure C-1 Relationship between speed limit and highway safety.

jective view of traffic safety. By combining to determine a driver's optimal speed in each travel environment, these objective and subjective factors produce a distribution of speeds on the roadway and a set of safety outcomes (e.g., number and type of crashes, number and type of injuries).

Notice also that a driver's optimal speed is a latent variable. Although analysts can observe posted speed limits, measure the distribution of speeds on roadways, and observe safety outcomes, analysts cannot directly observe a driver's optimal speed. However, analysts can potentially (i.e., under certain conditions) infer the empirical effect of highway safety policy on a typical driver's optimal speed by examining the effect of policy on the road's distribution of speeds.

In addition to direct links between causal or determining factors, denoted by dotted-line boxes, and determined factors, denoted by solid-line boxes, there are indirect links that represent feedback effects. The figure shows the feedback roles that speed distributions and highway safety play on roads. Not only does speed distribution affect highway safety, but also a road's safety record has a feedback effect on the road's distribution of speeds (through its effect on individual drivers' optimal speed decisions). Further, a road's safety record will ultimately have long-term effects on highway and vehicle design, governmental policy, and the topic of this review—posted speed limits.

Two other points about Figure C-1 are worth mentioning. First, if, as hypothesized, the indicated linkages represent a given type of road (e.g., rural Interstate highway) in the system, then similar linkages will characterize other roads in the system (e.g., urban Interstate highways, arterials). Each road does not operate in isolation but is linked with other roads in the network, which implies that policy changes specific to one type of road are not likely to produce effects specific to that road but will influence travel behavior on other roads in the network. *Traffic diversion,* reflecting changes in route choice, *traffic generation,* reflecting latent travel demands, and *spillover effects,* whereby travel behavior on the affected road carries over onto other roads, are indicators of these secondary or indirect effects of a targeted highway policy.

Second, most empirical studies of highway safety, particularly as they relate to the 65-mph (105-km/h) speed limit, fall into one of three general categories. A relatively small group of studies examines how posted speed limits are set—in practice, what factors traffic engineers take into account when posting speed limits on alternative roadways. A related question concerns the effect of changes in the posted speed limit on speed distributions and driver compliance with the posted speed limit. A second group of empirical studies examines the relationship between attributes of the speed distribution, specifically average speed and speed dispersion, and highway safety. An important issue in this research is the role that average speed plays in highway safety after controlling for the statistical effect of speed dispersion. The last, and largest, set of empirical studies focuses on the effect of changes in the posted speed limit on highway safety. In Figure C-1, this is the direct link between the Speed Limit box and the Highway Safety box (indicated by the dashes). Although a large body of research on this issue is extant, a consensus has yet to form on whether increasing speed limits, particularly on limited-access roads, deteriorates safety. Part of the current debate in this area concerns how the law affected alternative highway safety measures.

METHODOLOGICAL CONSIDERATIONS

Empirical studies examining the effect of changes in posted speed limits on speed distributions or highway safety generally identify the primary null hypothesis as either (or at times both) of the following:

H_{01}: Increased speed limits have no effect on highway speed distributions.

H_{02}: Increased speed limits have no effect on highway safety outcomes.

The respective alternative hypotheses are as follows:

H_{A1}: Increased speed limits have a nonzero effect on highway speed distributions.

H_{A2}: Increased speed limits have a nonzero effect on highway safety outcomes.

Depending on the analyses' objectives, there are numerous variations of these hypotheses. Highway speed limits, for example, may be referred to as having "direct" or "indirect" effects. A direct effect refers to the highway directly affected by the speed limit change. Indirect effects, on the other hand, correspond to speeds on highways whose speed limits have not changed. The direct effect of the STURA Act in 1987, for example, is the effect of a 65-mph (105-km/h) speed limit on rural Interstate speed distributions; the effect on speed distributions of all other roads is the indirect effect. If, all else being constant, relaxed speed limits on one road produce changes in the distribution of speeds on other road networks whose speed limits have not changed, there is said to be a "spillover" or "tainting" effect associated with the speed limit change. Often, various null hypotheses are tested on characteristics of the distribution of speeds (on the affected and unaffected roads), including average speed, speed dispersion, 85th percentile speed, and the proportion of drivers traveling above a given speed. Also of interest are hypotheses related to a speed limit's effect on highway speeds by type of vehicle, road type, time of day, and a variety of other factors that differentiate travel in the highway system.

Similarly, numerous hypotheses concerning the effect of relaxed speed limits on highway safety outcomes are tested. As with highway speed distributions, these hypotheses often focus on direct and indirect effects, as well as the effects by vehicle type, road type, time of travel, location, alcohol consumption, and socioeconomic factors (e.g., age and gender). Although most of the attention is on fatal crashes and fatalities, some studies also identify the effect of relaxed speed limits on the severity of crashes.

In the empirical literature on speed limits and their effects, three methodological approaches have typically been used to test hypotheses concerning the effects of changes in posted speed limits: paired comparisons, regression analysis, and time series analysis.

Paired Comparisons

Ideally, testing null hypotheses on the effects of altered posted speed limits would require an experimental design whereby the analyst randomly selects a set of homogeneous roads (i.e., roads that are physically identical and that have an identical user profile) for analysis. The analyst randomly divides the set of roads into two subsets, a control group and an experimental group. The analyst then alters the speed limit for those roads in the experimental group, observes speed distributions and safety outcomes, and tests whether these outcomes are statistically different from similar measures for the control group. A benefit of this methodology is that the analyst can then draw inferences for the population of roads under study [e.g., a 10-mph (16-km/h) increase in rural Interstate speed limits increases average rural Interstate speeds by 3.2 mph (5.1 km/h), all else held constant]. Depending on whether the null hypothesis is accepted (rejected), the analyst concludes that the results are not (are) consistent with an altered speed limit having an effect on speed distributions and highway safety. Often, to obtain additional insights on the extent to which the observed effect is (is not) close to 0, the analyst reports confidence intervals.

Unfortunately, use of an experimental design approach to analyze the effect of speed limit changes is not generally feasible. Even assuming that one could sufficiently control for differences in a set of randomly selected roads to isolate the effect of changing speed limits, transportation agencies are reluctant to participate in such experiments for a variety of reasons. The alternative to an experimental design approach is a quasi-experimental methodology, which recognizes that speed limit changes do occur on some roads while not on others. In quasi-experimental procedures, there is a set of nonrandomly chosen roads (e.g., rural Interstate highways) on which the speed limit has changed—the experimental group—and a set of nonrandomly chosen roads on which the speed limit has not changed (e.g., rural non-Interstate highways)—the comparison group. After controlling for confounding factors that reflect heterogeneity across roads and road users, the analyst tests whether there are statistically significant differences between speed distributions and highway safety outcomes on the affected and unaffected roads. Depending on whether the null hypothesis is accepted, the analyst concludes that the change in speed limit has or has not had an effect.

Paired comparison approaches come in many forms. In some cases, the analyst draws conclusions from simple comparisons of average speeds and safety outcomes for the affected and unaffected roads. Other applications use more formal testing procedures to determine whether there is a statistically significant difference in speeds or safety, or both. Further, the approach is used across roads at a given point in time (e.g., a comparison between states that did and did not increase rural Interstate speeds) or across time (a comparison of affected states before and after the speed limit change).

A common approach is the use of odds ratios. Consider the following table:

	After Speed Limit Increase	*Before Speed Limit Increase*
65-mph (105-km/h) rural Interstate states	n_{11}	n_{12}
55-mph (89-km/h) rural Interstate states	n_{21}	n_{22}

where n_{ij} $(i, j = 1, 2)$ is the number of fatal crashes in state type i and speed limit environment j. Relative to 55-mph (89-km/h) states, the odds of a fatal crash in a 65-mph (105-km/h) state prior to the speed limit increase are (n_{12}/n_{22}). After the speed limit increase, the odds of a fatal crash in a 65-mph state relative to 55-mph states are (n_{11}/n_{21}). Thus, the odds ratio is $(n_{11}/n_{21})/(n_{12}/n_{22})$. If the speed limit increase in 65-mph states has no effect on fatal crashes, then the odds ratio will be 1. Alternatively, if the law significantly increased (decreased) fatal crashes, then the ratio would be greater (less) than 1. Analysts typically calculate chi-square tests and confidence intervals to test null hypotheses using these methods.

A primary advantage of quasi-experimental methodologies based on paired comparison approaches is that very little information is needed to conduct the test. In the preceding example, four bits of information are sufficient to test the hypothesis. However, the example, as with all paired comparison analyses, has a maintained hypothesis that relating outcomes in the experimental group [i.e., fatal crashes in 65-mph (105-km/h) states] to those in the comparison group [i.e., 55-mph (89-km/h) states] controls for all differences between the two groups in all other determining factors. Whether these techniques provide sufficient control for confounding factors that may influence the variable of interest and, accordingly, affect the test results and the associated policy implications is an important empirical issue. Analysts often stratify the sample by other variables (e.g., highway exposure, socioeconomic characteristics) to explicitly control for other determining factors. In most cases, however, the analyst uses univariate stratification, that is, stratification of the sample one variable at a time. Simultaneously stratifying by multiple variables would enable an analyst to better isolate the effect of altered speed limits, although a practical limitation of multivariate stratification is that it generates many empty cells.

Regression Models

An alternative procedure for analyzing the effect of altered speed limits on highway speeds and safety is to develop a statistical model that not only includes the relevant policy variable but also controls for other confounding factors. This is the regression approach, whose aim is to estimate equations of the following general form:

$$H_{it} = \sum_{i=1}^{N} \alpha_i + \sum_{j=1}^{k} \beta_j x_{it,j} + \varepsilon_{it}$$

where

- H_{it} = highway outcome (e.g., fatal crashes, fatality rate, injury crashes, injury rate) for cross section i and time period t ($i = 1,\ldots, N$; $t = 1,\ldots, T$),
- $x_{it,j}$ = jth explanatory variable for cross section i and time period t ($i = 1,\ldots, N$; $t = 1,\ldots, T$; $j = 1,\ldots, k$),
- β_j = parameter reflecting the marginal effect of the jth explanatory variable on the highway outcome ($j = 1,\ldots, k$), and
- ε_{it} = error term for cross section i and time period t ($i = 1,\ldots, N$; $t = 1,\ldots,T$).

The data for this regression are cross sections over a period of time, called a pooled data set, an example of which is the number of annual fatal crashes in each state from 1970 through 1995.

The formulation in the preceding equation is often referred to as a *fixed effects* specification because the model includes separate parameters (α_i) to reflect each of the cross sections included in the analysis. This pooled data formulation is a general specification that, depending on one's data set, collapses to simpler econometric models. The two most common are time series regression models and cross-section models. In a time series regression model, $N = 1$ and there is a single cross section (e.g., annual nationwide fatal crashes from 1970 through 1997, or the monthly fatality rate from January

1980 through December 1992). Further, if the model included only a constant term and a time trend as the only explanatory variable, then the regression equation would model historical trends. Alternatively, a cross-section model is based on a cross section of observations at a single point in time (e.g., fatal crashes in each county for 1994, or total crashes for each state in the nation in 1996).

To the extent that the analyst can obtain accurate information on other confounding factors that affect the dependent variable of interest, a well-specified regression model controls for the statistical influence of the confounding factors and better isolates the independent effect of the policy. In general, there are two difficulties with this approach. First, estimation of regression models is subject to several statistical pitfalls. In time series analysis, for example, error terms may be serially correlated, which, if not corrected, invalidates hypothesis tests. Alternatively, regression models based on highly collinear data are generally unable to isolate the independent effects of the collinear variables. Thus, the potential advantages of regression model approaches will be realized to the extent that the analyst tests and, if necessary, corrects for statistical and other problems encountered in regression techniques. Second, the ability of the regression model approach to control for other determining factors implies that regression analysis is generally more data intensive. Unavailable, inappropriate, or unreliable data as well as time or resource constraints on data collection may cause researchers to develop and estimate relatively simple models that fail to adequately control for a larger set of relevant determining factors.

Similar to a paired comparison methodology, regression models may also reflect a quasi-experimental approach. Consider, for example, a regression analysis of fatalities on 50 observations, where each observation represents the number of fatalities in a state during 1990. Because not all states with eligible mileage increased their rural Interstate speed limits when Congress passed STURA, the sample of observations includes states with 65-mph (105-km/h) highways and states with 55-mph (89-km/h) highways. Typically, a variable is included in the model to reflect a state's maximum speed limit status; the variable is equal to 1 if the state increased its speed limit on rural Interstate highways and 0 otherwise. Because the sample includes experimental states along with comparison states, the approach is quasi-experimental. If the analyst cannot reject the null hypothesis that the coefficient on the 0-1 speed limit variable equals 0, the inference is that the enactment of STURA is consistent with a null hypothesis that the act had no effect on fatalities, holding all else constant.

Another example of a quasi-experimental approach within a regression framework occurs when there are no explanatory variables in the model. In this case, the model includes a constant, which reflects the overall mean of the dependent variable, and a set of 0-1 variables that reflect treatments. The analyst estimates this model, called analysis of variance (ANOVA), to examine whether the treatments (e.g., relaxing speed limits on rural Interstates, type of road) in the experimental states have a significant effect on the overall mean relative to the comparison states.

Interrupted Time Series Analysis

A third methodology often used to analyze the effect of altered speed limits on speed distributions and highway safety is time series intervention models. If a time series of the monthly fatalities from 1976 to 1990 were examined, two features would probably be immediately apparent. First, the series would exhibit a declining trend. Second, a repeating cyclical pattern that reflects seasonal variations in fatalities would appear. An analyst's objective is to develop an autoregressive integrated moving average (ARIMA) model that accounts for the trend of the series, seasonal patterns, and any serial dependencies that exist in the series itself or in the error term. In effect, ARIMA models decompose the behavior of the series into three components: trend, which is captured by an integrated component of the model; autoregressive and moving average components that explain the current observation in terms of past observations and random shocks; and seasonal terms that capture the regularities in the series. The model is initially estimated for the preintervention period. Assuming that the process, in the absence of the intervention, would continue in accordance with the preintervention model, the model is then estimated with an additional function to identify the effect of the intervention (e.g., relaxed speed limit). There are several possibilities for modeling the intervention. An "abrupt permanent" function reflects an intervention that has an immediate and permanent effect on the series, whereas an "abrupt temporary" function is one that immediately affects the series but whose effect decays over time. Or there could be no initial effect but a gradual buildup to a permanent effect.

A significant advantage of ARIMA time series models is data economy. In contrast to regression time series models that require data on the dependent variable and each of the explanatory variables, ARIMA models only require data on the dependent variable series and knowledge of when the intervention occurred. This can yield considerable savings on resources expended to collect the necessary data for analysis.

However, the implications that ARIMA models have for data collection are not free. In time series models, a maintained hypothesis is that the effect of other determining factors is captured and that there are no disruptions in these series over the relevant period of analysis. Essentially, the assumption is made that the disruption occurring in the series is due only to the policy under study. For example, consider the effect that relaxed rural Interstate speed limits have on fatalities. An analyst estimates an ARIMA model of the process and finds that relaxed speed limits significantly reduced fatalities. This assumes that all other determining factors, including, for example, vehicle miles traveled, evolved during the postintervention period as it had during the preintervention period. Suppose, however, that gasoline prices significantly rose in the third quarter of 1987, shortly after relaxed speed limits were implemented. The assumption that preintervention vehicle miles traveled evolved in a manner consistent with postintervention miles traveled is no longer tenable and the drop in fatalities would be inappropriately attributed to the relaxed speed limits. In recent work, researchers have included additional variables in ARIMA models, referred to as ARIMAX models, to explicitly test the hypothesis that other determining factors have no effect on the series.

POSTED SPEED LIMITS AND SPEEDING BEHAVIOR

Figure C-1 indicates that changes in posted speed limits alter the distribution of speeds on a road to the extent that changed limits alter drivers' optimal speed choices. Holding all else constant, if altered speed limits have no effect on optimal speeds, speed distributions will be unaffected. Although conceptually this is straightforward, empirically the issue revolves around the analyst's ability to isolate the specific effect of posted speed limits from the effects of other confounding factors that influence optimal speed decisions, including traffic enforcement, environmental attributes, and public safety campaigns. Because roads are linked in a network, a related issue is whether a change in posted speed limits on one road alters drivers' optimal speeds on other roads, the spillover effect.

Studies that have addressed the effects of changing posted speed limits on speed distributions can be usefully divided by two road types, nonlimited-access and limited-access roads.

Nonlimited-Access Roads

Table C-1 identifies recent studies that have examined the speed distribution effects of posted speed limits on nonlimited-access roads. A study by Parker (1997) included 100 experimental [172 mi (277 km)] and 83 comparison [132 mi (212 km)] nonlimited-access sites in 22 states between June 1986 and July 1989. The primary objective in selecting a comparison site was to match as closely as possible the design, volume, and speed characteristics of the associated experimental site. In general, posted speed limits on the comparison sites included in the study were set at the 45th percentile speed.

The following information is given for the experimental sites:

- Sixty-three of the 100 experimental sites and 80 percent of the total mileage for the study were located in rural areas with populations less than 5,000. Fifteen sites were located in urban areas with 50,000 persons or more.
- Posted speed limits were lowered at 59 sites and raised at 41 sites. The most frequent speed limit decrease was 10 mph (16 km/h) (35 sites), whereas the prevailing increase was 5 mph (8 km/h) (26 sites). The maximum decrease in the posted limit was 20 mph (32 km/h) (three sites), and the maximum increase was 15 mph (24 km/h) (three sites). Before the speed limit change, the typical

Table C-1 U.S. Research on Speed Limits and Speeds—Nonlimited-Access Roads

Study	Database for Speeds	Methodology	Major Findings	Comments
Casey and Lund 1987[a]	Experimental/comparison site data, 55-mph[b] freeways to connecting roads, CA 1985	ANOVA Multiple regression	Supports speed adaptation, 0 to 4 percent increase mitigated by environmental factors	Tested three road configurations Lower speeds for commercial vehicles Differences in the effects of age and gender across field studies What is the geographical extent of adaptation?
Casey and Lund 1992	Experimental/comparison site data Reanalysis of 1985 CA study 1988	ANOVA Multiple regression	Increase in average speeds with no change in speed limits Continued support for speed adaptation No increase in adapted speeds	Retested road configurations from 1987 study Lower speeds for commercial vehicles Sronger evidence that younger drivers and female drivers travel faster What is the geographical extent of adaptation?

Ullman and Dudek 1987[a]	Six urban fringe 55-mph[b] sites in Texas	Before/after analysis	Lowering speed limits from 55[b] to 45 mph[b] had little effect on speed distributions	No control for confounding factors
Parker 1997[a]	Experimental/comparison site data, 22 states June 1986–July 1988 Aug. 1987–July 1989	Quasi-experimental	Increased speed limits have significant but small absolute effect on speeds Change in speed alone has little effect on driver behavior No apparent speed adaptation	100 experimental sites; 83 comparison sites Nonrandom site selection No control for cross-site and cross-state differences (e.g. enforcement, vehicles, drivers, education) Many results statistically significant but interpreted as "not practically meaningful"

[a]The text covers this study in more detail.
[b]55 mph = 89 km/h; 45 mph = 72 km/h.

posted speed limit for the experimental sites was set at the 20th percentile speed; after the speed limit change, this increased to the 43rd percentile speed.

• Sites whose speed limits were lowered by 15 mph (24 km/h) or more had the highest "before change" posted speed limits. Sites whose speed limits were increased by 10 mph (16 km/h) or more had the lowest "before change" speed limits.

• Average 24-h volume at the experimental sites was 4,500 vehicles. For the comparison sites, the average 24-h volume was 3,400.

In general, Parker's study found little evidence of a relationship between posted speed limits and speed distributions. The study's primary findings with respect to speed distributions are as follows:

• There was generally less than a 2-mph (3-km/h) difference in average speeds, speed standard deviation, and 85th percentile speed between the before and after speeds. These changes were statistically significant but were interpreted as "not sufficiently large to be of practical significance" (Parker 1997, 86).

• There was little evidence of spillover effects.

• Changes in posted speed limits led to changes in driver compliance, but this reflects the definition of compliance as driving at or below the posted speed limit rather than changes in driver behavior.

In sum, Parker's study found that changing posted speed limits on nonlimited-access roads had little effect on speed distributions. It was further concluded that changes in posted speed limits had little effect on highway safety. The latter result is expected given the finding that altered limits had little effect on speed distributions.

To the extent possible, Parker's study matches experimental with comparison sites to isolate the effect that posted speed limit changes have on driver behavior and speed distributions. At the start, Parker proposed an experimental design methodology for studying the effects of posted speed limit changes. However, because of legal, safety, and other concerns, state departments of transportation would only agree to participate if sites were nonrandomly selected. In particular, experimental sites were not randomly chosen from the population of nonlimited-access roads but from a set of sites whose posted speed limits were to be changed. Thus, the methodology actually used in the study was quasi-experimental. This has two implications:

- Nonrandom selection of sites implies that the results emanating from a study of these sites cannot be generalized to a population of nonlimited-access roads. Inferences can only be drawn for the 172 mi (277 km) of experimental site roads included in the analysis.
- Since, for all experimental sites included in the study, speed limits were to be changed, the posted speed limit changes may have simply rationalized observed behavior.

The first point is explicitly recognized in the study, which states: "The findings may apply to similar sites where the speed limits are changed for similar reasons. Generalizations to other roadways are not appropriate" (Parker 1997, 5). There is an allusion to but relatively little discussion of the second point—the study recognizes that "speed limit changes at the study sites were not made for the purpose of experimentation" (Parker 1997, 6). Reasons cited in the study for changing speed limits included requests from the public, leaders, or enforcement personnel; consistency of speed limits with traffic conditions; high incidence of crashes; compliance with local ordinances; and changing traffic volume and land use patterns. According to the study, the researchers were not aware of any major differences in enforcement or public information campaigns between the pre- and postchange environments. However, there was no attempt to explicitly evaluate whether traffic enforcement at the experimental sites differed between the pre- and postchange periods. This is potentially important, since differences in enforcement affect drivers' optimal speeds and, accordingly, speed distributions. Higher (lower) posted speed limits combined with greater (less) enforcement could produce little difference in observed speeds.

Further, if changes in the posted speed limit simply legalized existing behavior, the findings would be significantly biased toward accepting the null hypothesis that altered speed limits have no effect on driver behavior, and little insight would be offered into the independent effect of changing posted speed limits on speed distributions or highway safety.

The study also notes that the modest changes in the speed distributions, on the order of 2 mph (3 km/h) or less, are statistically significant but not practically meaningful. An implication is that a statistically significant 2-mph increase in average speeds will have no effect on highway safety regardless of whether the road is posted at 20 or 40 mph (32 or 64 km/h), representing a 10 percent and 5 percent change, respectively, in average speed. The researchers do not comment on how large the distribution change must be to be "of practical significance."

Ullman and Dudek (1987) examined the effect of lowering the speed limit from 55 to 45 mph (89 to 72 km/h) at six urban fringe highway sites in Texas where rapid urban development was occurring. On the basis of 1 year pre– and 1 year post–speed limit change data, the authors generally find little change in average speed, 85th percentile speed, the proportion of drivers traveling above 60 mph (97 km/h), acceleration, or skewness. However, there was no control for other confounding factors, including population changes, traffic congestion, and traffic enforcement, which weakens the authors' conclusions that lowering speed limits below the 85th percentile speed had no "conclusive effect on absolute speeds, speed distributions, or speed-changing activities" (Ullman and Dudek 1987, 48).

In related studies, Casey and Lund (1987, 1992) analyzed the extent to which drivers who are exposed to and have adapted to higher-speed environments drive faster when entering lower-speed environments compared with drivers who have not been exposed to higher-speed environments. Holding all else constant, the null hypothesis is that driver speeds in low-speed environments will be no different whether or not these drivers were previously exposed to a higher-speed environment. Rejection of the null hypothesis is consistent with speed adaptation. In their 1987 paper, Casey and Lund tested three California field locations (representing six sites), reflecting rural and urban settings and alternative connecting road configurations and speed limits. Casey and Lund reached the following conclusions:

• Drivers traveled more slowly on the connecting roads. However, drivers exiting an expressway generally traveled faster on the connecting road than those not exiting an expressway. At one site there was no difference between adapted and nonadapted speeds; at the other five sites, the difference ranged between 1.8 and 4.7 percent.

• At two of the three field locales, close to 100 percent of the drivers were required to stop before entering the connecting road. This provides stronger evidence of speed adaptation behavior, since the observed speed behavior on the connecting road was not simply an uninterrupted continuation from the higher-speed road, a phenomenon often referred to as speed perpetuation.

• In a 1992 study, the authors retested these sites to assess the effect of the 65-mph (105-km/h) speed limit that California implemented on a portion of its eligible roads. Although none of the sites included in the study were eligible for the higher speed limit, the authors found that average speed increased at two of the three freeway sites and three of the four connecting roads in the study. Speed adaptation continued to be observed but did not worsen in the post-65-mph environment.

The results reported in these studies are consistent with previous research [e.g., Matthews (1978)], although the extent of speed adaptation is less in Casey and Lund's work, which may reflect better control of confounding factors. This suggests the need for similar studies in different areas and with different road configurations to determine whether Casey and Lund's results are representative or, for some reason, unique to the location and set of roads studied. Further, a potentially important question that this study raises is the extent to which the speed adaptation effect continues. In the study, drivers are either "adapted" or "nonadapted," reflecting the freeway exposure of the "adapted" drivers. If speed adaptation is a general phenomenon, will expressway drivers adapt to the lower speeds on the connecting road? If so, we might expect to initially see higher speeds for the adapted drivers on exiting the expressway but little difference in speeds between the adapted and nonadapted drivers after a time.

Limited-Access Roads

Table C-2 summarizes recent research on the effect of increased speed limits, and specifically the 65-mph (105-km/h) speed limit embodied in the STURA Act, on limited-access roads. Significant aspects of these studies are as follows:

- Regardless of research methodology, unit of observation, or time period, the 65-mph (105-km/h) speed limit generally led to an increase in average speeds on the rural Interstate systems. In various studies, the National Highway Traffic Safety Administration (NHTSA) and others consistently measured significant speed increases in the post-65-mph environment. For example, between the fourth quarter of 1986 and the fourth quarter of 1990, NHTSA (1992) estimated a 3.4-mph (5.5-km/h) increase in average speeds, from 60.6 mph (97.5 km/h) to 64 mph (103 km/h).
- Consistent with the increase in average speeds has been a general increase in speed dispersion, 85th percentile speed, and the proportion of drivers traveling over 65 mph (105 km/h).
- Virtually no study explicitly controlled for other confounding factors across either time or unit of observation, although some studies used 55-mph (89-km/h) environments to normalize for other factors.
- Although average speeds increased after states implemented 65-mph (105-km/h) speed limits on eligible parts of their Interstate systems, average speeds did not increase by the amount of the speed limit increase.
- There is mixed evidence on the effect that relaxed rural Interstate speed limits had on speed distributions in 55-mph (89-km/h) states or on 55-mph highways in 65-mph (105-km/h) states.

Similar to most studies in the highway safety literature, the studies cited in Table C-2 use a quasi-experimental design methodology, and none sufficiently controls for other factors that may influence speed distributions. Although one cannot conclude from the existing evidence that, all else constant, an increase in rural Interstate speed limits caused an increase in mean and 85th percentile speeds, the immediate and persistent increase in speeds identified in this work is

Table C-2 U.S. Research on Speed Limits and Speeds—Limited-Access Roads

Study	Database for Speeds	Methodology	Major Findings	Comments
NHTSA 1989[a]	Thirteen 65-mph[b] states Eight 55-mph[b] states 3rd qtr. 1982–1987 4th qtr. 1985–1st qtr. 1988	Before/after analysis Regression trend analysis	Increased average speed in 65-mph[b] states Increased 85th percentile speed in 65-mph[b] states	Time series, based on averages across states Limited sample
NHTSA 1990	Eighteen 65-mph[b] states continuing to monitor speeds 4th qtr. 1985–1st qtr. 1990	Before/after analysis Regression	Increased speeds by 0.25 mph[b] per year Increased 85th percentile speed by 0.30 mph[b] per year Significant (but unreported) effect of speed limit on average speed and 85th percentile speed	Update of 1989 study No control found differences across states
NHTSA 1992	Eighteen 65-mph[b] states monitoring speeds, two periods 4th qtr. 1986, 4th qtr. 1990	Before/after analysis	Increased average speed from 60.6[b] to 64 mph[b] Increased 85th percentile speed from 66.6[b] to 70.7 mph[b] Increased speed dispersion by 0.7 mph[b]	Update of 1990 study No control found differences across states

(continued on next page)

Table C-2 *(continued)*

Study	Database for Speeds	Methodology	Major Findings	Comments
FHWA 1995	State-monitored 55-mph[b] roads 1993	Reports 1993 statistics	Average speed = 56.9 mph,[b] range = (49.4, 59.6)[b] 85th percentile speed = 64.0,[b] range = (56.4, 68.3)[b] 6.5 million citations, range = (2,081, 980,258)	No statistical analysis
McKnight et al. 1989[a]	Nine 65-mph[b] states Seven 55-mph[b] states Quarterly data, 1982–1988	Quasi-experimental ARIMA models	65-mph[b] states, percent driving over 65 mph[b] 48.2% increase on rural Interstates 9.1% increase on 55-mph[b] roads 55-mph[b] states, percent driving over 65 mph[b] 18% increase on rural Interstates 37% increase on other 55-mph[b] roads	Aggregates over all 55-mph[b] and 65-mph[b] states Analyzed percentage of drivers traveling above 65 mph[b] Data could not answer why speeds in the 55-mph[b] states increased No control for differences across states or systems

Freedman and Esterlitz 1990	Rural Interstates (MD, NM, VA) Urban Interstate (NM) April 1987–July 1989	Quasi-experimental	Average and 85th percentile speed increase in 65-mph[b] rural Interstate states (VA, NM) Little change in 55-mph[b] rural Interstate state (MD) Little change on urban Interstate (NM) Similar increase in tractor-trailer speeds (MD, VA)	No data on estimated trends No statistical tests No control for differences across states or systems Differentiates speeds by vehicle type
Mace and Heckard 1991	51 rural Interstate speed study sites in AL, AZ, CA, FL, IL, OH, TN, TX 1986, 1988/1989	Before/after analysis	3.9-mph[b] increase in rural Interstate speeds 4.3-mph[b] increase in rural Interstate 85th percentile speed 0.65-mph[b] increase in rural Interstate speed dispersion Little change in speeds from 1988 to 1989 Lttle local spillover effect observed and no evidence of spillover onto urban Interstates	No control for confounding effects For spillover analysis, "toward/away" approach used for some states Small number of spillover sites Detailed analysis of Illinois data Dual speed limits inhibit car speeds
Freedman and Williams 1992	Northeastern states (CT, MD, MA, NJ, NY, PA, NH, OH, VT, VA, WV) Oct. 1989–Jan. 1990	Quasi-experimental	Increased rural Interstate speeds in 65-mph[b] states No effect on rural Interstate speeds in 55-mph[b] states Lower truck speeds in dual limit states	Average car speed in 65-mph[b] states less than in dual speed limit states No statistical tests No control for differences across states or systems Differentiates speeds by vehicle type

(continued on next page)

Table C-2 *(continued)*

Study	Database for Speeds	Methodology	Major Findings	Comments
Parker 1997	Experimental/comparison site data, 10 sites, 4 states (CA, MD, MI, VA) April 1989–August 1989	Quasi-experimental	Increased average speed at experimental sites, range = (0.2, 2.3)[b] Decrease in speed standard deviation at three of four experimental sites, range = (–0.9, 0.2)[b] Changes in average speed and 85th percentile speed less than 0.5 mph[b] at comparison sites	Nonrandom site selection Small sample size No control for differences across states or systems

[a] The text covers this study in more detail.

[b] Measurements given in miles per hour in this table are converted to kilometers per hour as follows:

mph	*km/h*	*mph*	*km/h*	*mph*	*km/h*
-0.1	-0.2	2.3	3.7	59.6	95.9
0.2	0.3	3.9	6.3	60.6	97.5
0.25	0.40	4.3	6.9	64	103
0.3	0.5	49.4	79.5	65	105
0.5	0.8	55	89	66.6	107.2
0.65	1.05	56.4	90.8	68.3	109.9
0.7	1.1	56.9	91.6	70.7	113.8

certainly consistent with this hypothesis. The evidence strongly suggests that drivers' optimal speeds on rural Interstate systems in states whose speed limits did rise lies above 55 mph (89 km/h) and for some drivers may lie above 65 mph (105 km/h). This further implies that an enforced 55-mph NMSL did constrain rural Interstate drivers' speed decisions.

On the other hand, the mixed evidence on speed distributions in 55-mph (89-km/h) environments, combined with a lack of control for other confounding factors, precludes the drawing of any firm conclusions from these studies concerning the spillover effects of relaxed rural Interstate speed limits.

As indicated in Table C-2, NHTSA produced a series of studies on the speed distribution effects of the 65-mph (105-km/h) speed limit. Relative to speeds expected from historical trends, average and 85th percentile speeds on rural Interstate systems that raised the speed limits consistently rose. Average and 85th percentile rural Interstate speeds in thirteen 65-mph states increased 1.9 and 1.3 mph (3.1 and 2.1 km/h), respectively, in 1987 over 1986 (NHTSA 1989a, 56–57). Average speeds in eight states that did not raise rural Interstate speed limits also increased, but the increase was much less. Rural Interstate average speeds in the 13 states, which had been trending upwards by about 0.2 mph (0.3 km/h) per year, appeared to have gotten a boost from the STURA Act in 1987.

But there are inconsistencies even in these data. Of the thirteen 65-mph (105-km/h) states in the study, average speeds increased in 8 (Arizona, Arkansas, California, Colorado, Illinois, Iowa, Nevada, and Washington) but actually fell in 4 (Indiana, Mississippi, South Dakota, and Tennessee) and did not change in 1 (Wisconsin) between the first quarter of 1987 and the first quarter of 1988. Eighty-fifth percentile speeds increased in nine but fell in four states (Indiana, Mississippi, South Dakota, and Tennessee). A similar phenomenon occurred in the eight 55-mph (89-km/h) states in the study. Between the first quarter of 1987 and the first quarter of 1988, average speeds rose in five states and fell in four (Connecticut, New Jersey, New York, and Rhode Island). Eighty-fifth percentile speeds fell in the same four states. On the basis of individual state data, the apparently strong national evidence that relaxed rural Interstate speed limits led to a uniform rise in speeds weakens. These findings emphasize the need to develop models that sufficiently control for confounding factors in order to accurately identify the isolated effect of the relaxed speed limits on speed distributions. They also imply that conclusions based on aggregates may be oversimplified and that aggregation masks the underlying mechanisms through which speed limit changes affect speed distributions.

The analysis by McKnight et al. (1989) of 55- and 65-mph (89- and 105-km/h) states gives limited speed distribution data, but the information provided is consistent with NHTSA's research. There is no information on differences in average speeds or 85th percentile speeds between the 65-mph and 55-mph states. However, McKnight et al. provide information on the proportion of drivers traveling over 65 mph. On the basis of 16 states providing quarterly speed information between 1982 and 1989, McKnight et al. found that, between 1986 and 1988, the ratio of rural Interstate drivers to 55-mph road drivers traveling over 65 mph significantly increased in 65-mph states but fell in 55-mph states This is not a surprising result for the 65-mph states, given the observed increase in average speeds in the 65-mph environments.

An intriguing finding of the study by McKnight et al. is that, in the post-65-mph (105-km/h) environment, the percentage of drivers exceeding 65 mph in 55-mph (89-km/h) states increased 18 percent on rural Interstate systems and 37 percent on other 55-mph highways. By comparison, in 65-mph states, there were 48 and 9 percent increases. The authors suggest that this may reflect a tainting or spillover effect but provide no evidence of this. Traffic diversion may explain the large difference in 65-mph states but does not explain the findings in the 55-mph environments. These findings again demonstrate the need to develop models that sufficiently control for relevant confounding factors in order to fully understand the mechanisms at work.

Summary

From the work cited, several conclusions can be drawn concerning the effect on speed distributions of increasing speed limits from 55 mph (89 km/h) to 65 mph (105 km/h).

• On nonlimited-access roads, evidence suggests that changes in speed limits affect average speeds and speed dispersions, but the magnitude of these changes appears to be small, and possibly much smaller than the change in speed limit.

• Drivers exhibit speed adaptation, but the difference between adapted and nonadapted speeds is less than 5 percent. The extent of speed adaptation appears not to worsen with increasing speed limits on limited-access high-speed roads.

• On limited-access high-speed roads, work indicates that increased speed limits lead to higher average speeds [on the order of 4 mph (6 km/h) or less for a 10-mph (16-km/h) increase in the speed limit] and increased 85th percentile speeds (of a similar magnitude) with small increases in speed dispersion [by less than 1 mph (2 km/h)], but these findings are based on limited control for other confounding factors. The effects that increased speed limits on limited-access roads have on speed distributions of nonlimited-access roads are considerably more ambiguous.

• Many of these studies comment on the importance of speed enforcement in determining the effects of speed limit changes on speed distributions, but there is little empirical evidence on the explicit role that enforcement plays.

SPEED DISTRIBUTION AND HIGHWAY SAFETY

Studies

The preceding section summarized a set of empirical studies examining the effect of changes in speed limits on speed distributions on nonlimited-access and limited-access roads. Particularly for relaxed rural Interstate speed limits passed in 1987, there is evidence, albeit not consistent, that relaxed speed limits on rural Interstate highways increased mean and 85th percentile speeds as well as speed dispersion on these roads. The effect that speed limits have on roads' speed distributions, however, is primarily relevant because of its implications for highway safety. A critical question then is, What effect do speed distributions have on highway safety? Since speed distributions can be characterized by average speed, speed dispersion, 85th percentile speed, and the proportion of traffic traveling above some speed, it is important to understand whether there is an identifiable relationship between a road's speed distribution and highway safety.

Unfortunately, relatively little research has focused on the relationship between a road's speed distribution and measures of the road's safety. Recent work, identified in Table C-3, has typically centered on the highway safety effects of average speeds versus speed dispersion. In contrast, as will be seen in the next section, a significant amount of research exists on the effect of speed limits on highway safety. For much of this research, the hypothesis of interest is that an increase in speed limits leads to a deterioration in highway safety. The implication is that increases in speed limits induce drivers to travel faster, which leads to crashes involving more serious injuries and more fatalities. That is, "speed kills."

Solomon (1964) initially investigated the relationship between crash involvement rate and speed dispersion, finding that the involvement rate is lowest very near average speeds. At speeds significantly lower or higher than average speed, involvement rates increase. According to Solomon's findings, slower drivers can be just as dangerous as faster drivers. Cerrelli (1981) also found a U-shaped curve between crash rates and deviations from average speeds. In related work, Garber and Gadiraju (1988) found a U-shaped relationship between speed dispersion and the difference between a road's design speed and the posted speed limit. Minimum speed dispersion tends to occur when the design speed is 5 to 10 mph (8 to 16 km/h) higher than the posted speed limit. The authors also estimated a positive but not U-shaped relationship between speed dispersion and the crash rate.

There are relatively few empirical studies that examine the direct relationship between speed distribution and highway safety after controlling for other relevant determinants. Lave (1985) explored the effects of average speed and speed dispersion on rural and urban fatality rates for Interstate systems, arterial roads, and collector roads. Each of the 6 models was estimated for 1981 and 1982, for a total of 12 models. Lave's basic hypothesis is

$$\text{Fatality rate} = f(\text{crash severity, crash involvement})$$

Table C-3 U.S. Research on Speed, Speed Dispersion, and Highway Safety

Study	Database for Speeds	Methodology	Major Findings	Comments
Lave 1985[a]	Statewide, by functional class 1981, 1982	Regression analysis	After controlling for speed dispersion, average speed had little effect on fatality rates More emphasis on speed dispersion as a coordinating device	Controlled for enforcement and hospital access Limited control for other factors
Garber and Gadiraju 1988[a]	Interstate, arterial, and major rural collector test sites in Virginia	Regression analysis ANOVA	Crash rates increase with increasing speed dispersion on all roads Relationship between speed dispersion and (design speed – posted speed limit) is U shaped	Speed dispersion is lowest when difference is between 5 and 10 mph[b] Crash rate is not necessarily positively related to average speed
McCarthy 1988	Countywide State of Indiana, 1987	Regression analysis	After controlling for speed dispersion, average speed had little effect on safety	Controls for a variety of socioeconomic factors Limited sample

(continued on next page)

Table C-3 *(continued)*

Study	Database for Speeds	Methodology	Major Findings	Comments
Levy and Asch 1989	Statewide data for 1985	Regression analysis	Average speed, speed dispersion, and their interaction have important effects on the fatality rate	Controls for a variety of socioeconomic factors Speed dispersion significantly increased Interstate fatality rates when average speed $\geq$ 63.8 mph[b] Average speed significantly increased Interstate fatality rates when speed dispersion $\geq$ 8.2 mph[b] Similar results for total fatality rates Significant speed effect results from weighted average speed measures (Lave 1989)

Fowles and Loeb 1989	Statewide data for 1979	Regression analysis	Speed and speed dispersion consistently significant determinants of fatalities	Results robust to model specification Controls for a variety of socioeconomic factors Uses Interstate speeds to explain total statewide fatalities (Lave 1989)
Snyder 1989	Primary federal-aid rural highways Annual data: 1972–1974 for 26 states	Regression analysis	Average speed and speed dispersion for the fastest vehicles are significant determinants of fatalities Speed dispersion for the slowest vehicles is unimportant	Lack of control for confounding effects offset, to some degree, by fixed effects model Rural speed data reflect Interstates, rural primary and secondary roads (Lave 1989) Use of 1974 data is a complicating factor (Lave 1989)

[a]The text covers this study in more detail.
[b]5 mph = 8 km/h; 10 mph = 16 km/h; 8.2 mph = 13.2 km/h; 63.8 mph = 102.7 km/h.

arguing that crash involvement depends on whether traffic is flowing smoothly (smoothness varies inversely with speed dispersion) and that crash severity depends on how fast traffic is moving—which is a positive function of average speed. Since smoother traffic flows imply lower speed dispersions, Lave posited that speed dispersion reflects a coordinating mechanism whereas average speed reflects a limiting mechanism on highway traffic. Lave's empirical formulation of the above model is

$$\text{Fatality rate} = f(\text{average speed, speed dispersion, other factors})$$

In defining the fatality rate as the dependent variable, Lave controlled for exposure. He included two other variables in the empirical equation to control for other determining influences of highway fatality rates, enforcement and access to medical care. Average speed and speed dispersion (measured as the difference between 85th percentile speed and average speed) are the two variables of most interest, and both are expected to have a nonnegative coefficient.

From this research, Lave reached the following conclusions:

- After controlling for speed dispersion and other determining factors of the fatality rate, "there is no discernible effect of speed on the fatality rate" (Lave 1985, 1162). In all 12 equations, average speed is not statistically significant, and in 10 of 12 equations, the coefficient of average speed is negative.
- Speed law enforcement should focus on reducing speed dispersion to maintain a smoother traffic flow rather than on speed per se. Slow drivers as well as fast drivers are hazardous to public safety.

Lave did not use these findings to support higher posted speed limits because there is little information on the relationship between speed dispersion and average speed. For his data, there was "generally a negative correlation" between the two, but he took this only as suggestive of a negative relationship. Supporting Lave, Garber and Gadiraju (1988) also found an inverse relationship between average speed and speed dispersion, but their model fails to control for other confounding factors.

Lave's general conclusion that average speed has little effect after controlling for speed dispersion is not fully supported by the estimation results. Of the 12 final regression equations reported, speed dispersion is consistently insignificant in half, corresponding to rural collectors, urban freeways, and urban Interstate roads. For these systems, the result is counterintuitive—neither speed dispersion nor average speed has any effect on the fatality rate. High correlation among explanatory variables will drive down t-statistics and could explain the insignificance in some of Lave's equations. However, arguing against this is the nonuniform correlation between speed and variance (negative correlation in eight cases, nonnegative in four) as well as the generally low reported values of R^2 (ranging between .019 and .269 when neither speed measure is significant). In only two equations, those for rural Interstate highways in each year, do the included explanatory variables explain more than half of the variation in the fatality rate.

An alternative explanation for the poor performance of some models may be the omission of other factors that explain the fatality rate. Levy and Asch (1989) and Fowles and Loeb (1989) estimated regression models with a larger set of explanatory variables that captured additional influences including gender, age distribution of drivers, income, alcohol, and population. Enforcement, however, was absent in both studies. Both of these studies focused on the role of average speed in highway safety. Snyder (1989), on the other hand, estimated a fixed effects model (to account for the absence of controlling factors) that differed from the others in explicitly considering whether the effect of speed dispersion was symmetric for slower and faster drivers. Among the findings from these studies are the following:

- After controlling for other influences on safety, average speed and speed dispersion are both important determinants of highway safety.
- Levy and Asch (1989) found that the interaction between average speed and speed dispersion has a positive effect on fatality rates. Speed dispersion significantly increases the fatality rate when average speed reaches 63.8 mph (102.7 km/h), considerably higher than the sample average speed of 55.2 mph (88.8 km/h).

• Speed dispersion has an asymmetric effect. Snyder (1989) found that the effect of speed dispersion for the slower drivers (measured as median speed minus 15th percentile speed) had no effect on fatalities, whereas speed dispersion for faster drivers (measured as 85th percentile speed minus median speed) had a positive and significant effect on fatalities.

These results are both consistent and inconsistent with those of Lave. In that speed dispersion is found to be an important influence on highway safety, these studies support Lave's findings. However, in contrast to Lave, each study concludes that average speed is separately important. Further, Snyder's results call into question Lave's conclusion that speed dispersion is symmetric for slow- as well as fast-moving traffic. In a response, Lave (1989) argued that the contradictory findings in each of these analyses could be attributed to aggregation problems in that either the fatality measures or speed measures were inappropriately aggregated across road types. He reported the empirical results of alternative specifications of the authors' models that demonstrated the implications of alternative aggregation schemes and produced results generally consistent with his 1985 study.

All of these studies produce strong evidence that speed dispersion is an important influence on highway safety. Although the outcome of a crash is more severe the higher the speed, all else being constant, there is greater uncertainty as to the effects of average speed on crash probability. As noted by Lave, there is a need to obtain improved data on a road's speed characteristics as well as associated data that control for other determining factors of highway safety. This would reduce potential aggregation problems and enable researchers to better isolate the effects of average speed and speed dispersion on highway safety.

Additional work is needed on the appropriate level of aggregation. In some cases, aggregation may be more beneficial than harmful. Does the speed distribution on a collector road affect speed distributions on Interstate highways? Probably not. However, much of the current debate on rural Interstate speed limits concerns speed adaptation, whereby drivers adapted to higher speeds on roads posted with high speed limits will also drive at higher speeds on roads posted with lower speed limits. In other words, the speed distribution on higher-speed rural Interstate roads will affect speed distributions on other road systems with lower posted speed limits. Empirically, this implies that rural Interstate speed measures may be appropriate variables in models that analyze total fatality rates. And the finding that rural Interstate speeds affect the total fatality measures, rather than reflecting spurious correlation, may be capturing relationships between driving activities on road networks.

Summary

Among the implications from this discussion are the following:

- There is a positive relationship between crash severity and speed dispersion, particularly for rural Interstate roads. Also, evidence suggests that minimum speed dispersion occurs when the difference between a road's design speed and the posted limit lies between 5 and 10 mph (8 and 16 km/h).
- There is some evidence for the notion that the marginal effect of average speed (speed dispersion) on highway safety depends on the level of speed dispersion (average speed).
- The safety effect of speed dispersion appears to be most important for the fastest rather than the slowest drivers, thus suggesting the need for maximum speed limits. Minimum speed limits could also reduce speed dispersion, but more research is needed to evaluate the effects of minimum speed limits on speed distribution and highway safety.
- More detailed and informative data should be collected to better understand the relationship between average speed, speed dispersion, and highway safety. Speed distribution measures that characterize the environment of the safety outcome (e.g., late night crashes on arterial roads) would be ideal. Existing measures, however, are typically highly aggregated proxies, and the extent to which these proxies bias the results and lead to inappropriate inferences is not known.
- There is a need for research on the aggregation issue and specifically what level of aggregation is appropriate for accurately charac-

terizing the relationship between speed distribution and highway safety.

• Literature on average speed and speed dispersion focuses primarily on fatality measures. With the exception of McCarthy (1988), who found that speed dispersion is a significant determinant of total and injury as well as fatality measures, current literature is silent on the effect of speed distribution on the spectrum of crashes.

RELAXED RURAL INTERSTATE SPEED LIMITS AND HIGHWAY SAFETY

Preceding sections have reviewed the empirical literature on the effects of posted speed limits on speed distributions and work on how changes in speed distributions affect highway safety. As shown in Figure C-1, the extent to which changes in posted speed limits affect highway safety depends on their effects on drivers' optimal speeds and, therefore, on the distribution of speeds. The two preceding sections have identified a body of research that addresses these questions, but the literature on these issues is not extensive. In contrast, a large body of work on the relationship between posted speed limits and highway safety exists. Much of the difference reflects the availability of data. Speed distribution information is not widely available and, when available, may not be appropriate to the study's objectives.

Highway safety data and information on changes in speed limits, particularly those initiated or facilitated at the federal level that are likely to have a broad influence on highway safety, are readily available and amenable to time series, cross section, panel data, or simply before-and-after analyses. For the 55-mph (89-km/h) NMSL and the relaxed 65-mph (105-km/h) speed limit on rural Interstate roads embodied in the EHEC and STURA Acts, respectively, the availability of data has had the positive effect of generating many studies on the relationship between changes in speed limits and highway safety. However, empirically establishing a relationship (or the absence of one) presents a difficult task. In addition to the hypothesized effects of changes in posted speed limits on speed distributions and, therefore, highway safety, account must be taken of a multitude of confounding factors, identified in Figure C-1, that influence highway safety.

Recent literature analyzing the highway safety effects of an increase to 65 mph (105 km/h) in the posted speed limit on rural Interstate highways that Congress permitted in the STURA Act is reviewed in this section. The review is divided into two subsections depending on whether the study is national in scope or concentrates on a single state. Further, to more reliably evaluate the effects of relaxed rural Interstate speed limits, the review concentrates, with some exceptions, on studies based on a postenactment environment of at least 2 years.

Rural Interstate Speed Limits of 65 mph (105 km/h) and Highway Safety—National Perspective

Table C-4 identifies 14 studies analyzing the overall effects of relaxed rural Interstate (RI) speed limits on highway safety. Immediately after passage of the STURA Act in 1987, 38 states raised speed limits on some portion of, if not all, eligible RI mileage, and 2 other states increased their limits in 1988. Among the salient points in Table C-4 are the following:

- Compared with 55-mph (89-km/h) states, most studies concluded that highway safety on RI highways deteriorated with the higher speed limits.
- Most of the studies fail to adequately control for other factors that determine RI fatalities and fatality rates.
- The primary focus of many studies is the direct effect of the speed limit law to the exclusion of the law's systemwide effect.
- There is relatively little attention given to nonfatal crashes, nonfatality measures, or the distribution effect of the speed limit on crash and injury severity.
- The bulk of the studies occurred in the late 1980s and early 1990s, with relatively few studies in the past 2 to 3 years.

Since passage of the law, NHTSA has completed a number of studies on the law's effects. In the appendices of its first assessment

Table C-4 Research on 65-mph[a] Speed Limit and Highway Safety—U.S. National Perspective

Study	Database for Study	Methodology	Major Findings	Comments
NHTSA 1989a[b]	Thirty-eight 65-mph[a] states Ten 55-mph[a] states Annual data: 1975–1987	Before/after Regression analysis with comparison series	65-mph[a] states 19% increase in RI fatalities, 1986–1987 7% decrease in UI fatalities, 1986–1987 55-mph[a] states 7% increase in RI fatalities, 1986–1987 10% increase in UI fatalities, 1986–1987	Inconclusive results on selective speed limit increases and dual speed limits Limited control for confounding factors Small numbers problem for some state analysis 55-mph[a] states—East Coast Limited evidence of increases in nonfatal injuries
NHTSA 1990	Thirty-eight 65-mph[a] states Ten 55-mph[a] states Annual data: 1975–1988	Before/after analysis Regression analysis with comparison series	65-mph[a] states 13% increase in RI fatalities, 1987–1988; 2% decrease, 1988–1989 7% increase in RI fatality rate, 1987–1988; 7% decrease, 1988–1989 55-mph[a] states 12% decrease in RI fatalities, 1986–1989 13% increase in UI fatalities, 1986–1989 Monthly changes mirror annual changes	Updates 1989 study Limited control for confounding factors Variability across states 20% increase in RI vehicle miles traveled, 1986–1989, and accounts for one-third of increase in fatalities Small numbers problem for individual states Weak information on total crashes and nonfatal injuries

NHTSA 1992	Thirty-eight 65-mph[a] states Ten 55-mph[a] states Annual data: 1975–1990	Before/after analysis Regression analysis with comparison series	65-mph[a] states 4% decrease in RI fatalities, 1989–1990; 27% increase, 1986–1990 19% decrease in RI fatality rate, 1989–1990; 0% change, 1986–1990 55-mph[a] states 17% increase in RI fatalities, 1989–1990; 3% increase, 1986–1990	Updates 1990 study Limited control for confounding factors Variability across states
FHWA 1995	All states, 1993	Reports 1993 statistics	65-mph[a] states 2.4% increase in RI fatalities, 1992–1993 55-mph[a] states 4.5% decrease in RI fatalities, 1992–1993	No analysis
Garber and Graham 1989[b]	Forty 65-mph[a] states Monthly data: Jan. 1976–Nov. 1988	Regression analysis	Estimated median effect of law on RI fatalities—15% increase Estimated median effect of law on non-RI fatalities—5% increase	Controlled for seasonal effects, safety belt law, economy, and exposure (i.e., trend term) Large differences across individual states Only considered fatalities

(continued on next page)

Table C-4 *(continued)*

Study	Database for Study	Methodology	Major Findings	Comments
McKnight et al. 1989[b]	Twenty 65-mph[a] states Eight 55-mph[a] states Six dual limit states Six experimental states Monthly data: Jan. 1982–July 1989	Before/after analysis Quasi-experimental ARIMA models	65-mph[a] states 21.8% increase in RI fatal crashes 1.2% increase in fatal crashes on other 55-mph[a] roads 55-mph[a] states 10.4% increase in RI fatal crashes 12.7% increase in fatal crashes on other 55-mph[a] roads Limited positive effect on injury crashes	Aggregate model over states Identified nonuniform changes over states Before/after analysis identified regional differences Safety belt laws and traffic density not important in explaining law's effects Abrupt intervention Dual limit and experimental states, significant fatality increase on RI and other 55-mph[a] roads
Baum et al. 1989	Thirty-eight 65-mph[a] states Eight 55-mph[a] states Annual data: 1982–1987	Before/after odds ratio 1982–1986 versus 1987	65-mph[a] states 15% increase in RI fatalities relative to other rural roads (odds ratio = 1.15) 55-mph[a] states No effect on RI odds ratio (odds ratio = .94) (4% increase in all RI fatalities; 12% increase in fatalities on other rural roads)	Odds ratio assumes independent series Similar results for uniform versus dual speed limit laws, safety belt/no safety belt law, daytime/nighttime crashes, and single/multiple vehicle crashes Odds ratio increased in 24 of 38 states Analyzed fatalities only

Baum et al. 1990[b], 1991[b]	Forty 65-mph[a] states Eight 55-mph[a] states Annual data: 1982–1989	Before/after odds ratio 1982–1986 versus 1988 1982–1986 versus 1989	65-mph[a] states (1991 study) 29% increase (19% after adjustments for VMT and passenger vehicle occupancy rates) in RI fatalities relative to other rural roads (odds ratio = 1.29) 55-mph[a] states (1991 study) No effect on RI odds ratio	Updates of 1988 study Odds ratio assumes independent series Adjusted for VMT increases and changes in vehicle occupancy No adjustment for other confounding factors Analyzed fatalities only
Mace and Heckard 1991	Twenty-eight rural Interstate speed study sites in IL, OH, TX Annual data: 1986, 1988	Before/after analysis	General increase in total and injury crashes Insufficient data on fatal crashes	No control for confounding effects
Chang et al. 1991[b]	Thirty-two 65-mph[a] states Six 55-mph[a] states Monthly data Jan. 1975–Dec. 1989	Before/after analysis ARIMA models	No effect of the speed limit on Interstate fatalities for larger states Increase in Interstate fatalities, with some decaying effects, for smaller states An initial increase with decaying effects occurred in the 55-mph[a] states	Aggregate model over states Investigated alternative intervention functional forms Significant change in fatalities compounded by change in unknown exogenous factors

(continued on next page)

Table C-4 *(continued)*

Study	Database for Study	Methodology	Major Findings	Comments
Lave 1992 (published with Godwin 1992)	Thirty-eight 65-mph[a] states Eight 55-mph[a] states Annual data: 1986, 1988	Before/after analysis	Systemwide, the law decreased fatalities	Comment on Godwin's (1992) literature review Decrease due to traffic diversion and more efficient allocation of policing resources Other than VMT, no control for confounding factors How comparable is the comparison group?
Godwin 1992[b]	Thirty-eight 65-mph[a] states Eight 55-mph[a] states Annual data: 1986, 1988	Before/after analysis	Decreased fatalities systemwide implies unreasonably high VMT shift from non-RI to RI roads	Comment on Lave's (1992) finding Other than VMT, no control for confounding factors How comparable is the comparison group?

McCoy et al. 1993	19 pairs of state highway urban speed zones 1985–1988	Quasi-experimental Poisson regression	Speed zones with "reasonable" posted speed limits have lower crash rates than zones with lower "unreasonable" limits	Focused on urban areas Reasonable and unreasonable speeds based on zone's prevailing speed and test run speed Comparison of reasonable and unreasonable zones with same proposed speeds Regression controlled for AADT, length, and number of businesses
Lave and Elias 1994[b]	Thirty-eight 65-mph[a] states Eight 55-mph[a] states Annual data: 1986, 1988 Monthly data: Jan. 1976–Dec. 1990	Before/after analysis Regression analysis	Systemwide, 3.4% to 5.1% decrease in the fatality rate	Updates and extends Lave's (1992) comment Systemwide approach State analysis controls for seasonal effects, safety belt law, and the economy

Note: AADT = average annual daily traffic; RI = rural Interstate; UI = urban Interstate; VMT = vehicle miles traveled.

[a]55 mph = 89 km/h; 65 mph = 105 km/h.

[b]The text covers this study in more detail.

of the law, NHTSA (1989a) discusses the analytical methodology used in the first and subsequent updates to the 1989 study (NHTSA 1989b; NHTSA 1990; NHTSA 1992). In a before-and-after comparison, NHTSA (1989a) found that RI fatalities in 65-mph (105-km/h) states were 18 percent higher between 1986 and 1987, which compared with a 7 percent increase in 55-mph (89-km/h) states. Similarly, in its 1992 study, 65-mph states experienced a 27 percent increase in fatalities between 1986 and 1990 compared with a much smaller 3 percent increase in the 55-mph states. However, between 1989 and 1990, RI fatalities in 65-mph states decreased 4 percent compared with a 17 percent increase in 55-mph states.

By not adequately controlling for other influences on highway safety, before-and-after comparisons can produce a distorted picture of the law's effects. To control for the effects of confounding factors, NHTSA relates changes in RI fatalities to changes in a companion series. An ideal companion series would have the following attributes: (*a*) the companion series is conceptually related to the RI series, (*b*) it is statistically related to the RI series over time, and (*c*) it is not contaminated by the intervention in the RI fatality series. According to the study (p. II-7),

> the basic assumption is that the rural Interstate series and the companion series move well enough together historically that a deviation in the historical pattern can be interpreted as the result of a higher speed limit in 1987. This assumption is justified *as long as no other changes affected the relationship between the two series.* This assumption is not a statistical concern but one requiring knowledge about the highway safety environment. [Emphasis added.]

NHTSA experimented with various companion series and found that "fatalities on other roads" worked best. An ideal companion series enables the analyst to control for other confounding factors that influence both series. However, underlying this methodology are two important assumptions. First, no other changes occurred that affected one series but not the other. If this does not hold, the model does not sufficiently account for the influence of other confounding factors. Second, there are no spillover effects. As Attribute *c* indicates, the ideal companion series is not contaminated by the intervention, an assumption that is unlikely to be satisfied. There is sufficient evidence in the literature [e.g., Garber and Graham (1989)] to seriously question the assumption of no spillover effects. The fact that the implications of these assumptions are only discussed in the appendix is unfortunate, since readers will likely place greater importance on the reported 18 percent increase in fatalities between 1986 and 1987 than may be justified by the analysis.

NHTSA (1989a) also explores the effects of the speed limit by state and finds that most states, although not all, experienced an increase in fatalities. The change in the ratio of RI fatalities to all other fatalities between 1986 and 1987 ranged from a low of –.053 for Montana to a high of .1483 for Wyoming. Of the 21 states included in this analysis, 9 states had ratios less than .01. Whether these changes are statistically different from 0 is not reported.

Subsequent studies by NHTSA (1989b; 1990; 1992) used similar methodologies and newly available data to update the estimates reported in the 1989 study. One difference in the 1992 study is the explicit control for vehicles miles traveled (VMT). According to NHTSA, the 20 percent increase in RI VMT between 1986 and 1990 accounted for one-third of the increase in fatalities on these roads, once again signifying the importance of appropriately controlling for other factors.

Baum et al. (1989; 1990; 1991) used a before-and-after analysis based on odds ratios to assess the effect of higher RI speed limits on highway safety. The studies defined two groups —38 (or 40, depending on the study) 65-mph (105-km/h) states that raised the speed limit in the post-STURA environment and eight 55-mph (89-km/h) states—and two time periods, 1982 through 1986 versus the year of study (1987, 1988, or 1989). Similar to NHTSA's regression strategy, the odds ratio identifies a companion series and statistically investigates whether the change in the odds ratio of RI to other rural fatalities was significantly different between 65-mph and 55-mph states. Overall, Baum et al. (1989) found that relaxed speed limits significantly increased the odds of an RI fatality in 65-mph states, whereas in the 55-mph states, no significant effect was found. In 65-mph states, fatalities increased 19 and 4 percent on RI and other rural roads, respectively, yielding a net 15 percent increase in fatalities, a result similar to the 18 percent initially estimated by NHTSA (1989a). Similar results were found for comparisons of 55-mph states with and without dual speed limits, states with and without safety belt laws, and daytime versus nighttime crashes. However, in a state-by-state analysis, the study observed that 24 of the 38 states had an odds ratio greater than 1. This implies a decline in the odds ratio in 14 of the 38 states, suggesting that safety improved in those locales. This reflects, at least in part, the lack of control for other factors that influence highway safety.

In contrast to the 1989 study, Baum et al. (1991) controlled for changes in VMT and vehicle occupancy. With no adjustment, the study found that, relative to 1982–1986, the odds of an RI fatality in 65-mph (105-km/h) states in 1989 increased 29 percent. After adjustment for changes in VMT and vehicle occupancy, the percentage increase was 19 percent. The qualitative importance of this finding is twofold. First, the 1991 study again stresses the importance of controlling for other determining factors and implies that, by not controlling for them, the initial estimates of the law's general effect were biased upward. Second, it raises the question, How would these estimated effects change if the study included controls for changes in other known influences on highway safety such as alcohol consumption and traffic enforcement?

In a widely cited paper, Garber and Graham (1989) estimated separate regression models based on monthly data for the 40 states that raised RI speed limits. In the study, the authors explicitly controlled for a subset of determining factors for which monthly data were available, including economic performance, seasonal effects, weekend travel, and safety belt laws. The models also included a time trend to capture the influence of VMT. Consistent with NHTSA's estimates and those of Baum et al. (1991), Garber and Graham estimated that the median effect of the higher speed limit law was a 15 percent increase in fatalities on RI highways. The median effect on rural non-Interstate roads was a 5 percent increase in fatalities. From their work, the authors reached the following conclusions:

- The 65-mph (105-km/h) speed limit did not have uniform effects across the 40 states. All else being constant, fatalities increased in 28 of the 40 states and either decreased or were unchanged in 12 states.
- The higher speed limit generally increased rural non-Interstate fatalities, implying that the spillover effects from the law dominated the law's traffic diversion effects.
- There is a need for additional research on identifying factors that explain cross-state heterogeneity, which implies the need to collect more detailed state-level data and to develop more reliable models of highway safety.

Although they controlled for a subset of determining factors, the authors expressed concern about the extent to which the variables included sufficiently control for other determinants of highway fatalities.

Garber and Graham's finding of positive and negative effects of the speed limit on statewide fatalities is consistent with the notion that existing studies have not sufficiently identified or controlled for the influence of other factors on state fatalities. If a model adequately accounted for these differences, the speed limit law could be expected to have the same effect on highway safety in different states. Whether it is possible to control for the various effects is an empirical issue, but future research should move in this direction.

McKnight et al. (1989) and Chang et al. (1991) estimated ARIMA intervention time series models to assess the effect of the 65-mph (105-km/h) speed limit. McKnight et al. (1989) aggregated over twenty 65-mph states from January 1982 through July 1989. They eliminated observations prior to 1982 due to "major shifts in crash trends occurring in the years prior to 1982" (McKnight et al. 1989, 10), although there was no discussion of the nature of these shifts or why they could not be included in the empirical models. As indicated in Table C-4, McKnight et al. estimated a significant increase in RI fatal crashes in 65-mph states but no effect on non-rural Interstate roads in these states, a finding that suggests the possibility of traffic diversion toward 65-mph RI highways in the 65-mph states. Dual limit states and experimental states exhibited similar effects. Further, as confounding factors, neither safety belt use nor traffic density affected the results. In 55-mph (89-km/h) states, on the other hand, there was an inexplicably significant increase in both RI and nonrural Interstate fatal crashes.

These findings, and particularly the significant fatal crash increase in 55-mph (89-km/h) states, raise more questions than they answer. How would the results change if a longer time series were used? What role does aggregation of 65-mph (105-km/h) and 55-mph states, respectively, have on the results? Would the results change if factors in addition to safety belt use and traffic density were accounted for in the analysis? Are the results for the 55-mph states the result of spillover effects and speed adaptation or do they reflect uncontrolled-for heterogeneity?

In a related analysis, Chang et al. (1991) used ARIMA time series intervention methodology that included a longer monthly time series, January 1975 to December 1989, to estimate fatality models for 32 states with a 65-mph (105-km/h) limit and 6 states with a 55-mph (89-km/h) limit. In contrast to McKnight et al.'s abrupt permanent intervention, Chang et al. tested alternative formulations of the intervention, including abrupt permanent, abrupt temporary, an increasing effect up to a permanent level, and so forth. Further, the authors tested the sensitivity of the interventions to alternative starting and ending periods (if appropriate). Overall, the authors concluded that the 65-mph speed limit had a statistically significant effect on fatalities, but after a year's "learning period" the effect decayed over time. In separate analyses based on state clusters, similar effects were present in smaller states; large states, on the other hand, were "virtually insensitive to the speed limit change" (Chang et al. 1991, 68).

On the basis of their sensitivity analyses, which identified significant effects on fatalities prior to implementation of the speed limit, Chang et al. (p. 68) concluded that "the level of impacts exhibited in the 'after' fatality records . . . represented the compounded effects of the increased speed limit and some other exogenous factors. . . . *Those unknown factors have consistently caused an increase in fatality numbers since 1986. . . .*" (emphasis added).

In contrast, one could argue that driver anticipation of higher speeds, rather than changes in exogenous factors, generated the fatality increases in the months preceding the 65-mph (105-km/h) limits. The proximity between 1986 and the speed limit law in 1987 raises the question of what other exogenous factors could have resulted in the observed increase in fatalities. Without further and more explicit information concerning the "unknown" exogenous factors and an explanation of the mechanism through which changes in these factors generated the increase in fatalities, the evidence does not support the authors' conclusions that the exogenous factors have consistently increased fatalities since 1986. This again underscores the need to appropriately account for determinants of highway safety not related to speed limits. Also, Chang et al.'s analysis finds that speed limit effects are not uniform across relatively homogeneous groups of 65-mph states, which, similar to other studies, raises important issues of the appropriate level of aggregation and heterogeneity.

RI Speed Limits of 65 mph (105 km/h) and Highway Safety—Statewide Perspective

Table C-5 summarizes a number of state-specific studies on the effects of the 65-mph (105-km/h) speed limit, most but not all of which are for the more populous states. Similar to the national studies, the state-specific analyses use a variety of methodological approaches, but the state-specific studies are typically more general in that many examine the effects of the speed limit on fatal as well as nonfatal measures of highway safety. Some relevant points from Table C-5 are the following:

- With the exception of a study of Illinois by Pfefer et al. (1991), the speed limit significantly increased RI fatality measures. Fatal crashes on 65-mph (105-km/h) roads increased by as much as 45 percent.
- Fatal crashes on 65-mph (105-km/h) roads increased by 45 percent in Iowa (Ledolter and Chan 1994), and fatalities increased by as much as 40 percent in Illinois (Rock 1995).
- On 55-mph (89-km/h) roads, effects of the speed limit law were mixed. Streff and Schultz (1990) found no effect on 55-mph roads in

Table C-5 U.S. Research on Speed Limits and Highway Safety—State-Specific Studies

Study	Database for Study	Methodology	Major Findings	Comments
Wagenaar et al. 1989	Michigan Jan. 1978–Dec. 1988 Monthly	ARIMAX intervention analysis	19% increase in fatalities on 65-mph[a] roads 40% increase in serious injuries on 65-mph[a] roads 38% increase in fatalities on 55-mph[a] roads	Controls for various confounding effects but some are significant with perverse signs Models variable levels only Large confidence intervals Fatality equation: R^2 = .03 Limited postenactment sample
Streff and Schultz 1990	Michigan Jan. 1978–Dec. 1989 Monthly	ARIMAX intervention analysis	28% increase in fatalities 39% increase in serious injuries No effect on 55-mph[a] roads or other roads	Extends Wagenaar et al. (1989) study No effect on number of vehicles involved, implying that main effect is on severity Wide confidence intervals, often including 0 Why include insignificant covariates? Small number problem?

Pant et al. 1991	Ohio July 1984–June 1987 versus Aug. 1987–July 1990	Quasi-experimental Before/after analysis Poisson analysis	Increase in injuries and PDO crashes on 65-mph[a] roads Increase in fatal, decrease in injury and PDO crashes on 55-mph[a] RI roads Decrease in injury and PDO crashes on non-RI 55-mph[a] roads	Interesting findings but no attempt to explain Levels only Little control for confounding factors
Pfefer et al. 1991	Illinois Jan. 1983–July 1988 Monthly	ARIMA intervention analysis	No significant effect on passenger car crash rate Decrease in fatal-injury car-truck crash rate	Only considered rural Interstate crashes How sensitive are results to intervention month?
McCarthy 1993	Indiana Countywide data 1981–1989	Regression analysis	Increase in total, fatal/injury, and PDO alcohol-related crashes Redistribution of alcohol-related crashes from higher-speed to lower-speed environments	Fixed effects model Controlled for exposure, age distribution, population, economy, alcohol availability, and enforcement Similar effects for most categories of alcohol-related crashes (e.g., daytime, single-vehicle, non-truck-involved)

(continued on next page)

Table C-5 *(continued)*

Study	Database for Study	Methodology	Major Findings	Comments
Jernigan et al. 1994	Virginia 1985–1987 versus 1989–1992	Before/after analysis ANOVA	Increase in RI fatalities Decrease in systemwide fatalities	Levels only No control for confounding factors Effect on RI fatalities stabilized in 1990–1991 Dual speed limit had no effect on car-truck crashes
Khorashadi 1994	California RI 65-mph[a] roads, 1,155 mi[a] RI 55-mph[a] roads, 343 mi[a] RNI 65-mph[a] roads, 132 mi[a] 1982–1986 versus 1988–1992	Before/after analysis ANOVA	Increase in fatal crashes on 65-mph[a] roads, RI and RNI Increase in total, fatal, injury, and fatal and injury crashes on 65-mph[a] roads relative to 55-mph[a] roads	Fixed versus random effects ANOVA Examined various crash causes but no control for VMT or other confounding effects

Ledolter and Chan 1994	Iowa Quarterly, 1981–1991	Regression time series Seemingly unrelated regression	Systemwide 18% increase in fatal crashes 2.4% increase in major injury crashes Rural roads 45% increase in RI fatal crashes 17% increase in rural primary road fatal crashes 12% increase in rural secondary road fatal crashes	Implications for law's effect on severity not discussed No control for confounding factors Possible small number problem for road type analysis
McCarthy 1994b	California Jan. 1981–Dec 1989 Monthly	Regression analysis	Systemwide No effect on total, fatal, injury, PDO crashes Road type Law had no effect on injury or fatal crashes on Interstate roads, U.S. highways, state highways, or county roads	Garber and Graham (1989) type specification Results not completely consistent with panel data analysis (by county by year) over the same period. McCarthy (1994a) found redistribution away from counties with and toward counties without Interstate roads

(continued on next page)

Table C-5 *(continued)*

Study	Database for Study	Methodology	Major Findings	Comments
Rock 1995	Illinois May 1982–April 1991 Monthly	ARIMA intervention analysis	40% increase in RI fatalities, 65-mph[a] roads 25% increase in RI fatalities, 55-mph[a] roads	Modeled levels Abrupt permanent intervention Considered only rural highways

Note: PDO = property damage only; RI = rural Interstate; RNI = rural non-Interstate; VMT = vehicle miles traveled.
[a]55 mph = 89 km/h; 65 mph = 105 km/h; 132 mi = 212 km; 343 mi = 552 km; 1,155 mi = 1859 km.

Michigan, and Pant et al. (1991) obtained mixed results, increased fatal crashes but decreased injury and property damage crashes.

- Most studies did not control for confounding factors.
- Wagenaar et al. (1989) and Streff and Schultz (1990) estimated time series ARIMAX models (ARIMA models that include explanatory variables), but the confidence intervals were often wide and the coefficients of other determinants often carried perverse signs.
- Only one study, McCarthy (1993), investigated the effect of the law on a subset of crashes, those that were alcohol related. He found no systemwide effect but significant redistribution of crashes away from higher-speed environments and toward lower-speed environments.
- In a time series study of California, McCarthy (1994b) found that the law had a statistically insignificant effect on fatal and nonfatal injury crashes on Interstate roads, U.S. highways, state highways, and county roads.
- For the smaller states that experience few fatal crashes and fatalities, a small number of crashes involving many fatalities could significantly affect observed percentage changes. Also, with a small number of incidents, classical regression models [e.g., Garber and Graham (1989)] are inferior to other modeling procedures. Poisson regression, for example, explicitly accounts for the fact that the dependent variable represents count data, which are likely to include a large number of zeroes. Since fatal crash or fatality data are often more consistent with Poisson rather than classical regression models, Poisson regression is a more appropriate framework for analysis.

Local Versus Systemwide Effects

An interesting twist in this literature occurred in 1992 when Lave, in a response published with a survey paper by Godwin (1992) on the effects of the 65-mph (105-km/h) speed limit, commented that the new law could have actually saved lives. Using data from an NHTSA (1989b) study, Godwin presented information that, between 1986 and 1988, RI and non-Interstate fatalities increased 35 and 0 percent, respectively, in 65-mph states; in 55-mph (89-km/h) states, the respective increases were 9 and 2 percent. These data are consistent with much of the literature (as indicated in Table C-4) that 65-mph states experienced a disproportionate increase in RI fatalities. Lave's twist had two points, one theoretical and one empirical. The theoretical point was that the 65-mph law, by reducing the relative generalized cost of driving on RI highways, would alter drivers' route choices away from the less safe non-Interstate roads to the safer RI highways. That is, traffic would be diverted to the RI roads. Further, by removing the threat of cutting off funding if states did not enforce the 55-mph speed limit, the law enabled enforcement agencies to optimally reallocate traffic resources from catching speeders to more productive traffic activities such as targeting DUI drivers. Lave argued that these two effects would produce a systemwide decrease in fatalities.

Empirically, Lave demonstrated this by reworking the numbers in Godwin's Table 2. Overall, fatalities in 1988 were 1.86 percent higher in 65-mph (105-km/h) states but 1.92 percent higher in 55-mph (89-km/h) states. Alternatively, to account for exposure, Lave considered fatality rates and found that, for the 65-mph states, the 1988 fatality rate was 2.42 per 100 million VMT (1.50 per 100 million VKT) compared with 2.57 per 100 million VMT (1.60 per 100 million VKT) in 1986. There was no change in the fatality rate for the 55-mph states. Lave concluded that "if the 1986 fatality rate had still prevailed in 1988, there would have been 2206 more fatalities" (p. 12). Lave attributed the reduction to the 65-mph speed limit since fatality rates in the 55-mph states remained constant.

In a reply, Godwin (1992) pointed out that if the fatality savings occurred because of traffic diversion, the required shift in traffic to generate the expected savings would be 88.5 million VMT (142.4 million VKT), much higher than the observed 14.8 percent increase in RI VMT.

Lave and Elias (1994) refined Lave's 1992 argument. Using updated data, they estimated models of the Garber and Graham type using systemwide fatalities and fatality rates rather than RI fatality measures as the dependent variable. Separate models were fitted to each of 46 states. Consistent with Lave's earlier comment, the authors in this study concluded that systemwide fatality rates in 65-mph (105-km/h) states fell between 3.4 and 5.1 percent (significant in 14 of 40 states). Reasons cited for the decline included traffic diversion, reallocation of enforcement resources, and possible declines in speed dispersion.

Griffith (1995) and Lave (in a response published with Griffith's comment) discussed issues concerning Lave and Elias's 1994 paper. Two of the more important concerns raised by Griffith, relative to the time series regression results, and Lave's responses are as follows:

- Concern: Statewide fatality rates may be too broad to capture systemwide effects of the speed limit.

  Response: The error associated with too narrow a definition of systemwide effects will miss some of the law's effects, whereas too general a definition will reduce the model's explanatory power by adding noise to the model. If the additional error is systematic, that is, the model missed some strong influence that occurred independently of the speed limit law but had a negative effect on the fatality measure, then it is important to identify an alternative explanation for the observed results.
- Concern: The use of fatality rates assumes that fatalities and VMT move proportionately, contrary to empirical findings that the fatality rate decreases with traffic density.

  Response: Fatality rates control for exposure, and if the speed limit law diverted traffic to the higher-density Interstate highways, then the law should be credited with the associated lower fatality rates.

In general, both of these issues are empirical and can be subjected to hypothesis testing. The first point suggests that other excluded determinants of fatality rates may be responsible for the observed results. Garber and Graham (1989) found considerable heterogeneity across states, as did Lave and Elias, and raise the specification issue in the concluding remarks of their initial state-by-state analysis. Although Lave and Elias (1994, 53) claim that Garber and Graham's empirical model is the "most sophisticated analysis" of the effects of the 65-mph (105-km/h) limit, an unnecessarily strong statement that even Garber and Graham may question, Lave's basic point is relevant. Lave and Elias have proposed a theory that identifies the expected systemwide effects of the 65-mph speed limit. As with all empirical models, their model does not prove the theory but is consistent with it. To falsify their theory, it is not sufficient to argue that some other factors may be responsible. Indeed, this was also a point of criticism for the unwarranted conclusion of Chang et al. (1991) that some exogenous factors, not the speed limit change, drove the observed change in fatalities.

Whether VMT is proportional to fatalities is also testable. Estimating, for example, a double-log model and testing the null hypothesis that the coefficient of VMT is 1 is a test of the proportionality hypothesis.

Although concerns about the direction and size of Lave and Elias's quantitative results are likely to continue, their analysis is important because it tends to reorient one's perspective on the various effects of the speed limit change. There has been a significant amount of research on the direct effects of the higher speed limits. The results of the research suggest that the higher speed limits have increased fatalities on RI highways. As indicated in Table C-4, many studies have also found various effects on 55-mph (89-km/h) roads (or in 55-mph states) and interpret them as detrimental spillover effects of the law. There has been relatively little discussion of traffic diversion or, for that matter, traffic generation effects of the higher speed limits. Consider two sets of hypotheses, A and B. Hypothesis Set A is as follows:

H_0: The 65-mph (105-km/h) speed limit had no effect on systemwide highway safety.

H_1: The 65-mph speed limit decreased systemwide highway safety.

Hypothesis Set B is as follows:

H_0: The 65-mph speed limit had no effect on systemwide highway safety.

H_1: The 65-mph speed limit increased or decreased systemwide highway safety.

If the direct and spillover effects of the law are emphasized to the exclusion of the traffic diversion effects, highway safety is expected to fall, consistent with Hypothesis Set A. Contrary to most work in the area, Lave and Elias identify a mechanism, based less on speed adaptation and more on traffic diversion, that supports Hypothesis Set B. In other words, their perspective focuses more on traffic diversion (complemented with a reallocation of enforcement resources). This allows a trade-off between the deteriorating and enhancing effects of the law and produces an alternative hypothesis that admits the possibility of systemwide highway safety improvements as a result of the law. On the basis of time series and panel data for California, McCarthy (1994a, 1994b), consistent with Lave and Elias, found no systemwide effect from the 65-mph (105-km/h) speed limit law.

Lave and Elias's paper and subsequent comments and replies generate a number of research questions on the effects of speed limits:

- Is it possible to validate Lave and Elias's underlying assumptions on traffic diversion and reallocation of resources?
- What role do other confounding factors not included in Lave and Elias's models have on the systemwide highway safety–enhancing effects of the 65-mph (105-km/h) speed limit law?
- What is the appropriate geographic size for internalizing the systemwide effects of the law and what are its determinants?
- To what extent do national or statewide speed limit laws produce traffic generation effects as the generalized trip cost falls below a road user's reservation price (i.e., the price at which trip demand is zero) or as users shift from nonhighway to highway modes?
- As with most work in this area, Lave and Elias's model examines only fatality measures. What effect would a systemwide approach have on the distribution of nonfatal injuries and property damage crashes?
- Would multiequation frameworks that modeled highway safety on alternative road types improve our understanding of the mechanisms that link changes in speed limits on high-speed roads to systemwide highway safety?

Summary

To sum up, evidence on the effect of higher RI speed limits on highway safety indicates the following:

• The higher RI speed limits initiated in mid-1987 have generally led to an increase in RI fatalities and fatal crashes. Because other determining factors were not appropriately controlled for, however, initial study estimates of fatality increases in the range of 15 to 30 percent were too high.

• The effects of the speed limit exhibited considerable heterogeneity across states. Part of this may reflect the fact that small states with few crashes will have large proportional changes relative to larger states. However, part also reflects differences across states that are not adequately accounted for in the empirical models.

• Similar to the law's mixed effects on the speed distributions of nonlimited-access roads, the higher RI speed limits have produced mixed highway safety effects on nonrural Interstate roads.

• There is sufficient evidence in the literature to seriously question whether the net effect of the law is unambiguously negative. More work is needed on the distribution effects and the overall net effects of higher speed limits on limited-access roads.

INTERNATIONAL WORK ON SPEED LIMITS

In addition to U.S. work on the linkages between speed limits and highway safety, a number of international studies examined this issue. Tables C-6 and C-7 summarize the findings of recent international analyses for lower- and higher-speed roads, respectively.

Lower-Speed Roads

Table C-6 indicates that, unlike the United States, substantial work has been done in international studies on the effects of speed limits on lower-speed roads [roads ranging from 19 mph (30 km/h) to 50 mph (80 km/h)]. In general, the analysis in these studies is very similar to that used in many U.S. studies, namely, quasi-experimental approaches dominated by a paired comparisons methodology. As such, these studies tend to generate similar effects and suffer the same drawbacks. On the positive side, the imposition of speed limits in lower-speed environments is typically associated with a decrease in crashes and crash severity. However, these analyses generally suffer

Table C-6 International Research on Speed Limits and Highway Safety—Lower-Speed Roads

Study	Database for Study	Methodology	Major Findings	*Comments*
Engel and Thomsen 1988	Denmark Introduced a 31-mph[a] speed limit, urban areas Quarterly data, Oct. 1985–Oct. 1987	Logit regression	9% decrease in crashes 24% decrease in fatalities	Prior speed limits were 37 mph[a] Limited sample size No control for confounding factors Assumes that the proportion of urban to rural miles traveled is the same before and after the law change
Schleicher-Jester 1990	Germany Implemented 19-mph[a] speed zones 1983–1986	Before/after analysis	General decrease in speeds and crash severity	Prior speed limits were 31 mph[a] Speed limit decreases combined with public information, traffic control, speed control, and street design changes

(continued on next page)

Table C-6 *(continued)*

Study	Database for Study	Methodology	Major Findings	Comments
Vis et al. 1992	Netherlands, 15 municipal areas Implemented 19-mph[a] speed zones 1980s	Before/after analysis Quasi-experimental	20% speed reduction, generally resulting in an 85th percentile speed of 19 mph[a] Traffic volume fell 5% to 30% 5% trend-adjusted decrease in all crashes 25% trend-adjusted decrease in injury crashes	No information on prior speed limits Speed limit aimed to "integrate" road user categories, where the motorist identifies 19 mph[a] as the appropriate speed Combined with engineering measures to slow traffic (e.g., humps, axis realignments, traffic islands) Where did the decreased traffic go? No experimental site; changed only the speed limit sign

Engel and Thomsen 1992	Denmark, residential areas Introduced 19-mph[a] speed zones 44 experimental areas, 53 control areas 1980s	Quasi-experimental Before/after analysis Regression analysis	18.4% decrease in control group adjusted crashes 21.1% decrease in control group adjusted injuries 72% decrease in casualties per road user, experimental areas No change in crash risk per user in experimental areas 96% increase in casualties per road user, just outside experimental areas	No information on prior speed limits 3 years of before data, 3 years of after data 139 mi,[a] experimental group; 11,766 mi,[a] control group Status of streets changed from "traffic streets" to "living areas" Speed-reducing measures also implemented 0.4-in.[a] increase in height of hump decreased speed by 0.6 mph[a] Road narrowing decreased speed by 2.9 mph[a] No discussion of effect on casualties per road user in outer areas

(continued on next page)

Table C-6 *(continued)*

Study	Database for Study	Methodology	Major Findings	Comments
Cairney and Fackrell 1993	City of Unley, Australia 25-mph[a] speed zone 1991–1993	Before/after analysis	25-mph[a] limit led to permanent 3-mph[a] reduction in speed Initial temporary fall in traffic volume Effect of increased enforcement ambiguous	No information on prior speed limits 2-mi[a] by 660-ft[a] study area in Unley Size of speed reduction at experimental sites varied Examines effects of speed limit changes with and without speed camera enforcement Authors question whether changes in economic factors may have affected results
Newstead and Mullan 1996	Victoria, Australia 31-,[a] 43-,[a] and 50-mph[a] speed limit zones 1992–1993, 1994–1995	Before/after analysis Quasi-experimental	No systemwide effect 6.9% increase in injury crashes for metropolitan Melbourne, marginally significant 32.9% reduction in injury crashes in the rest of Victoria, marginally significant	Speed limits increased on 1,196 mi[a] of roads, decreased on 342 mi[a] of roads For Melbourne, 47% decrease in injury crashes when limit increased from 37 mph[a] to 50 mph[a] and a 10.5% increase when limit increased from 47 mph[a] to 50 mph[a] No control for other confounding factors

[a]Study used Standard International units, which were converted to U.S. equivalents in the table. Correspondences are as follows: 0.4 in. = 1 cm; 660 ft = 200 m.

mi or mph	*km or km/h*	*mi or mph*	*km or km/h*
0.6	1	43	70
2	4	47	75
2.9	4.7	50	80
3	5	139	223
19	30	342	550
25	40	1,196	1925
31	50	11,766	18935
37	60		

Table C-7 International Research on Speed Limits and Highway Safety—Higher-Speed Roads

Study	Database for Study	Methodology	Major Findings	Comments
Fieldwick and Brown 1987	Europe and the United States 1984	Regression cross-section analysis	Decrease in urban speed limit from 37 mph[a] to 31 mph[a] would decrease fatal and nonfatal injuries 25% Similar but smaller effect if rural speed limits decrease from 62 mph[a] to 56 mph[a]	Confidence interval for predicted effects not given No control for cross-section heterogeneity Authors caution that other excluded variables could reduce the beneficial effects found in their analysis
Nilsson 1990	Sweden 56-mph[a] speed limit on 3,400 mi[a] of roads 1988, 1989	Before/after analysis	Decrease in average speed by less than speed limit decrease Relative to other 56-mph[a] roads, 15% (11%) decrease in injury crashes (injuries), neither effect statistically significant	Assumes that speed limit change had no effect on previous 56-mph[a] roads No control for accompanying changes in public information and enforcement or other confounding factors
Sliogeris 1992	Victoria, Australia Imposition and removal of a 68-mph[a] speed limit 1985–1991	Before/after analysis Regression analysis	Statistically significant 24% increase in injury crashes per mile after introduction of 68-mph[a] speed limit Statistically significant 19% decrease in injury crashes per mile after removal of 68-mph[a] speed limit	Controlled speed limit was 62 mph[a] No control for other factors Control group is all other 62-mph[a] signed roads in Victoria Similar results for rural and urban roads

Borsje 1995	Netherlands Introduction of general 75-mph[a] speed limit 1988–1992	Before/after analysis	Differentiated speeds on motorways decreased average speed and had a nonincreasing effect on speed dispersion for 62-mph[a] and 75-mph[a] roads Positive effect on crash incidence	75 mph[a] on 80% of motorways, 62 mph[a] on 20% of motorways Statistical significance of results not reported Accompanying policies included greater enforcement, media campaigns, infrastructure changes
Johansson 1996	Sweden 56-mph[a] speed limit Monthly, 1982–1991	Poisson time series analysis	No statistically significant effect on fatal or serious injury crashes Statistically significant decrease in minor injury and vehicle damage crashes	Methodology accounts for overdispersion and serial correlation Controls for exposure (through economic variables), seasonal effects, safety belt law

[a]Study used Standard International units, which were converted to U.S. equivalents in the table. Correspondences are as follows:

mi or mph	*km or km/h*
31	50
37	60
56	90
62	100
75	120
3,400	5500

from not appropriately accounting for confounding factors and using a comparison series that may also be affected by the speed limit change.

There are interesting and unique aspects to some of these experiments. First, three European countries—Germany, the Netherlands, and Denmark—have analyzed the effects of a 19-mph (30-km/h) speed zone in urban areas. In each of these cases, the speed limit was part of an urban planning policy whereby traffic users shared the streets with other users. Complementing the reduced limit were other actions, including public information campaigns, increased enforcement, engineering speed measures, and so forth, intended to inform the public (directly or indirectly) that the appropriate speed on the affected roads was lower than in the surrounding areas. Moreover, in the Netherlands study, Vis et al. (1992) report that for all experimental sites a combination of actions was taken. In other words, in no case did the speed limit change simply involve a speed limit sign change. Thus, it is not possible in these studies to draw any conclusions concerning the effect of a speed limit sign change only. However, there were differential effects, depending on the specific combination of actions taken, which suggests that effective speed limit changes involve the implementation of reinforcing policies. Faure and de Neuville (1992) also make this point in a description of France's "Safer City, Accident-Free Districts" program.

A second point of interest is that part of the decrease in crashes in some studies was due to a decrease in traffic volume, which raises the question of the traffic distribution effects of the speed limit. An illustration of this was Denmark's 19-mph (30-km/h) speed zone in residential areas. In areas just outside the speed limit effect area, Engel and Thomsen (1992) report (with no discussion) a 96 percent increase (significance level not reported) in casualties per road user. This leads to the question of whether the 30-km/h zone has sufficiently diverted traffic to outer areas that the net effect is a deterioration of safety.

Local versus systemwide effects are also present in Newstead and Mullan's (1996) recent study of the speed limit policy of Victoria, Australia, which attempted to rationalize speed limits on more than 1,550 mi (2500 km) of its roads. The authors found that differentiated speed limits increased injury crashes in metropolitan Melbourne, decreased injury crashes in the rest of Victoria, and produced no overall systemwide effect.

Pedestrian Safety

There has been some but not much work on the relationship between speed limits and pedestrian safety. The evidence leads to an expected positive relationship between vehicular speed and the incidence and severity of pedestrian crashes:

- Ashton and Mackay (1979) report that 5, 45, and 85 percent of pedestrians hit by vehicles traveling 20, 30, and 40 mph (32, 48, and 64 km/h), respectively, end in a fatality. Pasanen (1992) makes a similar point in a Finnish study, finding that the risk of fatality when a pedestrian is hit by a vehicle traveling 31 mph (50 km/h) is nearly 8 times higher than when a pedestrian is hit by a vehicle traveling 19 mph (30 km/h). In a study of 118 speed-related pedestrian fatalities in Adelaide, Anderson et al. (1997) found that a small reduction in vehicle speed could produce a large decrease in pedestrian crash risk by decreasing vehicle impact speed. In a 37-mph (60-km/h) speed zone, for example, the authors determined that a 6-mph (10-km/h) fall in traveling speed would produce 48 percent fewer pedestrian fatalities, and that for 22 percent of the cases, the pedestrian-related crash would not have occurred at the lower speed limit.
- Pasanen (1992) found that pedestrians were at fault in 84 percent of the crashes. In many of these cases, the pedestrian was not aware of an approaching vehicle.

Higher-Speed Roads

The relatively few recent international studies on higher speed limits, reported in Table C-7, indicate a positive correlation between relaxed speed limits and average speeds and crashes. Nilsson (1990) found, for example, that Sweden's speed limit reduction (implemented in June 1989) from 68 to 56 mph (110 to 90 km/h) had beneficial effects. On the basis of speed and crash information in 1988 (before the change) and 1989 (after the change), average speeds fell, but not by as much as the speed limit reduction. Total and injury crashes fell 15 and 11 percent, respectively. However, since there was not an attempt to control for changes in enforcement, public information, or other confounding factors, the extent to which the observed beneficial effects are specific to speed limit changes is unclear. Johansson's (1996) analysis of the same event sheds additional light on the law's effects. On the basis of monthly data covering the period January 1982 through December 1991, Johansson estimated a Poisson time series model, which controlled for serial correlation, seasonal effects, safety belt legislation, and exposure. Although citing alcohol and driver age as potential determinants of safety, Johansson excluded each from the analysis, the former because alcohol policy had not changed in Sweden during the analysis period and the latter because data were unavailable. Like Nilsson, Johansson found that the speed limit reduction was beneficial in that the number of minor injuries and property damage only crashes fell. However, unlike Nilsson, Johansson found that the law had no effect on the number of fatal or serious injury crashes.

In addition to the studies reported in Table C-7, there has been considerable work in Finland on the effects of speed limit changes on higher-speed roads. From the 1960s through the 1970s, Finland undertook a series of speed limit experiments, the results of which were broadly consistent with the findings reported in Table C-7 (Salusjarvi 1988). In addition, between 1987 and 1988, Finland initiated a series of seasonal speed limit experiments (Finch et al. 1994) that included (*a*) reducing speed limits on 1,200 mi (2000 km) of roads from 62 to 50 mph (100 to 80 km/h) in the winter of 1987 [in the winter of 1988, speed limits on an additional 1,200 mi (2000 km) of roads were similarly reduced], (*b*) reducing speed limits on all 75-mph (120-km/h) motorways to 62 mph (100 km/h) during each winter period, and (*c*) increasing speed limits on 870 mi (1400 km) of roads from 50 to 62 mph (80 to 100 km/h) in the summers of 1988 and 1989, half each summer. Findings from these experiments indicated that reductions (increases) in speed limits were associated with decreases (increases) in average speed and speed dispersion. In addition, there was a positive correlation between the direction of the speed limit change and the effect on crashes. The extent to which other factors may have affected these results, however, is not known.

Summary

This group of international studies yields the following insights in setting speed limits:

- For nonlimited-access urban roads, local speed limit zones were successful in reducing speeds and crashes when implemented with complementary policies such as public information campaigns, greater enforcement, and engineering measures. However, part of the improvement in urban speed zones was due to reduced volumes, and there was little analysis of where the traffic went, that is, the policy's effects outside the zones. Limited evidence suggests that the systemwide effects may be zero.
- For nonlimited-access roads, there is limited evidence that enforcement is an important determinant of safety. This is consistent with more recent work by Elvik (1997), who used meta-analysis to explore the effect of automated speed enforcement on traffic safety. On the basis of work in Norway, Germany, Sweden, England, the Netherlands, and Australia, Elvik estimated that automated speed enforcement reduced injury crashes by 17 percent.
- On higher-speed roads, the international work is broadly consistent with that in the United States. With little control for other confounding factors, higher (lower) speed limits generally lead to higher (lower) speeds and more (fewer) crashes. The absolute change in speed is less than the absolute change in the speed limit.

As a final point, there has been limited international work on the role of enforcement in highway safety.

CONCLUSIONS AND AREAS FOR FUTURE RESEARCH

The purpose of this review is to provide an overview of recent empirical research on the effect of changes in posted speed limits on speed distributions and highway safety. To provide a contextual basis for the review, the conceptual framework and statistical methodologies common to many of the reviewed studies were summarized. Recent domestic and international research on the effects of posted speed limits was reviewed.

What implications does this work have for determining speed limit policies? This section focuses on two areas. First, notwithstanding the often significant differences in geographic and temporal scope as well as methodological approach, can anything specific be said about the effect of alternative speed limits? Second, although there has been a significant amount of work on speed limits, are there important gaps in existing research that future research should address?

Conclusions

With regard to specific implications for speed limit policy, existing studies provide support for the following conclusions:

- Speed limits must be perceived by the traveling public as "reasonable," that is, as consistent with the enforced traffic conditions experienced by the typical driver. To the extent that this is not true, more drivers will be noncompliant, which could compromise highway safety.
- On nonlimited-access roads, speed limit changes of 5 to 10 mph (8 to 16 km/h) "for cause" (e.g., based on crash experience, increased pedestrian traffic, more businesses) will likely have little effect on speed distribution and highway safety.
- For nonlimited-access roads, the greatest effect on speed distributions and highway safety occurs when a speed zone is implemented as part of an urban planning policy that simultaneously introduces complementary measures (e.g., greater enforcement, public information campaigns, engineering measures) to slow drivers down.
- For limited-access roads, a 10-mph (16-km/h) increase in RI speed limits from 55 mph (89 km/h) to 65 mph (105 km/h) has generally increased nationwide average speeds by less than 4 mph (6 km/h) and increased nationwide speed dispersion by less than 1 mph (2 km/h). But there is considerable cross-state variation in these effects.

- For limited-access roads, both average speed and speed dispersion are inversely related to highway safety in general and fatalities in particular. The effect of speed dispersion is most important for RI roads. Drivers traveling in the top 15th percentile appear to compromise highway safety more than those traveling in the lowest 15th percentile.
- The increase in RI speed limits from 55 to 65 mph (89 to 105 km/h) has generated mixed results with respect to its effect on nonrural Interstate roads whose speed limits remained the same.
- Although increasing RI speed limits from 55 to 65 mph (89 to 105 km/h) produces highway fatality distribution effects, the evidence is consistent with (at least) a zero net systemwide effect.
- Evidence indicates that speed adaptation occurs, but the effect appears to be small, suggesting that the highway safety effect will also be small.
- The few studies that have analyzed the effects of alternative enforcement levels indicate that traffic enforcement is an important determinant of highway safety.

Areas for Future Research

There are a number of areas in which additional research could significantly contribute to an understanding of the effect of speed limits on speed distributions and highway safety. These areas are discussed in the remainder of this section.

Data Collection

Common among many, if not most, of the studies reviewed in this paper was either the absence of or insufficient control of confounding factors that affect speed distributions and highway safety. Studies that do not adequately control for these related factors will likely be biased and lead to improper inferences. Although in some cases it is not possible to obtain additional information, in most cases there is at least some possibility of improved specification to better isolate the true effect of speed limit changes. An important omission in most analyses is enforcement, yet the few studies that include this variable find that enforcement is an important determinant of highway safety.

Much of the data on speed distributions is highly aggregated. Future research should aim to generate speed distribution data that are better aligned with the environment in which the crash occurred (e.g., late-night crashes on rural two-lane roads). Further, free-flow data are often collected to generate measures of speed distribution, but how useful are these data in determining highway safety outcomes in non-free-flow periods (i.e., during congested periods)? This is an open question. Also, since travel occurs on a network of interconnected roads, are existing aggregate measures of highway safety reasonable speed distribution proxies for different functional road types, or does use of these measures cause important biases?

Methodology

As noted earlier, existing research on speed limits generally uses univariate classification procedures, regression analysis, or ARIMA time series models. Multivariate classification models are rarely used to analyze the effects of highway safety. Among simple regression models, there is often a surprising lack of diagnostics and, if necessary, correction for common statistical problems (e.g., serial correlation in time series analysis).

The relationship between speed limits, speed distribution, and highway safety would likely be better understood if researchers experimented more with more general models of highway safety or alternative methodologies. The infrequency of fatal crashes and fatalities is amenable to Poisson regression techniques, yet these methods have been used less frequently than might be expected. In addition, there has been little work on developing and estimating simultaneous frameworks to capture the interaction between the demand for road space and highway safety. A third area is the use of various probability models. Ordered probit (Greene 1997), for example, is one methodology that could be used to examine the effect of speed limits on crash severity.

To date, most work on speed limits applies a particular methodology to a particular data set (e.g., regression analysis on cross-section data from California or ARIMA models on monthly time series data from Michigan). Given the availability of state and national data and computing technology, developing multiple data sets from a given base of information is relatively easy and would enable researchers to make different passes at the same underlying information. Using data from 1980 through 1996 for a given state that raised its speed limit in 1987, for example, would an aggregate regression model based on annual data produce similar effects of the law as would an ARIMA model for that state based on monthly data over the same time period? Would the effects be similar to those generated from univariate classification models that compare crash rates between 1980 and 1986 with those between 1987 and 1996? Such analyses may produce dramatically different estimates of the law's effects and, in so doing, identify potentially fruitful areas for further research.

Unresolved Research Issues

Following are a number of issues on which some research exists but on which further research is warranted.

- How robust is the empirical finding that a 10-mph (16-km/h) increase in RI speed limits leads to an increase in average speed and speed dispersion, respectively, of around 4 mph (6 km/h) and under 1 mph (2 km/h), particularly if there is greater control of other determining factors? This is particularly important given the recent increase in speed limits to 70 mph (113 km/h) that some states implemented following passage of the National Highway System Designation Act in 1995.
- How important is enforcement in determining speed distribution properties and highway safety when speed limits change?
- Although there is some information on the relationship between average speed, speed dispersion, and highway safety, much additional work is needed to improve the understanding of these relationships. Are average speed and speed dispersion negatively related? If so, does this relationship hold at all speeds or is there a nonlinear (or independent) relationship between these measures at other speeds? A related question is whether speed dispersion is only important on

high-speed RI highways, as suggested in some research, and less important on lower-speed nonlimited-access roads.

- What level of aggregation is appropriate for accurately characterizing the relationship between speed distribution and highway safety?
- More information is needed on how speed limit laws affect the spectrum of crashes, injury related as well as noninjury related. Although nonfatal crash and nonfatal injury data are less reliable, this does not justify ignoring all the available information.
- Additional research is needed on the spillover effects associated with speed limit changes for both limited- and nonlimited-access roads. The literature on this issue is mixed, and there is no consensus on either the direction or the magnitude of the effect. Better models are needed to identify the linkages that produce spillover effects.
- In addition to hypothesized spillover effects, speed limit changes, particularly on limited-access high-speed roads, are likely to produce traffic generation effects. It is not known whether these effects exist and, if so, how important they are in determining the highway safety effects of speed limit changes.
- Sufficient evidence exists to question whether the net effect on highway safety of speed limit laws is to deteriorate highway safety. More research is needed on the distribution effects of speed limit laws to evaluate their net effects on highway safety.
- Reducing the impact speed of vehicles can have a significant effect on pedestrian crashes and fatalities. For the United States there is little information on the extent to which pedestrian fatalities are an important consideration when speed limits change.

REFERENCES

ABBREVIATIONS

FHWA	Federal Highway Administration
NHTSA	National Highway Traffic Safety Administration
TRB	Transportation Research Board

Anderson, R. W. G., et al. 1997. Vehicle Travel Speeds and the Incidence of Fatal Pedestrian Crashes. *Accident Analysis and Prevention*, Vol. 29, pp. 667–674.

Ashton, S. J., and G.M. Mackay. 1979. Some Characteristics of the Population Who Suffer Trauma as Pedestrians When Hit by Cars and Some Resulting Implications. *Proceedings of the IRCOBI Conference*, Gothenburg, Sweden.

Baum, H., et al. 1989. The Mortality Consequences of Raising the Speed Limit to 65 mph on Rural Interstates. *American Journal of Public Health*, Vol. 79, pp. 1392–1395.

Baum, H., et al. 1990. Motor Vehicle Crash Fatalities in the Second Year of 65 mph Speed Limits. *Journal of Safety Research*, Vol. 21, pp. 1–8.

Baum, H., et al. 1991. The Fatality Consequences of the 65 mph Speed Limits, 1989. *Journal of Safety Research*, Vol. 22, pp. 171–177.

Borsje, J. F. 1995. The Effects of the 1988 Differentiation of Speed Limits in the Netherlands. *Proceedings, Road Safety in Europe and Strategic Highway Research Program (SHRP)*, Swedish Road and Transport Research Institute Conference 2A, Part 4, Lille, France, Sept. 26-28, 1994, pp. 25–36.

Cairney, P. T., and H. L. Fackrell. 1993. *The Effects of a 40 km/h Local Area Speed Limit on Traffic Behaviour and Community Perceptions and Opinion*. Research Report ARR 243. Australian Road Research Board Ltd., July.

Casey, S. M., and A. K. Lund. 1987. Three Field Studies of Driver Speed Adaptation. *Human Factors*, Vol. 23, pp. 541–550.

Casey, S. M., and A. K. Lund. 1992. Changes in Speed and Speed Adaptation Following Increase in National Maximum Speed Limit. *Journal of Safety Research*, Vol. 23, pp. 135–146.

Cerrelli, E. C. 1981. *Safety Consequences of Raising the National Speed Limit from 55 mph to 60 mph*. National Highway Traffic Safety Administration, U.S. Department of Transportation.

Chang, G. L., et al. 1991. *Safety Impacts of the 65-mph Speed Limit on Interstate Highways*. AAA Foundation for Traffic Safety, Aug.

Elvik, R. 1997. Effects on Accidents of Automatic Speed Enforcement in Norway. Presented at 76th Annual Meeting of Transportation Research Board, Washington, D.C.

Engel, U., and L. Thomsen. 1988. Speeds, Speed Limits, and Accidents. The Road Trend in Built Up Areas after the Introduction of the 50 km/h Limit. Technical Report 3/1988. Danish Council of Road Safety Research, Oct.

Engel, U., and L. K. Thomsen. 1992. Safety Effects of Speed Reducing Measures in Danish Residential Areas. *Accident Analysis and Prevention*, Vol. 24, pp. 17–28.

Faure, A., and A. de Neuville. 1992. Safety in Urban Areas: The French Program "Safer City, Accident-Free Districts." *Accident Analysis and Prevention*, Vol. 24, pp. 39–44.

FHWA. 1995. *Travel Speeds, Enforcement Efforts, and Speed-Related Highway Statistics*. FHWA-SA-95-051. U.S. Department of Transportation, Oct.

Fieldwick, R., and R. J. Brown. 1987. The Effect of Speed Limits on Road Casualties. *Traffic Engineering Control*, Vol. 28, pp. 635–640.

Fildes, B. N., and S. J. Lee. 1993. *The Speed Review: Road Environment, Behaviour, Speed Limits, Enforcement and Crashes*. Roads and Traffic Authority of New South Wales and the Department of Transport and Communications, Australia, Sept.

Finch, D. J., et al. 1994. *Speed, Speed Limits, and Accidents*. Project Report 58. Safety Resource Centre, Transport Research Laboratory, United Kingdom.

Fowles, R., and P. D. Loeb. 1989. Speeding, Coordination, and the 55 mph Limit: Comment. *American Economic Review*, Vol. 79, pp. 916–921.

Freedman, M., and A. F. Williams. 1992. Speeds Associated with 55-mph and 65-mph Speed Limits in Northeastern States. *ITE Journal*, Feb., pp. 17–21.

Freedman, M., and J. R. Esterlitz. 1990. Human Factors and Safety Research Related to Highway Design and Operation. In *Transportation Research Record 1281*, Transportation Research Board, National Research Council, Washington, D.C., pp. 52–61.

Garber, N., and R. Gadiraju. 1988. *Speed Dispersion and Its Influence on Accidents*. AAA Foundation for Traffic Safety, July.

Garber, S., and J. D. Graham. 1989. *The Effects of the New 65 Mile-per-Hour Speed Limit on Rural Highway Fatalities: A State-By-State Analysis*. Final Grant Report DOT HS 807 452, July.

Godwin, S. R. 1992. Effect of the 65 m.p.h. Speed Limit on Highway Safety in the U.S.A. With comments by C. Lave and reply to comments. *Transport Reviews*, Vol. 12, pp. 1–14.

Greene, W. H. 1997. *Econometric Analysis* (third edition). Prentice-Hall, Inc., Upper Saddle River, N.J.

Griffith, M. S. 1995. Discussion of "Did the 65 mph Speed Limit Save Lives?" With response by C. Lave. News, Queries & Comment Section, *Accident Analysis and Prevention*, Vol. 27, pp. 137–140.

Jernigan, J. D., et al. 1994. *Impact of 65-mph Speed Limit on Virginia's Rural Interstate Highways: 1989–1992*. Final Report VTRC 95-R7. Virginia Transportation Research Council, Nov.

Johansson, P. 1996. Speed Limitation and Motorway Casualties: A Time Series Count Data Regression Approach. *Accident Analysis and Prevention*, Vol. 28, pp. 73–87.

Khorashadi, A. 1994. *Accidents Before and After the 65 mph Speed Limit in California*. Final Report CA-TO-94-1. California Department of Transportation, Sacramento, June.

Knowles, V., B. Persaud, M. Parker, and G. Wilde. 1997. *Safety, Speed and Speed Management: A Canadian Review*. Final Report, Contract T8080-5-6858. Transport Canada, March.

Lave, C. 1985. Speeding, Coordination, and the 55 mph Limit. *American Economic Review*, Vol. 75, pp. 1159–1164.

Lave, C. 1989. Speeding, Coordination, and the 55 mph Limit: Reply. *American Economic Review*, Vol. 79, pp. 926–931.

Lave, C., and P. Elias. 1994. Did the 65 mph Speed Limit Save Lives? *Accident Analysis and Prevention*, Vol. 26, pp. 49–62.

Ledolter, J., and K. S. Chan. 1994. *Safety Impact of the Increased 65 mph Speed Limit on Iowa Rural Interstates*. Midwest Transportation Center, University of Iowa, Iowa City, July.

Levy, D. T., and P. Asch. 1989. Speeding, Coordination, and the 55 mph Limit: Comment. *American Economic Review*, Vol. 79, pp. 913–915.

Mace, D. J., and R. Heckard. 1991. *Effect of the 65 mph Speed Limit on Travel Speeds and Related Crashes.* Final Report DOT HS 807 764, March.

Matthews, M. L. 1978. A Field Study of the Effects of Drivers' Adaptation to Automobile Velocity. *Human Factors*, Vol. 20, No. 6, pp. 709–716.

McCarthy, P. S. 1988. *Highway Safety and the 65 mph Maximum Speed Limit: An Empirical Study.* AAA Foundation for Traffic Safety, Oct.

McCarthy, P. S. 1993. The Effect of Higher Rural Interstate Speed Limits in Alcohol Related Accidents. *Journal of Health Economics*, Vol. 11, pp. 281–299.

McCarthy, P. S. 1994a. An Empirical Analysis of the Direct and Indirect Effects of Relaxed Interstate Speed Limits on Highway Safety. *Journal of Urban Economics*, Vol. 36, pp. 353–364.

McCarthy, P. S. 1994b. Relaxed Speed Limits and Highway Safety: New Evidence from California. *Economics Letters*, Vol. 46, pp. 173–179.

McCoy, P. T., et al. 1993. *Evaluation of Lower Speed Limits on Urban Highways.* Research Report TRP-02-26-92. Nebraska Department of Roads, May.

McKnight, A. J., et al. 1989. *The Effect of the 65 mph Limit on Speeds and Accidents.* Final Grant Report DOT HS 807 463, Aug.

NHTSA. 1989a. *The Effects of the 65 mph Speed Limit During 1987: A Report to Congress.* U.S. Department of Transportation, Jan.

NHTSA. 1989b. *The Effects of the 65 mph Speed Limit Through 1988: A Report to Congress.* U.S. Department of Transportation, Oct.

NHTSA. 1990. *The Effects of the 65 mph Speed Limit Through 1989: A Report to Congress.* U.S. Department of Transportation, Dec.

NHTSA. 1992. *The Effects of the 65 mph Speed Limit Through 1990: A Report to Congress.* U.S. Department of Transportation, May.

Newstead, S., and N. Mullan. 1996. *Evaluation of the Crash Effects of the Changes in Speed Zones in Victoria During 1993-94 (Excluding 100 to 110 km/h).* Report 93. VicRoads, Australia, June.

Nilsson, G. 1990. *Reduction in the Speed Limit from 110 km/h to 90 km/h During Summer 1989.* VTI Report 358A. Swedish Road Safety Office.

Pant, P. D., et al. 1991. Effects of the 65-mph Speed Limit on Traffic Accidents in Ohio. In *Transportation Research Record 1375*, Transportation Research Board, National Research Council, Washington, D.C., pp. 53–60.

Parker, M. R., Jr. 1997. *Effects of Raising and Lowering Speed Limits on Selected Roadway Sections.* Final Report FHWA-RD-92-084. Federal Highway Administration, U.S. Department of Transportation, Jan.

Pasanen, E. 1992. *Driving Speeds and Pedestrian Safety: A Mathematical Model.* Transportation Engineering Publication 77. Helsinki University of Technology, Finland.

Pfefer, R. C., W. W. Stenzel, and B. D. Lee. 1991. Safety Impact of the 65-mph Speed Limit: A Time Series Analysis. In *Transportation Research Record 1318*, Transportation Research Board, National Research Council, Washington, D.C., pp. 22–33.

Rock, S. M. 1995. Impact of the 65 mph Speed Limit on Accidents, Deaths, and Injuries in Illinois. *Accident Analysis and Prevention*, Vol. 27, pp. 207–214.

Salusjarvi, M. 1988. The Speed Limit Experiments on Public Roads in Finland. In *Proceedings of Roads and Traffic Safety on Two Continents*, VTI Report 332A, Vagoch Trafik Institute, Linkoping, Sweden.

Schleicher-Jester, F. 1990. TEMPO 30 in Towns—Results of a German Experiment. *Living and Moving in Cities.* Centre d'Études des Transports Urbans, Bagneux, France, pp. 100–107.

Sliogeris, J. 1992. *100 Kilometre per Hour Speed Limit—Evaluation of Road Safety Effects.* Report GR 92-8. VicRoads, Australia, Aug.

Snyder, D. 1989. Speeding, Coordination, and the 55 mph Limit: Comment. *American Economic Review*, Vol. 79, pp. 922-925.

Solomon, D. 1964. *Accidents on Main Rural Highways Related to Speed, Driver, and Vehicle.* Federal Highway Administration, U.S. Department of Transportation, July.

Streff, F. M., and R. H. Schultz. 1990. *The 65-mph Speed Limit in Michigan: A Second Year Analysis of the Effects on Crashes and Crash Casualties.* Final Report UMTRI-90-37. The University of Michigan Transportation Research Institute, Sept.

TRB. 1984. *Special Report 204: 55: A Decade of Experience.* National Research Council, Washington, D.C.

Ullman, G. L., and C. L. Dudek. 1987. Effects of Reduced Speed Limits in Rapidly Developing Urban Fringe Areas. In *Transportation Research Record 1114*, Transportation Research Board, National Research Council, Washington, D.C., pp. 45–53.

Vis, A. A., et al. 1992. Safety Effects of 30 km/h Zones in the Netherlands. *Accident Analysis and Prevention*, Vol. 24, pp. 75–86.

Wagenaar, A. C., et al. 1989. *The 65 mph Speed Limit in Michigan: Effects on Injury and Death.* Final Report UMTRI-89-28. The University of Michigan Transportation Research Institute, Dec.

Appendix D

Review of Automated Technologies for Speed Management and Enforcement

William D. Glauz
Midwest Research Institute

Speeding (traveling faster than the posted speed limit) is apparently becoming more and more common throughout the world, particularly excessive speeding [exceeding the speed limit by 20 mph (32 km/h) or more]. Many countries have recognized this and have undertaken comprehensive programs to reduce speeding and the traffic crashes to which it contributes. Such programs are in existence in Victoria and New South Wales, Australia; British Columbia and Ontario, Canada; the Netherlands; Sweden; and perhaps others.

In the United States, speed management and speed enforcement are the responsibilities of the states and communities, although the federal government can pass legislation requiring the states to take certain actions concerning speeding and traffic. Most recently, for example, the federal government canceled its mandatory maximum speed limit of 55 mph (89 km/h), allowing the states to set higher limits.

Speeding, especially excessive speeding, is apparently becoming more common in the United States. On September 19, 1997, the newspaper *USA TODAY* reported the results of a study it performed on some 2.3 million speeding tickets from 11 states between 1991 and 1996. The study indicates that the percentage of tickets written for speeding over 80 mph (129 km/h) rose from 15 percent in 1991 to 25 percent in 1996. Of course, many speed limits increased during this interval. The study also reported on speeding levels as a function of the local speed limit. In 55-mph (89-km/h) zones, the percentage of tickets written for speeding in excess of 75 mph (121 km/h) rose from 21 to 27 percent during this interval, and the percentage exceeding 80 mph (129 km/h) in these zones rose from 7 to 9 percent. In 65-mph (105-km/h) zones the percentage exceeding 85 mph (137 km/h) rose from 8 to 10 percent. It is not stated whether the level of enforcement, as indicated by the total number of speeding tickets written, had changed during this period, or whether the changes observed were statistically significant, although on the basis of the sample sizes they undoubtedly were.

Activities in other countries indicate that speeds and speed-related crashes can be reduced by a combination of speed management and speed enforcement programs. Speed management programs alone were ineffective due to the lack of concomitant enforcement, and speed enforcement programs alone were ineffective because they were too manpower intensive and thus costly. The use of automation has been shown to increase effectiveness, especially for enforcement.

In this review the experiences of automated speed management technologies and programs around the world are examined. Then a brief overview of automated photo radar technologies is given, followed by a presentation of experiences with automated speed enforcement, mostly using photo radar. Finally, some of the political and legal issues associated with the use of photo radar are discussed, and thoughts on the most effective types of implementation of automated speed management and speed enforcement are expressed.

EXPERIENCE WITH AUTOMATED SPEED MANAGEMENT

Speed management may be defined as a process designed to control or affect vehicle speeds, both the average speeds and the dispersion of speeds. *Automated* speed management is a speed management process that uses automation in some form (usually electronics and other advanced technologies). Police enforcement (with or without automation) is not included in this discussion of speed management; police enforcement (with automation) is treated as a special topic later in this review.

This section of the review is organized as follows. First, the earlier work in speed management is discussed, focusing on automated speed management. Two major types of automated speed management are identified: speed monitoring and warning systems, and variable speed limit systems. Following the review of the early work, more recent experiences of speed monitoring and warning systems and, on a country-by-country basis, of variable speed limit systems are examined. Finally, another type of automated speed management system, drone radar, is reviewed.

Early Experience

An early study of speed management systems was reported by Parker and Tsuchiyama (1985). They examined a broad spectrum of speed management concepts, ranging from static methods such as fixed maximum and minimum speed limit signs to the automated highways of the future. In between are a number of methods mentioned only to illustrate the scope of the options presented; they are not discussed further in this paper:

- Dummy police cars,
- Oversized speed limit signs,
- Painting or striping to create illusions of narrower roads or increasing speed,
- Speed bumps and rumble strips,
- Economic approaches (e.g., tolls increased if elapsed time is too short),
- Legislative approaches (e.g., prohibition of radar detectors), and

• In-vehicle devices ranging from current cruise control systems to future speed-limit-sensing engine governors.

Of all the methods examined, two are most relevant to this review—speed monitoring and warning systems, and variable speed limits.

Parker and Tsuchiyama (1985) state, "The purpose of speed warning systems is to continuously monitor vehicle speeds and provide speed-related informational or warning messages to aid motorists in the selection of appropriate travel speeds." Two general types of systems are distinguished—those providing group speed information and those providing overspeed or underspeed warnings.

The group speed information systems display average vehicle speeds on the theory that motorists will then check their speedometers and adjust their speeds to more closely match the average. The warning systems provide individualized information to vehicles traveling too fast or too slow in the hope that the drivers will respond appropriately by either slowing down or speeding up.

The researchers identified only two group speed information systems existing at the time of their study, one in Calgary, Canada, and one on the "Maine Facility." Both displayed data that were updated frequently as real-time data were collected. Effectiveness data were available only from the Canadian facility. They found that whereas average speeds were reduced only 4 percent, the proportion of drivers traveling more than 10 mph (16 km/h) over the speed limit decreased 35 percent, speed violations were reduced 40 percent, and total crashes were reduced 57 percent. Moreover, public reaction was positive.

A number of overspeed and underspeed warning systems were identified in the United States, Canada, and the United Kingdom. Evaluation data were limited. Some sites had no data; the others indicated only modest reductions in average speeds [2 to 4 mph (3 to 6 km/h)] but greater reductions in percentages of speeding vehicles (15 to 24 percent).

Parker and Tsuchiyama (1985) state, "The concept of variable speed limits involves setting minimum and maximum speed limits based on real-time monitoring of prevailing traffic and roadway conditions and using dynamic information displays to inform motorists of the appropriate limits." They go on to state that no existing systems (at that time, 1984) fulfilled that concept, but they then examine the five existing systems that came closest to doing so:

- New Jersey Turnpike Control System, United States;
- National Motorway Communication System, United Kingdom;
- Corridor Control System north of Marseilles, France;
- Motorway Control and Signaling System, the Netherlands; and
- Self-Sufficient Speed Control System, Germany.

All five systems used speed and volume data. The English and Dutch systems used incident detection data along with speed and volume data. The German system used speed and volume data along with daylight (day/night) and rainfall (wet/dry). The English system required manual changing of the speed limits; the U.S. and French systems allowed manual override of the automated speed settings. The automated German system had many built-in backup features such as duplicate computers and message-lighting systems.

Effectiveness data were very limited. The Germans believed that drivers perceived the displayed speed as a recommendation, not a limit; nevertheless they determined that the differences in speeds of consecutive vehicles were decreased, as was the frequency of short headways, and there was a slight increase in the traffic flow rate. The British system produced larger speed reductions with lower speed restrictions, but the speed standard deviation remained constant at about one-seventh of the average speed. The U.S. system (the oldest of these five systems) was judged less sophisticated than the European systems in terms of backup capabilities and the ability to store historical data (which all the European systems had), which would be needed if enforcement were to accompany the use of variable speed limits.

Additional technical details about these variable speed limit systems are provided in a second report by Parker (1985).

Speed Monitoring and Warning Systems

Roqué and Roberts (1989) reported on experiments in Alabama, wherein an automated system collected data on traffic speeds a day at a time. After a day of collection, the percentage of vehicles exceeding the speed limit was determined and displayed on variable message signs the next day. Both truthful and inaccurate results were displayed, in accordance with an experimental design. The hope was that drivers would modify their speeds to provide better compliance than had been observed. No significant changes were observed.

Casey and Lund (1993) examined the effectiveness of "mobile roadside speedometers" in reducing traffic speeds in California. The speedometer used an "undetectable" radar to measure speeds of individual vehicles, which the system displayed to the motorists. The system was deployed at five urban sites with speed limits from 30 to 45 mph (48 to 72 km/h) and at five school zones with speed limits of 25 mph (40 km/h). Significant but modest speed reductions were noted at three of the five urban sites while the system was in place, but the reductions disappeared the following week. Statistically significant speed reductions were found at all five school zone sites, with greater reductions at sites with higher prior average speeds. The researchers also examined the longer-term effectiveness of this system by coupling it with downstream enforcement. They found that adding downstream enforcement greatly increased the longevity of the system's effectiveness.

Garber and Patel (1994) reported on a very thorough evaluation of the use of variable message signs designed to control driver speeds in work zones. They deployed the system at seven work zone sites in Virginia and collected extensive driver response data. The system determined individual vehicle speeds with radar and then, in accordance with the experimental design, either did nothing (baseline) or displayed one of four predetermined messages for high-speed drivers:

- Excessive Speed Slow Down,
- High Speed Slow Down,
- Reduce Speed in Work Zone, or
- You Are Speeding Slow Down.

Data were collected by roadway sensors and by videotape and were analyzed in detail using formal statistical methods. Effectiveness was judged by the reduction in the percentage of speeders (typically about 50 percent before implementation of the speed warning system), the percentage of vehicles speeding by 5 mph (8 km/h), the percentage of vehicles speeding by 10 mph (16 km/h) or more, average speeds, 85th percentile speeds, and speed variance. All of the warning messages were effective, although the last was the most effective and the second was second-most effective.

Oei (1996), in a comprehensive report of experiences with automatic speed management in the Netherlands, discusses two types of installations, one to reduce speeds in school zones and one to reduce speeds on two-lane rural roads. For the school zones, three types of speed signs were used: a permanent 31-mph (50-km/h) sign, a 31-mph sign illuminated only during school hours, and a 31-mph sign that flashed only when an approaching vehicle was exceeding the speed limit. The latter was the most effective, reducing average speeds by 3 mph (5 km/h) and producing a theoretical reduction in crashes of 24 to 65 percent. The two-lane road installations covered stretches from 5 to 9 mi (8 to 15 km) in length and cost an average of U.S. $40,000. They consisted of static signs indicating the speed limits [minimum of 37 and maximum of 50 mph (60 and 80 km/h, respectively)], an automated, illuminated, switchable sign saying "60-80" displayed for vehicles outside of these limits, and downstream automatic signs saying "You Are Speeding" (in Dutch) for vehicles still exceeding the speed limit. Evaluations indicated significant reductions in average speeds, 85th percentile speeds, percentages of speeders, and the standard deviation of speeds.

Variable Speed Limit Systems

In this section findings on the use of variable speed limit systems are presented alphabetically by country.

Australia

Coleman et al. (1996), in their report on speed management and enforcement technology in four countries, include a brief discussion of the use of automated speed management in Australia. At the time of their investigation (1995), although Australia had a major speed management program in place, only one automated component was documented. A fog warning and speed advisory system was installed south of Sydney. The speed of a vehicle passing through a detector is displayed to the next vehicle as an advisory speed. A prototype of the system installed in 1993 notified motorists traveling more than 6 mph (10 km/h) over the speed limit. That system resulted in a 60 percent reduction in the number of speeders, but the effect was temporary; there was no reduction in speeding 1,000 ft (300 m) downstream.

Finland

Pilli-Sihvola and Taskula (1996) reported on a Finnish system to warn drivers of black ice and other hazards with a variable speed limit system. Installed on a section of roadway 9 mi (14 km) long, the system includes 36 variable speed limit signs. Sensors detect ice or snow, wet pavement, heavy rain, fog, and high winds. The speed limit is varied between 50, 62, and 75 mph (80, 100, and 120 km/h), depending on conditions. A 3-year evaluation was under way at the time of the report (1996).

Germany

Coleman et al. (1996) reported that Germany is a world leader in the application of advanced traffic management technology, with 70 traffic management facilities in operation on the autobahns at the time of the study (1995) and another 60 planned to be in operation by the end of 1997. These systems are located where hazardous conditions exist, especially hazardous environmental conditions. A typical system has variable speed limit signage that displays not only the current speed limit but also its reason. Reasons such as construction, fog, crash ahead, ice, and high winds are included. The researchers report a crash reduction of about 25 percent. The cost of these systems ranged from U.S. $0.6 million to $1.1 million per mile ($0.4 million to $0.7 million per kilometer).

The Netherlands

Wilkie (1997), in her review of variable speed limit systems, included a discussion of the Dutch speed management system installed in

1992 on the A2 highway between Amsterdam and Utrecht, which was still in operation in 1997. The system covers a 12-mi (20-km) length of highway with three interchanges, with signs spaced at intervals of about 0.6 mi (1 km). The main reason for the installation was frequent congestion at one of the interchanges and resultant traffic backups. The normal speed limit is 75 mph (120 km/h), but lower limits of 56, 43, or 31 mph (90, 70, or 50 km/h) are displayed depending on sensed traffic conditions. The goal was not so much to reduce average speeds as to narrow speed dispersion. Evaluation found that the system was well received by motorists, speeds were effectively reduced in all lanes, the number and severity of shock waves were reduced, the percentage of small headways was reduced, the average headway increased, and the average roadway occupancy increased. More details on this system are provided by van den Hoogen and Smulders (1994).

Coleman et al. (1996) report on a fog advisory system and on the more extensive Motorway Signaling System in the Netherlands. The fog advisory system reduces the speed limit from 62 mph (100 km/h) to 50 or 37 mph (80 or 60 km/h), depending on visibility. The system proved to be effective, reducing average speeds by 5 to 6 mph (8 to 10 km/h) (though the speeds remained higher than the displayed speed limit), reducing the standard deviation of speeds, and reducing the percentage of vehicles with very small headways. The Motor Signaling System, begun in 1981, in 1995 covered about 120 mi (200 km) of highways and is planned to cover 560 mi (900 km) by 2000. Displayed speed limits are reduced depending on traffic and weather conditions. Evaluations indicate a reduction of 50 percent in secondary crashes (when speed limits are reduced because of a crash ahead) and a decrease of 5 to 15 percent in lost travel time. The system costs are U.S. $1.1 million to $1.6 million per mile ($0.7 million to $1.0 million per kilometer).

United Kingdom

Wilkie (1997) reported on British work on the "Controlled Motorway Pilot Scheme." The Department of Transport established this system on a 14-mi (23-km) section of M25 outside of London;

it was extended in 1995. The system was designed to minimize stop-and-go driving during heavy traffic (one-way peak volumes reach 10,000 vehicles per hour). The system senses volume and reduces the speed limit from 70 to 60 mph (113 to 97 km/h), then further to 50 mph (80 km/h), as volume thresholds are reached. The speed limits are displayed on changeable message signs spaced at 0.6-mi (1-km) intervals. (The speed limits can also be changed manually by the police.) The speed limits are enforced by photo radar. Formal evaluation is under way by the Transportation Research Laboratory, but preliminary results indicate that police are impressed by the system and the obedience of the drivers, compliance is about 98 percent, lane usage is more even, and average headways have increased.

United States

Wilkie (1997) included information on two early installations in the United States. One was on the John C. Lodge freeway in Detroit. It was installed in 1962 and dismantled sometime after 1967. The system was intended to display variable speed limits and lane-control information in response to congestion ahead. It was an advisory system, not an enforceable system. It consisted of 21 variable speed signs at 1,600-ft (500-m) intervals, 11 lane control locations at 2,600-ft (800-m) intervals, and 14 television camera locations at 1,300-ft (400-m) intervals. Evaluation found that aspects of the system, especially the lane-control information, were confusing to drivers, and that the variable speed limits did not induce any changes in driver speeds.

In 1986 the U.S. Federal Highway Administration contracted with Farradyne Systems, Inc., to develop a variable speed limit system (VSLS). The system is described in a report by Sumner and Andrews (1990). It appears that the VSLS was well designed and was intended to be flexible in its modes of operation and in the environmental conditions it could sense and act upon. It was estimated that future systems could be built and installed for $30,000 per station, plus $20,000 for the central hardware. The system's software and hardware were tested in the field in Albuquerque and found to be operating correctly. The system was then turned over to the state of New

Mexico for longer-term evaluation. Whether any further reports are available on the operation of this system is unknown. Some limited applications of VSLSs are under development as part of the Intelligent Transportation Systems program. For example, the Nevada Department of Transportation in conjunction with the U.S. Department of Transportation is developing a VSLS that reflects actual traffic speeds and weather conditions on a stretch of Interstate highway that is frequently subject to adverse weather. Deployment of the system will be accompanied by a monitoring effort to assess effects on driving speeds and crash experience.

Drone Radar

The use of drone (unattended, continuously operating) radar to control driver speeds has been studied in the United States by several authors, including Pigman et al., whose early work was reported in 1989. Two of the most recent reports are those of Streff et al. (1995) and Freedman et al. (1994).

Streff et al. (1995) installed drone radars in 1993 at two freeway sites and one construction zone in Michigan and compared their effectiveness with traditional police enforcement and with no enforcement. Speeds were measured at the drone location and upstream and downstream of the drone location. Overall effects of the drone radar were small [typically 1.5-mph (2.4-km/h) decrease with drone radar present] but statistically significant due to the very large sample sizes. The effects were about the same as those with police presence. Some reductions in the speeds of the highest-speed vehicles, especially trucks [reductions from 30 to 70 percent of trucks exceeding the speed limit by 10 mph (16 km/h) at some sites and times], were found. It was determined that about 5 percent of the cars had radar detectors and that between 19 percent (day) and 28 percent (night) of the trucks had radar detectors.

Freedman et al. (1994) did a similar study in Missouri, comparing speeds of traffic with and without the presence of operational drone radar. Twelve sites were investigated, covering rural construction zones, rural and urban temporary work zones, and rural and urban locations with high crash rates. They also found only modest changes in average speeds but a greater change in truck speeds than in car speeds. The proportions of vehicles with excessive speeds were often reduced by one-third to one-half when the drone radar devices were activated.

OVERVIEW OF AUTOMATED SPEED ENFORCEMENT TECHNOLOGIES

Automated speed enforcement (ASE) equipment has been in use for more than 30 years (Blackburn and Bauer 1995). Most of it uses some form of radar to sense vehicle speed, although pavement sensors and optical sensors are also used. (The author is unaware of any commercially available automated equipment that uses laser technology.) The remainder of this discussion will focus on photo radar ASE equipment.

The concept of the photo radar equipment has not changed during its period of use, although the technologies have improved greatly. The heart of the photo radar is the radar unit. It is much different from the radar guns traditionally used in the United States and elsewhere. Traditional radar produces a powerful but wide beam aimed down the road that can detect speeding vehicles as much as 1 mi (1.6 km) away. Unfortunately, it is not selective and does not identify which of the vehicles in its field of view is the speeder. Furthermore, drivers with radar detectors can usually detect the beam and slow down before they are detected speeding.

The radar used with ASE equipment is usually a type called "cross-the-road" radar. It produces a low-powered, narrow beam that is aimed at a 20- to 25-degree angle to the direction of the road. It is undetectable to drivers until they are within the beam, by which time their speed has been determined. This technology also enables vehicle identification for vehicles with headways of more than about ½ s.

The radar unit is connected to a computer that determines whether the vehicle's speed is greater than a predetermined threshold. If so, the computer triggers a camera (and a flash if necessary) to photograph the vehicle and its license plate. The photograph has superimposed on it the time, date, recorded speed, location, officer, and so forth. Typically, the film is processed to the negative stage and the license number of the offending vehicle determined. If the speeder is unambiguously identified in the photo and the license number can be read, a search of files is conducted and the owner identified. A ticket is then mailed to the owner. Depending on local laws, the owner may be required to pay the fine or may be given the opportunity to review the film at the police station or otherwise identify the driver, who then must pay the fine. Appeals are allowed, but they are rare.

As stated, the concepts have not changed over the years, but the technologies have improved. Improved electronics have allowed the units to be made much smaller. The use of lenses with longer focal length and better film (including some units that use a 70-mm format and color rather than black and white) has enabled license plates to be more readily identified. Some units have used video film.

Until recently, all of the equipment development and sales have been from overseas. More recently, a U.S. firm has designed and now builds complete photo radar systems (American Traffic Systems 1997). The systems feature their own military-grade camera with advanced photoelectronic imaging capabilities. They then use a proprietary system to rapidly scan the negatives into a computer (or read digital camera images directly), conduct digital enhancement procedures, read the image of the license plate by the use of optical character recognition, and produce printed traffic tickets if the system is tied to an owner's license database.

EXPERIENCE WITH ASE

ASE using photo radar has been in existence since the 1970s. The experience has been documented by Glauz and Blackburn (1980), Fitzpatrick (1991), Zaal (1994), and Blackburn and Gilbert (1995). At the time of this review, there are reportedly 75 countries using automated speed enforcement (American Traffic Systems 1997). This review is mainly concerned with the most recent research reports, although some of the more unusual early work is included. The experience is presented in alphabetical order by country.

Australia

Victoria, Australia, has perhaps the most extensive photo radar enforcement program of any jurisdiction in the world. The program was launched in December 1989, and by January 1991 there were 54 speed cameras in operation across Victoria (Cameron et al. 1992). The program included massive publicity both to increase the level of perception of the use of the cameras and to build a community agenda about speeding and safety. The enforcement occurred primarily on arterial roads with 37-mph (60-km/h) speed limits in both metropolitan and country areas.

The rate of issuance of speeding tickets increased from around 20,000 per month prior to the program to 40,000 to 80,000 per month during the program (Cameron et al. 1992). Over the 2-year period, more than 20 percent of all drivers received at least one speeding ticket. The penalties ranged from a small fine and demerit points to license suspension for speeding 19 mph (30 km/h) over the limit. The incidence of crashes and their severity were carefully analyzed statistically. For these analyses, crashes were separated into "low-alcohol hours," basically daytime hours, and nighttime hours, to distinguish causality between the speed program and a concurrent drinking/driving campaign; drinking had been shown not to be a concern during the low-alcohol hours prior to 1990. New South Wales was used as a "control" since it had no photo radar program, at least initially.

The frequency of casualty crashes compared with that in New South Wales decreased around 30 percent in Victoria because of the combination of the speed enforcement and publicity programs. The percentage of crashes resulting in serious injury also declined significantly. Most of the reductions occurred on arterial roads in Melbourne and on 37-mph (60-km/h) roads in rural Victoria, where the photo radar operations were conducted. The comparisons did not indicate a like reduction during the last 6 months of this 2-year period, during which time New South Wales also introduced a photo radar program and its crash rate dropped.

Rogerson et al. (1994) further analyzed data from the 2-year Victoria experience. One type of analysis used just the crash data from within 0.6 mi (1 km) of each of the 1,699 photo radar camera sites. The crashes were separated into "influenced" and "not influenced" time periods, where "influenced" was defined to be within 7 days after photo radar operations at the site or within 2 weeks after the traffic tickets were mailed (which usually occurred several weeks after photo radar operations). There were no control sites; the enforcement sites served as their own controls. As before, the times of the crashes were separated into low-alcohol hours and high-alcohol hours. The only statistically significant reductions in crash frequency found were during the days influenced by mailing of traffic tickets, and then only during the high-alcohol hours.

The second set of analyses presented by Rogerson et al. (1994) dealt with the effects of photo radar on speeds in Melbourne and the rest of Victoria. The researchers analyzed a sample of speeds taken from 44 locations and continuous speed data taken from 8 permanent monitoring sites. They found little change in average speeds or in 85th percentile speeds but significant reductions in the percentage of vehicles exceeding the speed limit by at least 9 mph (15 km/h) (from 11.3 percent to 5.5 percent) and in the percentage exceeding the speed limit by at least 19 mph (30 km/h) (from 2.5 to 3 percent to 1 to 1.5 percent). These reductions were observed on roads with speed limits of 37 and 47 mph (60 and 75 km/h); there were insufficient data on roads with a speed limit of 62 mph (100 km/h) to draw similar conclusions.

An update to the Victoria program was provided by Coleman et al. (1996). In the 5 years since the program was begun (December 1989), the percentage of vehicles exceeding the speed limit tolerance (10 percent above the speed limit) decreased from 23 to 2.9 percent, and virtually no drivers exceeded this tolerance by more than 25 percent. There was a 30 percent reduction in casualty crashes on arterial roads in Melbourne and a 20 percent reduction on the 37-mph (60-km/h) rural roads. In 1989 the safety management plan, which included the photo radar speed enforcement, had a goal of reducing Victoria fatalities to 500 per year by 2000. This goal was met in 1992. In 1994 there were 378 fatalities.

Additional data were provided on the Victoria program by Sinclair (1996). Reported traffic collisions dropped from more than 5,400 per year in 1989 to about 4,000 per year in 1996; fatalities dropped from about 1,050 per year to about 700 per year during the same period, with serious injuries dropping correspondingly. In December 1989, 23.9 percent of vehicles exceeded the camera threshold speeds. This percentage dropped to 13 percent in December 1990 and to 5 percent in December 1996. The percentage of all tickets written that were for speeds more than 19 mph (30 km/h) above the limit (at which level the driver's license is suspended) dropped from 1.6 percent in December 1989 to about 0.4 percent in 1996.

Coleman et al. (1996) also reported on the photo radar program in New South Wales, which was begun in mid-1991. As of 1995, 21 speed cameras were operating at 809 sites throughout the state. A 22 percent reduction in serious crashes and a decrease in excessive speeding [6 or 12 mph (10 or 20 km/h) above the limit] were realized. The targeted reduction in fatalities for 2000 was surpassed in 1994.

Canada

An early, limited experiment in Vancouver, British Columbia, was reported by Pedersen-Handrahan (1991) and by Pedersen and McDavid (1994). The Vancouver police used photo radar at a site in Vancouver during fall 1990, and data from that site were compared with a control site. The analyses indicated that both average speeds and the percentage of drivers exceeding the speed limit of 31 mph (50 km/h) decreased during the enforcement period but increased again after enforcement ended.

The use of photo radar has increased substantially in more recent times (personal communication, F. Navin, 1997). Photo radar is in widespread use in British Columbia in a program that is patterned after the Australian experience. The effect on high-speed driver behavior is reportedly very noticeable. At the time of writing this review, results of this program had not yet been published. A report is expected from Peter Cooper of the Insurance Corporation of British Columbia.

The Ontario government developed a program "to make Ontario's roads the safest in North America" (Ontario Ministry of Transportation 1995). As part of this program, a 1-year pilot project was designed to evaluate the effectiveness of photo radar. Photo radar was deployed at three experimental sites [six-lane 62-mph (100-km/h) divided freeway, four-lane 62-mph divided highway, two-lane 50-mph (80-km/h) undivided urban highway] and three control sites. The ministry's report covers the effects on speeds after 4 months of operation. Significant decreases in average vehicle speeds, and even more profound declines in the percentages of vehicles speeding by various amounts, especially the highest speeds, were found. Decreases were also noted at the control sites, but they were of lesser magnitude. The control site decreases were attributed to extensive media attention to the use of photo radar and to campaigns against speeding in general. Analyses of changes in crash rates await the accumulation of more data.

Germany

One of the earliest studies of the effect of photo radar on speeds and crashes was reported by Glauz and Blackburn (1980); a more detailed study was reported by Lamm and Kloeckner (1984). A section of southbound autobahn A3 between Cologne and Frankfurt experienced crash rates ranging from 5 to 10 times that of the rest of the autobahn system. The section was on a long, steep downgrade (the Elzer Berg) and experienced 85th percentile speeds of 93 mph (150 km/h), compared with the local design speed of 62 mph (100 km/h). Therefore, a speed limit of 62 mph for cars (lower for trucks) was put in place. In conjunction with that, automatic photo radar was installed over each of the three lanes. The 85th percentile speed dropped quickly to about 65 mph (105 km/h) in the left lane and remained at that level for at least 10 years. Total crashes dropped from about 300 per year to under 30 per year, and injury crashes dropped by a factor of 20.

Coleman et al. (1996) indicate that photo radar is now used in Germany only on a limited basis. The reason for this, they indicate, is that under German law the driver, not the owner, is liable to pay the fine. The author's experience, based on travel there in 1997, is that photo radar is much in evidence. It was particularly evident on autobahn A6 from Cologne to Hannover to Berlin, especially in conjunction with reduced speed limits in construction zones. This observation has been confirmed by the coordinator for police traffic activities in the state of Niedersachsen, with headquarters in Hannover (personal communication, E. Klein, 1997). He agrees that enforcement is more difficult because of the German legal system, but "even given these drawbacks, we will not stop using the automatic speed control on autobahns, since it is pretty successful."

Correspondence received on December 15, 1997, prepared by Herr Brackemeyer of the German Police Academy in Münster provided additional detail. Frontal photos are taken in hopes of identifying the driver. If the registered owner will not identify the driver, and the driver is repeatedly detected speeding, German law enables the police to require the owner to keep a log of all trips and their drivers for later reference. Photo radar is being used in conjunction with the variable speed limit program described in the previous section. In addition, photo radar is used by local communities, although by law they cannot stop vehicles for speeding (only "the police service" can do that).

The Police Academy also furnished statistics on the prevalence of photo radar units in Germany. As of April 1996, there were 593 photo radar units in the 16 states of Germany, of several different manufacturers and models. The states with the most were Nordrhein-Westfalen (104), Bayren (95), Baden-Württemburg (69), and Niedersachsen (67). Each of the states has at least a few.

Kuwait

Ali et al. (1997) report that Kuwait installed 10 automatic (unmanned) photo radar units for speed enforcement purposes. The researchers determined that drivers slow down dramatically as they approach the units, whose permanent locations are now well known, then speed up immediately after passing them. This behavior is attributed to the general lack of visible law enforcement in the Persian Gulf countries. (Ali et al. quote another study involving 112 h of traffic observation by researchers at a number of intersections over a 3-month period, during which they observed more than 10,000 traffic violations and 3 crashes, but never saw a police officer.) Ali et al. believe that photo radar will not be effective in Kuwait unless it is accompanied by a much greater police presence.

The Netherlands

Oei (1996) presents information and data on speed management and speed enforcement in the Netherlands. The government instituted a Multiyear Road Safety Program with the goals of reducing fatalities by 25 percent between 1985 and 2000, the average speed by 5 to 10 percent, and the number of speeders to less than 10 percent. Photo radar was installed at four locations that also had speed warning systems in place. The 85th percentile speed was reduced by 2 mph (3 km/h) with warning signs alone and by 5 mph (8 km/h) with signs and photo radar enforcement. The percentage of speeders dropped from 38 percent initially to 28 percent with signs only and to 11 percent with enforcement. The latter percentage increased slightly from 11 percent speeders to 16 percent after 3 years of operation. A small experiment using moveable photo radar in unmarked cars was also reported; it had smaller but measurable beneficial effects on speeds.

Coleman et al. (1996) provide additional information on photo radar enforcement in the Netherlands. They point out that recent enabling legislation that holds vehicle owners, as opposed to drivers, liable for speeding violations makes their program more effective. They also quote additional research by Oei, reported by the Dutch Institute for Road Research, that shows the efficiency in the use of automated speed enforcement as compared with manual enforcement, and they quote other research that shows that automated enforcement can be ineffective without accompanying media publicity.

Norway

Elvik (1997) reported on automatic speed enforcement in Norway. Photo radar was deployed at 64 road sections that were classified according to whether they met certain warrants. One warrant was based on crash rates (crashes per million vehicle kilometers before deployment); the other was crash density (crashes per kilometer before deployment) The analyses corrected for regression to the mean, and the effects at each site were weighted statistically. He found a statistically significant reduction in injury crashes of 20 percent for all 64 sections combined. The largest reduction, 26 percent, was found for sections meeting both warrants, and the smallest, 5 percent, was found for sections meeting neither of the warrants.

Elvik (1997) also used a statistical approach to combine his data with 15 other data sets of reported effectiveness of automatic speed enforcement from Germany, Australia, England, Sweden, and the

Netherlands. The weighted mean change (based on the size of the crash sample) was a highly significant 17 percent decline, with 95 percent confidence bounds of 16 to 19 percent.

Sweden

A test program of the use of automatic speed enforcement in Sweden was reported by Nilsson (1992). For a 2-year period, 8, and later 16, test sites comprising a total of 68 mi (110 km) of rural road and 11 mi (17 km) of urban main roads had cameras installed; a like number of control sites were also identified. These cameras were tied to sensors buried in the road, not radar (personal communication, G. Nilsson, 1997). They were placed into use according to a plan, for 4 to 6 h at a time, spread over the 24 h of the day and all days of the week. During this period, 14,000 photos were taken of incidents in which the driver exceeded the speed limit of 31 mph (50 km/h) by at least 8 mph (13 km/h), or the speed limit of 56 mph (90 km/h) by at least 9 mph (14 km/h).

The researchers found that average speeds dropped by 3 to 6 mph (5 to 10 km/h) at the experimental sites. The speed reductions started about 0.3 mi (500 m) upstream of the radar units and continued to about 0.6 mi (1 km) past the units. Over the 2-year period the range of influence diminished to be more in the immediate vicinity of the cameras. A reduction in injury crashes and fatalities was also observed, but these changes were too small to be statistically significant.

Additional information is provided by Coleman et al. (1996) and by Nilsson (personal communication, 1997). Photo radar usage in Sweden is now rather limited. Where it is used, it is usually mounted in a police van that can be moved from site to site. Most speed enforcement there is not automated but uses manned radar (without a camera) or manned laser guns. In fact, the use of manned lasers is increasing dramatically in Sweden, as reported by Andersson and Nilsson (1997). The percentage of all tickets written using lasers increased from 36 percent to 53 percent from 1994 to 1995. This enforcement is part of Sweden's national road safety program, intended to decrease the proportion of drivers exceeding the speed limits by 35 percent by 2000.

United Kingdom

The effects of the use of automated photo enforcement (speed cameras, using radar and other speed-sensing systems) on trunk roads in West London were reported by Swali (1993) and later with additional data by Winnett (1994). The early results reported by Swali indicated very significant reductions in speeds; one site with a 40-mph (64-km/h) speed limit indicated a change from 1,090 drivers per day traveling more than 20 mph (32 km/h) over the limit before enforcement to 30 drivers per day after, a reduction of 97 percent. For all sites combined, total crashes were reduced by 22 percent, and fatal plus serious injury crashes were reduced by 38 percent.

The later report by Winnett (1994) indicates that, after correcting for general crash trends, total crashes at speed camera sites declined 14 percent, significant at the 1 percent level. Furthermore, the decrease in fatal and serious injury crashes was highly significant, whereas the 8 percent decrease in slight crashes was not statistically significant.

United States

The first use of ASE in the United States was in Arlington, Texas, in 1976 (Blackburn and Gilbert 1995). For a 3-month period a photo radar system known as Orbis III was used. Photo radar was not used again for actual enforcement until 1986, although, as will be noted, there was much field testing of various systems. In July 1986, Precinct 8 of Galveston County, Texas, began an ASE program that lasted for 1 year. In 1987 the city police of La Marque, Texas, used ASE equipment for a 3-month period. Both programs were stopped because of adverse public opinion.

Blackburn and Gilbert (1995) report that, as of about 1994, 13 additional U.S. communities used photo radar for speed enforcement for some period. At the time they wrote their report, the ASE programs in 6 of the 13 communities had ceased for a variety of reasons. Programs still operational at that time were Paradise Valley, Arizona; Campbell, National City, and Riverside, California; and Garland, Wellington, and West Valley, Utah. The Pasadena program, no longer operational, was well known for its intensity and the fact that it was in a fairly large community. It ran for 4 years until it ended in 1992 for several reasons (judicial and public support eroded, the equipment vendor went out of business, police manpower was reduced, and the cost of the program was excessive).

At the present time the following U.S. communities are using ASE: Portland, Oregon; Scottsdale, Mesa, Tempe, and Paradise Valley, Arizona; National City and perhaps San Jose, California; and Fort Collins and Commerce City, Colorado (personal communication, A. Tuton, 1997). (Canadian locations with current ASE programs include British Columbia and Edmonton, Calgary, and Lethbridge, Alberta.) Boulder and Denver, Colorado, have issued RFPs to establish ASE programs.

Generally, the U.S. programs did not receive as much evaluation as many of the foreign programs did. However, some data are presented by Blackburn and Gilbert (1995). In Paradise Valley (the longest running of any U.S. ASE program) the annual number of crashes went from 460 in 1986, the year before the program was begun, to 224 in 1992, the last year data were available to the authors. In West Valley, Utah, the annual number of crashes fell from 2,130 to 1,710 after 2 years of ASE use. The police of National City, California, reported a 26 percent decline in crashes during the first 10 months of photo radar use.

The Scottsdale ASE program was begun in 1996. American Traffic Systems (1997) reports that crashes declined from 181 to 120 during comparable 10-week periods before and after enforcement. Similarly, an 81 percent drop in speeding violations, from about 6.6 percent to about 1.2 percent as a percent of all vehicles, was reported in Commerce City, Colorado (American Traffic Systems 1997).

Midwest Research Institute provided an evaluation of the ASE program in Riverside, California (Blackburn and Bauer 1995). Data were obtained from 13 test sites in the community by the police department. Unfortunately, broad generalizations are not possible because the amount of data collected varied greatly from site to site and at different times of the day; at some sites no data were obtained after the beginning of enforcement and at some sites there were no before-enforcement data. Following are some of the findings:

- Average speeds were changed by an amount ranging from a decrease of 14 mph (23 km/h) (at a school zone) to an increase of 1.1 mph (1.8 km/h).
- The 85th percentile speed (calculated as the mean plus one standard deviation) was reduced at all sites and times of day for which data are available by a maximum of 16.4 mph (26.4 km/h) (at the school zone) and a minimum of 0.2 mph (0.3 km/h).
- The percentage of vehicles exceeding the speed limits by various amounts was examined. For example, the percentage speeding by 11 mph (18 km/h) or more decreased in all but 1 of the 39 site/time combinations for which data were available. Again, the largest reduction was at the school zone, where, in the a.m. peak, for example, the percentage dropped from 77.7 to 19.9. [At this 25-mph (40-km/h) speed zone, nearly everyone was speeding before the ASE program; some speeds of 70 to 80 mph (113 to 129 km/h) were recorded.]
- Reductions in crashes in Riverside were compared with those in a control city, Santa Ana. The monthly average of speed-related (by police report) fatal and injury crashes decreased by 5.3 in Riverside, while it increased by 2.4 in Santa Ana. The total number of speed-related crashes dropped by 14.2 per month in Riverside and increased by 1.1 per month in Santa Ana.
- The percentage reduction in speed-related fatal and injury crashes in Riverside was 14.7, whereas the comparable reduction in fatal and injury crashes judged not to be speed related was 18.1 percent. Similar results were obtained for total crashes.

Finally, it is of interest to report the number of evaluations of photo radar systems in the United States that stopped short of issuing speeding citations. Pilot tests of ASE equipment are reported by Blackburn and Gilbert (1995) in the early 1980s by state police agencies in Washington, Michigan, and New Jersey. Lynn et al. (1992) report on feasibility studies conducted in Virginia and Maryland, with the intent of ultimately installing such systems on the Capital Beltway (which has not happened).

SUMMARY OF LEGAL AND POLITICAL ISSUES ASSOCIATED WITH ASE

A short selection of some of the more commonly discussed legal and political issues is presented here, with brief discussions of each. Much of this material is taken from Blackburn and Gilbert (1995).

Constitutional Issues

Issues such as right to privacy and illegal search and seizure have been raised from time to time. Many state and Supreme Court decisions have consistently found that the use of photo radar does not violate rights under the Fourth Amendment.

Admissibility of Photographic Evidence

Some have argued that photographs taken by photo radar should not be allowed as evidence in a courtroom. This issue has been addressed by a number of state supreme courts and appellate courts, and it was found consistently that photographic evidence of this type, if it can be shown to be authentic and competent, is admissible.

Scientific Reliability

The issue here is whether the photo radar equipment can be shown to be scientifically valid and reliable. In some countries the equipment (not just a sample, but every single device) must be tested periodically by a government testing agency and certified to be accurate. In the United States a formal set of standards for such equipment is under development and should be available soon (personal communication, A. Tuton, 1997).

Frontal Versus Rear Photographs

There was much debate on this issue 15 years ago, and some continues. The argument is that a frontal photograph is required to provide some identification of the driver. Others argue that such photographs have occasionally created unpleasant repercussions if a motorist was shown in a potentially embarrassing situation. If the owner of the vehicle can be made liable for the speeding infraction (see next issue), then frontal photographs would not be necessary since it would only be necessary to identify the vehicle. A related issue is that some states do not require front license plates, so a frontal photograph would not identify the vehicle. In other states that require front plates, the police find that a significant fraction of vehicles (10 to 20 percent) do not display such plates. Therefore, they set up their photo radar with two cameras and manually take a second photo of the rear of the vehicle if the front plate is missing. It is also possible for an automatic system to routinely take both front and rear photos of detected speeders.

Owner Liability

In most jurisdictions where photo radar is used, the legal system makes the driver, not the owner, liable for the violation. Exceptions include Australia, the Netherlands, and Paradise Valley, Arizona, where the owner is held responsible (vicarious liability). Otherwise, the police can mail the registered owner the ticket and the owner has the option of paying the fine, identifying the driver, coming to the police station to view the photograph (most jurisdictions do not mail the photos), or contesting the ticket and going to court. Laws in some countries require owners to follow these steps; in others such as Germany they are voluntary, but the majority of owners pay the fine.

Penalties

In some jurisdictions the fines for speeding when detected by photo radar are modest, and the violations are considered civil (not criminal) offenses. As such, they are treated much like parking tickets; this approach makes it easier for the jurisdiction to hold the owner vicariously liable. In many European countries and in Australia, the fines can be stiff (hundreds of dollars). Moreover, points may be assessed against the driver's record. It is not uncommon for countries to impose license suspension for excessive speeding [19 mph (30 km/h) over the limit, for example].

Manned Versus Unmanned Operation

It is possible for photo radar to be operated in a totally automatic, unmanned mode. In this mode, a large spool of film is placed in the camera, the system is placed in a roadside box or cabinet, power is supplied, and the system then operates by itself until an officer comes to retrieve the film. With this mode, many boxes are usually installed at the locations to be used for speed enforcement, the locations being evident to the motorists. However, there are far fewer photo radar units than boxes, so the photo radar units are rotated among the boxes. This mode can be effective because the motorists do not know which boxes are active. Experience indicates that vandalism can be expected, however.

Alternatively, a manned operation requires an officer to be present with the equipment. Some jurisdictions require this, so the officer can vouch for the operation and that the photographed vehicles were witnessed by the officer. The equipment can either be set up alongside the road on a stand or tripod or, more commonly, mounted in the back of a police van, enabling rapid mobility.

Public Opinion

The demise of a photo radar program is often the result of adverse public opinion being brought to the attention of the community officials (city council, mayor, etc.), causing them to cancel the program. This happens not only in the United States but also on occasion in foreign countries.

There have been only two formal surveys of public opinion about photo radar in North America in recent years. A well-publicized survey by the Insurance Institute for Highway Safety was conducted in 1989, using random digit dialing in two communities with ongoing photo radar programs, Paradise Valley, Arizona, and Pasadena, California, and in the surrounding areas (Freedman et al. 1990). There was great awareness of the ongoing programs in both communities and in the surrounding areas. In all, 58 percent either approved or strongly approved of the program, with the residents of Paradise Valley and Pasadena more likely to approve than those in the nearby communities. (However, the majority of all subpopulations approved, after removing those who had no opinion.) The percentage of those interviewed who strongly disapproved ranged from 12 percent in the two communities with active enforcement to 15 and 20 percent, respectively, in the surrounding areas of the two communities. Reasons given by those who disapproved were that the wrong person may be ticketed, it gives police an unfair advantage, it violates rights to privacy, it does not give the driver a chance to explain, and it is not effective in reducing speeds.

A later survey was conducted in British Columbia by Zuo and Cooper (1991). Surveys of randomly selected drivers in British Columbia during the period 1988 to 1990 were conducted about red light cameras. Roughly 500 to 600 driver responses were obtained in telephone interviews in each of the 3 years. In 1989 and 1990, questions about photo radar were added. The positive response to photo radar increased from 71 percent in 1989 to 74 percent in 1990, which was not statistically significant. Drivers who were against photo radar tended to be young to middle-aged males with two or more moving violations in the past 3 years and who tend to respond more aggressively to frustrating traffic situations.

In a parallel survey in 1990, drivers were presented with a hypothetical situation where they were speeding to "keep up with traffic" (Zuo and Cooper 1991). If they received a ticket from a policeman using conventional enforcement, 39 percent felt that the ticket was unfair, and 51 percent said that it would make them angry. If they received the ticket because of photo radar enforcement, 45 percent said that it would be unfair and 60 percent said that it would make them angry. The authors conclude that "there are obviously a number of drivers whose attitude towards the cameras simply reflects their attitude towards enforcement in general."

DEPLOYMENT STRATEGIES FOR ASE

Automated Speed Monitoring and Warning Systems

Experience with these systems indicates that they can be effective at selective locations, such as in school zones and work zones. They must react to the speeds of individual vehicles. They must display messages dynamically, by flashing or giving appropriate messages. They must be enforceable speeds, not advisory speeds, and they must be backed up by enforcement, at least occasionally.

Variable Speed Limit Systems

These systems can be effective when installed at locations where the public senses that they are believable. Locations where there is frequent fog or traffic backups are prime candidates. (At a cost on the order of $1 million per installation, they must be used selectively.) Dynamically displaying the reason for a reduced speed limit is recommended. The displayed speeds must be appropriate to the conditions of the moment and enforceable. Actual enforcement must accompany the reduced speed limit, at least some of the time, and must be accompanied by publicity about both the variable speed limit and the presence of enforcement.

Automated Speed Enforcement

ASE and, in particular, photo radar can be effective in detecting and convicting drivers traveling at excessive speeds, provided that enabling legislation that is supported by the politicians and the courts is in force. It is critical that public support be gained before the legislation is implemented. The public must be convinced that there is a safety problem, that high speeds are a primary cause of the problem, and that enforcement is aimed at only a small minority of drivers (the focus population of automated enforcement travel at very high speeds). If the public becomes convinced that ASE is being used to generate revenue, the program is doomed to failure.

ASE should be used where there is a perceived speeding problem. Candidates include school zones (during hours when students are likely to be about), work zones (when there is actually work going on or where the road geometrics have been temporarily and radically modified), and known high-crash locations. Especially appropriate are high-crash locations where traditional police enforcement is not feasible due to lack of adequate shoulders, high traffic volumes, and so forth. The installations must be publicized and defended. Signage upstream or downstream of the actual installation is often used to allay driver complaints of police unfairness. It must be understood that the purpose of the enforcement is to reduce high speeds, not to "catch" speeders.

The ASE equipment should be used, at least initially, with a fairly high threshold—say, 20 mph (32 km/h) over the limit. It has been found that there are enough drivers with such speeds to keep the equipment, the police, and the courts busy. As the public becomes more used to the equipment, it may be possible to reduce the threshold.

If a state, a community, or the nation decides on a major program to reduce speeding in general and not just at selected locations as part of a greater program to reduce serious crashes, then a wider deployment of ASE would be in order. Either a large number of boxes or cabinets could be installed to house ASE equipment on a rotating basis or mobile equipment housed in police vans could be used. The public must be convinced of the importance of the program and know that they cannot predict where the equipment might be located on a day-by-day or hour-by-hour basis. The types of roads where such equipment is deployed should be determined on the basis of speed surveys; the road class in itself is not particularly important. Modern ASE equipment can easily be deployed to survey two or three lanes of traffic in one direction, perhaps more. If the jurisdiction is serious about the program, convictions should be accompanied not only by fines but also by points, and consideration should be given to license suspension if the violation is serious enough.

REFERENCES

Ali, S. Y., O. Al-Saleh, and P. A. Koushki. 1997. Effectiveness of Automated Speed-Monitoring Cameras in Kuwait. In *Transportation Research Record 1595*, Transportation Research Board, National Research Council, Washington, D.C., pp. 20–26.

American Traffic Systems. 1997. http://www.traffic.com (Oct.).

Andersson, G., and G. Nilsson. 1997. Speed Limits, Speeds and Safety. In *Speed Management and Enforcement*, Swedish National Road and Transport Research Institute, Linköping, Sweden, June.

Blackburn, R. R., and K. M. Bauer. 1995. *Field Tests of Automated Speed Enforcement Programs.* Final report, NHTSA Contract DTNH22-90-C-07290, April.

Blackburn, R. R., and D. T. Gilbert. 1995. *NCHRP Synthesis of Highway Practice 219: Photographic Enforcement of Traffic Laws.* Transportation Research Board, National Research Council, Washington, D.C.

Cameron, M. H., A. Cavallo, and A. Gilbert. 1992. *Crash-Based Evaluation of the Speed Camera Program in Victoria 1990–1991; Phases I and II.* Accident Research Centre, Monash University, Victoria, Australia, Dec.

Casey, S. M., and A. K. Lund. 1993. The Effects of Mobile Roadside Speedometers on Traffic Speeds. *Accident Analysis and Prevention*, Vol. 25, No. 5, pp. 627–634.

Coleman, J. A., et al. 1996. *FHWA Study Tour for Speed Management and Enforcement Technology.* FHWA-PL-96-006. Federal Highway Administration, U.S. Department of Transportation, Feb.

Elvik, R. 1997. Effects on Accidents of Automatic Speed Enforcement in Norway. In *Transportation Research Record 1595*, Transportation Research Board, National Research Council, Washington, D.C., pp. 14–19.

Fitzpatrick, K. 1991. *A Review of Automated Enforcement.* Report FHWA/TX-92/1232-5. Austin, Tex., Nov.

Freedman, M., A. F. Williams, and A. K. Lund. 1990. Public Opinion Regarding Photo Radar. In *Transportation Research Record 1270*, Transportation Research Board, National Research Council, Washington, D.C., pp. 59–65.

Freedman, M., N. Teed, and J. Migletz. 1994. Effect of Radar Drone Operation on Speeds at High Crash Risk Locations. In *Transportation Research Record 1464*, Transportation Research Board, National Research Council, Washington, D.C., pp. 69–80.

Garber, N. J., and S. T. Patel. 1994. *Effectiveness of Changeable Message Signs on Controlling Vehicle Speeds in Work Zones.* Report FHWA/VA-95-R4. Virginia Transportation Research Council, Sept.

Glauz, W. D., and R. R. Blackburn. 1980. *Technology for Use in "Automated" Speed Enforcement.* Report DOT-HS-805454. National Highway Traffic Safety Administration, U.S. Department of Transportation, June.

Lamm, R., and J. H. Kloeckner. 1984. Increase of Traffic Safety by Surveillance of Speed Limits with Automatic Radar Devices on a Dangerous Section of a German Autobahn: A Long-Term Investigation. In *Transportation Research Record 974*, Transportation Research Board, National Research Council, Washington, D.C., pp. 8–16.

Lynn, C. W., W. S. Ferguson, and N. J. Garber. 1992. Feasibility of Photo-Radar for Traffic Speed Enforcement in Virginia. In *Transportation Research Record 1375*, Transportation Research Board, National Research Council, Washington, D.C., pp. 11-16.

Nilsson, G. 1992. *Försök med Automatisk Hastighetsövervakning 1990–1992 (Trials with Automatic Speed Surveillance 1990-1992)* (in Swedish with English summary). Report VTI 378. Swedish Road and Traffic Research Institute, Linköping, Sweden.

Oei, H.. 1996. Automatic Speed Management in the Netherlands. In *Transportation Research Record 1560*, Transportation Research Board, National Research Council, Washington, D.C., pp. 57–64.

Ontario Ministry of Transportation. 1995. *Photo Radar Safety Evaluation Preliminary 4-Month Speed Results.* Report SRO-101/95, Jan.

Parker, M. R., Jr., and K. H. Tsuchiyama. 1985. *Methods for Reducing Large Speed Differences in Traffic Streams, Volume I—Inventory of Methods.* Report FHWA/RD-85/103. Federal Highway Administration, U.S. Department of Transportation, Aug.

Parker, M. R., Jr. 1985. *Methods for Reducing Large Speed Differences in Traffic Streams, Volume II—Final Report.* Report FHWA/RD-85/104. Federal Highway Administration, U.S. Department of Transportation, Aug.

Pedersen, K. S., and J. C. McDavid. 1994. The Impact of Radar Cameras on Traffic Speed: A Quasi-Experimental Evaluation. *The Canadian Journal of Program Evaluation*, Vol. 9, No. 1, pp. 51–68.

Pedersen-Handrahan, K. 1991. An Evaluation of the Radar Camera on Traffic Speed. *Proceedings of the Canadian Multidisciplinary Road Safety Conference VII*, Vancouver, British Columbia, Canada, June.

Pigman, J. G., K. R. Agent, J. A. Deacon, and R. J. Kryscio. 1989. Evaluation of Unmanned Radar Installations. In *Transportation Research Record 1244*, Transportation Research Board, National Research Council, Washington, D.C., pp. 7–16.

Pilli-Sihvola, Y., and K. Taskula. 1996. Mustaa Jäätä and Finland's Weather-Controlled Road. In *Traffic Technology International '96*, UK & International Press, Surrey, United Kingdom, pp. 204–206.

Rogerson, P., S. Newstead, and M. Cameron. 1994. *Evaluation of the Speed Camera Program in Victoria 1990–1991.* Phase 3 and Phase 4. Report 54. Accident Research Centre, Monash University, Victoria, Australia, Feb.

Roqué, G. M., and M. C. Roberts. 1989. A Replication of the Use of Public Posting in Traffic Speed Control. *Journal of Applied Behavior Analysis*, Vol. 22, No. 3, Fall.

Sinclair, G. I. 1996. Information from the Victoria, Australia, Traffic Camera Office. 1996. http://yarra.vicnet.net.au/~tco/html/ (Oct.).

Streff, F. M., L. P. Kostyniuk, and C. Christoff. 1995. *Effects of Drone Radar and Police Enforcement on Travel Speeds: Test on a 65 MPH Freeway and 55 MPH Construction Zone.* Report UMTRI-95-22. University of Michigan Transportation Research Institute, June.

Sumner, R. L., and C. M. Andrews. 1990. *Variable Speed Limit System.* Report FHWA RD-89-001. Federal Highway Administration, U.S. Department of Transportation, March.

Swali, L. N. 1993. The Effect of Speed Cameras in West London. *Proceedings of Seminar C, Traffic Management and Road Safety*, PTRC Education and Research Services, Ltd., Vol. P365, University of Manchester, Sept.

Van den Hoogen, E., and S. Smulders. 1994. Control by Variable Speed Signs: Results of the Dutch Experiment. *Road Traffic Monitoring and Control*, IEE Conference Publication 391, April, pp. 145–149.

Wilkie, J. K. 1997. Using Variable Speed Limit Signs To Mitigate Speed Differentials Upstream of Reduced Flow Locations. In *Compendium of Graduate Student Papers on Advanced Surface Transportation Systems*, Texas Transportation Institute Report SWUTC/97/72840-00003-2, Aug.

Winnett, M. A. 1994. A Review of Speed Camera Operations in the U.K. *Proceedings of Seminar J of the 22nd European Transport Forum for Traffic Management and Road Safety*, PTRC Education and Research Services, Ltd., Vol. P381, Sept.

Zaal, D. 1994. *Traffic Law Enforcement: A Review of the Literature.* Report 53. Accident Research Centre, Monash University, Victoria, Australia, April.

Zuo, Y., and P. J. Cooper. 1991. Public Reaction to Police Use of Automatic Cameras To Reduce Traffic Control Infractions and Driving Speeds in British Columbia. *Proceedings of the Canadian Multidisciplinary Road Safety Conference VII*, Vancouver, British Columbia, Canada, June.

Appendix E

Glossary

The terminology required for a comprehensive discussion of the relationship between vehicle speed and safety has specific technical connotations that may differ from the meanings of these words in the vernacular. This glossary describes several terms associated with vehicle speeds on streets and highways, and with highway and traffic engineering. Speed parameters customarily expressed in miles per hour (mph) are cited in these units in this glossary (1 mph = 1.609 km/h).

10-mph Pace

The 10-mph pace is the 10-mph range encompassing the greatest percentage of all the measured speeds in a spot speed study. It is described by the speed value at the lower end of the range and the percentage of all vehicles that are within the range; as such, it is an alternative indicator of speed dispersion. Most engineers believe that safety is enhanced when the 10-mph pace includes a large percentage (more than 70 percent) of all the free-flowing vehicles at a location. (Note: 10 mph = 16 km/h.)

85th Percentile Speed

The 85th percentile speed is the speed at or below which 85 percent of the free-flowing vehicles travel. Traffic engineers have assumed that this high percentage of drivers will select a safe speed on the basis of the conditions at the site.

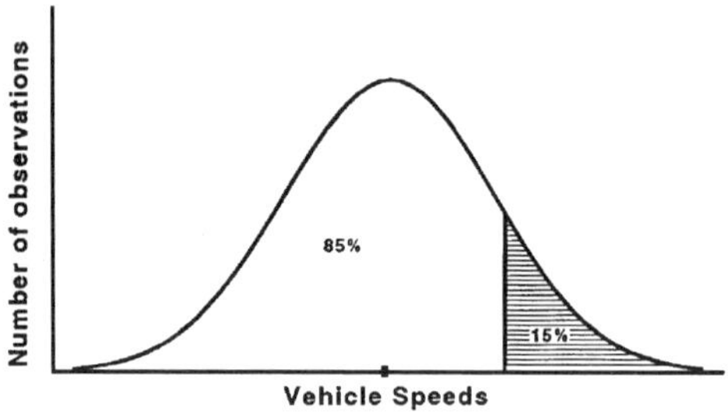

Figure E-1 Eighty-fifth percentile speed.

The 85th percentile speed has traditionally been considered in an engineering study to establish a speed limit. The 85th percentile speed for a normal distribution is shown in Figure E-1. In most cases, the difference between the 85th percentile speed and the average speed provides a good approximation of the speed sample's standard deviation.

Advisory Speed

At certain locations on the highway system, such as horizontal curves, intersections, or steep downgrades, the safe speed on the roadway may be less than the posted speed limit. Rather than lowering the regulatory speed limits at each of these locations, traffic engineers often place standard warning signs accompanied by a square black-and-yellow advisory speed plate as shown in Figure E-2. Although this sign provides a warning to approaching drivers, it is not legally enforceable.

Figure E-2 Advisory speed plate.

Arterial

Arterials provide the high-speed, high-volume network for travel between major points in rural areas. They generally have minimum design speeds of at least 37 mph (60 km/h). Most intersections are at grade (i.e., at the same level), and access to abutting property is permitted but controlled. Utilities are usually permitted within the right-of-way. All rural arterials, including freeways, constitute about 9 percent of the rural highway length in the United States and carry 64 percent of the rural vehicle miles of travel.

The principal purpose of urban arterials is to provide mobility. Design speeds may be as low as 31 to 37 mph (50 to 60 km/h), but higher speeds are common, particularly for principal arterials. In developed areas, principal arterials are often spaced at intervals of 0.6 to 1.2 mi (1 to 2 km). Principal arterials, including freeways, account for 9 percent of the urban street length and carry 58 percent of all urban travel.

Average Speed

The average (or mean) speed is the most common measure of central tendency. Using data from a spot speed study, the average is calculated by summing all the measured speeds and dividing by the sample size, *n*.

Basic Speed Law

The Uniform Vehicle Code (National Committee on Uniform Traffic Laws and Ordinances 1992) and most state motor vehicle laws include a basic speed law with wording similar to the following: No person shall drive a vehicle at a speed greater than is reasonable and prudent under the conditions and having regard for the weather, visibility, traffic, and the surface and width of the roadway.

Braking Distance

Braking distance, assumed for design purposes to be on a wet pavement surface, is the distance required to stop a vehicle from the instant brake application begins. The minimum braking distance for a vehicle on a level roadway increases with the square of the speed:

$$b = \frac{V^2}{254f}$$

where

b = braking distance (m),
V = initial speed (km/h), and
f = coefficient of friction between tires and roadway.

The dashed line in Figure E-3 shows braking distance as a function of a vehicle's initial speed. The solid line shows the total stopping distance.

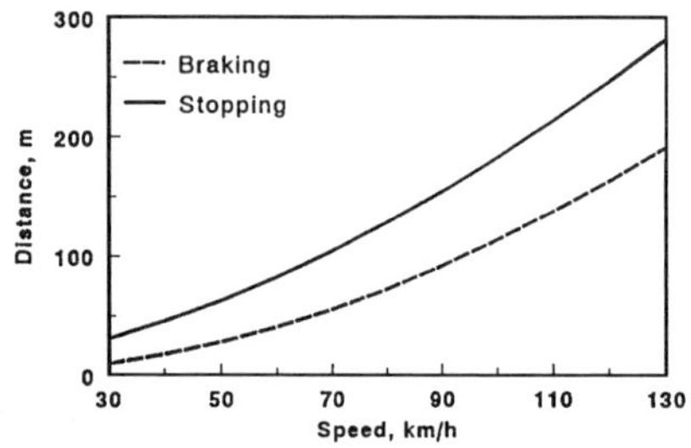

Figure E-3 Design values for braking and stopping distance. (Note: 1 m = 3.28 ft and 1 km/h = 0.62 mph.)

Business District

For the purpose of establishing statutory speed limits, the Uniform Vehicle Code (National Committee on Uniform Traffic Laws and Ordinances 1992) defines a business district as the territory contiguous to and including any highway when within any 180 m along such highway there are buildings in use for business or industrial purposes, including but not limited to hotels, banks, or office buildings that occupy at least 90 m of frontage on one side or 90 m collectively on both sides of the highway. (Note: 1 m = 3.28 ft.)

Collector Roads and Streets

Collector roads and streets collect vehicles from local roads and abutting properties and route them to arterials. Traffic volumes are relatively low and design speeds may be as low as 31 mph (50 km/h). Collectors have all intersections at grade and little access control. They may also have pedestrians and parked vehicles. Collectors represent 23 percent of the rural highway length and carry 25 percent of the rural vehicle miles of travel.

Collector streets in urban areas have design speeds of 31 mph (50 km/h) or greater. Their function is divided equally between mobility and access. Collectors are more likely than minor arterials to accommodate parking, pedestrians, bicycles, and local buses. Collectors and minor arterials account for 21 percent of urban street length and carry 28 percent of all urban travel.

Compliance with Speed Regulations

There is no commonly accepted definition of compliance with speed regulations. Motorists traveling less than the posted speed limit might appear to be in compliance, but under certain weather, visibility, or traffic conditions, they may be violating the basic speed law. In the more general case of free-flowing vehicles under favorable environmental conditions, measures of compliance (actually, noncompliance) include the percentage of vehicles exceeding the posted limit by 6 or 9 mph (10 or 15 km/h), or the percentage of vehicles exceeding the roadway's design speed.

Costs of Motor Vehicle Crashes

In highway safety analyses, it is often necessary to assign costs to traffic crashes. For example, the National Safety Council (NSC) recommends economic costs for crashes on the basis of productivity lost and expenses incurred because of collisions. NSC also estimated comprehensive costs for crashes, which included economic costs and a measure of the value of lost quality of life associated with deaths and injuries. The Federal Highway Administration (FHWA) has also suggested collision costs based on two different injury scales: (*a*) the KABC scale, with four injury levels ranging from Killed to Possible Injury; and (*b*) the Abbreviated Injury Scale, with six injury levels ranging from Killed to Minor. Table E-1 compares the costs recommended by NSC (1996) and FHWA (Judycki 1994).

Table E-1 National Safety Council and FHWA Traffic Crash Costs

	Type of Accident Cost ($)			
Type of Injury	Economic	Comprehensive	KABC Scale	Abbreviated Injury Scale
Fatal	790,000	2,790,000	2,600,000	2,600,000
Critical				1,980,000
Severe				490,000
Incapacitating	41,200	138,000	189,000	
Serious				150,000
Evident	13,900	35,700	36,000	
Moderate				40,000
Possible	7,900	17,000	19,000	
Minor				5,000
No injury—property damage only	6,000[a]	1,700[a]	2,000	

[a] NSC economic costs include minor injuries whereas comprehensive costs exclude all injuries.

Crash Probability

In typical use, crash probability refers to the long-term likelihood that a driver will be involved in a crash under a specified set of conditions (e.g., on a given trip, during the coming year). Estimates of national crash experience can be used to calculate average crash probabilities. However, crash probability is known to vary with driver characteristics, vehicle type, roadway features, and environmental factors, so the crash probability for an individual motorist may be substantially more or less than the average.

Crash Severity

A fatal crash is a crash that results in one or more deaths within 30 days of the crash. A nonfatal injury crash is a crash in which at least one person is injured, but no injury results in death. A property-damage-only (PDO) crash is a collision that results in property damage, but in which no person is injured.

Cross Section

The roadway cross section consists of those geometric features perpendicular to the direction of travel. Common cross-section elements include the following:

- Number of lanes—determined by the projected traffic volume for a facility.
- Lane width—must be sufficient to accommodate the design vehicle, allow for imprecise steering maneuvers, and provide clearance for traffic flow in adjacent lanes. It is dependent on the design vehicle, design speed, volume, the presence or absence of shoulders, horizontal alignment, and the presence of oncoming traffic.
- Cross slope—promotes drainage of surface water.
- Shoulders—used for emergency stopping and for lateral support of base and surface courses.
- Medians—used to separate opposing directions of traffic on multilane highways.
- Marginal elements—curbs, gutters, sidewalks, roadside slopes, and barriers.

Design Driver

A roadway's design must be compatible with drivers' capabilities and limitations. The design driver embodies those specific human characteristics that should be recognized in designing and operating the road. It is inappropriate to design for the median driver because this would potentially put half the drivers at risk. On the other hand, it is probably not realistic to design for the 99th percentile value of every human characteristic. Although the American Association of State Highway and Transportation Officials (AASHTO) does not provide an explicit description of the design driver, the following elements certainly should be included:

- Familiarity: The designer should assume that motorists are driving on a roadway for the first time and that they have no familiarity with its features.
- Driver age: Certain human performance characteristics deteriorate with age. Persons over the age of 65 constitute an increasing portion of the driving population, and their special needs must be considered in highway design.
- Vision: States specify a level of visual acuity (typically 20/30 corrected) that drivers must satisfy to retain their license. Designers must not only consider this requirement for their state, but also recognize that drivers from other jurisdictions with potentially inferior visual acuity standards will be using their roads. Most states do not test drivers for nighttime vision; nevertheless, the significant amount of travel during the hours of darkness suggests that designers should consider this factor.
- Eye height: The height of a driver's eye above the pavement affects the length of road ahead that a driver can see; eye height is a function of both the human and the vehicle. AASHTO's recommended value (AASHTO 1994) of 1070 mm corresponds to the 7th percentile driver in a passenger car.
- Impairment: Motorists may become impaired by fatigue, medication, alcohol, and drugs. These imperfections, at least to the extent that they are legal (e.g., a blood alcohol content below 0.08), should be recognized by the designer. As a consequence, engineers must design for the prudent, rather than the perfect, driver.

Design Speed

AASHTO defines a roadway's design speed as "the maximum safe speed that can be maintained over a specified section of highway when conditions are so favorable that the design features of the highway govern" (AASHTO 1994). This is the maximum speed prudent drivers would choose when environmental conditions are very good and traffic volumes are light. Subject to the constraints of environmental quality, economics, aesthetics, and social impacts, AASHTO recommends higher design speeds to promote safety, mobility, and efficiency. Certain highway design features, including curvature, sight distance, and roadside elements, are highly sensitive to the choice of design speed; others, including lane and shoulder widths, do not change appreciably with design speed. In planning a roadway, the engineer initially selects a design speed; that decision, in turn, establishes upper or lower bounds on the facility's geometric design parameters. This is the principal use of design speed. On a rural, level, straight roadway with no access points and obstacle-free roadsides, the concept of design speed is not meaningful.

Drivers exceeding the design speed by a small amount under favorable conditions will not necessarily have a crash, principally because AASHTO incorporates safety factors into its design recommendations. For example, the stopping sight distance model assumes a very conservative perception-reaction time and a wet roadway surface; an alert driver can react quicker and a vehicle on a dry roadway can decelerate to a stop in a much shorter distance than the design value. Likewise, an attentive motorist can exceed a horizontal curve's design speed without running off the roadway.

Higher design speeds enhance safety, principally by accommodating minor driver errors and providing greater opportunities for crash avoidance. AASHTO strongly recommends consistency in design speed along a roadway section to avoid misleading motorists. Although it appears reasonable that the posted speed limit should not exceed a highway's design speed, the existing roadway system includes countless horizontal curves with safe speeds below the design speed or posted speed limit; these situations are routinely handled with curve warning signs and advisory speed plates (see Figure E-2).

Engineering Study

The Uniform Vehicle Code (National Committee on Uniform Traffic Laws and Ordinances 1992) and state motor vehicle laws authorize state and local highway agencies to determine whether the statutory speed limit on a section of road is greater or less than is reasonable under the conditions that exist at the location. This determination must be based on an engineering study, which requires data collection and analysis in the determination of an appropriate limit. The data considered would typically include the following factors:

- Area—rural, suburban, or urban;
- Results of a spot speed study, principally the 85th percentile and 10-mph (16-km/h) pace speeds;
- Crash experience, with particular attention to speed-related crashes;
- Traffic volume and composition (i.e., types of vehicles);
- Existing traffic controls (regulatory and warning);
- Design features, including horizontal and vertical alignment, sight distance, and lane width;
- Pavement surface condition;
- Parking;
- Presence and usage of driveways;
- Roadside hazards;
- Pedestrians and bicycles;
- Speed limits on adjacent roadway sections; and
- Existing level of speed enforcement.

Typically, the speed data—particularly the 85th percentile speed—provide the first approximation of the speed zone limit. The limit may be adjusted from this value on the basis of the other factors.

Externalities

"Externalities" refers to the risks imposed on others not taken into account by an individual's decision. In the case of speed choice, the term refers to the risks imposed on other road users (e.g., other drivers and vehicle occupants, pedestrians, bicyclists) by an individual driver's selection of a driving speed. For example, a driver's decision to accept a higher risk of death or injury in exchange for a shorter trip time almost certainly increases the risk for other road users. Externalities are one of the primary reasons for regulating speed.

Fatality Rates

There are four common methods of calculating fatality rates:

- *Travel-based fatality rate*—fatalities per 100 million vehicle-mi of travel (100 mvm). In 1996, the United States had a travel-based fatality rate of 1.7 fatalities per 100 mvm. This rate is commonly used in the highway engineering community. (Note: 100 million vehicle-mi = 161 million vehicle-km.)
- *Registered vehicle fatality rate*—fatalities per 100,000 registered vehicles. In 1996, the United States had a registered vehicle death rate of 20.8 fatalities per 100,000 registered vehicles.
- *Population fatality rate*—fatalities per 100,000 population. In 1996, the United States had a population death rate of 15.8 fatalities per 100,000 people. This method of normalizing fatalities is commonly used by the health profession for infection and mortality rates.
- *Driver fatality rate*—fatalities per 100,000 licensed drivers. In 1996, the United States had a driver fatality rate of 23.3 fatalities per 100,000 licensed drivers.

Free Flow

A free-flowing vehicle is one whose driver has the ability to choose a speed of travel without undue influence from other traffic, conspicuous police presence, or environmental factors. In other words, the driver of a free-flowing vehicle chooses a speed that he or she finds comfortable on the basis of the appearance of the road.

In conducting a spot speed study, the field observer detects and records the speed of free-flowing vehicles. Vehicles operating under the following conditions are not free flowing and must be excluded from the sample:

- Two vehicles in the same lane have a headway (time from the front of one vehicle to the front of the following vehicle) of less than 4 s.

- A vehicle's brake lights are on.
- A vehicle is accelerating or decelerating; this includes a vehicle entering or leaving the roadway at nearby ramps, intersections, and driveways.
- Enforcement or emergency vehicles with flashing lights are nearby.
- Oversize loads or funeral convoys are present.
- Pedestrians, animals, debris, or disabled vehicles are on or adjacent to the roadway.
- There is interference from maintenance crews.

A field observer can monitor these conditions and select a sample of truly free-flowing vehicles. However, most automatic devices used to detect and record the speeds of passing vehicles are unable to detect these interfering factors. As a result, data from automatic speed monitoring stations underestimate the free-flow speed of traffic.

Freeway

A freeway is a type of principal arterial designed to move large traffic volumes at high speeds. It is characterized by limited access, grade separations rather than intersections at cross streets (i.e., intersecting traffic crosses the freeway at a different level), minimum design speed of 50 mph (80 km/h), and medians to separate opposing traffic flows. Because of their superior design features, freeways have low crash rates relative to other rural roads. They constitute only 1 percent of rural highway length but carry 24 percent of all rural travel.

Freeways in urban areas are intended to move large volumes of traffic at higher speed with limited access to adjacent property. Design speeds are similar to those of rural freeways, but urban freeways often have three or four lanes in each direction and interchanges spaced at less than 1.2 mi (2 km). Most traffic traveling through an urban area uses a freeway. Although urban freeways account for less than 3 percent of the street length in urban areas, they carry more than one-third of all urban travel.

Geometric Design Standards

The geometric design standards for streets and highways specify desirable and minimum values for most geometric features, including horizontal alignment, vertical alignment, cross section, and roadside elements.

Highway Capacity

All roads, streets, and freeways have an upper limit on the amount of traffic they can accommodate during an hour. For uninterrupted flow facilities (e.g., ones without traffic signals), this flow rate is related to speed as shown in Figure E-4. At very high flow rates, the speed of the traffic stream decreases slightly; under these conditions, even a small incident can cause the flow to become unstable, and both the volume and the speed will decrease. Traffic density is the number of vehicles in a single lane 0.6 mi (1 km) in length. At low densities, motorists are able to select their speed; as conditions become more congested density increases and speeds tend to decrease. The diagonal line in Figure E-4 shows the reciprocal of density as a function of the flow rate.

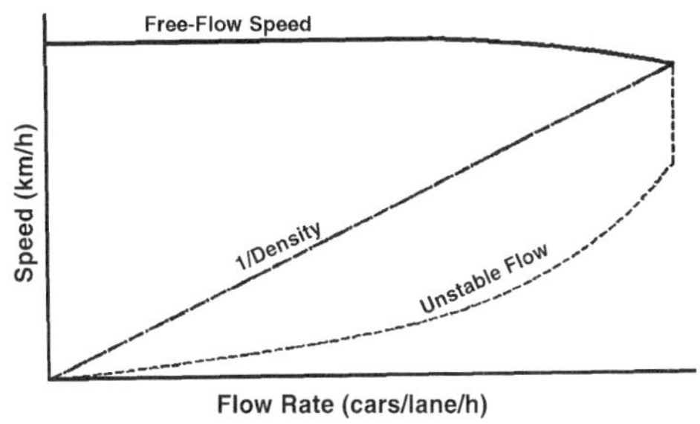

Figure E-4 Speed, flow rate, and density.

Highway Functional Classification

In designing a highway facility, the engineer initially defines the function that the facility will serve. The level of service required for the anticipated volume and composition of traffic determines the subsequent selection of design speed and geometric criteria. AASHTO recommends design characteristics for four classes of rural highway: freeway, arterial, collector, and local (AASHTO 1994).

The terminology used for roadway classification in urban areas is similar to that for rural areas. However, most urban areas have special conditions that can alter the design and operation of their roadways. Factors such as higher population density, one-way streets, parking, pedestrians, and transit influence urban street and roadway design.

Horizontal Alignment

Horizontal alignment parameters include the curve radii (*R*) and the roadway superelevation. To provide motorist comfort and permit higher operating speeds, road segments on horizontal curves are superelevated or banked. (See Figure E-5.) The superelevation rate (*e*) may be as high as 0.12, but it is typically limited to 0.08 in areas subject to ice and snow. The engineer selects *R* as a function of the highway's design speed and the superelevation.

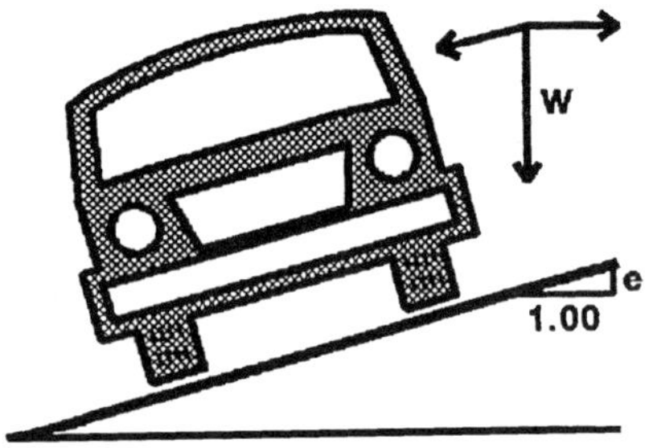

Figure E-5 Horizontal curve superelevation.

Level of Service

A roadway's operational condition as perceived by motorists is referred to as the level of service. In highway capacity analysis, this parameter has six designated levels, from A (the best condition with no congestion and higher operating speeds) to E (capacity) and F (the worst situation with extreme congestion and stop-and-go traffic). On a freeway section, most drivers judge the level of roadway performance by their travel speed. However, studies have documented that high speeds can be maintained on well-designed freeways over a considerable range of traffic volumes (see Figure E-4). As a result, the level of service for freeway sections is based on the density of traffic (vehicles per kilometer per lane); as density increases, the level of service deteriorates.

Local Roads and Streets

Local roads and streets primarily provide access to the farm, residence, business, or other abutting property. Because these facilities are not intended to accommodate much through traffic, they may have lower design speeds. Pedestrians, bicycles, and parked vehicles may use these facilities. Although 68 percent of all rural highway length in the United States is classified as local, these roads account for only 11 percent of all rural vehicle miles of travel.

Local urban streets provide access to property and connections to roadways of higher functional class. Design speeds are typically 37 mph (60 km/h) or less, and through traffic is discouraged. Traffic calming techniques are being used with increasing frequency to control vehicle volumes and speeds on local urban streets. Local streets account for 70 percent of the urban street length and carry 14 percent of all urban travel.

Median Speed

The median speed, another measure of central tendency, is the middle (or 50th percentile) value. It is readily determined by arranging all of the speed observations from low to high and then selecting the middle value. If the speed data are approximately symmetrical, the average and median will have similar values.

Operating Speed

Operating speed is the speed at which drivers of free-flowing vehicles choose to drive on a section of roadway. Figure F-6 compares the design speeds and two operating speeds (average and 95th percentile) at 12 two-lane study sites in Arkansas, Illinois, and Texas when the national 55-mph (89-km/h) speed limit was in effect (Messer et al. 1981). The dashed line represents the situation where the design and operating speeds are equal. On roadways with 50-mph (80-km/h) design speeds, average operating speeds exceeded the design speed by about 6 mph (10 km/h), and the 95th percentile speeds were 17 mph (27 km/h) greater than the design speed. These parameters increased by relatively small amounts on highways with design speeds of 60 and 70 mph (97 and 113 km/h).

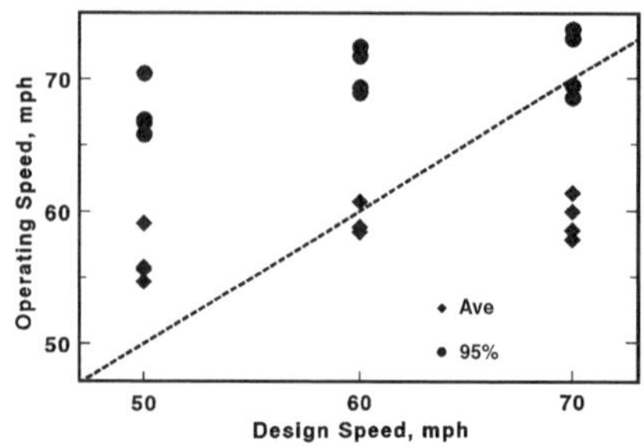

Figure E-6 Relationship between design and operating speeds (Messer et al. 1981). (Note: 1 mph = 1.609 km/h.)

Perception-Reaction Time

In the context of geometric design, perception-reaction time is the interval between the instant the motorist recognizes the existence of an object or hazard on the roadway ahead and the moment the driver actually applies the brakes or takes another action. Although most alert drivers have perception-reaction times of less than 1 s, AASHTO recommends a value for stopping sight distance calculations of 2.5 s (AASHTO 1994). Vehicle speed does not affect reaction time, but the distance traveled by a vehicle during a fixed time period obviously increases with speed.

Residence District

For the purpose of establishing statutory speed limits, the Uniform Vehicle Code (National Committee on Uniform Traffic Laws and Ordinances 1992) defines a residence district as the territory contiguous to and including a highway not comprising a business district when the property on such highway for a distance of 90 m or more is in the main improved with residences or residences and buildings in use for business. (Note: 1 m = 3.28 ft.)

Roadside Elements

Roadside elements consist of relatively flat slopes (which provide adequate recovery room for errant vehicles), ditches and other drainage features, highway appurtenances (e.g., signs, signals, and street lights), and traffic barriers to shield traffic from steep slopes or other potentially hazardous objects.

Safe Curve Speed

The safe speed through horizontal curves is often less than the design speed on adjacent sections of tangent roadway. However, the "safe speed" on a horizontal curve is much less than the speed at which a motorist would run off the roadway. Rather, it is the speed at which the unbalanced side force experienced by the driver and other vehicle occupants starts to become uncomfortable. To quantify this feeling, traffic engineers adapted the ball bank indicator from airplanes; a modern version of this device is shown in Figure E-7. This device is mounted in a typical passenger vehicle, and readings are taken as the vehicle negotiates a curve at progressively higher speeds. The readings, of course, increase with speed. The maximum recommended values, initially established around 1940, are 14 degrees for test speeds of less than 20 mph (32 km/h), 12 degrees for speeds between 22 and 37 mph (35 and 60 km/h), and 10 degrees for speeds of 40 mph (65 km/h) or greater. An FHWA study (Chowdhury et al. 1998) evaluated the behavior of contemporary drivers in horizontal curves and recommended raising these values.

Figure E-7 Ball bank indicator.

Sight Distance

Sight distance is the length of roadway ahead visible to the driver. AASHTO design standards discuss four types of sight distance–decision, intersection, passing, and stopping (AASHTO 1994).

Sight Distance, Decision

Decision sight distance is the length of roadway required for a driver to detect an unexpected hazard in the environment, recognize the hazard, select an appropriate speed and path, and initiate and complete the required maneuver safely and efficiently. In contrast to stopping sight distance, this model assumes that the driver will not simply slam on the brakes but rather will assess the situation, make an informed decision, and implement the action without interfering with other traffic. Table E-2 indicates decision sight distances on rural highways where the expected maneuvers are a controlled stop and a speed or path change.

Table E-2 Rural Decision Sight Distances

	Decision Sight Distance (m)	
Speed (km/h)	Stop	Path Change
50	75	145
60	95	175
70	125	200
80	155	230
90	185	275
100	225	315
110	265	335
120	305	375

Note: 1 m = 3.28 ft and 1 km/h = 0.62 mph.

Sight Distance, Intersection

AASHTO identifies several intersection sight distance criteria that must be considered by the designer (AASHTO 1994). At the risk of oversimplification, intersections on high-speed rural highways must provide sufficient sight distance for motorists under the following conditions:

• A driver approaching an intersection controlled by a Yield or Stop sign or a traffic signal must have sufficient distance to see and react to the traffic control.

• Drivers stopped at a Yield or Stop sign and preparing to cross or turn onto a through highway must be able to see a sufficient distance to make their maneuver with safety and without significantly interfering with motorists on the through road.

• Drivers on the major roadway intending to turn left onto a cross street must have adequate sight distance to make their maneuver with safety.

AASHTO prescribes numerical values for these and other situations at intersections; in all cases, the required sight distances increase with the speeds of traffic approaching the intersection on the controlled approaches and on the through highway. Many jurisdictions specify intersection sight distances that are less stringent than those recommended by AASHTO.

Sight Distance, Passing

Passing sight distance is the length of roadway that a motorist must be able to see ahead in order to safely complete a passing maneuver on a two-lane highway. The AASHTO model for passing sight distance design assumes that the passing maneuver, once initiated, will be completed (AASHTO 1994). The passing sight distance model uses a driver eye height of 1070 mm and a height for the opposing vehicle of 1300 mm. The model also makes assumptions about the relative speeds of the passing vehicle, the passed vehicle, and an oncoming vehicle. AASHTO's assumptions for design purposes are fairly conservative and result in long distances. By contrast, passing sight distances for operational purposes assume that a partially completed passing maneuver may be aborted if an opposing vehicle comes into view while the passing vehicle is in the left lane. This assumption shortens the necessary sight distance considerably. Values from the operational analysis are used by traffic engineers in establishing the location and length of marked no-passing zones. Table E-3 compares the passing sight distances for design and operational purposes.

Table E-3 Passing Sight Distances

	Minimum Sight Distance (m)	
Speed (km/h)	Design	Operation
50	345	150
60	407	170
70	482	200
80	541	240
90	605	280
100	670	320
110	728	360
120	792	

Note: 1 m = 3.28 ft and 1 km/h = 0.62 mph.

Sight Distance, Stopping

Stopping sight distance is the minimum distance for a vehicle traveling at or near a highway's design speed on wet pavement to come to a complete stop before reaching a stationary object (150 mm high) in its path (AASHTO 1994). Adequate stopping sight distance, which should be provided at every point along all roads, consists of two components—the motorist's perception-reaction distance and the vehicle's braking distance. Stopping sight distance may be calculated using the following formula:

$$d = 0.278tV + \frac{V^2}{254f}$$

where

d = minimum stopping sight distance (m);
t = perception-reaction time, assumed to be 2.5 s;
V = initial speed (km/h); and
f = coefficient of friction between tires and roadway.

The solid line in Figure E-3 shows the relationship between stopping sight distance and highway design speed. The difference between the stopping and braking distances is the length of highway traveled during the perception-reaction time.

Speed Change Lanes

Speed change lanes include acceleration and deceleration lanes, which are used in conjunction with interchange ramps to permit entering vehicles to attain the speed of the through traffic and exiting vehicles to decelerate outside of the through-traffic lanes.

Speed Dispersion

The speeds of individual vehicles on a street or highway vary, often in the manner suggested by Figure E-1. Speed dispersion refers to this spread in vehicle speeds. Speed dispersion can be quantified in various ways including the standard deviation, variance, 10-mph pace, or range (high minus low). There is general agreement that the safest conditions occur when all vehicles at a site are traveling at about the same speed.

Speed Limit, Absolute

An absolute speed limit specifies a numerical value, the exceeding of which is always in violation of the law, regardless of the conditions or hazards involved. Many enforcement officers prefer absolute speed limits because they reduce the incidence of challenged citations. However, absolute speed limits lack flexibility, particularly in those situations where traffic conditions vary widely. Approximately two-thirds of the states have absolute speed limits. Prima facie speed limits are the alternative to absolute limits.

Speed Limit, Differential

The motor vehicle codes in some states prescribe different speed limits for different classes of vehicles. For example, the maximum speed limit on a rural section of Interstate might be 75 mph (121 km/h) for cars, pickup trucks, and vans, but 65 mph (105 km/h) for large trucks. The primary rationale for this type of regulation is that large trucks have much longer stopping distance than cars. In the absence of differential speed limits, studies have found that large trucks travel 1 to 2 mph (2 to 3 km/h) slower than cars on level sections of rural

Interstate. This value may double when differential speed limits are introduced, but the actual difference between car and truck speeds rarely approaches the difference cited in the code.

Speed Limit, Posted

The posted speed limit is the value conveyed to the motorist on a black-on-white regulatory sign such as the one shown in Figure E-8. Standard engineering practice is to post speed limits for freeways, arterials, and any roadway or street where speed zoning has altered the limit from the statutory value. They are also used at any point where the speed limit changes, including points beyond major rural intersections where traffic may change from one road to another.

Figure E-8 Speed limit sign.

Speed Limit, Prima Facie

A prima facie speed limit is one above which drivers are presumed to be driving unlawfully. Nevertheless, if charged with a violation, drivers have the opportunity to demonstrate in court that their speed was safe for conditions at the time and not in violation of the basic speed limit, even though they may have exceeded the numerical limit. Approximately one-third of the states have prima facie speed limits or limits of each type (i.e., prima facie and absolute). Absolute speed limits are the alternative to prima facie limits.

Speed Limit, Statutory

State motor vehicle laws specify numerical values for speed limits on specific categories of streets and highways. For example, a code might limit speeds to 25 mph (40 km/h) in residential areas, 30 mph (48 km/h) in business districts, and 55 mph (89 km/h) on all other roads. Unless otherwise prohibited by law, these limits may be altered on the basis of an engineering study.

Speed Limit, Variable

The typical speed zoning process establishes a limit that is posted and enforceable 24 h/d. In reality, streets and highways experience conditions of traffic, weather, and incidents when lower limits would be appropriate. In some cases, the conditions will be such that motorists could not possibly travel at the posted speed limit. On the other hand, an urban speed limit established in part because of daytime pedestrian traffic may be unrealistically low for conditions at night. One method of addressing these types of situations is through the use of variable speed limits.

An urban freeway variable speed limit system would operate in the following manner. Detectors would monitor the actual volume, speed, and density of traffic in sections of the freeway. This information would be used to determine where congestion is causing traffic to slow. In advance of these locations, electronic speed limit signs (similar to Figure E-8, but with changeable numbers) would be remotely controlled to alter the posted speed limit. Motorists who comply with these regulations would decrease their speed and not approach the end of a stopped or slow-moving traffic queue at normal freeway speeds.

Speed Parameters

Field data from spot speed studies of free-flowing vehicles (see Figure E-9) are processed to determine typical data parameters of central tendency (average or median) and dispersion (standard deviation, variance, 10-mph pace, and range).

Speed Standard Deviation

The standard deviation, which has the units of speed (km/h), is the positive square root of the speed variance. Speed standard deviations are often 3.7 to 4.3 mph (6 to 7 km/h) on urban streets and 5.6 to 6.8 mph (9 to 11 km/h) on freeways. The standard deviation's value is strongly influenced by a few vehicles traveling at very high or very low speeds; elimination of these vehicles will reduce the standard deviation. The standard deviation is readily calculated from a sample of speed measurements such as those shown in Figure E-9. It may be roughly approximated by the speed range (largest observed speed minus the smallest) divided by 6. The standard deviation may also be estimated as the difference between the 85th percentile and average speeds.

SPOT SPEED SURVEY DATA FORM

Site Pennsylvania SB at Phoenix Speed Limit 50 km/h Date 07/13/97 Data Collector Bernie

Speed	Tally (5, 10)	(a) f_i	(b) Σf_i	(c) $f\mu_i$	(d) $f\mu_i^2$
35		0	0	0	0
36	✓✓	2	2	72	2,592
37	✓	1	3	37	1,369
38	✓✓✓	3	6	114	4,332
39	✓✓✓✓	4	10	156	6,084
40	✓	1	11	40	1,600
41	✓✓✓	3	14	123	5,043
42	✓✓✓	3	17	126	5,292
43	✓✓	2	19	86	3,698
44	✓✓✓✓✓✓✓	7	26	308	13,552
45	✓✓✓✓✓✓	6	32	270	12,150
46	✓✓✓✓✓	5	37	230	10,580
47	✓✓✓✓✓✓✓	7	44	329	15,463
48	✓✓✓✓✓✓✓✓✓	9	53	432	20,736
49	✓✓✓✓✓✓✓✓✓✓✓✓	12	65	588	28,812
50	✓✓✓✓✓✓✓✓✓✓	10	75	500	25,000
51	✓✓✓✓✓✓	6	81	306	15,606
52	✓✓✓✓✓✓✓✓	8	89	416	21,632
53	✓✓✓✓	4	93	212	11,236
54	✓✓✓✓✓✓	6	99	324	17,496
55	✓✓✓✓	4	103	220	12,100
56	✓✓	2	105	112	6,272
57	✓	1	106	57	3,249
58	✓✓	2	108	116	6,728
59	✓	1	109	59	3,481
60		0	109	0	0
61		0	109	0	0
62	✓	1	110	62	3,844
63		0	110	0	0
64		0	110	0	0
65		0	110	0	0
Total		110		5,295	257,947

Figure E-9 Sample speed data collection form.

Speed Variance

Speed variance for a spot speed study is calculated by summing the squares of the differences between each measured speed and the average speed, and dividing the total by the sample size minus one ($n - 1$). The variance, which is the square of the standard deviation, thus has units of speed squared (km^2/h^2). Speed variance has little practical value and is rarely cited as an output value from a spot speed study. The variance's principal application is in determining the standard deviation.

The technical literature includes studies in which analysts relied on selected speed parameters, rather than having the original data such as that shown in Figure E-9. Using speed study results that report only the average and the 85th percentile speeds, these analysts have attempted to quantify speed dispersion by calculating the numerical difference between these two values. Although this difference usually provides a good approximation of the speed sample's standard deviation, these analysts have unfortunately and incorrectly labeled this result as "speed variance." In reality, it is an estimate of standard deviation.

Speed Zone

Speed zoning is the process of establishing a reasonable and safe speed limit for a section of roadway where the statutory speed limits given in the motor vehicle laws [e.g., 30 mph (48 km/h) in business districts] do not fit the road or traffic conditions at a specific location. The limits may be altered on the basis of an engineering study. To be enforceable, the new limits must be posted along the roadway using a standard regulatory sign such as the one shown in Figure E-8. In addition, speed limits that are increased or decreased as a result of the speed zoning process must be recorded in documents maintained by an appropriate agency (e.g., state supreme court library). Speed zones should be periodically restudied.

The basic principles of speed zoning should also be applied to special situations such as school crossings and roadway construction areas. In addition, they may be used to establish minimum speed limits for freeways.

Spot Speed Study

Engineers conduct spot speed studies by measuring and recording the speeds of a sample of free-flowing vehicles as they pass a point on a street or highway. The measurements are usually made with a hand-held radar or laser speed meter. The field data are typically recorded on a data form similar to the one shown in Figure E-9. This study is an essential element in the more comprehensive engineering study required for speed zoning. Unless there is an interest in other conditions, a spot speed study is normally conducted on a straight, level road during daylight, off-peak hours. Speed data are collected separately by direction. Minimum sample sizes of at least 100 vehicles are necessary to properly represent the speed characteristics of the traffic at the study site.

Traffic Calming

Traffic calming is a term used to identify various engineering techniques to physically control vehicle speeds and/or volumes on local streets. The techniques, which include speed humps, traffic diverters, narrow roadways, and staggered alignment, are deployed in response to complaints by adjacent property owners of speeding traffic or excessive traffic volumes. Although these techniques have been found effective on local streets, they must be planned and implemented carefully to ensure that the original problems are not simply moved to another local street.

Vehicle Alignment

A roadway's vertical alignment consists of grades, where the elevation changes at a fixed rate per unit distance along the highway, and vertical curves, where the highway grade increases or decreases. These features are portrayed in Figure E-10. As indicated in Table E-4, AASHTO recommends maximum grades for rural highways as a function of highway classification and type of terrain (AASHTO 1994). Maximum grades on urban freeways are identical to those for rural freeways, but grades steeper than those given in Table E-4 are permitted on urban arterial, collector, and local streets. Minimum lengths of crest vertical curves are a function of the approach and departure grades as well as the stopping sight distance for the roadway's design speed.

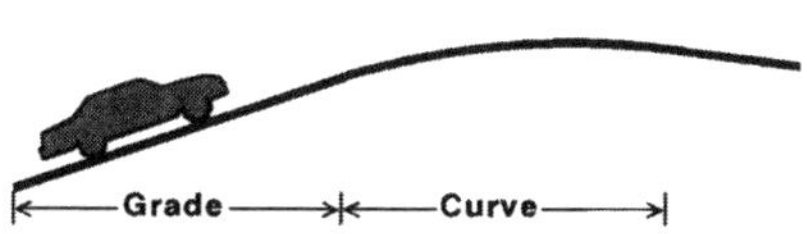

Figure E-10 Vertical alignment features.

Table E-4 Maximum Vertical Grades for Rural Roads

Terrain	Maximum Grade (%) Freeway	Arterial	Collector	Local
Level	3–4	3–5	4–7	5–8
Rolling	4–5	4–6	5–10	6–11
Mountainous	5–6	5–8	6–12	10–16

Vehicle Miles of Travel

The total amount of travel on a roadway segment or on an entire roadway system is typically expressed in vehicle miles of travel (VMT). The numerical value may be obtained by multiplying the length of a section (in miles) by average traffic volume (vehicles per day), summing these values for all sections of interest, and expanding the results to an annual value. VMT is commonly used to characterize the amount of travel on different classes of roadway and as a normalizing factor in calculating crash or fatality rates.

REFERENCES

ABBREVIATIONS

AASHTO	American Association of State Highway and Transportation Officials
NSC	National Safety Council

AASHTO.1994. *A Policy on Geometric Design of Highways and Streets.* Washington, D.C.

Chowdhury, M.A., D.L.Warren, H. Bissell, and S. Taori. 1998. Are the Criteria for Setting Advisory Speeds on Curves Still Relevant? *ITE Journal*, Vol. 68, No. 2, Feb., pp. 32–45.

Judycki, D. 1994. *Motor Vehicle Accident Costs.* HHS-10. Federal Highway Administration, U.S. Department of Transportation.

Messer, C., J. Mounce, and R. Brackett. 1981. *Highway Geometric Design Consistency Related to Driver Expectancy*, Volume 2. Report FHWA-RD-81-036. Federal Highway Administration, U.S. Department of Transportation.

National Committee on Uniform Traffic Laws and Ordinances. 1992. *Uniform Vehicle Code and Model Traffic Ordinance.*

National Safety Council. 1996. *Accident Facts.*

Study Committee Biographical Information

John G. Milliken, *Chairman*, is Partner at the firm of Venable, Baetjer & Howard with offices in Maryland, Virginia, and the District of Columbia. Mr. Milliken served as Secretary of Transportation for the Commonwealth of Virginia from 1990 to 1993 and on many local and regional governmental boards. He was a member of the Arlington County Board for 10 years, member and Chairman of the Board of the Washington Metropolitan Area Transit Authority, and member of the National Capital Interstate Air Quality Commission and Northern Virginia Transportation Commission. Mr. Milliken received his bachelor's degree from Haverford College and his law degree from the University of Virginia Law School. He recently served as a member of the Transportation Research Board (TRB) Study Committee on Urban Transportation Congestion Pricing.

Forrest M. Council is Director of the Highway Safety Research Center at the University of North Carolina, where he was Deputy Director and member of the research staff since 1967. Dr. Council's research interests include highway safety, crash records analysis, driver education, and crash protection. He received his bachelor of science and master of science degrees from North Carolina State University and his Ph.D. in civil engineering from the University of North Carolina. Dr. Council is a member and past president of the National Child Passenger Safety Association, Chairman of the TRB Committee on Methodology for Evaluating Highway Improvements, member of the Board of Directors and Editorial Board and Chairman of the Scientific Program Committee of the Association for the Advancement of Automotive Medicine, and member of TRB and U.S. Department of Transportation advisory panels concerned with future highway safety research needs, enforcement training for occupant restraint activities, large truck safety data needs, highway-related countermeasure analysis, occupant restraint research needs, and the safety relationship between vehicle configuration and highway design. He currently serves as a member of the TRB Research and Technology Coordinating Committee, which provides input to the Federal Highway Administration on its research activities.

Terrance W. Gainer is Executive Assistant Chief of Police of the Metropolitan Police Department of Washington, D.C., a position he assumed in May 1998. As second in command, he is responsible for a staff of 4,800. Before coming to Washington, he was Director of the Illinois State Police, where he managed the work of more than 3,700 employees engaged in patrol, criminal investigation, and police training. During his 30-year career in law enforcement, he served as Special Assistant to the Secretary and Director for Drug Enforcement and Program Compliance at the U.S. Department of Transportation; Deputy Inspector General, State of Illinois; and Chief Legal Officer, Homicide Detective, Patrol Officer, Supervisor and Commander in the Chicago Police Department. Mr. Gainer received his bachelor of art in sociology at St. Benedict's College and his master of science in management and public service and juris doctor at DePaul University. He is on the Executive Board of the International Association of Chiefs of Police and is Commissioner of the National Commission on Accreditation of Law Enforcement. Mr. Gainer is currently a Captain in the U.S. Navy Reserve.

Nicholas J. Garber is Chairman of the Department of Civil Engineering and Professor of Civil Engineering at the University of Virginia. For the past 15 years, he has been engaged in research in the areas of traffic operations and highway safety. Before joining the University of Virginia in 1980, Dr. Garber was a Professor of Civil Engineering and Dean of the Faculty of Engineering at the University of Sierra Leone. Before that, he taught at the State University of New York at Buffalo and worked as a design engineer in several consulting engineering firms. Dr. Garber received his bachelor of science in civil engineering from the University of London and his masters and doctorate from Carnegie-Mellon University. A registered professional engineer in the Commonwealth of Virginia and a chartered engineer of the United Kingdom, he is a member of the American Society of Civil Engineers (ASCE), the Institute of Transportation Engineers (ITE), the Institution of Civil Engineers of Great Britain, and TRB's Committee on Traffic Safety in Maintenance and Construction Operations.

Kristine M. Gebbie is Associate Professor of Nursing at the Columbia University School of Nursing. Before that she served as the first National AIDS Policy Coordinator under President Clinton, Secretary of the Department of Health for the State of Washington, where she helped establish a statewide trauma center system, Administrator of Public Health in Oregon, and Coordinator of Ambulatory Care for the St. Louis University Hospitals. Dr. Gebbie's research interests are focused on health policy and health services. She has a bachelor of science in nursing from St. Olaf College, a master of nursing from the University of California at Los Angeles, and a doctor of public health in health policy from the University of Michigan School of Public Health. Dr. Gebbie has served as a member of the Executive Board of the American Public Health Association and has chaired the Centers for Disease Control and Prevention Advisory Committee on the prevention of HIV infection, and the Environment, Safety, and Health Advisory Committee of the U.S. Department of Energy. She is also a member of the Institute of Medicine (IOM) and has served on several of its committees.

Jerome W. Hall is a Professor of Civil Engineering and past Chairman of the Department of Civil Engineering at the University of New Mexico, where he has taught and conducted research since 1977. Before that, he served for 7 years on the civil engineering faculty at the University of Maryland. Dr. Hall is an expert on the operational effects of roadway geometry and highway design, with particular emphasis on low-volume roads. He received his bachelor of science in physics at Harvey Mudd College and his master of science and Ph.D. in civil engineering at the University of Washington. Dr. Hall is a fellow in ITE. He has served on TRB's Study Committee on Truck Access, chaired TRB's Group 3 Council, and chaired National Cooperative Highway Research Program panels on stopping sight distance and resurfacing, restoration, and rehabilitation project effects.

Charles A. Lave is Professor of Economics, Director of the Graduate Program in Transportation Sciences, Associate Director of the Institute of Transportation Studies, and Faculty Assistant to the Chancellor at the University of California at Irvine. He has conducted research and published numerous articles about the effect of changes in speed limits on highway safety. Dr. Lave graduated with a bachelor of arts degree in political science from Reed College and a Ph.D. in economics from Stanford University. He is a member of the American Economics Association, the American Statistical Association, the American Association for the Advancement of Science, and the Association for Policy Analysis and Administration. He was also a member of the TRB Committee for the Study of the Benefits and Costs of the 55-mph National Maximum Speed Limit.

John M. Mason, Jr., is Associate Dean of Graduate Studies and Research in the College of Engineering and Professor of Civil Engineering at Pennsylvania State University. As a Faculty Research Associate at the Pennsylvania Transportation Institute, his research interests include geometric design, highway operations, and roadway safety, including the operational and geometric characteristics of heavy trucks. He has also provided expert testimony in highway tort-related litigation. Before coming to Pennsylvania State University, Dr. Mason served on the staff of the Texas Transportation Institute and the Department of Civil Engineering at Texas A&M University, where he held various research and teaching positions. In addition to his academic interests, Dr. Mason has had practical experience working with consulting engineering firms. He holds a bachelor's degree in transportation from The Pennsylvania State University, a master's degree in transportation engineering from Villanova University, and a

Ph.D. in civil engineering from Texas A&M University. Dr. Mason is a member of ASCE, ITE, the Tau Beta Pi National Engineering Honor Society, and TRB's Committee on Geometric Design.

Frederick Mosteller is Roger I. Lee Professor of Mathematical Statistics, Emeritus, at Harvard University. His research interests include theoretical and applied statistics, biostatistics, policy, public health and medicine, and social science. During his distinguished academic career, Dr. Mosteller served as Chairman of the Department of Statistics in the Faculty of Arts and Sciences, Director of the Technology Assessment Program, Chairman of the Department of Health Policy and Management, and Chairman of the Department of Biostatistics at the Harvard School of Public Health, and member of the faculty of the Harvard Medical School. He holds a bachelor's and master's degree in mathematics from the Carnegie Institute of Technology, and a master's and Ph.D. in mathematics from Princeton University. Dr. Mosteller is a member of the National Academy of Sciences and the IOM; a fellow of the American Academy of Arts and Sciences, the American Philosophical Society, the Institute of Mathematical Statistics, the American Statistical Association, and the American Association for the Advancement of Science; and an honorary fellow of the Royal Statistical Society. He has also served on numerous National Research Council and IOM committees.

Sharon D. Nichols is Executive Director of the Western Highway Institute (WHI), the trucking industry's research and educational resource in the Western United States and Canada. Prior to joining WHI, she served as Managing Director of the Wyoming Trucking Association. Her areas of expertise include truck size and weight, motor carrier taxation, and economic development. Ms. Nichols currently serves as a Governor's appointee to the Wyoming Water Development Commission and a cochairman of the Governor's Workers Insurance Task Force. She is a past chairman of the Wyoming Highway Users Federation, the Executive Council of the Western Trucking Associations, and the Job Service Employers

Committee. Ms. Nichols is a graduate of the University of Wyoming, with a bachelor of arts degree in English literature.

Clinton V. Oster is Professor of Public and Environmental Affairs and former Associate Dean of the School of Public and Environmental Affairs at Indiana University. He has also served as Director of the Indiana University Transportation Research Center, Research Director of the President's Aviation Safety Commission, and President of the Transportation Research Forum. Dr. Oster's research interests include aviation safety and the effects of government regulation on the private sector. He holds a B.S.E. from Princeton University, an M.S. from Carnegie-Mellon University, and a Ph.D. in economics from Harvard University. Dr. Oster chaired the TRB Committee for the Study of the Federal Employers' Liability Act and served on the TRB Committee for the Study on Air Passenger Service and Safety Since Deregulation.

Richard A. Retting is Senior Transportation Engineer with the Insurance Institute for Highway Safety (IIHS). His areas of research interest include speed limits and vehicle speeds, photo enforcement technology, traffic control devices, and pedestrian safety. Prior to joining IIHS in 1990, he served as Deputy Assistant Commissioner for the New York City Department of Transportation in charge of safety programs. Mr. Retting received a bachelor's degree in public administration from Baruch College, City University of New York, and a master's degree in transportation planning and engineering from Polytechnic University of New York. He is chairman of ITE's Transportation Safety Council and Secretary of TRB's Committee on Pedestrians. Mr. Retting was the 1989 recipient of the Volvo Traffic Safety Award.

Thomas B. Sheridan is Ford Professor of Engineering and Applied Psychology, Professor of Aeronautics and Astronautics, and Director of the Human-Machine Systems Laboratory at the Massachusetts

Institute of Technology (MIT), where he has spent most of his professional career. He is an expert in human factors, with research interests in modeling and design of human-machine systems in automobile driving, aviation, and other areas. Dr. Sheridan received his B.S. from Purdue University, his M.S. from the University of California at Los Angeles, and his ScD from MIT. He is a fellow of the Institute of Electrical and Electronics Engineers (IEEE) and past president of the IEEE Systems, Man and Cybernetics Society; fellow and past president of the Human Factors Society; and member of the National Academy of Engineering. He has served on numerous committees of the National Research Council and was a member of TRB's Committee for a Review of the National Automated Highway System Consortium Research Program.

William C. Taylor is Professor of Civil Engineering and previous Chairperson of the Department of Civil and Environmental Engineering at Michigan State University, where he has taught since 1972. Before that, Dr. Taylor was Executive Director of the Interagency Transportation Council for Michigan, Traffic Research Engineer for the Ohio Department of Highways, and Traffic Engineer for Cleveland. He received his bachelor's and master's degrees in civil engineering at Case Institute of Technology and his Ph.D. in civil engineering from Ohio State University. Dr. Taylor is a member of ITE and headed the technical committee that developed speed zone guidelines. He is also a member of ASCE and the National Society of Professional Engineers.

George Tsebelis is Professor of Political Science at the University of California at Los Angeles. He has also taught at Duke, Stanford, and Washington Universities and was a recipient of a Guggenheim fellowship. Dr. Tsebelis's areas of research include decision making in political systems and game theory as applied to enforcement strategies and sanctions. He received undergraduate degrees in engineering from the National Technical University of Athens and political science from the Institut d'Études Politiques de Paris, an engineering doctorate in mathematical statistics from the Pierre et Marie Curie University (Paris VI), and a Ph.D. in political science from Washington University. Dr. Tsebelis is on the Editorial Board of Governance and the Journal of Theoretical Politics.

David C. Viano is Principal Research Scientist in the Research and Development Center at General Motors Corporation (GMC), where he has worked as Assistant Department Head, Staff Research Engineer, and Senior Research Engineer since coming to GMC in 1974. Dr. Viano is an expert in the area of biomechanics and injury control. He received his bachelor of electrical engineering at Santa Clara University, his master's and Ph.D. in applied mathematics at the California Institute of Technology, his postdoctorate in biomedical science at the University and ETH Zurich, and his Doctor of Medicine from the Karolinska Institute of Medicine in Stockholm. Dr. Viano is a fellow of the Society of Automotive Engineers, the Association for the Advancement of Automotive Medicine, the American Society of Mechanical Engineers, the American Institute for Medical and Biological Engineering; he is a member of the American Trauma Society, the American Automobile Manufacturers Association, the American Society of Biomechanics, the American College of Surgeons, and the American Association for the Advancement of Science. He also served as a member of several National Research Council committees and two TRB study committees—the Committee To Identify Measures that May Improve the Safety of School Bus Transportation and the Committee To Identify Research Needs for Occupant Restraints.

Richard P. Weaver retired from the California Department of Transportation in September 1997 after a 36-year career. For the last 7½ years, he held the position of Deputy Director and Chief Engineer with responsibility for a staff of approximately 9,200 performing highway design, right-of-way construction, project management, and local programs—a $2.6 billion annual program. Before that, he served as District Director in Fresno, California, and Deputy Director for the

Fresno County Tax Initiative and held several positions related to construction of light rail projects in Sacramento and San Diego. Mr. Weaver holds a bachelor's degree in civil engineering from Sacramento State University, a master's degree in public administration from San Diego State University, and a graduate certificate in transportation from the California Community College system. He is a registered civil engineer and a registered traffic engineer in California. Mr. Weaver served as a member of TRB's Research and Technology Coordinating Committee and Strategic Highway Research Committee. He was also a member of the American Association of State Highway and Transportation Officials' (AASHTO's) Standing Committee on Highways, Chairman of the Subcommittee on Traffic Engineering, and Chairman of AASHTO's delegation to the National Committee to Rewrite the *Manual on Uniform Traffic Control Devices.*